NOV - 9 201

SIXTY-FIVE
PLATT BRANCH LIBRARY
23600 VICTORY BLVD
WOODLAND HILLS, CA 91367

CASE CLOSED

VOLUME

D0721159

740.9999
C3375
v.4

2109 64913

Gosho Aoyama

Case Briefing:

Subject: **Jimmy Kudo a.k.a. Conan Edogawa**
Occupation: **High School Student/Detective**
Special Skills: **Analytical thinking and deductive reasoning, Soccer**
Equipment: **Bow Tie Voice Transmitter, Super Sneakers,**
                   Homing Glasses, Stretchy Suspenders

The subject is hot on the trail of a pair of suspicious men in black when he is attacked from behind and administered a strange substance which physically transforms him into a first grader. When the subject confides in the eccentric inventor Dr. Agasa, they decide to keep the subject's true identity a secret for the safety of everyone around him. Assuming the new identity of first-grader Conan Edogawa, the subject continues to assist the police force on their most baffling cases. The only problem is that most crime-solving professionals won't take a little kid's advice.

Table of Contents

CASE CLOSED

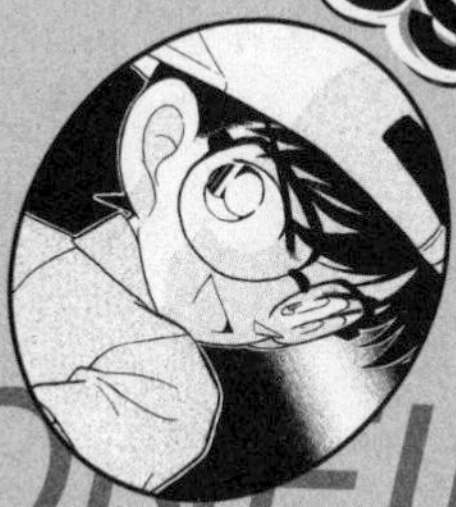

CONFIDENTIAL

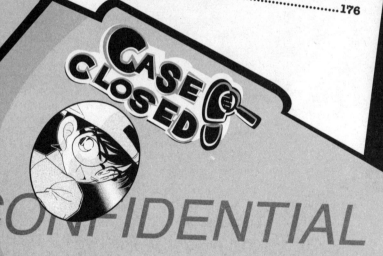

CASE CLOSED
Volume 4
Shonen Sunday Edition

Story and Art by GOSHO AOYAMA

© 1994 Gosho AOYAMA/Shogakukan
All rights reserved.
Original Japanese edition "MEITANTEI CONAN" published by SHOGAKUKAN Inc.

English Adaptation
Naoko Amemiya

Translation
Joe Yamazaki

Touch-up & Lettering
Walden Wong

Cover & Graphics Design
Veronica Casson

Editor
Andy Nakatani

The stories, characters and incidents mentioned in this publication are entirely fictional.

No portion of this book may be reproduced or transmitted in any form or by any means without written permission
from the copyright holders.

Printed in the U.S.A.

Published by VIZ Media, LLC
P.O. Box 77010
San Francisco, CA 94107

10 9 8 7 6 5 4
First printing, February 2005
Fourth printing, November 2014

RATED
T+
FOR OLDER TEEN

PARENTAL ADVISORY
CASE CLOSED is rated T+ for Older Teen
and is recommended for ages 16 and up.
This volume contains realistic and graphic
violence.
ratings.viz.com

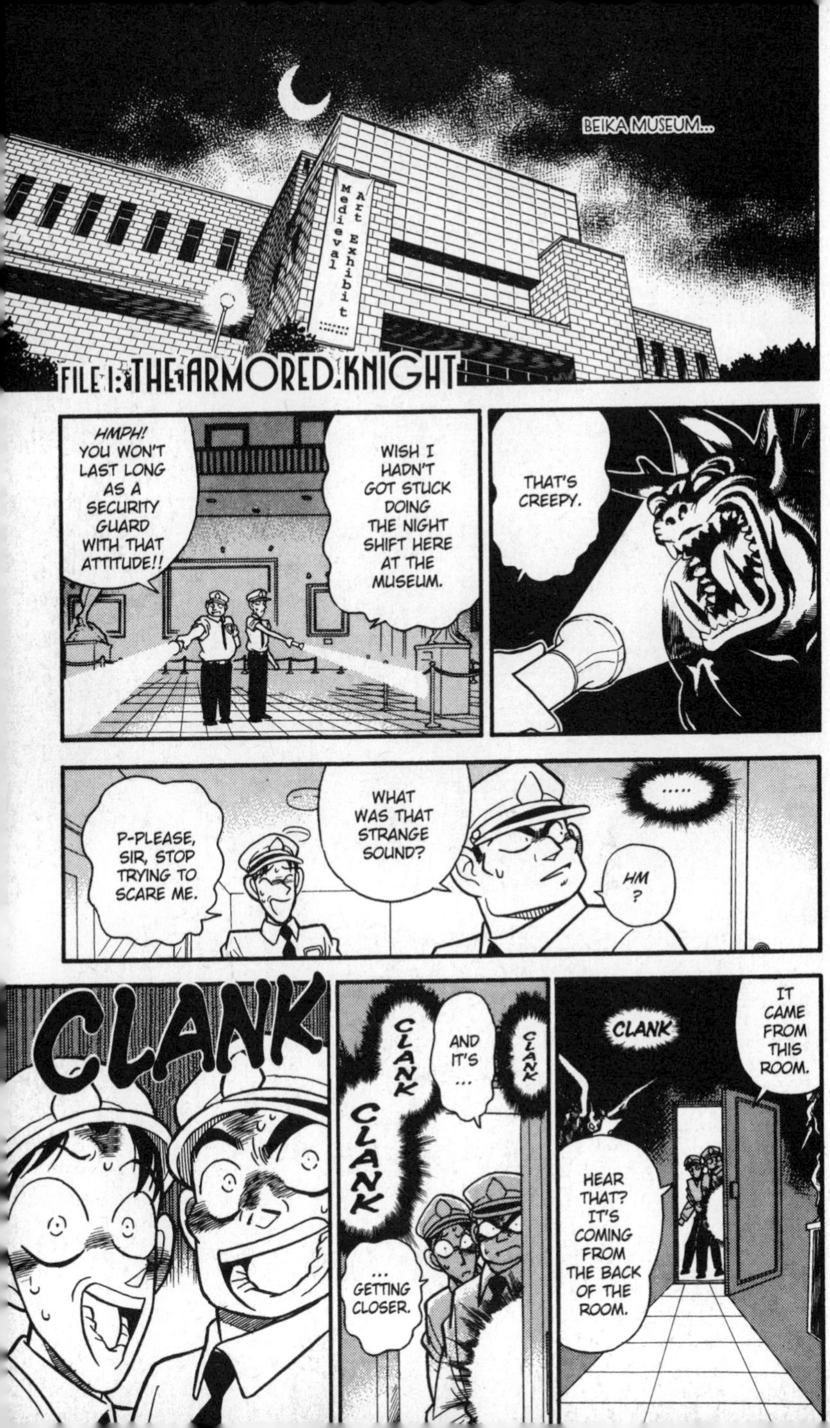
BEIKA MUSEUM...
Medieval Art Exhibit
FILE 1: THE ARMORED KNIGHT
THAT'S CREEPY.
WISH I HADN'T GOT STUCK DOING THE NIGHT SHIFT HERE AT THE MUSEUM.
HMPH! YOU WON'T LAST LONG AS A SECURITY GUARD WITH THAT ATTITUDE!!
......
HM ?
WHAT WAS THAT STRANGE SOUND?
P-PLEASE, SIR, STOP TRYING TO SCARE ME.
CLANK
IT CAME FROM THIS ROOM.
HEAR THAT? IT'S COMING FROM THE BACK OF THE ROOM.
CLANK
AND IT'S ...
CLANK CLANK
... GETTING CLOSER.
CLANK

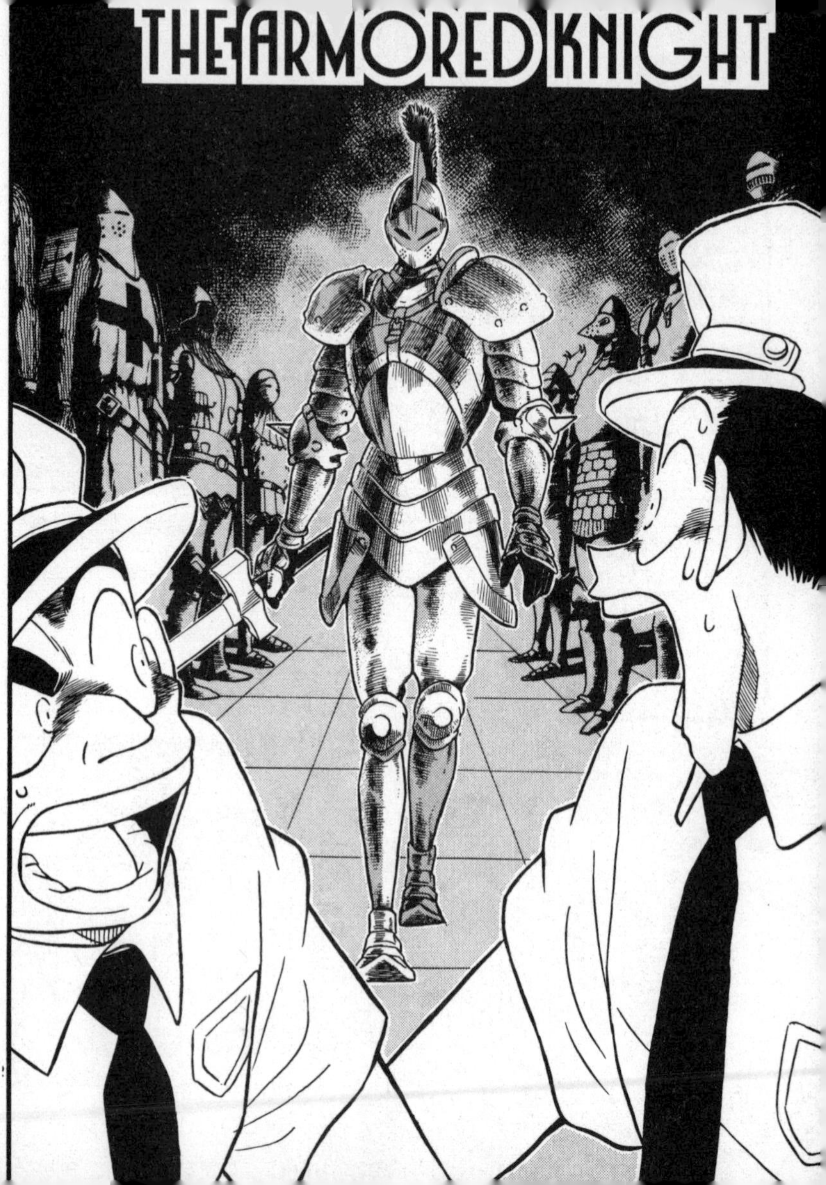
THE ARMORED KNIGHT

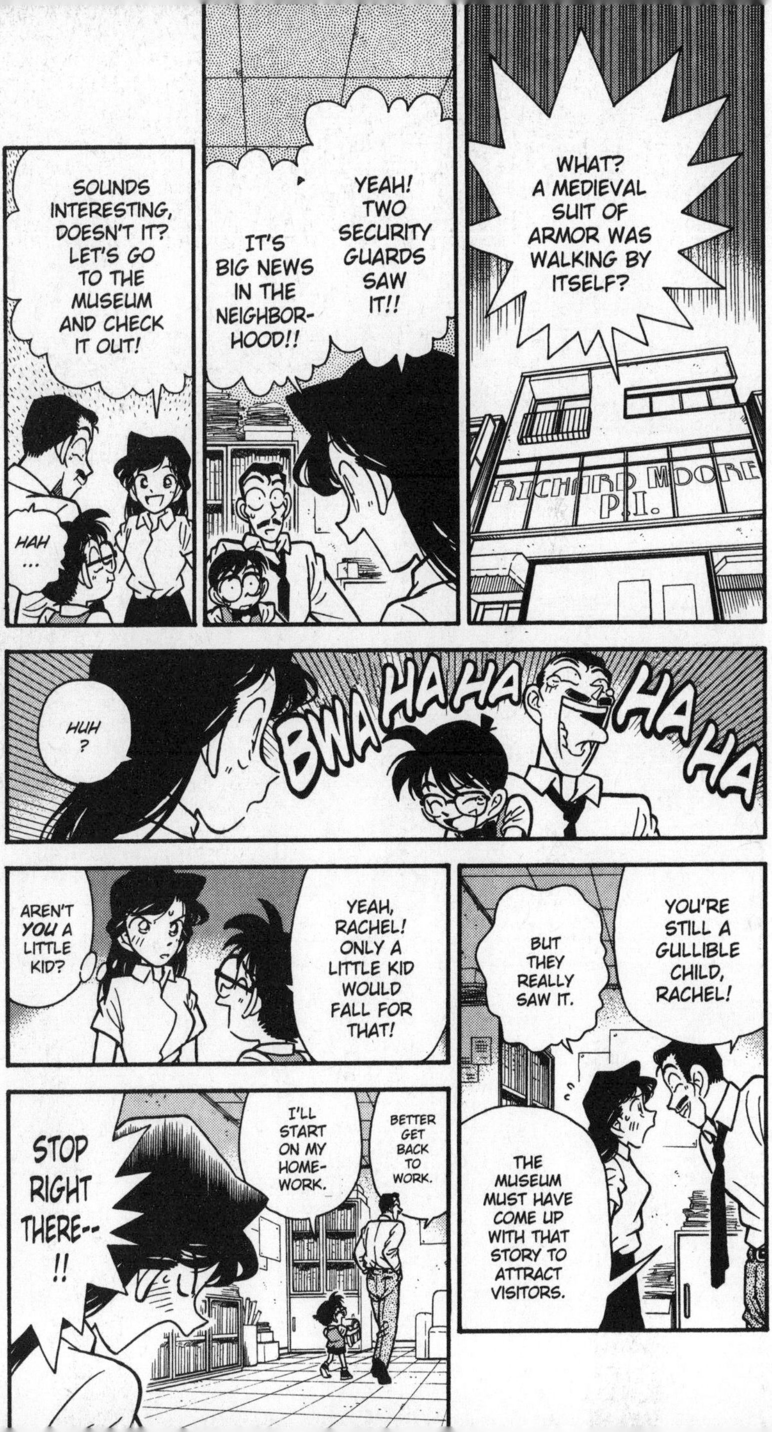
WHAT? A MEDIEVAL SUIT OF ARMOR WAS WALKING BY ITSELF?
RICHARD MOORE P.I.
YEAH! TWO SECURITY GUARDS SAW IT!!
IT'S BIG NEWS IN THE NEIGHBOR-HOOD!!
SOUNDS INTERESTING, DOESN'T IT? LET'S GO TO THE MUSEUM AND CHECK IT OUT!
HAH ...
BWA HA HA HA HA HA HA
HUH ?
YOU'RE STILL A GULLIBLE CHILD, RACHEL!
BUT THEY REALLY SAW IT.
THE MUSEUM MUST HAVE COME UP WITH THAT STORY TO ATTRACT VISITORS.
YEAH, RACHEL! ONLY A LITTLE KID WOULD FALL FOR THAT!
AREN'T *YOU* A LITTLE KID?
BETTER GET BACK TO WORK.
I'LL START ON MY HOME-WORK.
STOP RIGHT THERE-- !!

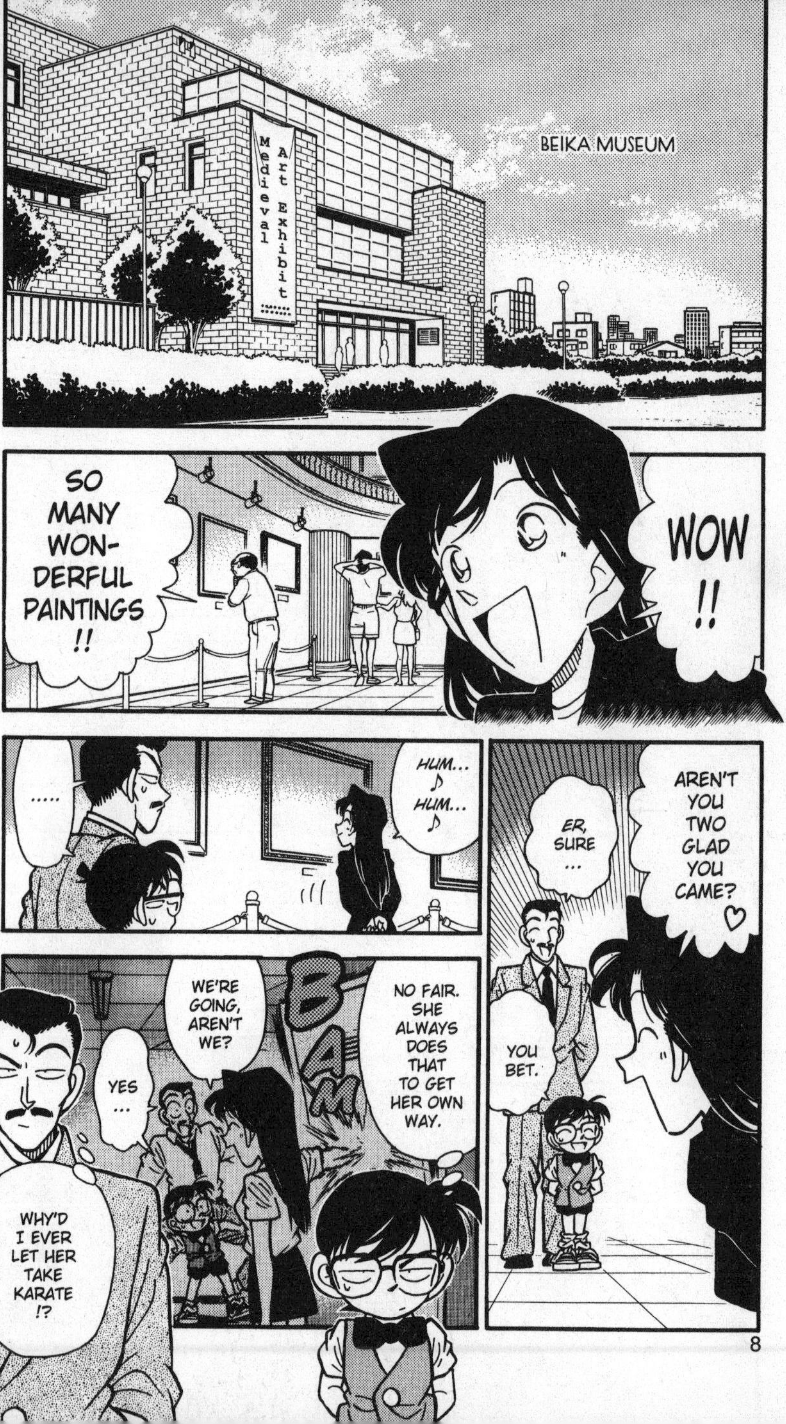
Medieval Art Exhibit
BEIKA MUSEUM
WOW!!
SO MANY WON-DERFUL PAINTINGS!!
AREN'T YOU TWO GLAD YOU CAME? ♡
ER, SURE...
YOU BET.
HUM... ♪ HUM... ♪
.....
NO FAIR. SHE ALWAYS DOES THAT TO GET HER OWN WAY.
BAM
WE'RE GOING, AREN'T WE?
YES...
WHY'D I EVER LET HER TAKE KARATE!?

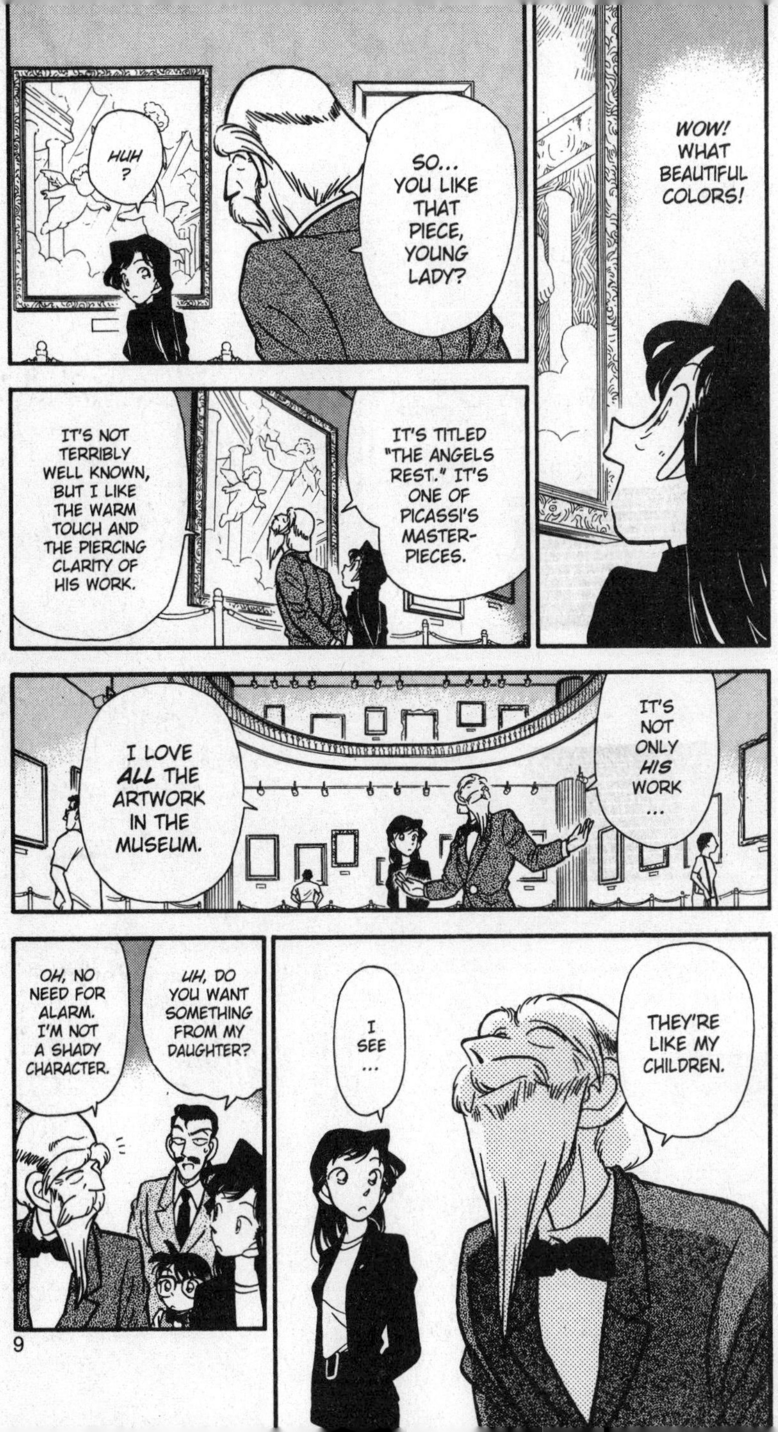
WOW! WHAT BEAUTIFUL COLORS!
SO... YOU LIKE THAT PIECE, YOUNG LADY?
HUH ?
IT'S TITLED "THE ANGELS REST." IT'S ONE OF PICASSI'S MASTER-PIECES.
IT'S NOT TERRIBLY WELL KNOWN, BUT I LIKE THE WARM TOUCH AND THE PIERCING CLARITY OF HIS WORK.
IT'S NOT ONLY HIS WORK ...
I LOVE ALL THE ARTWORK IN THE MUSEUM.
THEY'RE LIKE MY CHILDREN.
I SEE ...
UH, DO YOU WANT SOMETHING FROM MY DAUGHTER?
OH, NO NEED FOR ALARM. I'M NOT A SHADY CHARACTER.

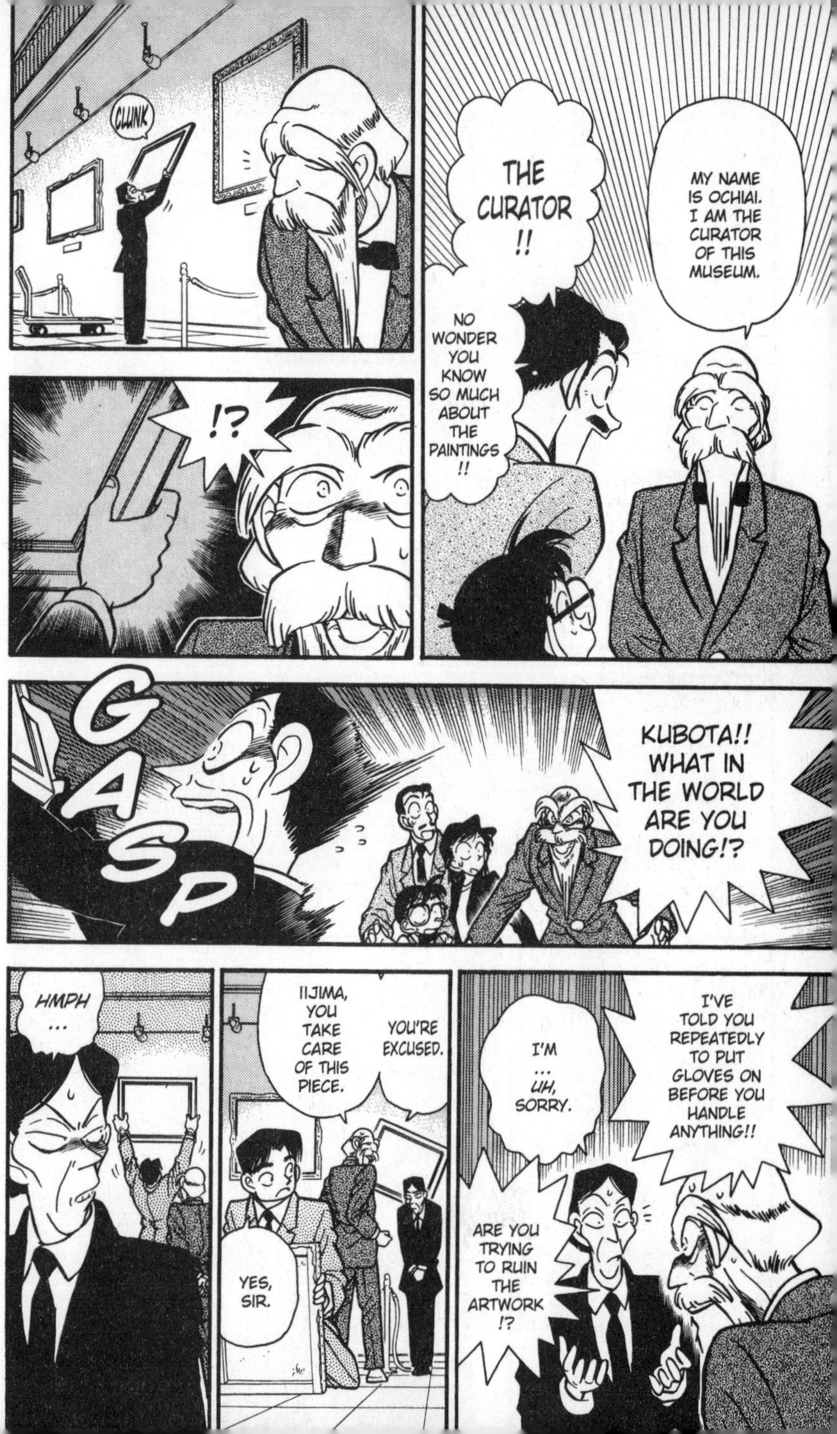
MY NAME IS OCHIAI. I AM THE CURATOR OF THIS MUSEUM.
THE CURATOR !!
NO WONDER YOU KNOW SO MUCH ABOUT THE PAINTINGS !!
CLUNK
!?
KUBOTA!! WHAT IN THE WORLD ARE YOU DOING!?
GASP
I'VE TOLD YOU REPEATEDLY TO PUT GLOVES ON BEFORE YOU HANDLE ANYTHING!!
I'M ... UH, SORRY.
ARE YOU TRYING TO RUIN THE ARTWORK !?
YOU'RE EXCUSED.
IIJIMA, YOU TAKE CARE OF THIS PIECE.
YES, SIR.
HMPH ...

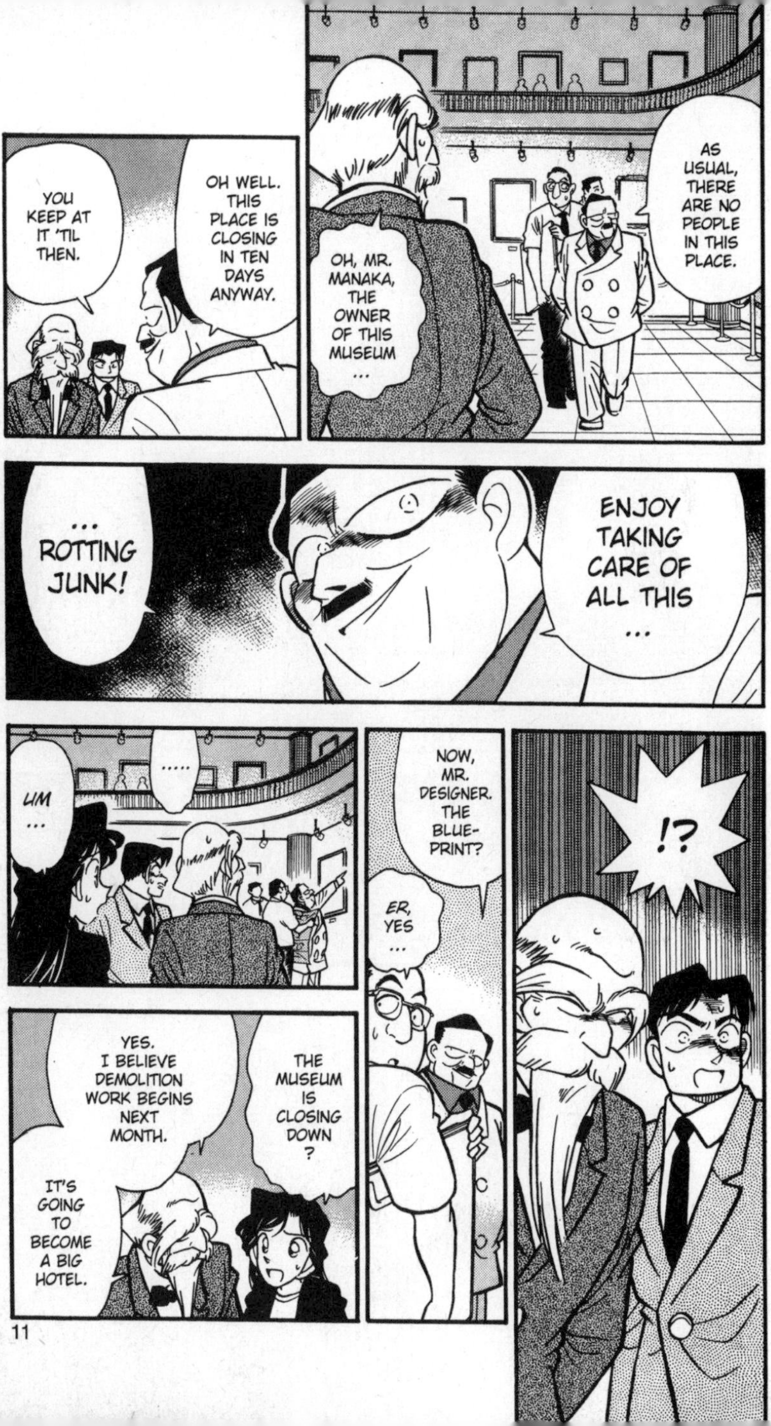
AS USUAL, THERE ARE NO PEOPLE IN THIS PLACE.
OH, MR. MANAKA, THE OWNER OF THIS MUSEUM ...
OH WELL. THIS PLACE IS CLOSING IN TEN DAYS ANYWAY.
YOU KEEP AT IT 'TIL THEN.
ENJOY TAKING CARE OF ALL THIS ...
... ROTTING JUNK!
!?
NOW, MR. DESIGNER. THE BLUE-PRINT?
ER, YES ...
.....
UM ...
THE MUSEUM IS CLOSING DOWN?
YES. I BELIEVE DEMOLITION WORK BEGINS NEXT MONTH.
IT'S GOING TO BECOME A BIG HOTEL.

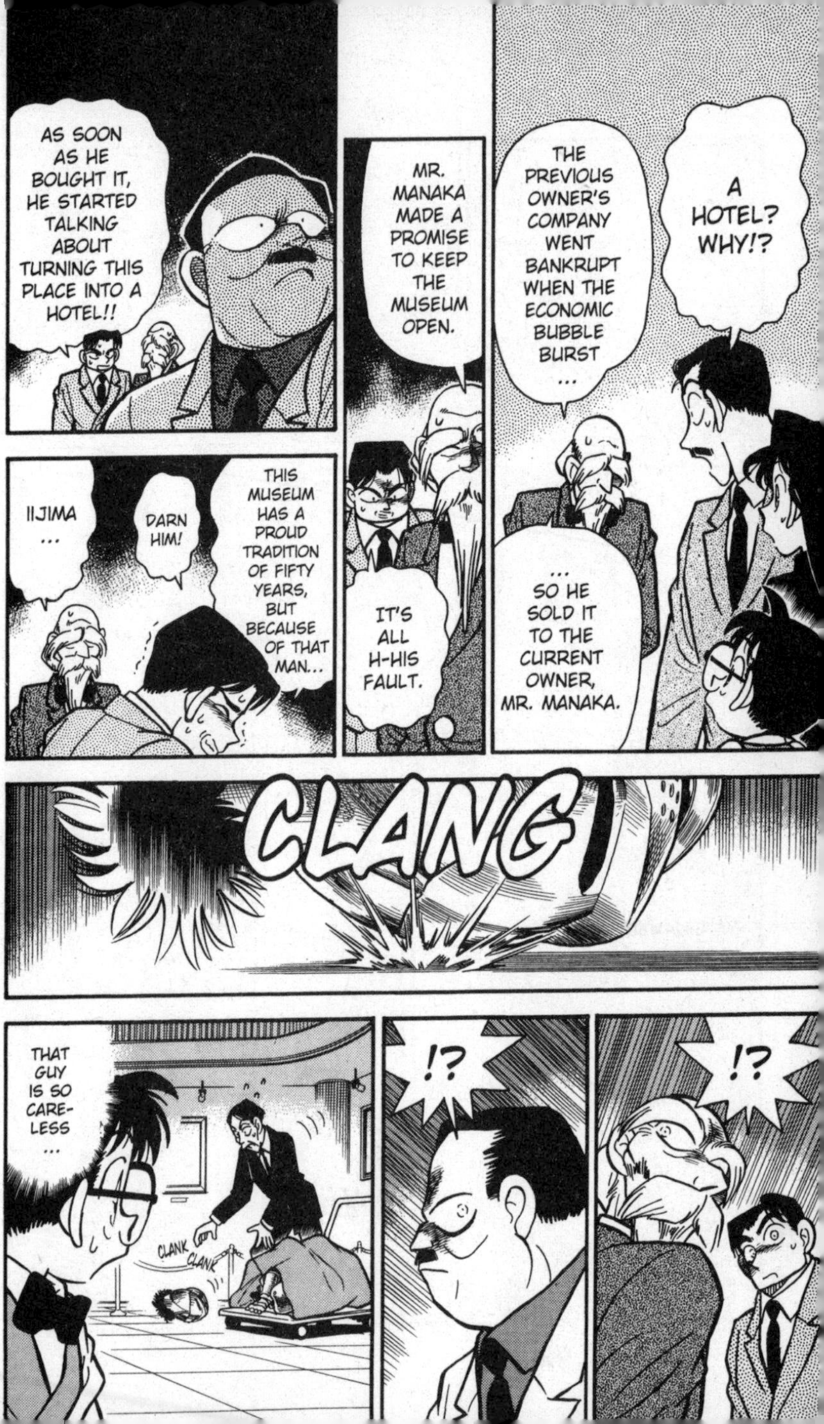
A HOTEL? WHY!?
THE PREVIOUS OWNER'S COMPANY WENT BANKRUPT WHEN THE ECONOMIC BUBBLE BURST ...
... SO HE SOLD IT TO THE CURRENT OWNER, MR. MANAKA.
MR. MANAKA MADE A PROMISE TO KEEP THE MUSEUM OPEN.
IT'S ALL H-HIS FAULT.
AS SOON AS HE BOUGHT IT, HE STARTED TALKING ABOUT TURNING THIS PLACE INTO A HOTEL!!
THIS MUSEUM HAS A PROUD TRADITION OF FIFTY YEARS, BUT BECAUSE OF THAT MAN...
DARN HIM!
IIJIMA ...
CLANG
!?
!?
THAT GUY IS SO CARE-LESS ...
CLANK
CLANK

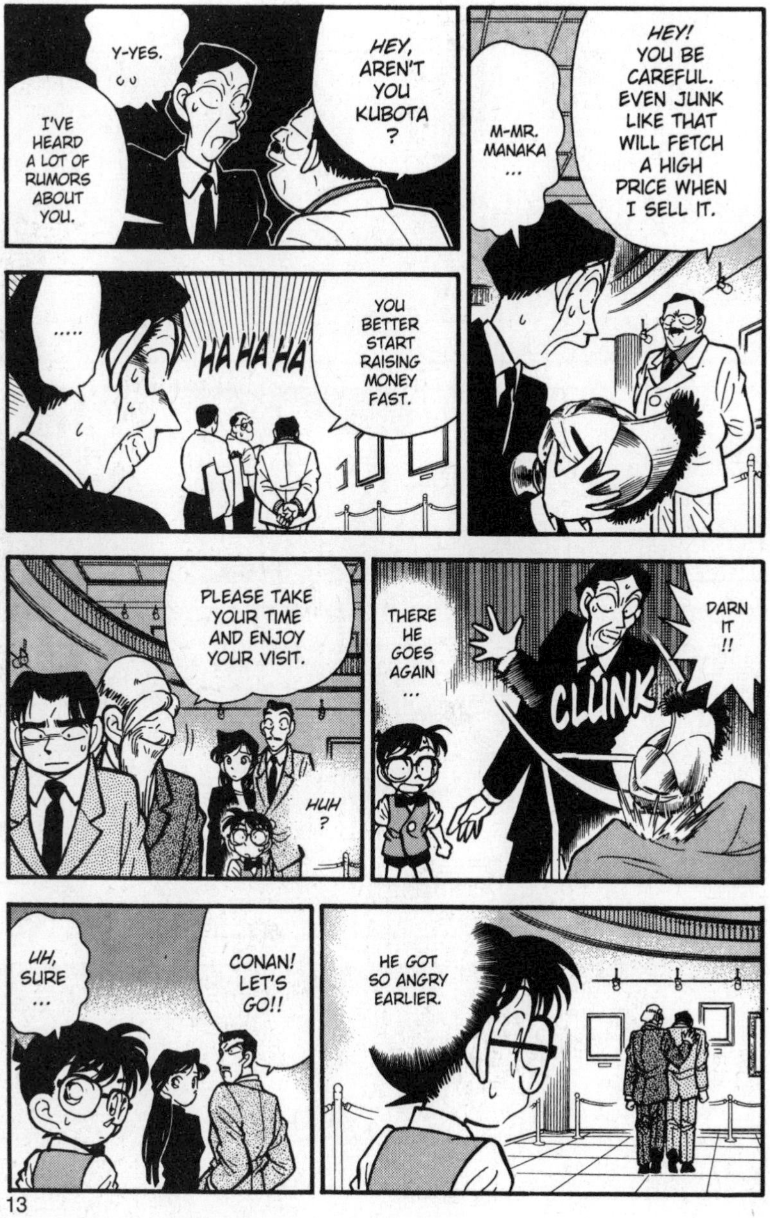
HEY! YOU BE CAREFUL. EVEN JUNK LIKE THAT WILL FETCH A HIGH PRICE WHEN I SELL IT.
M-MR. MANAKA ...
HEY, AREN'T YOU KUBOTA ?
Y-YES.
I'VE HEARD A LOT OF RUMORS ABOUT YOU.
YOU BETTER START RAISING MONEY FAST.
HA HA HA
.....
DARN IT !!
CLUNK
THERE HE GOES AGAIN ...
PLEASE TAKE YOUR TIME AND ENJOY YOUR VISIT.
HUH ?
HE GOT SO ANGRY EARLIER.
CONAN! LET'S GO!!
UH, SURE ...

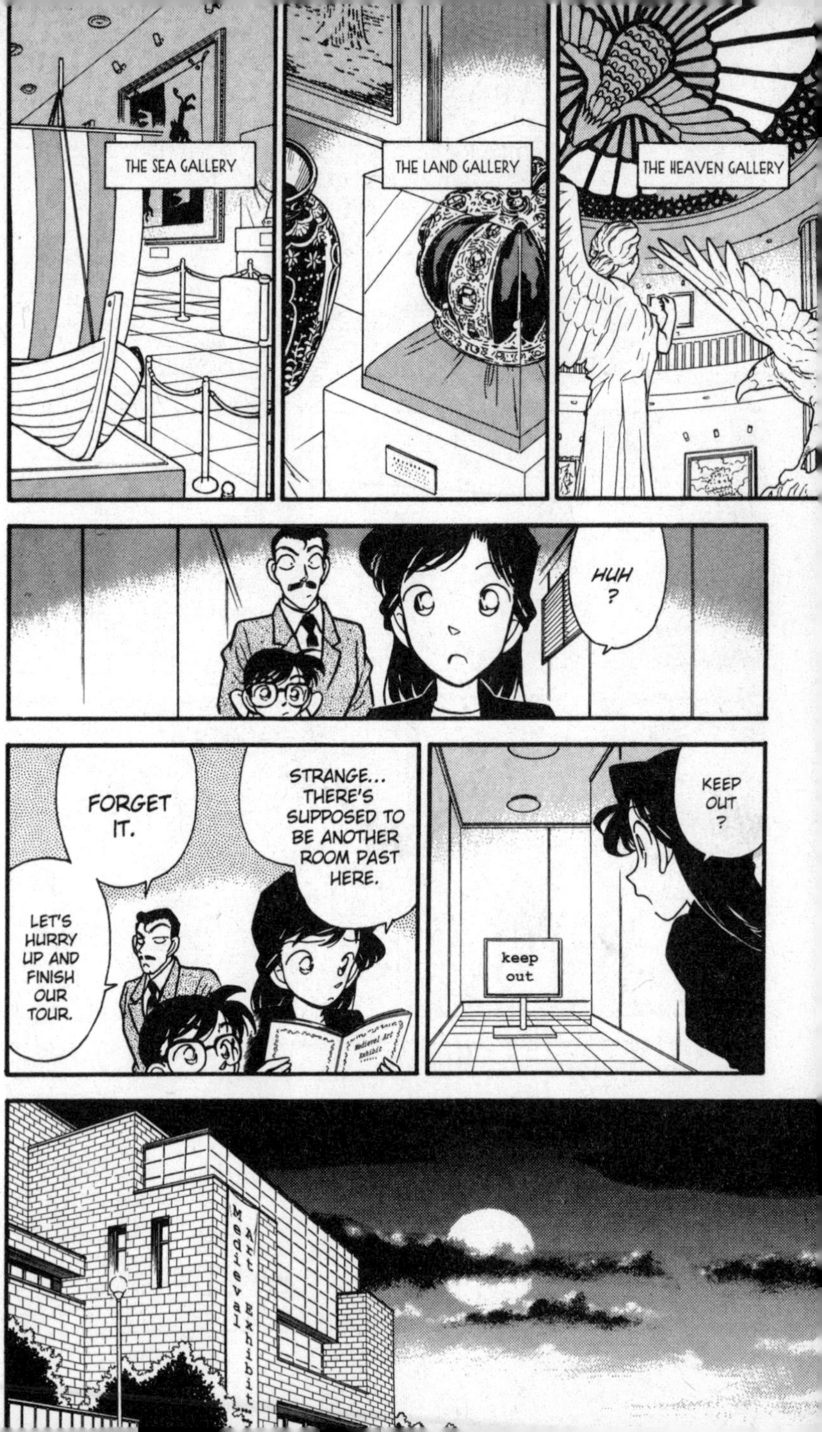
THE HEAVEN GALLERY
THE LAND GALLERY
THE SEA GALLERY
HUH?
KEEP OUT?
keep out
STRANGE... THERE'S SUPPOSED TO BE ANOTHER ROOM PAST HERE.
FORGET IT.
LET'S HURRY UP AND FINISH OUR TOUR.
Medieval Art Exhibit
Medieval Art Exhibit

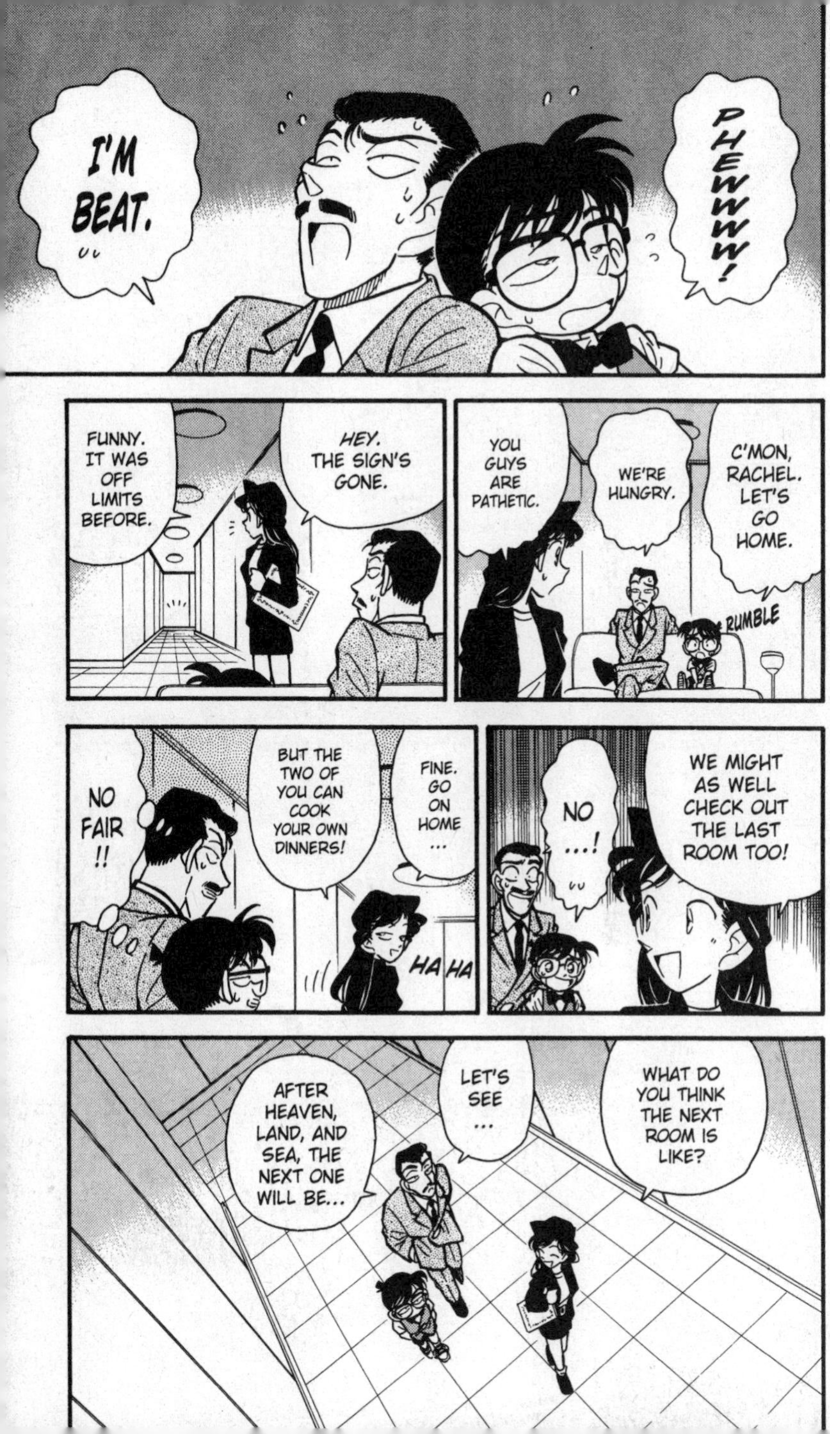
PHEWWWW!
I'M BEAT.
C'MON, RACHEL. LET'S GO HOME.
WE'RE HUNGRY.
RUMBLE
YOU GUYS ARE PATHETIC.
HEY. THE SIGN'S GONE.
FUNNY. IT WAS OFF LIMITS BEFORE.
WE MIGHT AS WELL CHECK OUT THE LAST ROOM TOO!
NO ...!
FINE. GO ON HOME ...
BUT THE TWO OF YOU CAN COOK YOUR OWN DINNERS!
HA HA
NO FAIR !!
WHAT DO YOU THINK THE NEXT ROOM IS LIKE?
LET'S SEE ...
AFTER HEAVEN, LAND, AND SEA, THE NEXT ONE WILL BE...

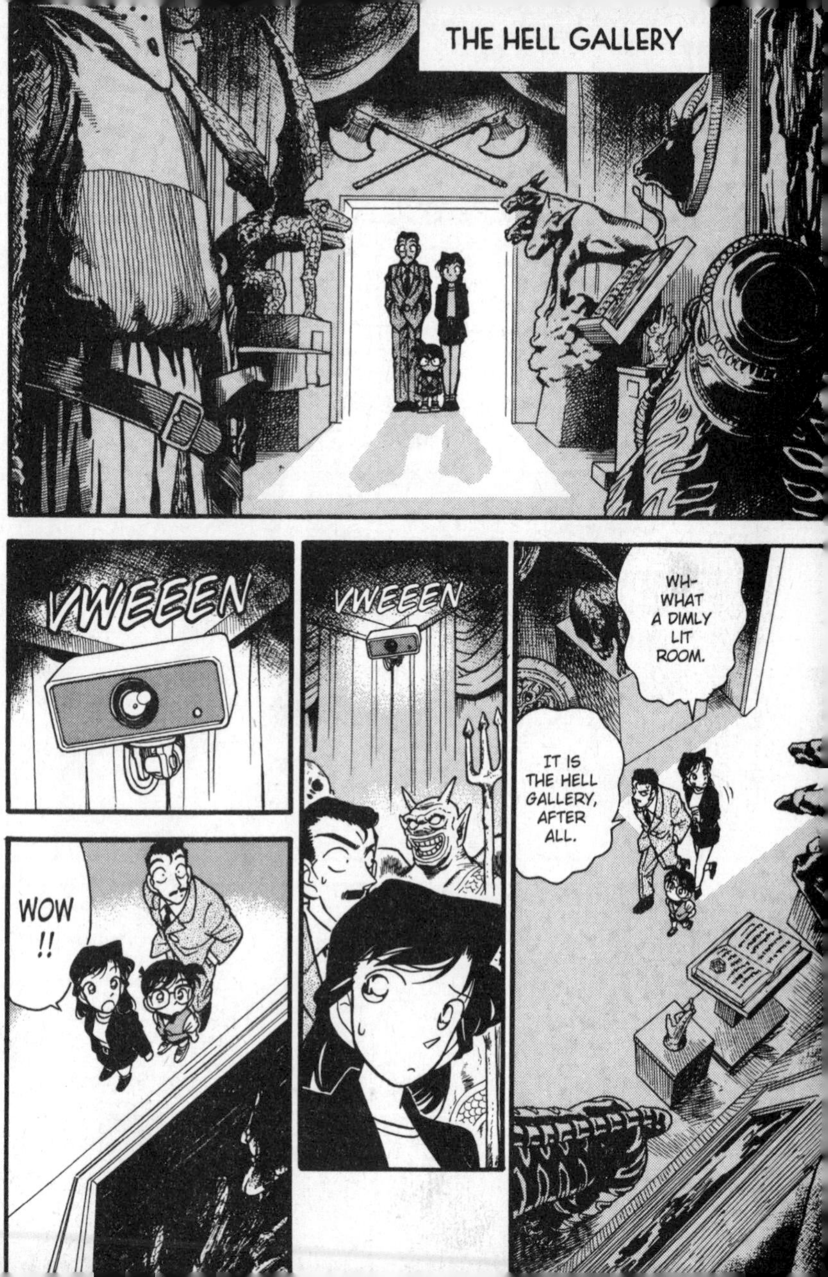
THE HELL GALLERY
WH- WHAT A DIMLY LIT ROOM.
IT IS THE HELL GALLERY, AFTER ALL.
VWEEEN
VWEEEN
WOW !!

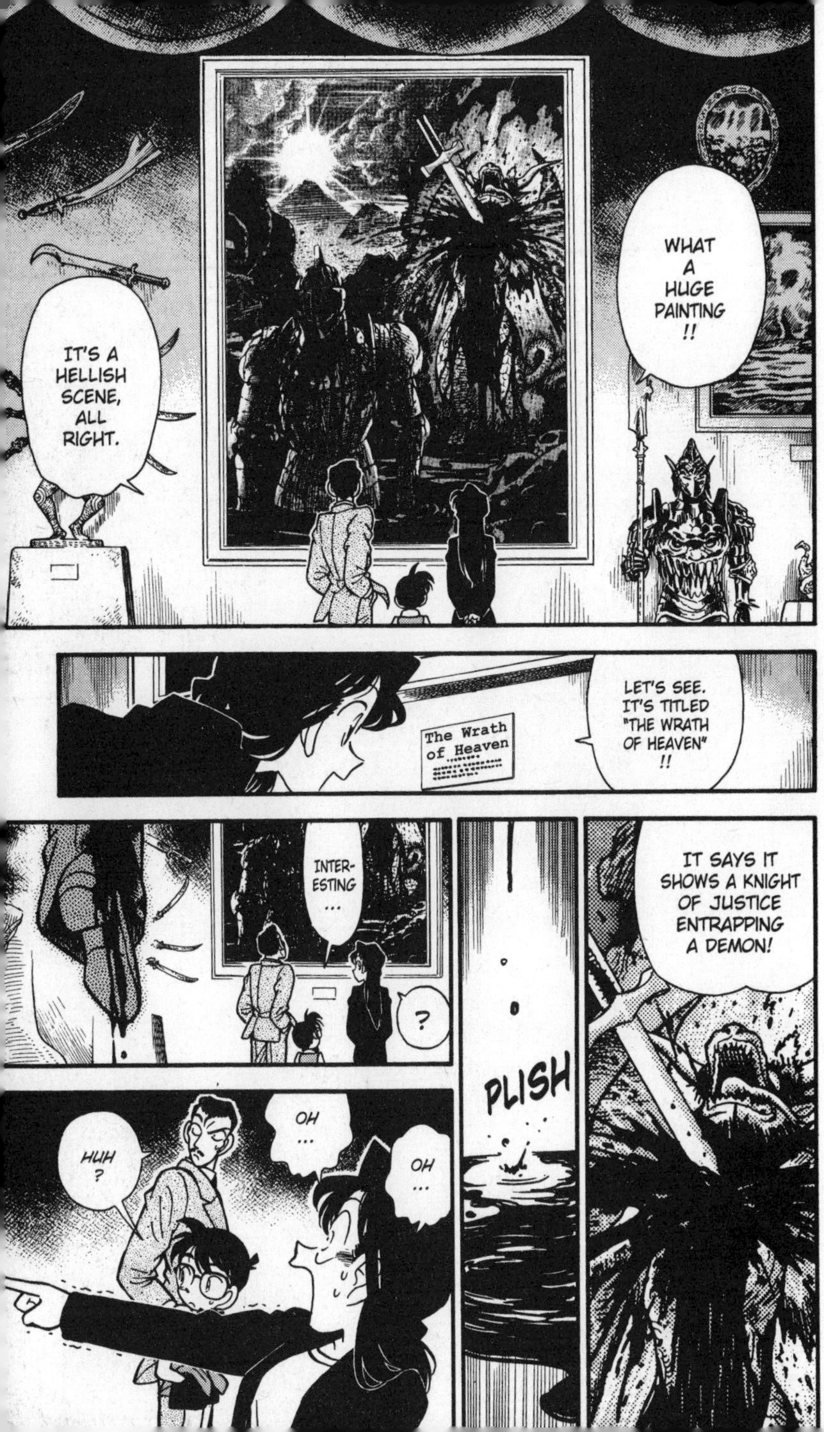
WHAT A HUGE PAINTING!!
IT'S A HELLISH SCENE, ALL RIGHT.
LET'S SEE. IT'S TITLED "THE WRATH OF HEAVEN"!!
The Wrath of Heaven
IT SAYS IT SHOWS A KNIGHT OF JUSTICE ENTRAPPING A DEMON!
PLISH
INTER-ESTING ...
?
OH ...
OH ...
HUH?

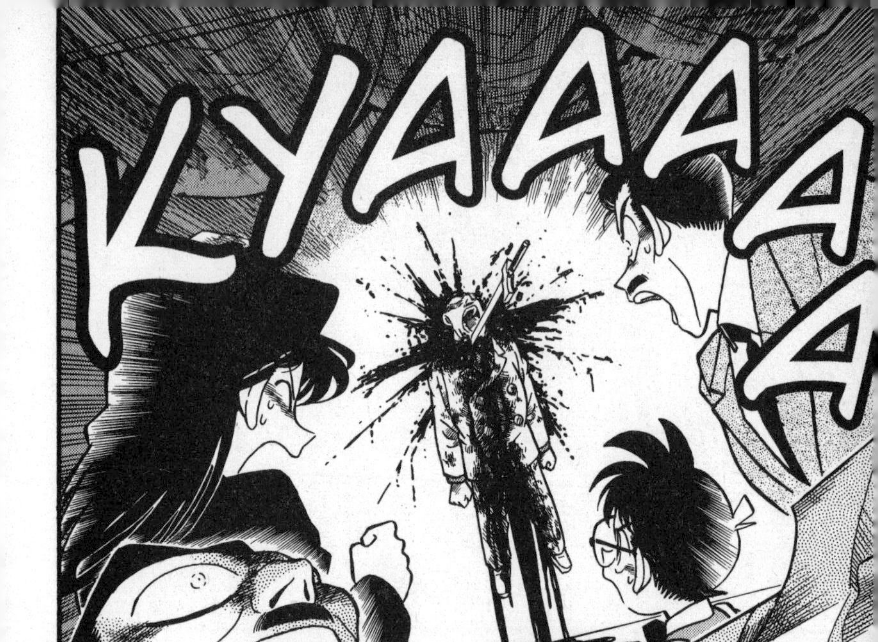
KYAAAAA

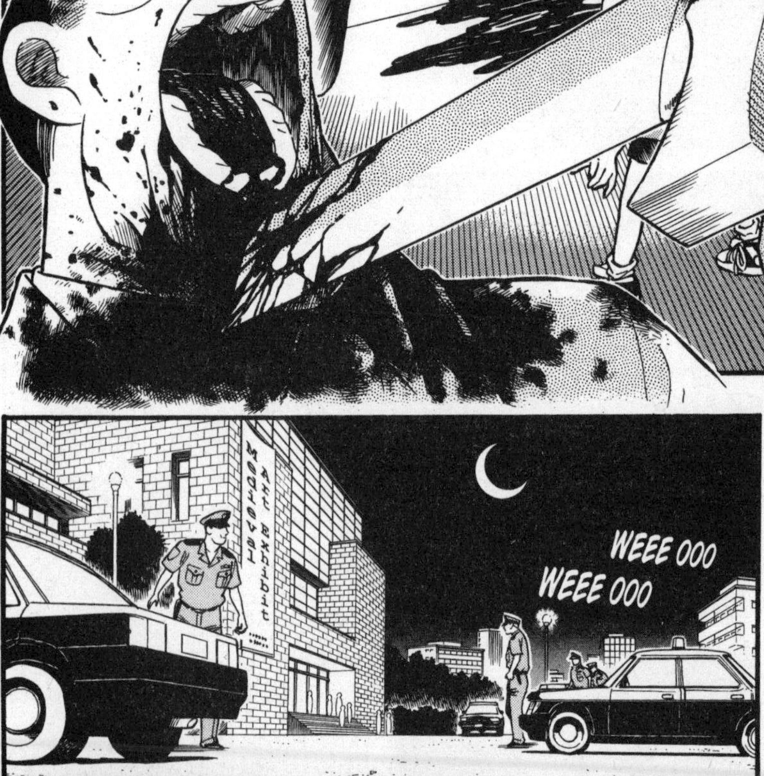
Medieval Art Exhibit
WEEE OOO
WEEE OOO

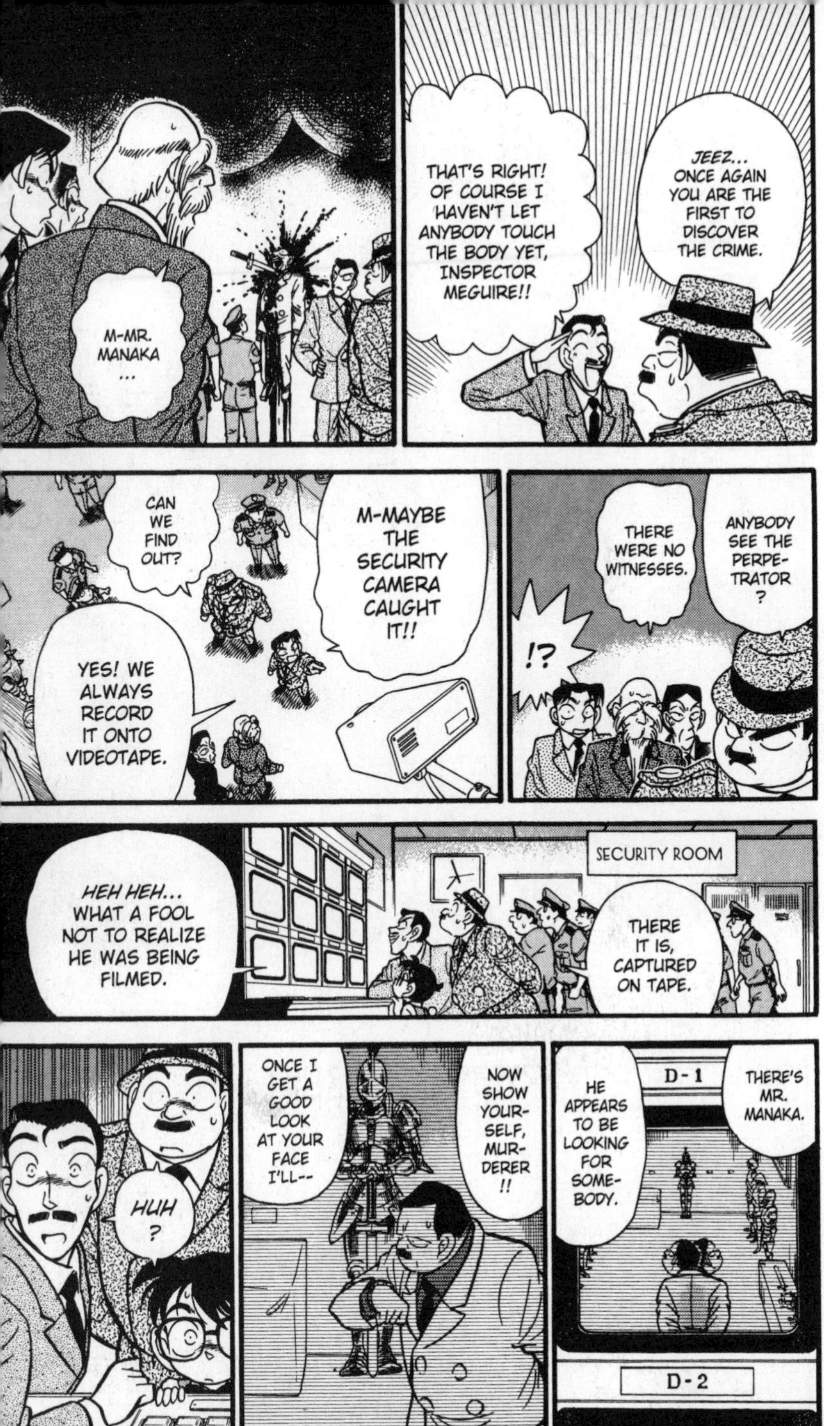
JEEZ... ONCE AGAIN YOU ARE THE FIRST TO DISCOVER THE CRIME.
THAT'S RIGHT! OF COURSE I HAVEN'T LET ANYBODY TOUCH THE BODY YET, INSPECTOR MEGUIRE!!
M-MR. MANAKA ...
ANYBODY SEE THE PERPE-TRATOR ?
THERE WERE NO WITNESSES.
!?
M-MAYBE THE SECURITY CAMERA CAUGHT IT!!
CAN WE FIND OUT?
YES! WE ALWAYS RECORD IT ONTO VIDEOTAPE.
SECURITY ROOM
THERE IT IS, CAPTURED ON TAPE.
HEH HEH... WHAT A FOOL NOT TO REALIZE HE WAS BEING FILMED.
THERE'S MR. MANAKA.
D-1
HE APPEARS TO BE LOOKING FOR SOME-BODY.
D-2
NOW SHOW YOUR-SELF, MUR-DERER !!
ONCE I GET A GOOD LOOK AT YOUR FACE I'LL--
HUH ?

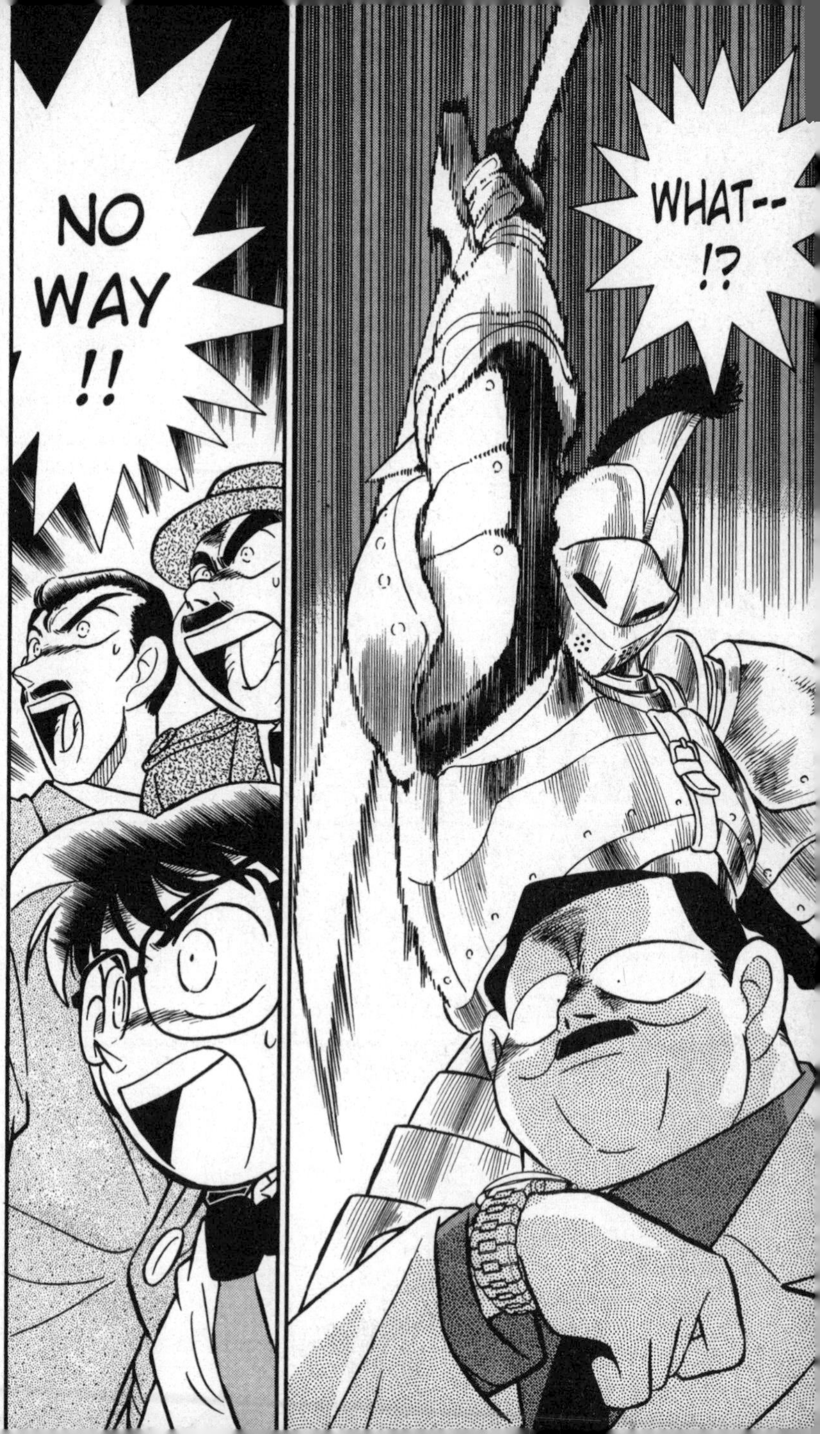
WHAT-- !?
NO WAY !!

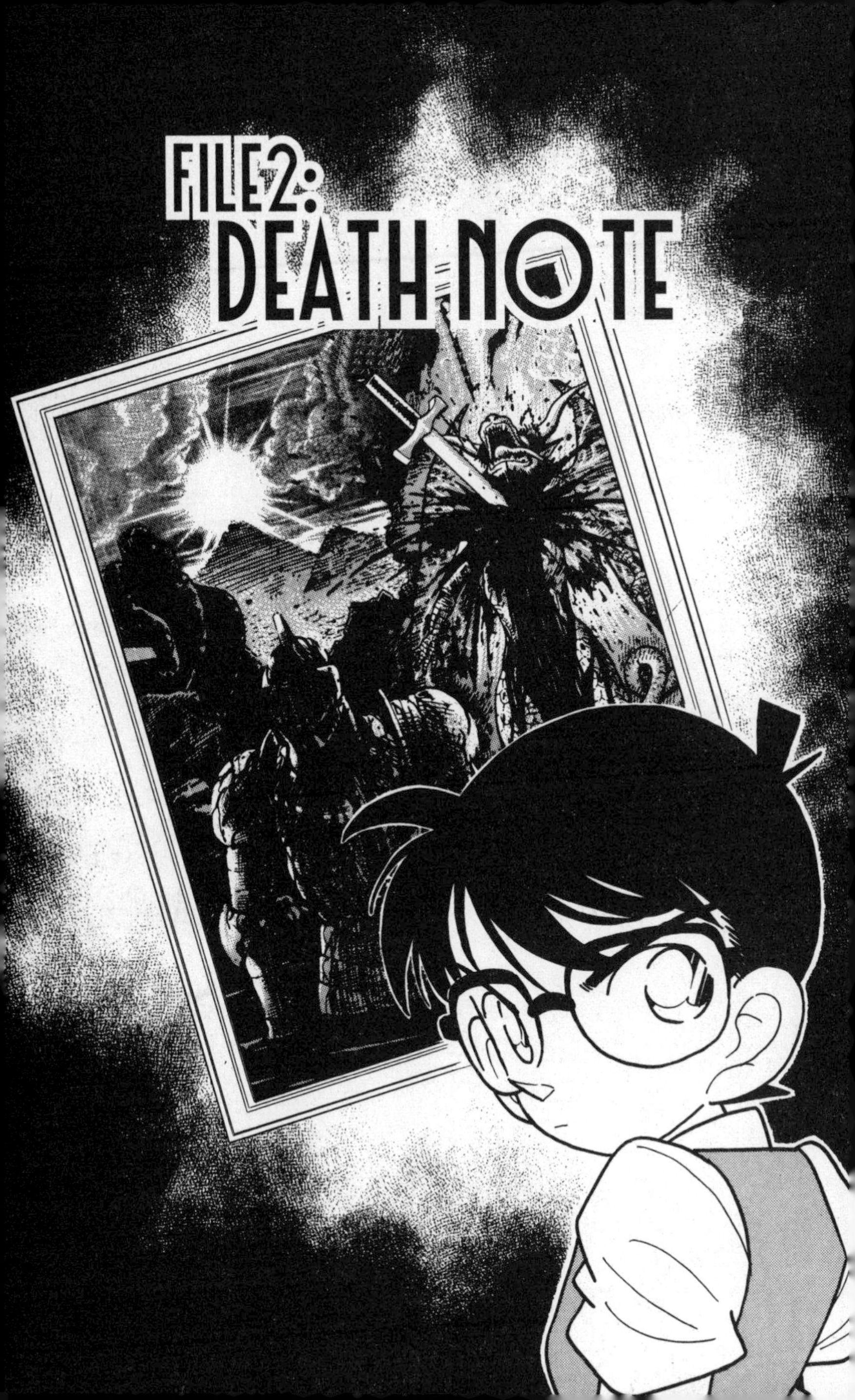
FILE 2:
DEATH NOTE

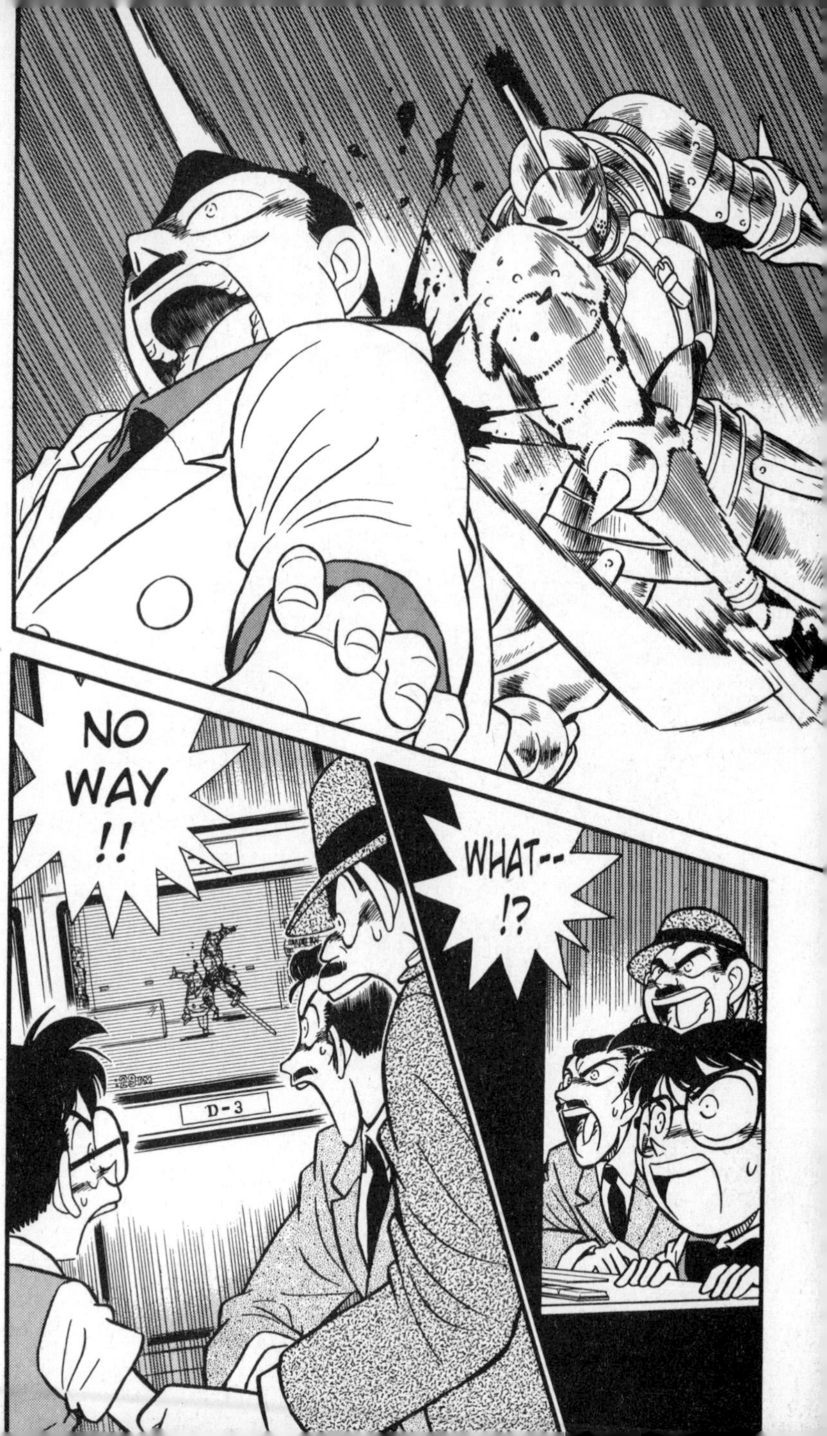
WHAT-- !?
NO WAY !!
D-3

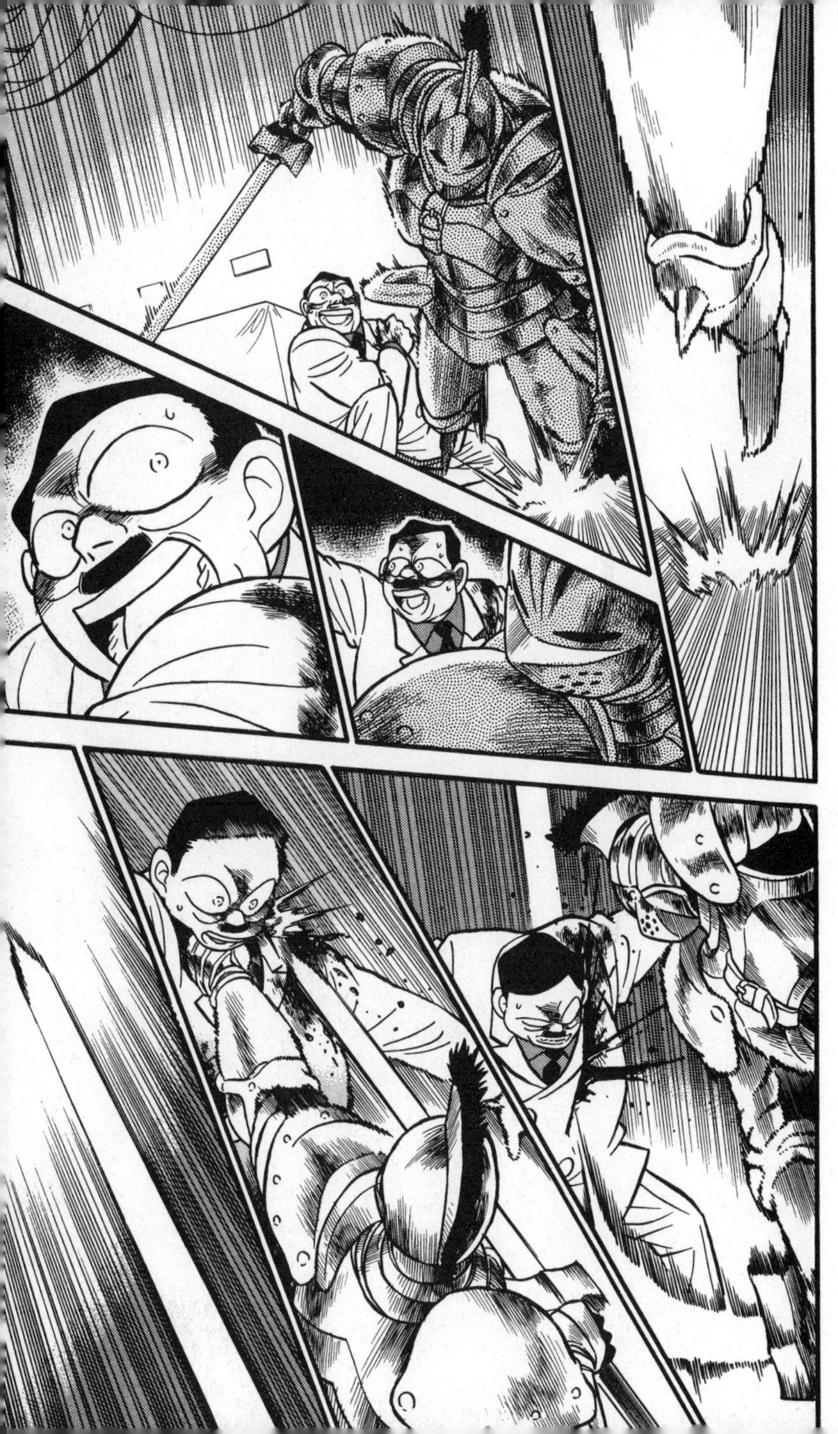

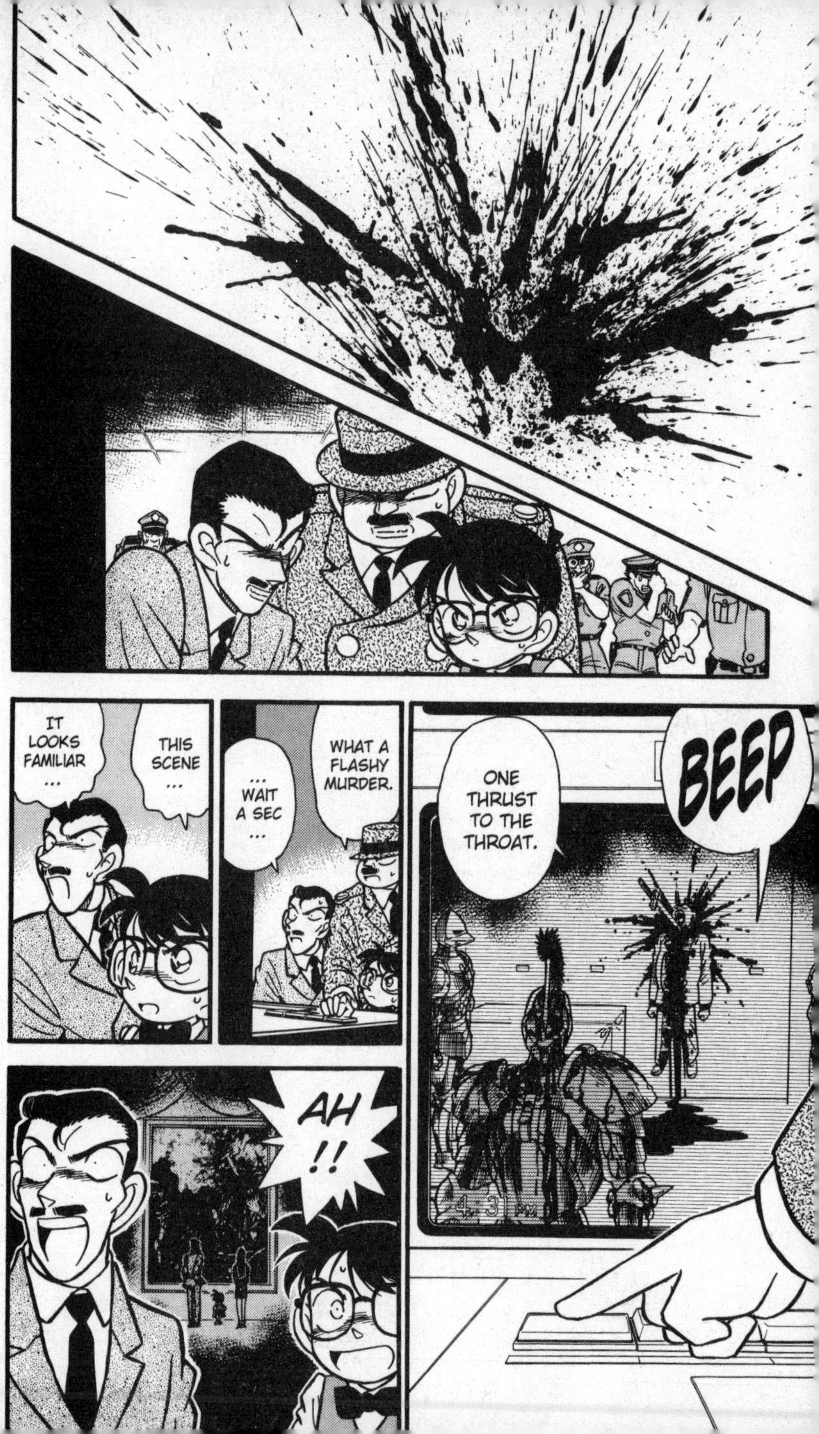
BEEP
ONE THRUST TO THE THROAT.
4:31 PM
WHAT A FLASHY MURDER.
... WAIT A SEC ...
THIS SCENE ...
IT LOOKS FAMILIAR ...
AH !!

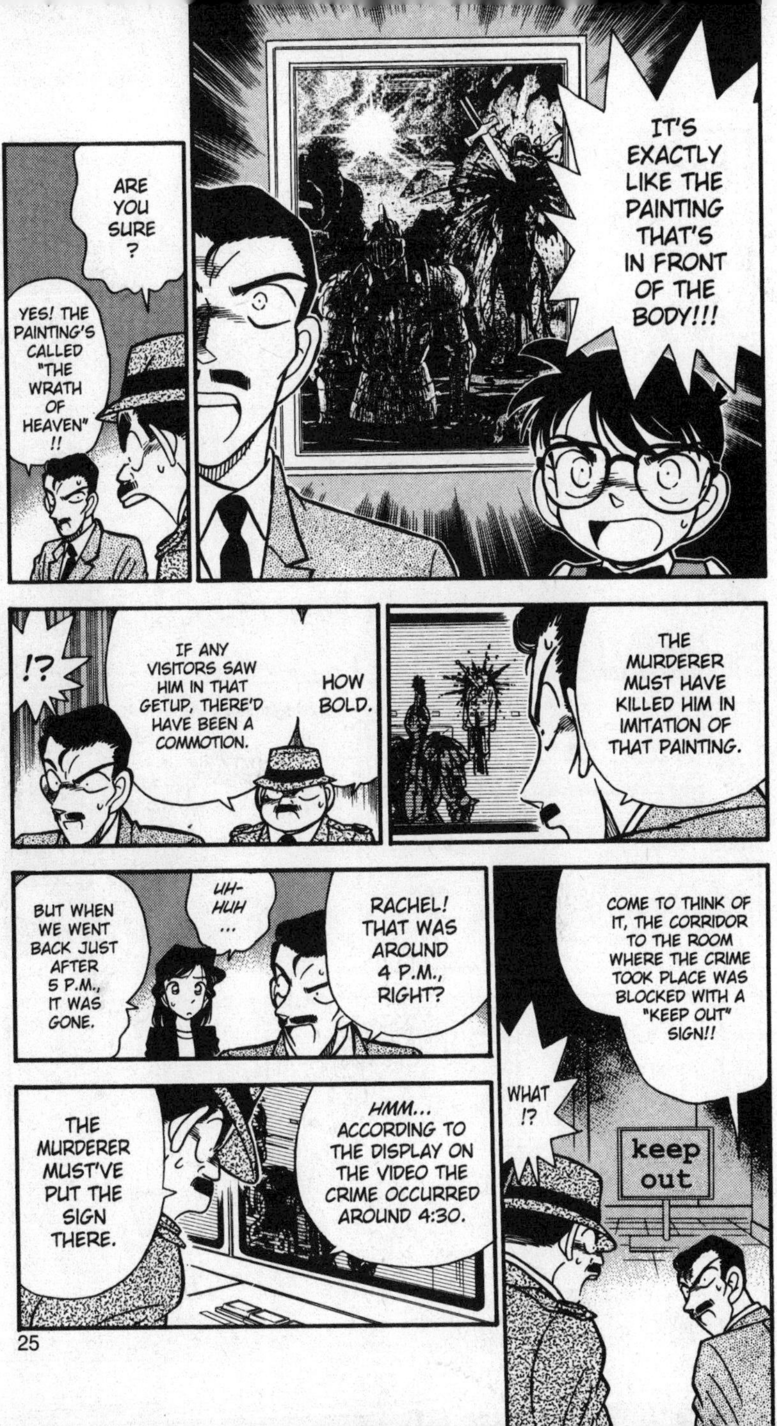
IT'S EXACTLY LIKE THE PAINTING THAT'S IN FRONT OF THE BODY!!!
ARE YOU SURE?
YES! THE PAINTING'S CALLED "THE WRATH OF HEAVEN"!!
THE MURDERER MUST HAVE KILLED HIM IN IMITATION OF THAT PAINTING.
HOW BOLD.
IF ANY VISITORS SAW HIM IN THAT GETUP, THERE'D HAVE BEEN A COMMOTION.
!?
COME TO THINK OF IT, THE CORRIDOR TO THE ROOM WHERE THE CRIME TOOK PLACE WAS BLOCKED WITH A "KEEP OUT" SIGN!!
WHAT!?
keep out
RACHEL! THAT WAS AROUND 4 P.M., RIGHT?
UH-HUH...
BUT WHEN WE WENT BACK JUST AFTER 5 P.M., IT WAS GONE.
HMM... ACCORDING TO THE DISPLAY ON THE VIDEO THE CRIME OCCURRED AROUND 4:30.
THE MURDERER MUST'VE PUT THE SIGN THERE.

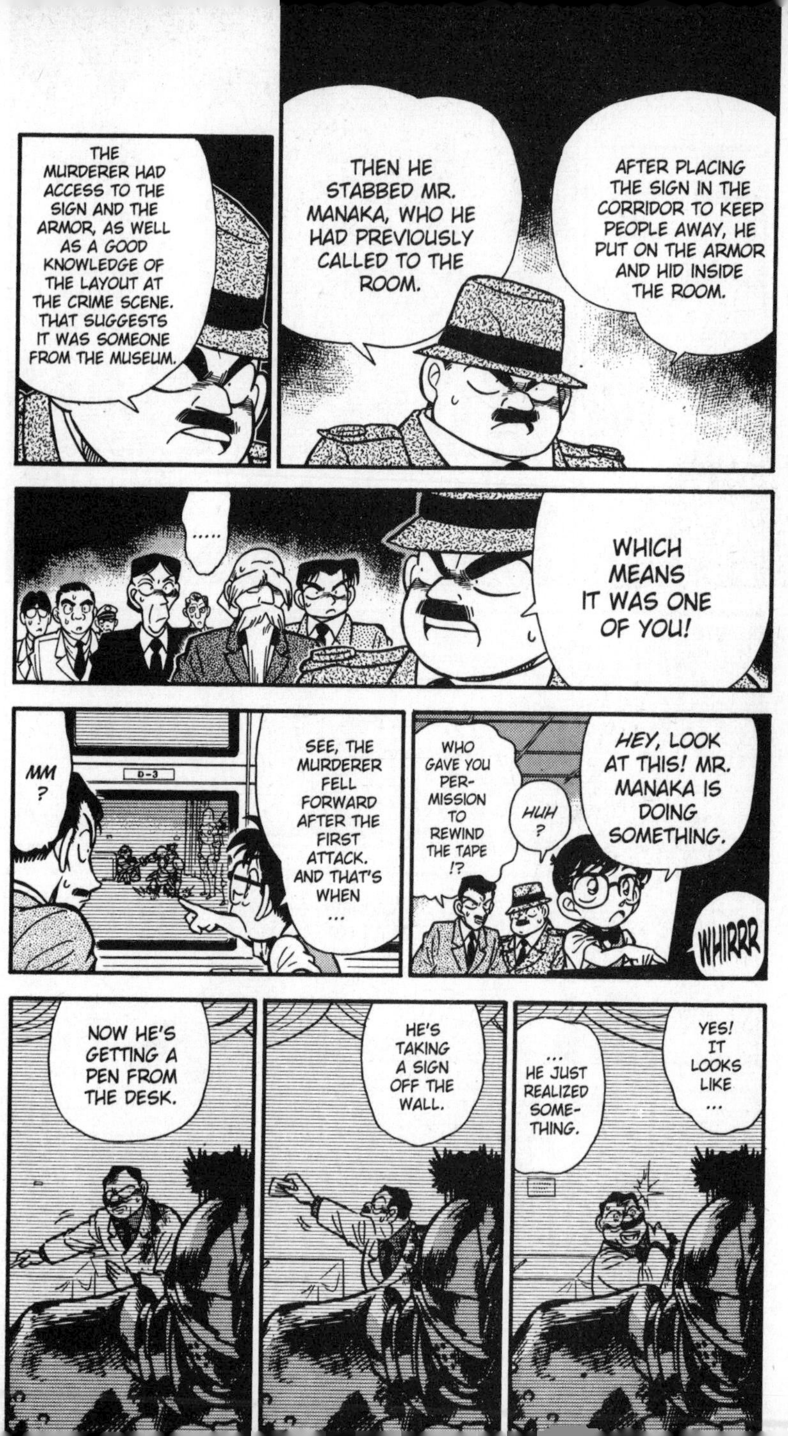
AFTER PLACING THE SIGN IN THE CORRIDOR TO KEEP PEOPLE AWAY, HE PUT ON THE ARMOR AND HID INSIDE THE ROOM.
THEN HE STABBED MR. MANAKA, WHO HE HAD PREVIOUSLY CALLED TO THE ROOM.
THE MURDERER HAD ACCESS TO THE SIGN AND THE ARMOR, AS WELL AS A GOOD KNOWLEDGE OF THE LAYOUT AT THE CRIME SCENE. THAT SUGGESTS IT WAS SOMEONE FROM THE MUSEUM.
WHICH MEANS IT WAS ONE OF YOU!
......
HEY, LOOK AT THIS! MR. MANAKA IS DOING SOMETHING.
HUH ?
WHO GAVE YOU PER-MISSION TO REWIND THE TAPE !?
WHIRRR
SEE, THE MURDERER FELL FORWARD AFTER THE FIRST ATTACK. AND THAT'S WHEN ...
MM ?
D-3
YES! IT LOOKS LIKE ...
... HE JUST REALIZED SOME-THING.
HE'S TAKING A SIGN OFF THE WALL.
NOW HE'S GETTING A PEN FROM THE DESK.

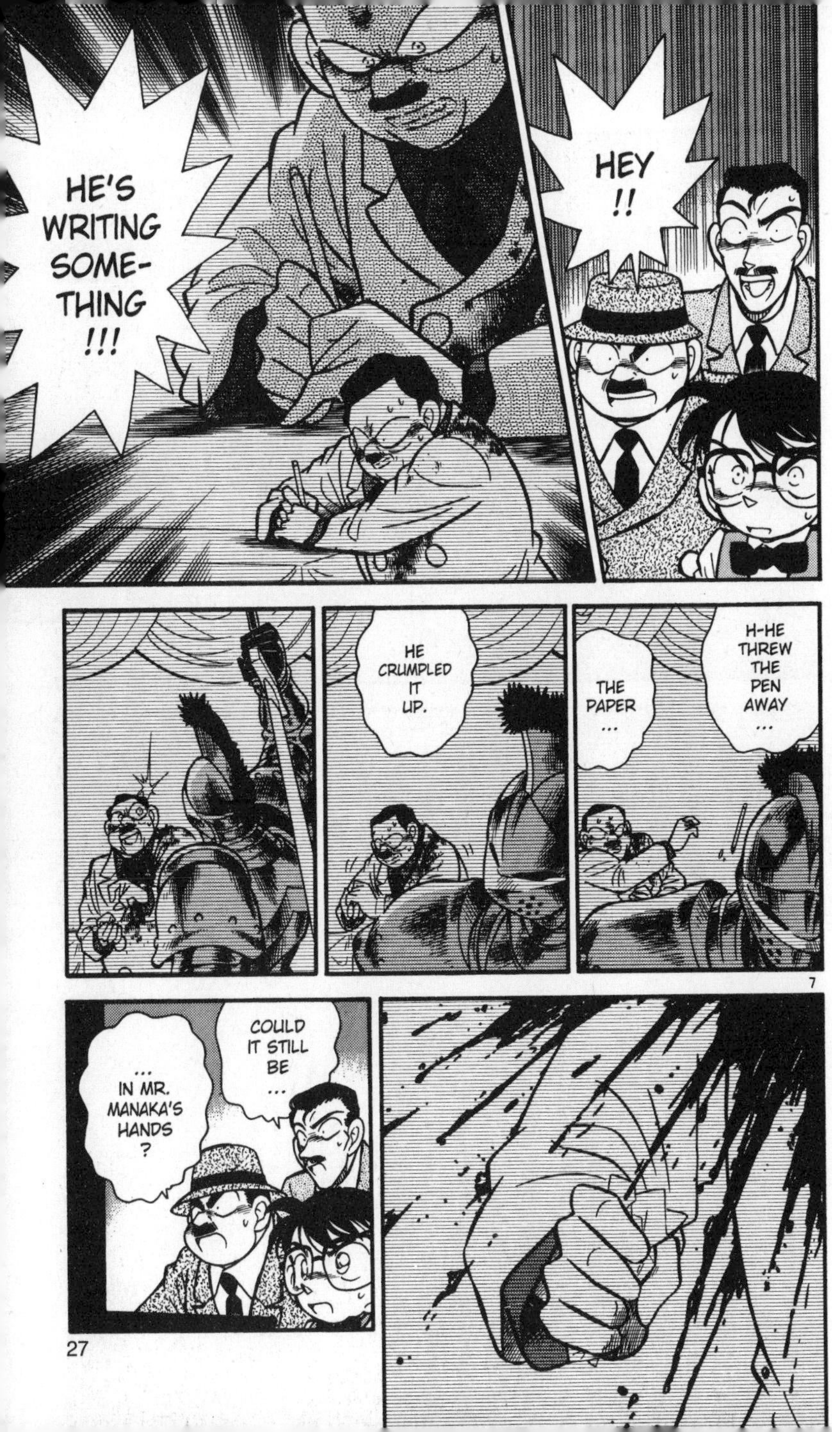
HEY!!
HE'S WRITING SOME-THING!!!
H-HE THREW THE PEN AWAY...
THE PAPER...
HE CRUMPLED IT UP.
COULD IT STILL BE...
...IN MR. MANAKA'S HANDS?

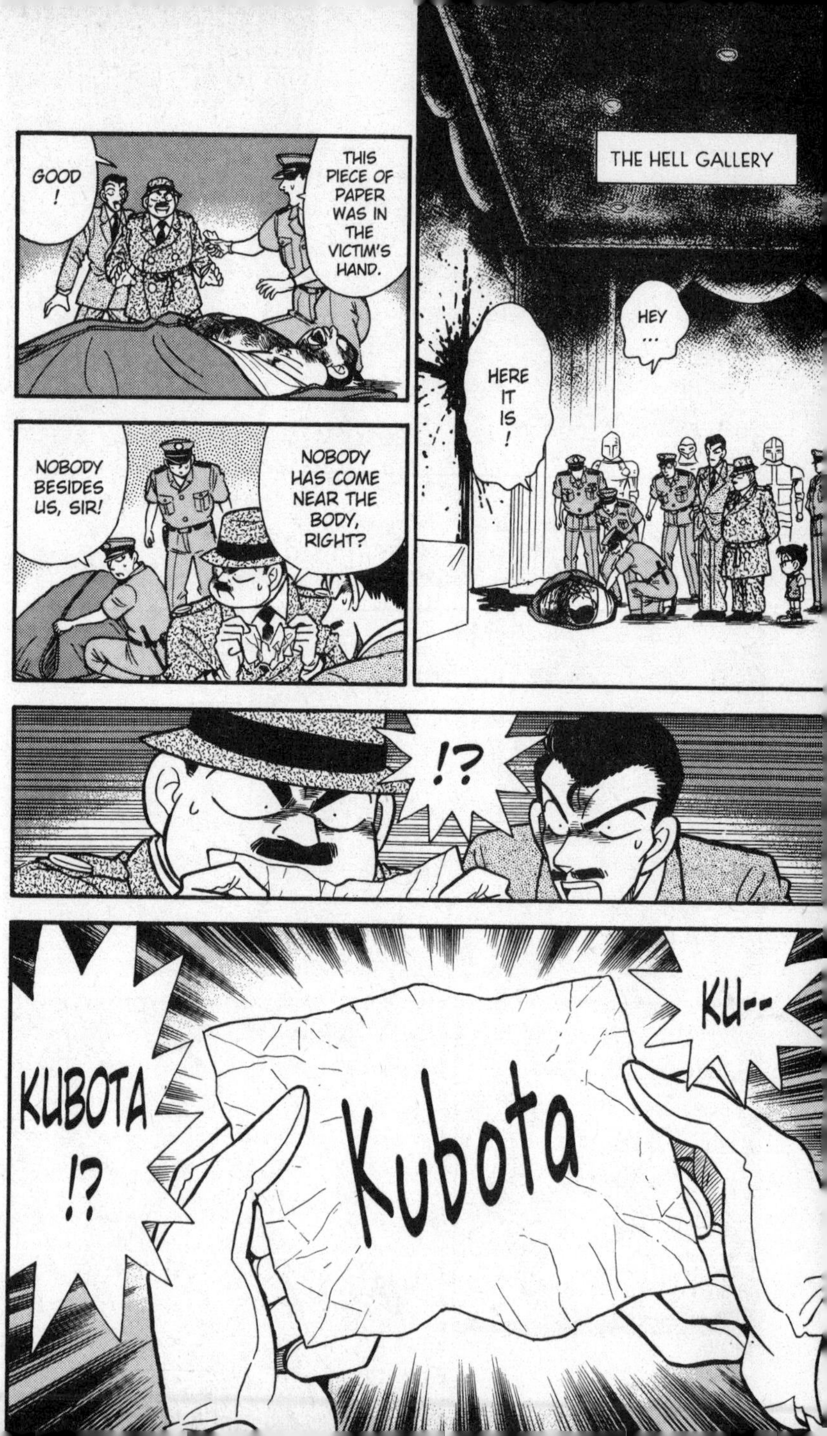
THE HELL GALLERY
HEY ...
HERE IT IS!
THIS PIECE OF PAPER WAS IN THE VICTIM'S HAND.
GOOD!
NOBODY HAS COME NEAR THE BODY, RIGHT?
NOBODY BESIDES US, SIR!
!?
KU--
Kubota
KUBOTA !?

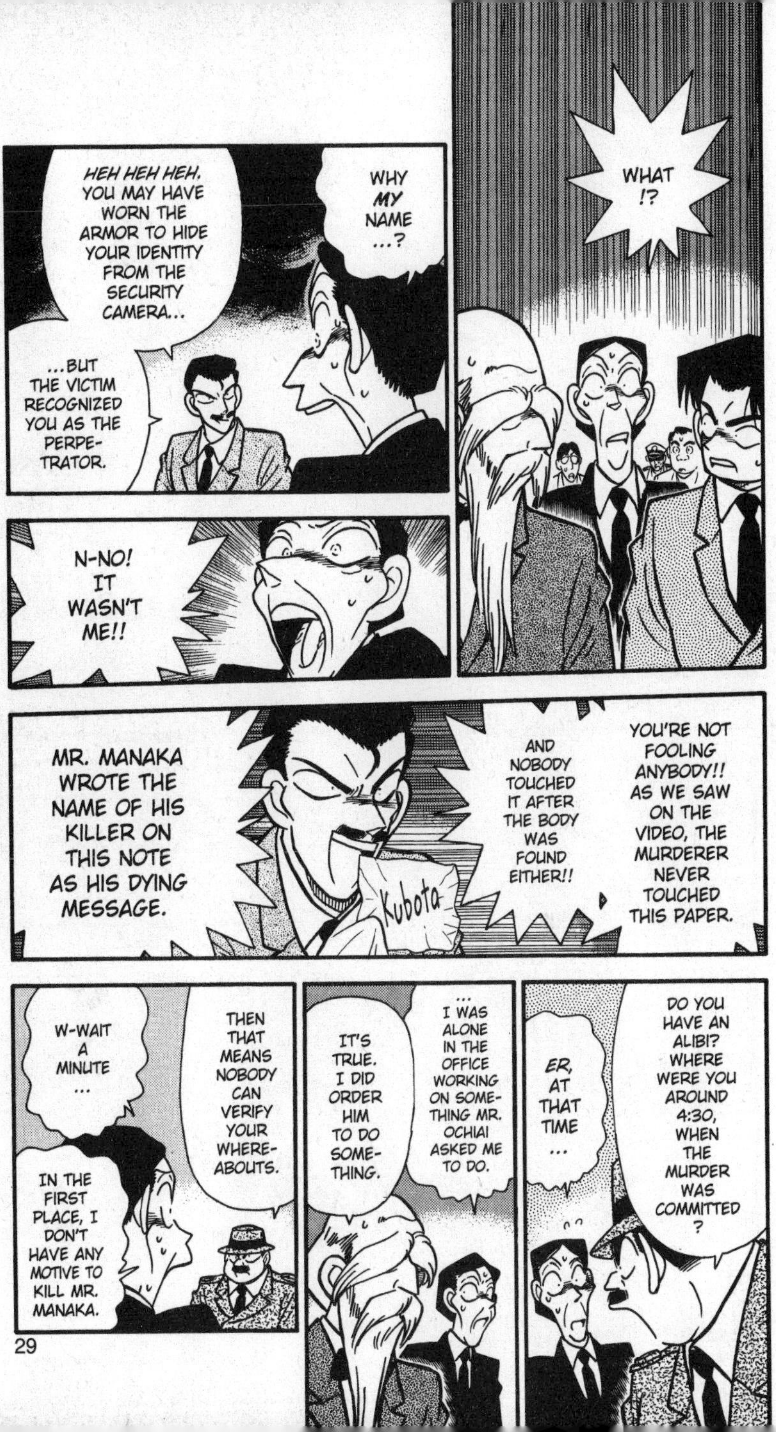
WHAT!?
WHY MY NAME ...?
HEH HEH HEH. YOU MAY HAVE WORN THE ARMOR TO HIDE YOUR IDENTITY FROM THE SECURITY CAMERA...
...BUT THE VICTIM RECOGNIZED YOU AS THE PERPE-TRATOR.
N-NO! IT WASN'T ME!!
YOU'RE NOT FOOLING ANYBODY!! AS WE SAW ON THE VIDEO, THE MURDERER NEVER TOUCHED THIS PAPER.
AND NOBODY TOUCHED IT AFTER THE BODY WAS FOUND EITHER!!
MR. MANAKA WROTE THE NAME OF HIS KILLER ON THIS NOTE AS HIS DYING MESSAGE.
Kubota
DO YOU HAVE AN ALIBI? WHERE WERE YOU AROUND 4:30, WHEN THE MURDER WAS COMMITTED?
ER, AT THAT TIME ...
... I WAS ALONE IN THE OFFICE WORKING ON SOME-THING MR. OCHIAI ASKED ME TO DO.
IT'S TRUE. I DID ORDER HIM TO DO SOME-THING.
THEN THAT MEANS NOBODY CAN VERIFY YOUR WHERE-ABOUTS.
W-WAIT A MINUTE ...
IN THE FIRST PLACE, I DON'T HAVE ANY MOTIVE TO KILL MR. MANAKA.

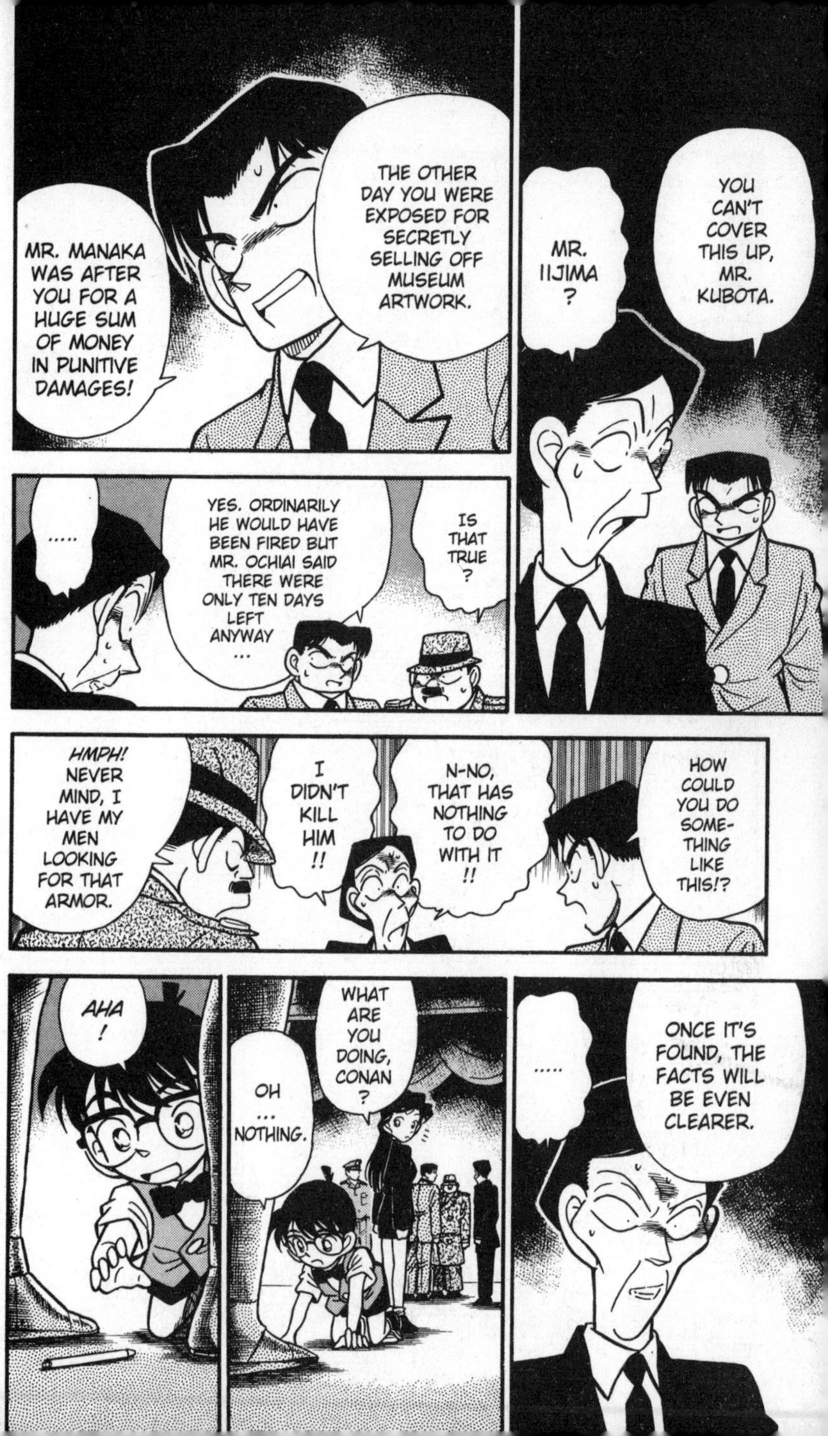
YOU CAN'T COVER THIS UP, MR. KUBOTA.
MR. IIJIMA?
THE OTHER DAY YOU WERE EXPOSED FOR SECRETLY SELLING OFF MUSEUM ARTWORK.
MR. MANAKA WAS AFTER YOU FOR A HUGE SUM OF MONEY IN PUNITIVE DAMAGES!
IS THAT TRUE?
YES. ORDINARILY HE WOULD HAVE BEEN FIRED BUT MR. OCHIAI SAID THERE WERE ONLY TEN DAYS LEFT ANYWAY ...
.....
HOW COULD YOU DO SOME-THING LIKE THIS!?
N-NO, THAT HAS NOTHING TO DO WITH IT!!
I DIDN'T KILL HIM!!
HMPH! NEVER MIND, I HAVE MY MEN LOOKING FOR THAT ARMOR.
ONCE IT'S FOUND, THE FACTS WILL BE EVEN CLEARER.
.....
WHAT ARE YOU DOING, CONAN?
OH ... NOTHING.
AHA!

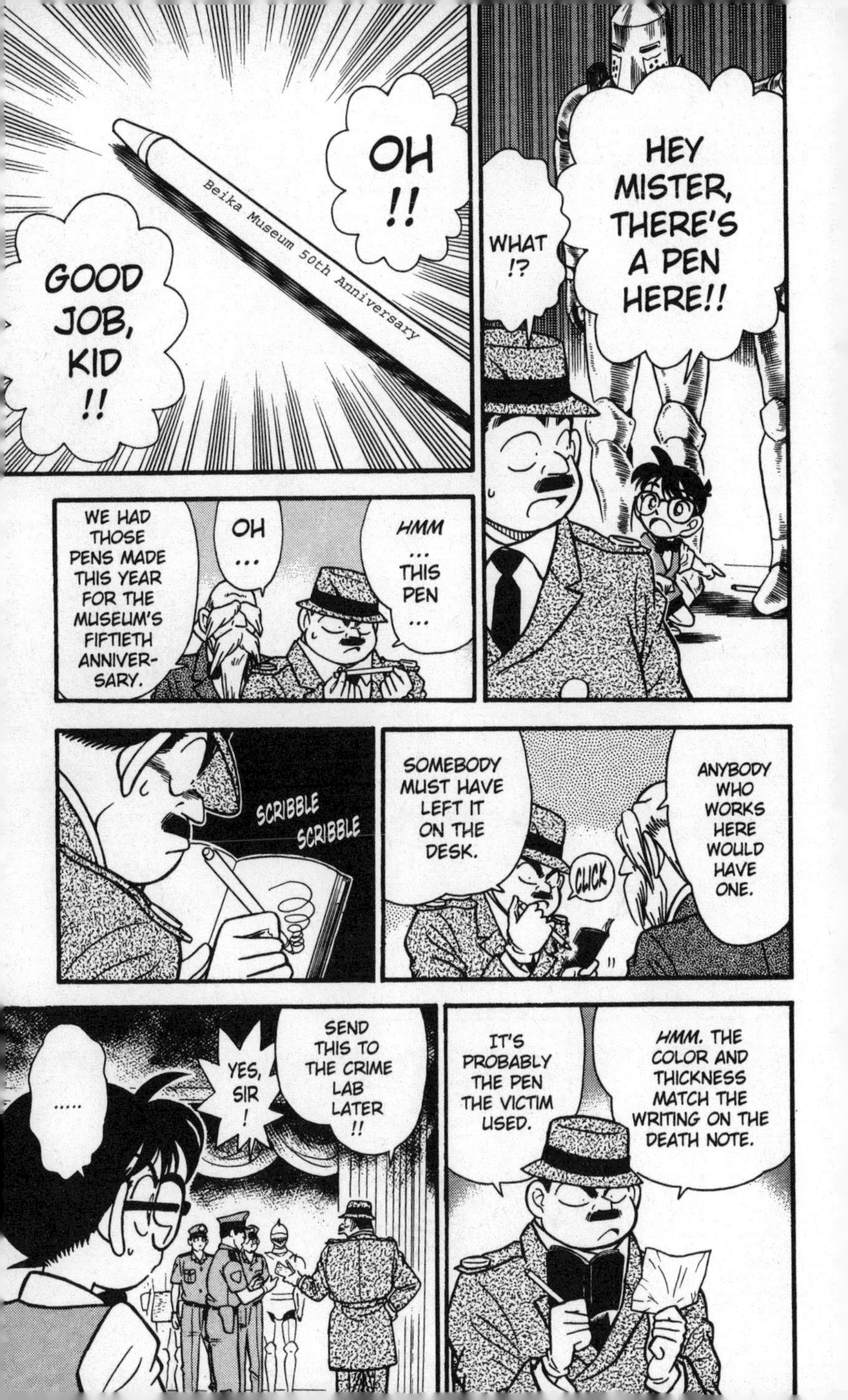
HEY MISTER, THERE'S A PEN HERE!!
WHAT !?
OH !!
Beika Museum 50th Anniversary
GOOD JOB, KID !!
HMM ... THIS PEN ...
OH ...
WE HAD THOSE PENS MADE THIS YEAR FOR THE MUSEUM'S FIFTIETH ANNIVER-SARY.
ANYBODY WHO WORKS HERE WOULD HAVE ONE.
CLICK
SOMEBODY MUST HAVE LEFT IT ON THE DESK.
SCRIBBLE SCRIBBLE
HMM. THE COLOR AND THICKNESS MATCH THE WRITING ON THE DEATH NOTE.
IT'S PROBABLY THE PEN THE VICTIM USED.
SEND THIS TO THE CRIME LAB LATER !!
YES, SIR !
.....

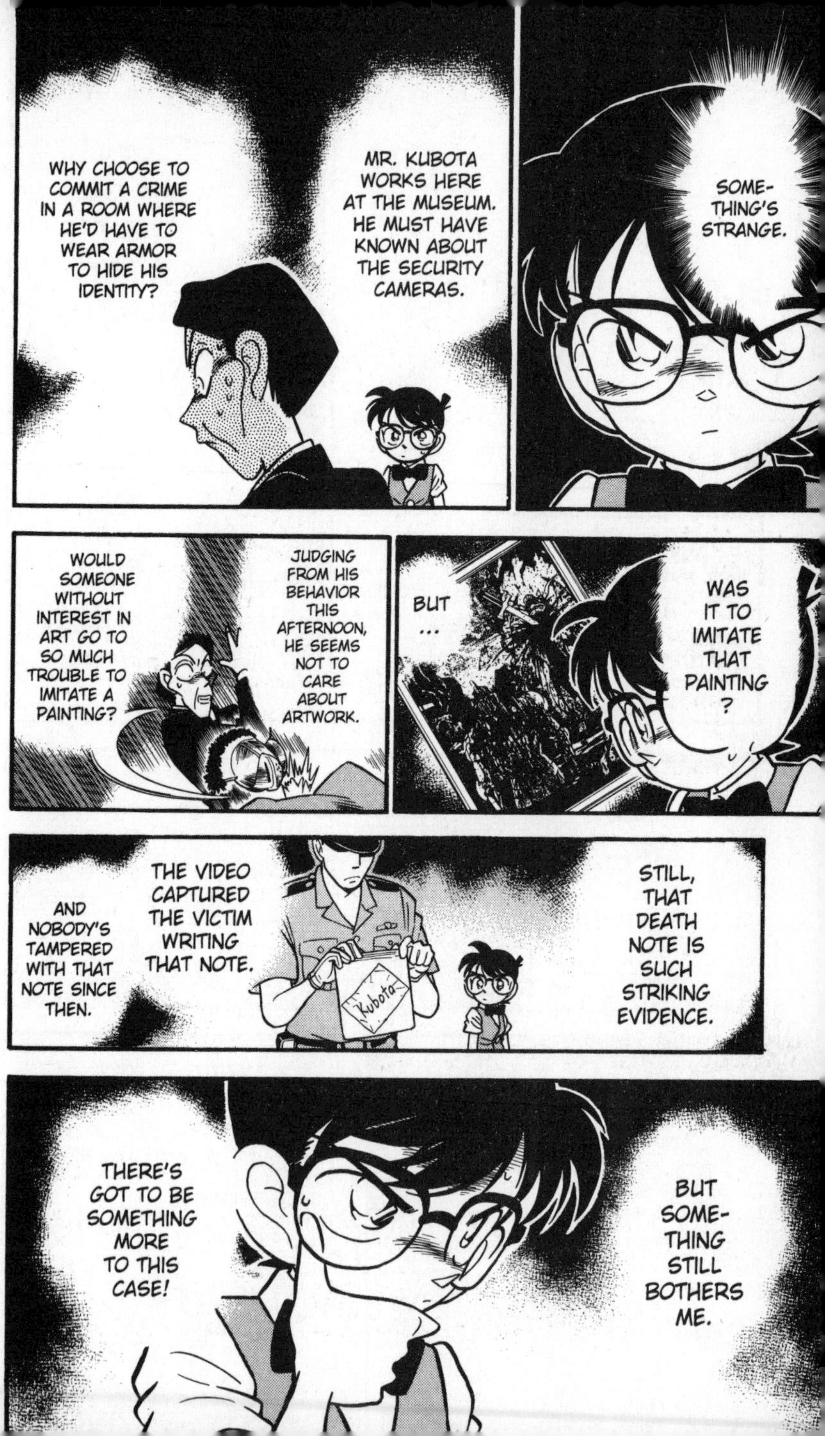
SOMETHING'S STRANGE.
MR. KUBOTA WORKS HERE AT THE MUSEUM. HE MUST HAVE KNOWN ABOUT THE SECURITY CAMERAS.
WHY CHOOSE TO COMMIT A CRIME IN A ROOM WHERE HE'D HAVE TO WEAR ARMOR TO HIDE HIS IDENTITY?
WAS IT TO IMITATE THAT PAINTING?
BUT ...
JUDGING FROM HIS BEHAVIOR THIS AFTERNOON, HE SEEMS NOT TO CARE ABOUT ARTWORK.
WOULD SOMEONE WITHOUT INTEREST IN ART GO TO SO MUCH TROUBLE TO IMITATE A PAINTING?
STILL, THAT DEATH NOTE IS SUCH STRIKING EVIDENCE.
THE VIDEO CAPTURED THE VICTIM WRITING THAT NOTE.
Kubota
AND NOBODY'S TAMPERED WITH THAT NOTE SINCE THEN.
BUT SOMETHING STILL BOTHERS ME.
THERE'S GOT TO BE SOMETHING MORE TO THIS CASE!

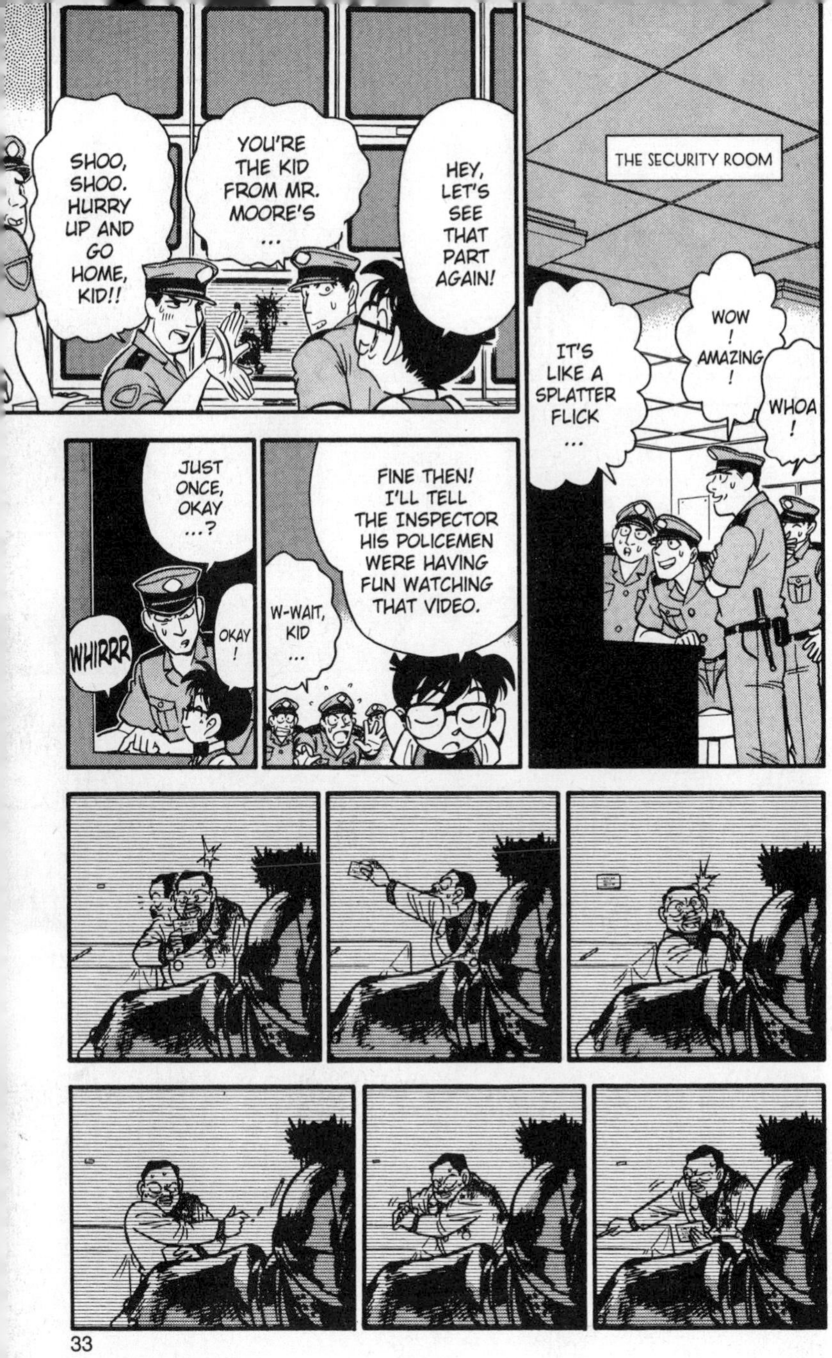
THE SECURITY ROOM
WOW! AMAZING!
WHOA!
IT'S LIKE A SPLATTER FLICK...
HEY, LET'S SEE THAT PART AGAIN!
YOU'RE THE KID FROM MR. MOORE'S...
SHOO, SHOO. HURRY UP AND GO HOME, KID!!
FINE THEN! I'LL TELL THE INSPECTOR HIS POLICEMEN WERE HAVING FUN WATCHING THAT VIDEO.
W-WAIT, KID...
JUST ONCE, OKAY...?
OKAY!
WHIRRR

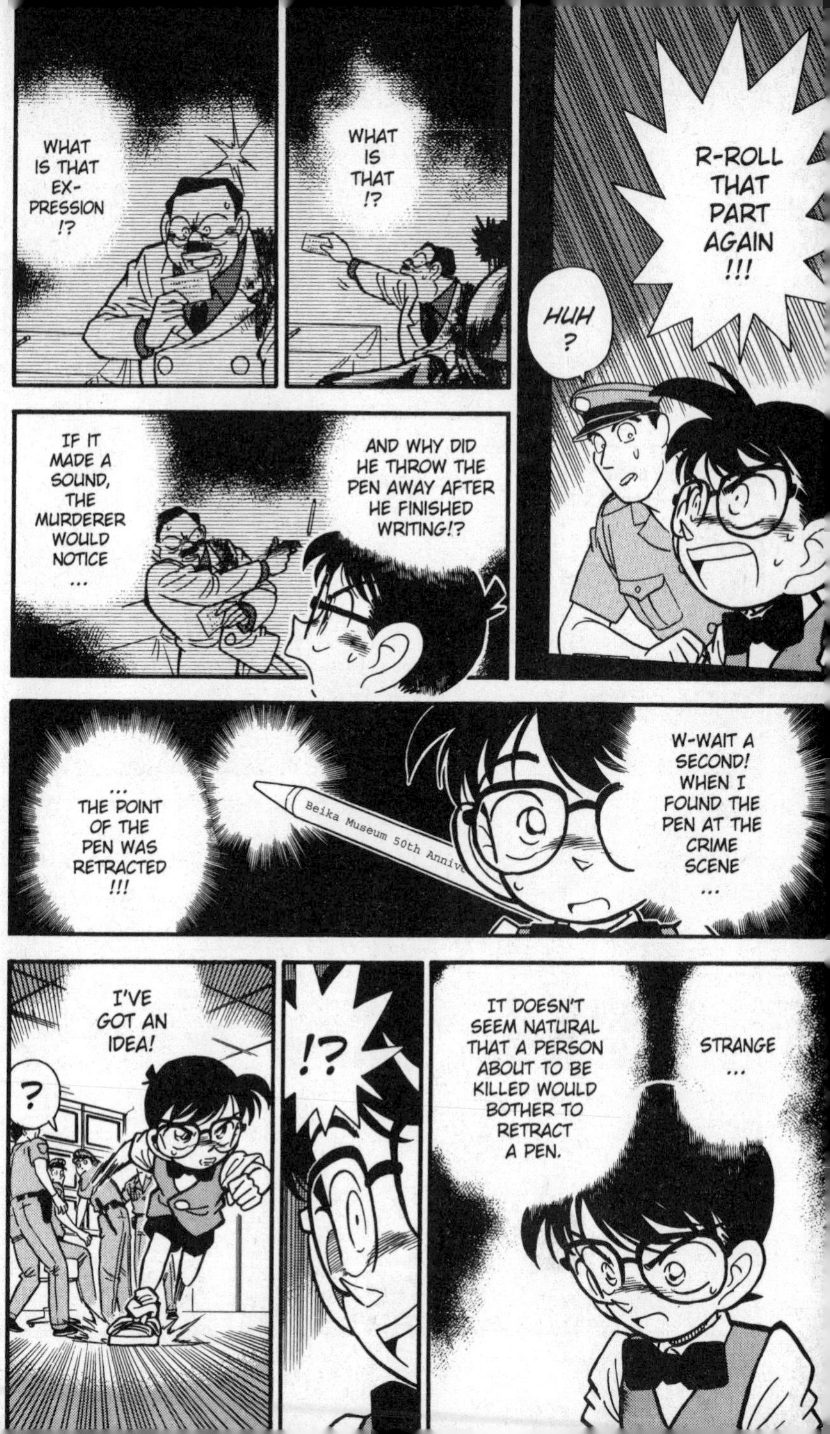
R-ROLL THAT PART AGAIN !!!
HUH ?
WHAT IS THAT !?
WHAT IS THAT EX-PRESSION !?
AND WHY DID HE THROW THE PEN AWAY AFTER HE FINISHED WRITING!?
IF IT MADE A SOUND, THE MURDERER WOULD NOTICE ...
W-WAIT A SECOND! WHEN I FOUND THE PEN AT THE CRIME SCENE ...
Beika Museum 50th Anniv
... THE POINT OF THE PEN WAS RETRACTED !!!
STRANGE ...
IT DOESN'T SEEM NATURAL THAT A PERSON ABOUT TO BE KILLED WOULD BOTHER TO RETRACT A PEN.
!?
I'VE GOT AN IDEA!
?

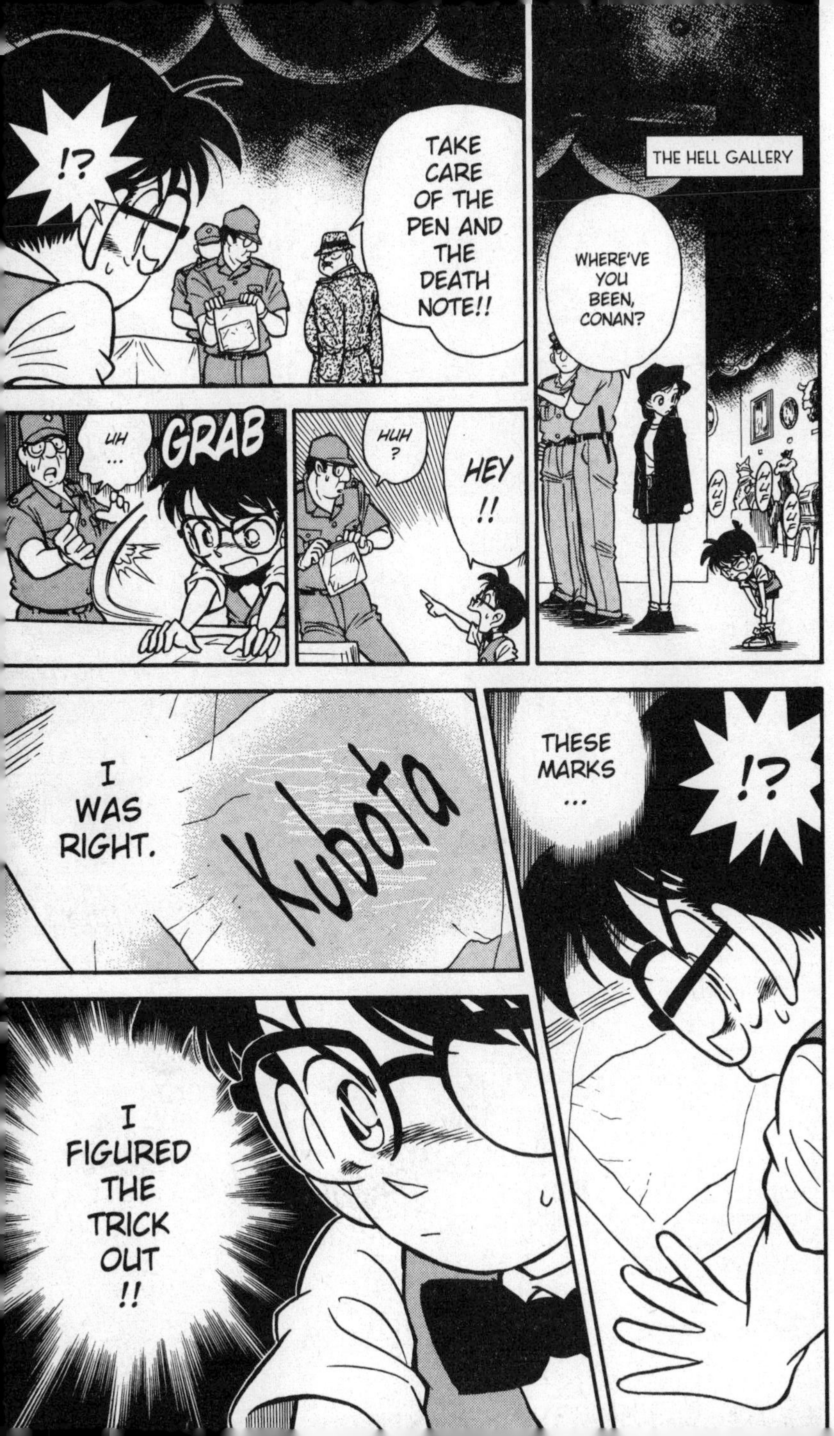
THE HELL GALLERY
WHERE'VE YOU BEEN, CONAN?
HUF
HUF
HUF
!?
TAKE CARE OF THE PEN AND THE DEATH NOTE!!
HEY !!
HUH ?
GRAB
UH ...
THESE MARKS ...
!?
I WAS RIGHT.
Kubota
I FIGURED THE TRICK OUT !!

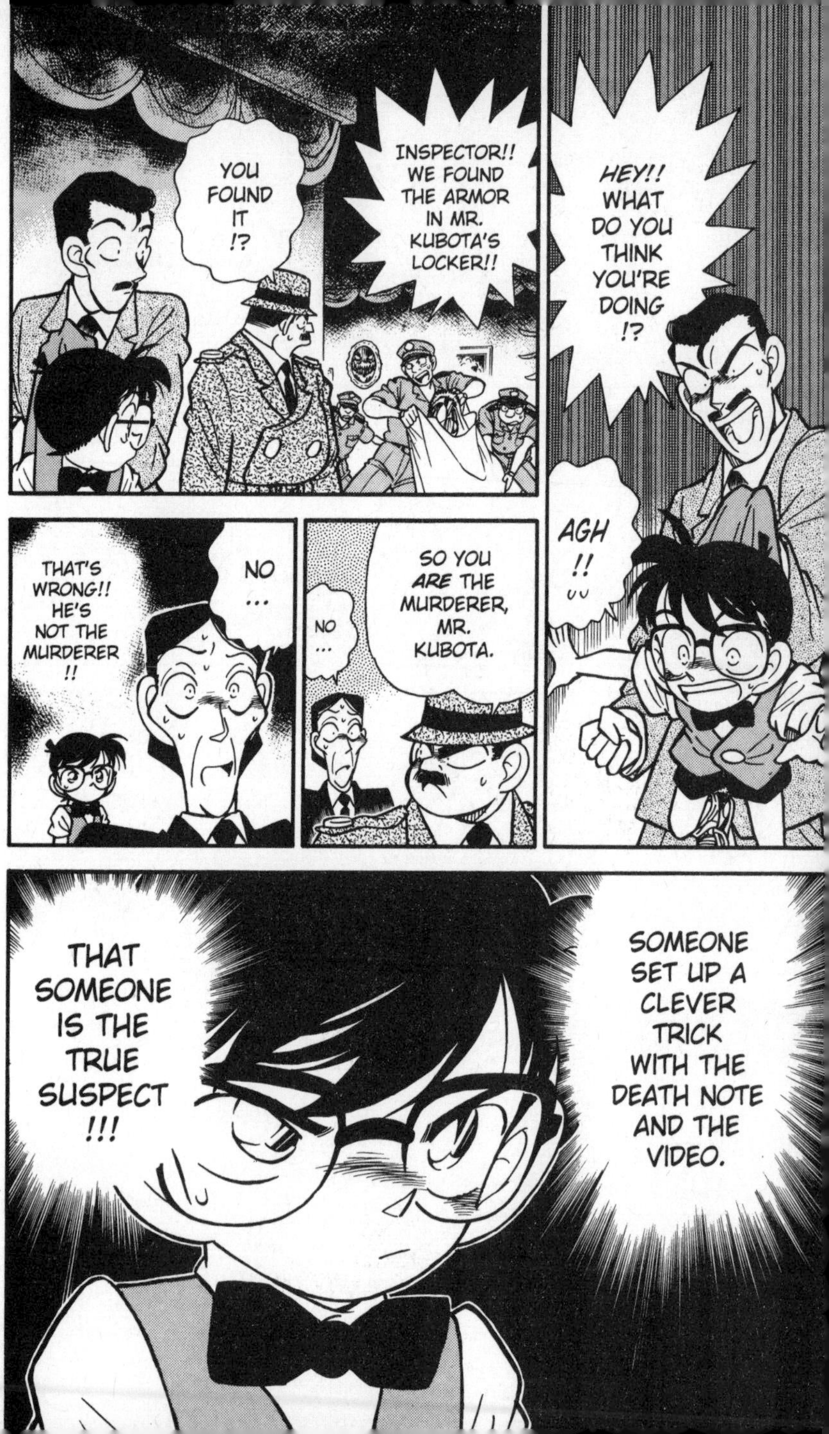
HEY!! WHAT DO YOU THINK YOU'RE DOING !?
AGH !!
INSPECTOR!! WE FOUND THE ARMOR IN MR. KUBOTA'S LOCKER!!
YOU FOUND IT !?
SO YOU *ARE* THE MURDERER, MR. KUBOTA.
NO ...
NO ...
THAT'S WRONG!! HE'S NOT THE MURDERER !!
SOMEONE SET UP A CLEVER TRICK WITH THE DEATH NOTE AND THE VIDEO.
THAT SOMEONE IS THE TRUE SUSPECT !!!

FILE 3:
OUT OF INK

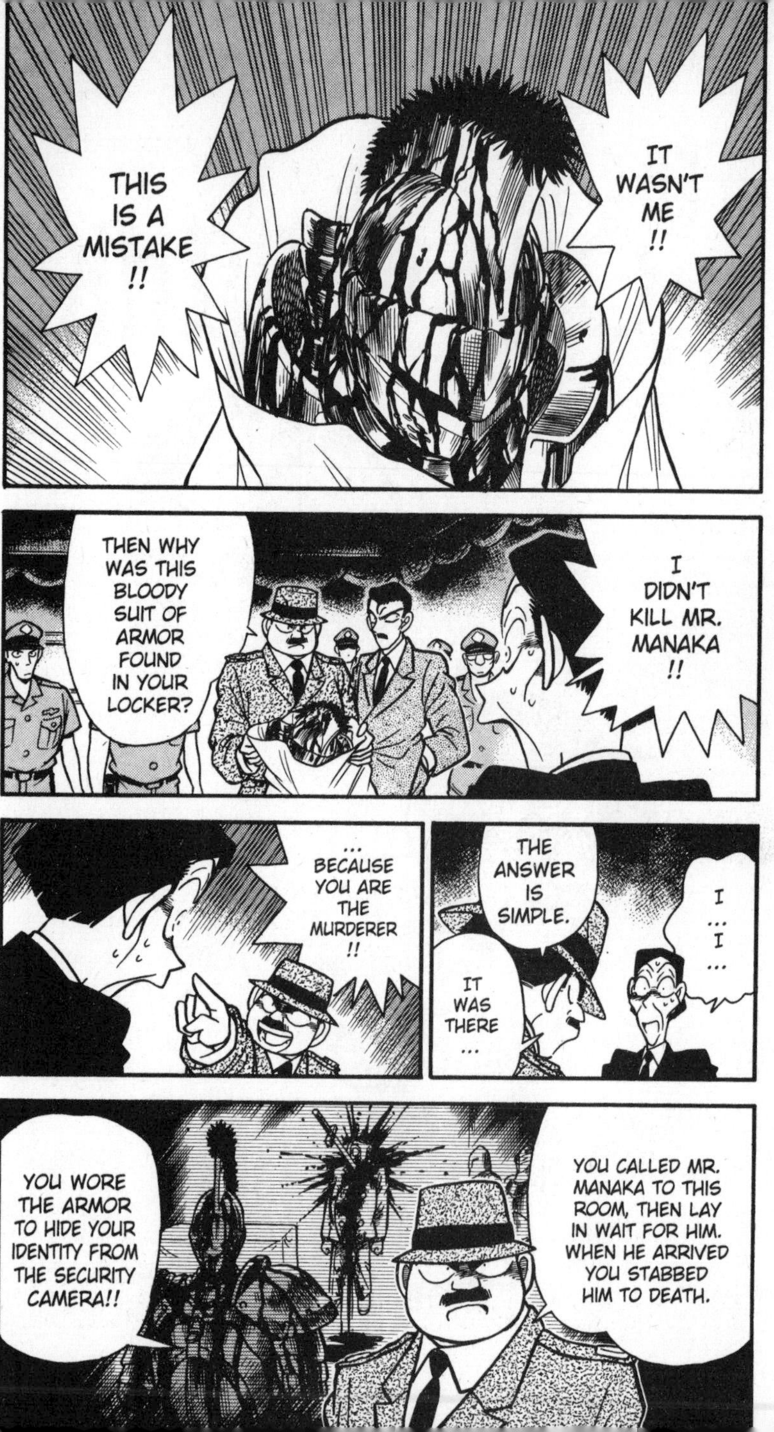
IT WASN'T ME !!
THIS IS A MISTAKE !!
I DIDN'T KILL MR. MANAKA !!
THEN WHY WAS THIS BLOODY SUIT OF ARMOR FOUND IN YOUR LOCKER?
I ... I ...
THE ANSWER IS SIMPLE.
IT WAS THERE ...
... BECAUSE YOU ARE THE MURDERER !!
YOU CALLED MR. MANAKA TO THIS ROOM, THEN LAY IN WAIT FOR HIM. WHEN HE ARRIVED YOU STABBED HIM TO DEATH.
YOU WORE THE ARMOR TO HIDE YOUR IDENTITY FROM THE SECURITY CAMERA!!

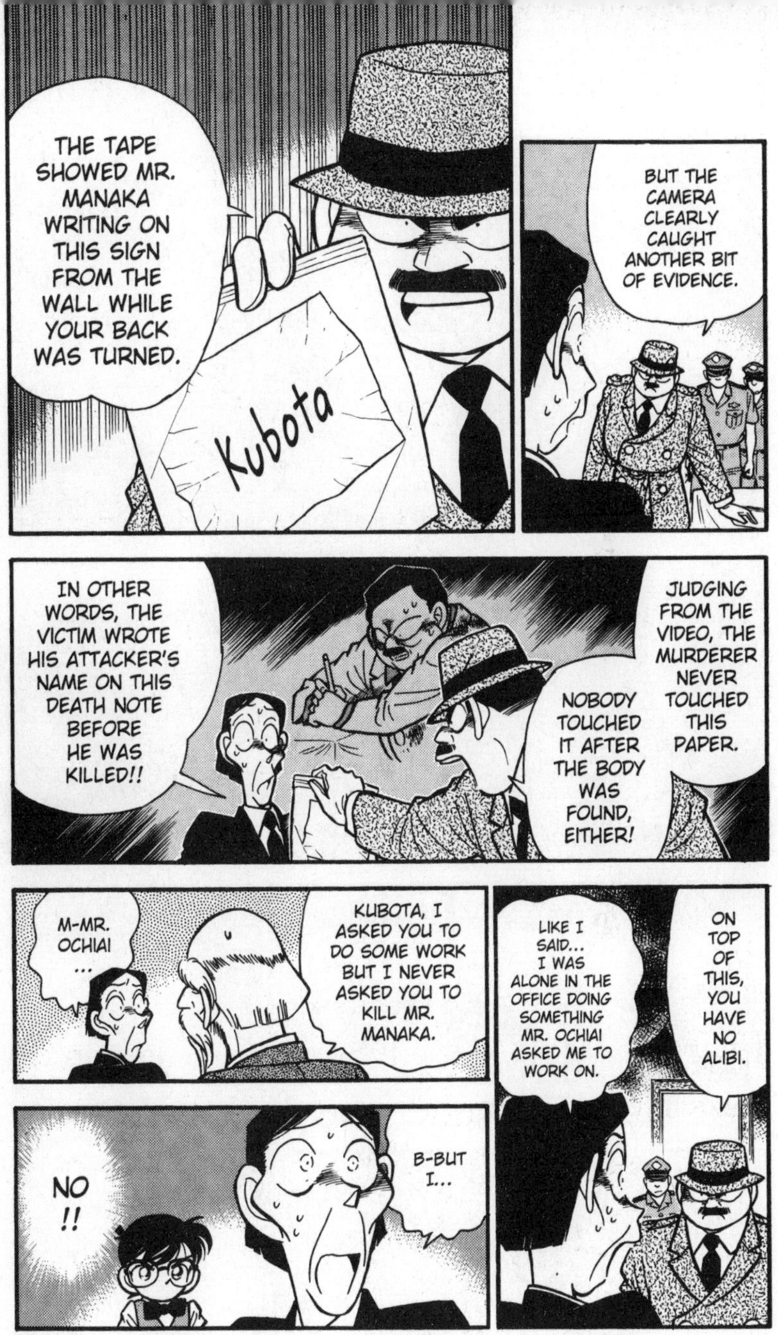
BUT THE CAMERA CLEARLY CAUGHT ANOTHER BIT OF EVIDENCE.
THE TAPE SHOWED MR. MANAKA WRITING ON THIS SIGN FROM THE WALL WHILE YOUR BACK WAS TURNED.
Kubota
JUDGING FROM THE VIDEO, THE MURDERER NEVER TOUCHED THIS PAPER.
NOBODY TOUCHED IT AFTER THE BODY WAS FOUND, EITHER!
IN OTHER WORDS, THE VICTIM WROTE HIS ATTACKER'S NAME ON THIS DEATH NOTE BEFORE HE WAS KILLED!!
ON TOP OF THIS, YOU HAVE NO ALIBI.
LIKE I SAID... I WAS ALONE IN THE OFFICE DOING SOMETHING MR. OCHIAI ASKED ME TO WORK ON.
KUBOTA, I ASKED YOU TO DO SOME WORK BUT I NEVER ASKED YOU TO KILL MR. MANAKA.
M-MR. OCHIAI ...
B-BUT I...
NO !!

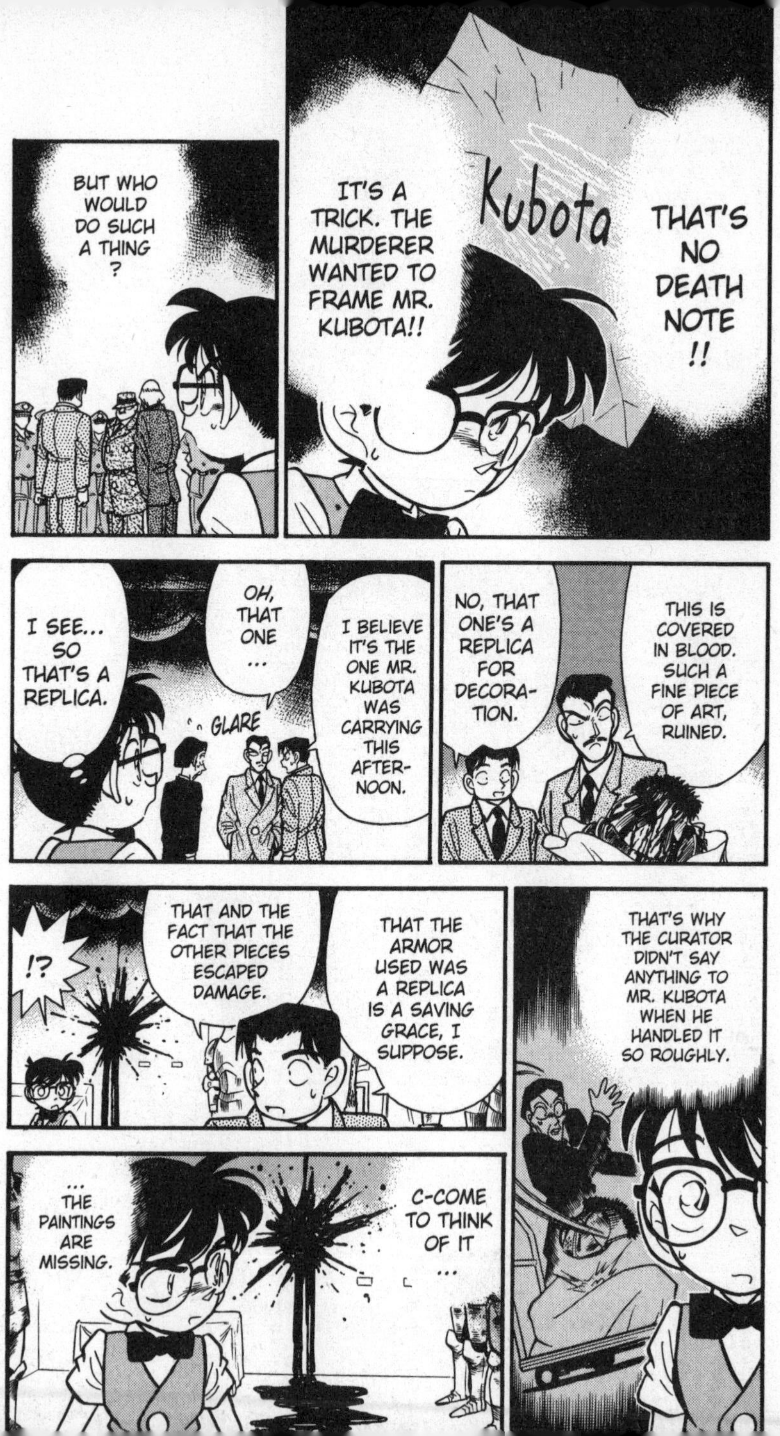
THAT'S NO DEATH NOTE !!
Kubota
IT'S A TRICK. THE MURDERER WANTED TO FRAME MR. KUBOTA!!
BUT WHO WOULD DO SUCH A THING ?
THIS IS COVERED IN BLOOD. SUCH A FINE PIECE OF ART, RUINED.
NO, THAT ONE'S A REPLICA FOR DECORATION.
I BELIEVE IT'S THE ONE MR. KUBOTA WAS CARRYING THIS AFTERNOON.
OH, THAT ONE ...
GLARE
I SEE... SO THAT'S A REPLICA.
THAT'S WHY THE CURATOR DIDN'T SAY ANYTHING TO MR. KUBOTA WHEN HE HANDLED IT SO ROUGHLY.
THAT THE ARMOR USED WAS A REPLICA IS A SAVING GRACE, I SUPPOSE.
THAT AND THE FACT THAT THE OTHER PIECES ESCAPED DAMAGE.
!?
C-COME TO THINK OF IT ...
... THE PAINTINGS ARE MISSING.

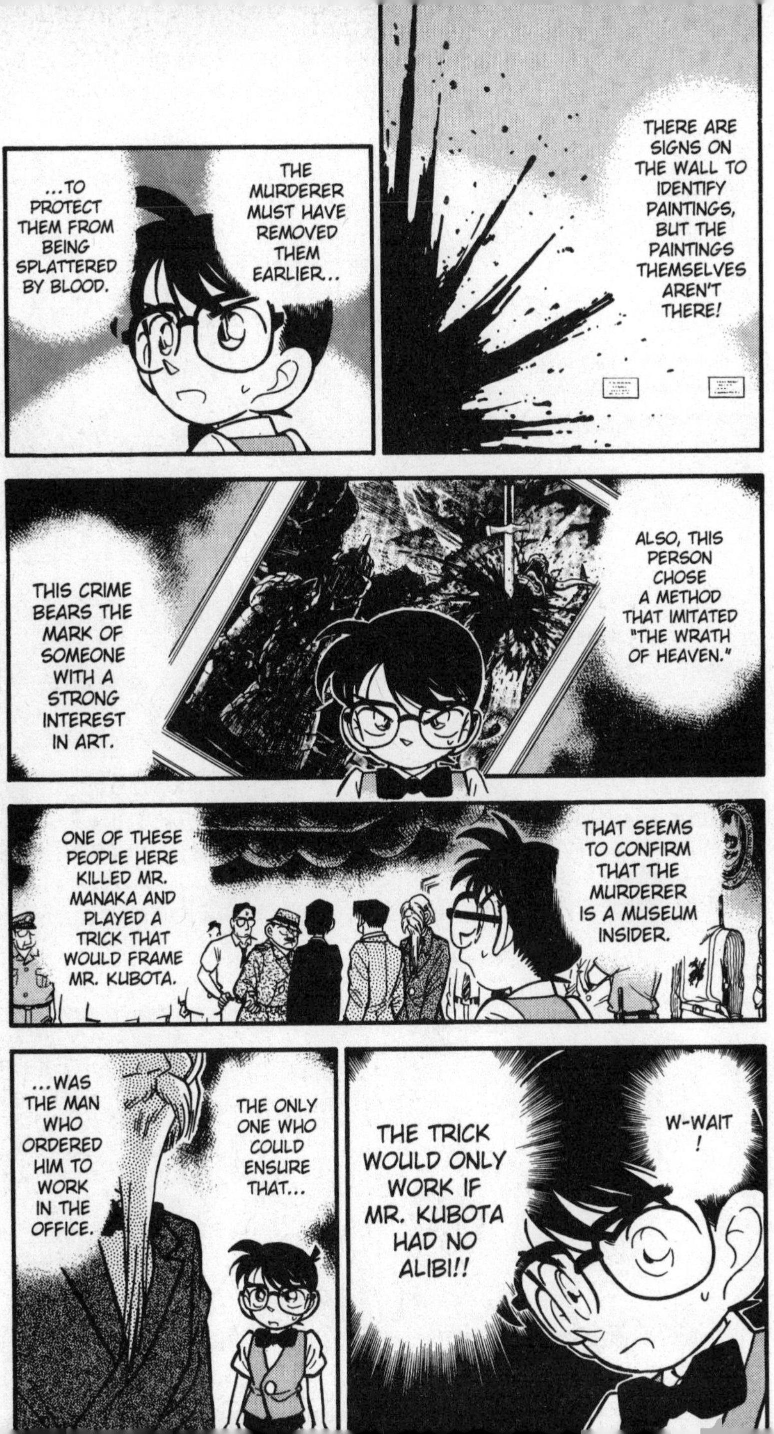
THERE ARE SIGNS ON THE WALL TO IDENTIFY PAINTINGS, BUT THE PAINTINGS THEMSELVES AREN'T THERE!
THE MURDERER MUST HAVE REMOVED THEM EARLIER...
...TO PROTECT THEM FROM BEING SPLATTERED BY BLOOD.
ALSO, THIS PERSON CHOSE A METHOD THAT IMITATED "THE WRATH OF HEAVEN."
THIS CRIME BEARS THE MARK OF SOMEONE WITH A STRONG INTEREST IN ART.
THAT SEEMS TO CONFIRM THAT THE MURDERER IS A MUSEUM INSIDER.
ONE OF THESE PEOPLE HERE KILLED MR. MANAKA AND PLAYED A TRICK THAT WOULD FRAME MR. KUBOTA.
W-WAIT!
THE TRICK WOULD ONLY WORK IF MR. KUBOTA HAD NO ALIBI!!
THE ONLY ONE WHO COULD ENSURE THAT...
...WAS THE MAN WHO ORDERED HIM TO WORK IN THE OFFICE.

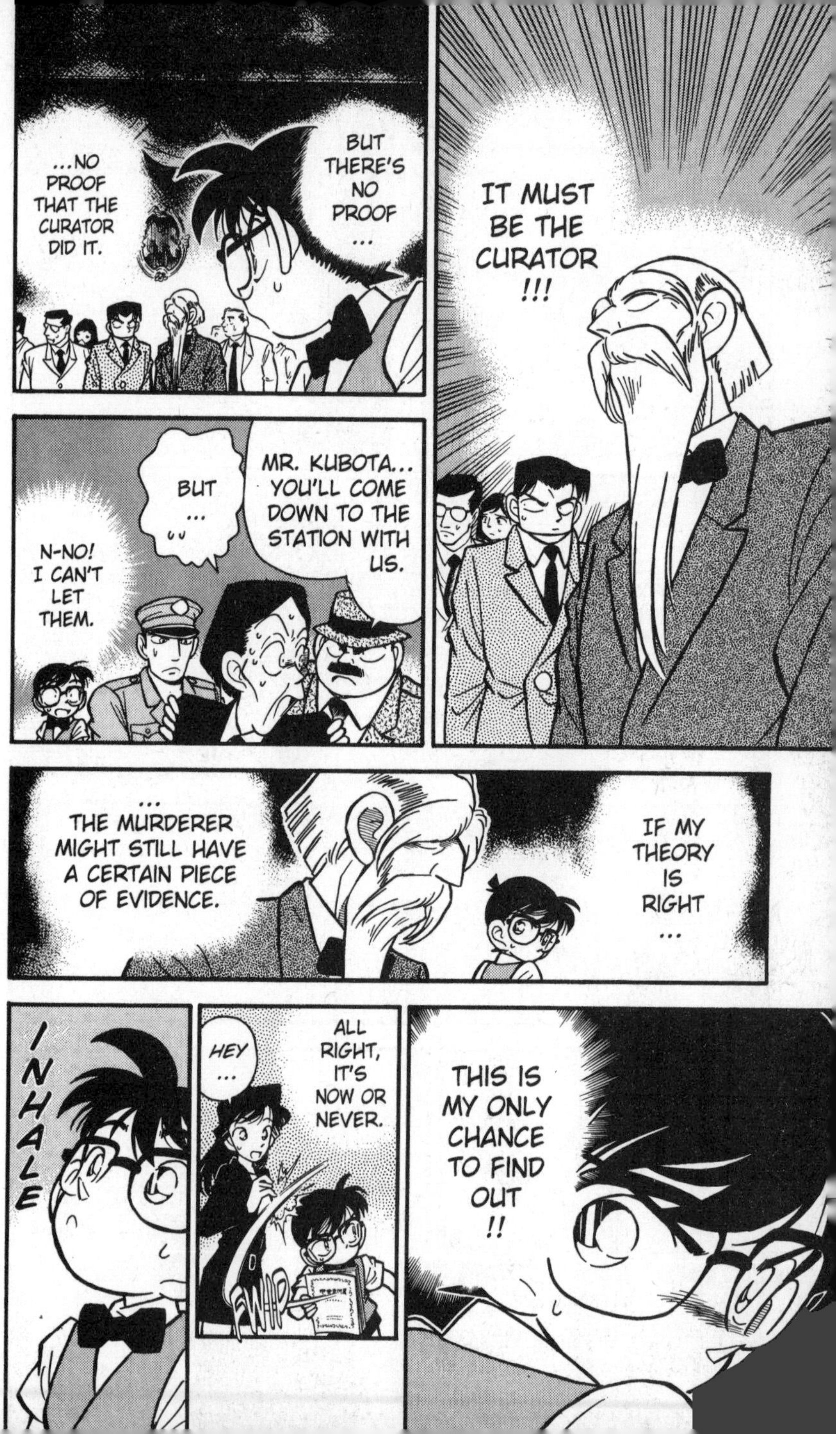
IT MUST BE THE CURATOR !!!
BUT THERE'S NO PROOF ...
...NO PROOF THAT THE CURATOR DID IT.
MR. KUBOTA... YOU'LL COME DOWN TO THE STATION WITH US.
BUT ...
N-NO! I CAN'T LET THEM.
IF MY THEORY IS RIGHT ...
... THE MURDERER MIGHT STILL HAVE A CERTAIN PIECE OF EVIDENCE.
THIS IS MY ONLY CHANCE TO FIND OUT !!
ALL RIGHT, IT'S NOW OR NEVER.
HEY ...
INHALE

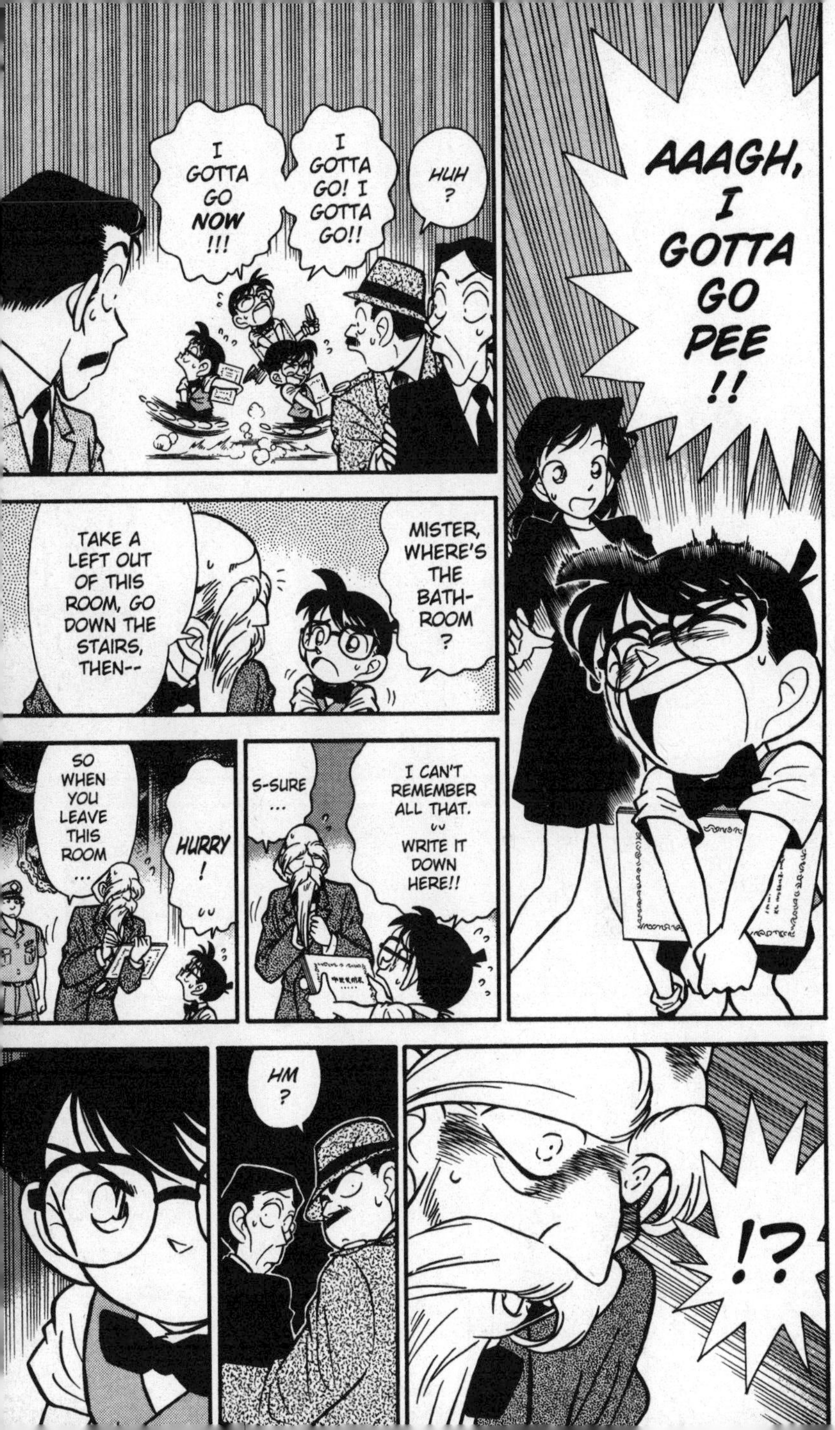
AAAGH, I GOTTA GO PEE!!
HUH?
I GOTTA GO! I GOTTA GO!!
I GOTTA GO NOW!!!
MISTER, WHERE'S THE BATHROOM?
TAKE A LEFT OUT OF THIS ROOM, GO DOWN THE STAIRS, THEN--
I CAN'T REMEMBER ALL THAT. WRITE IT DOWN HERE!!
S-SURE...
HURRY!
SO WHEN YOU LEAVE THIS ROOM...
!?
HM?

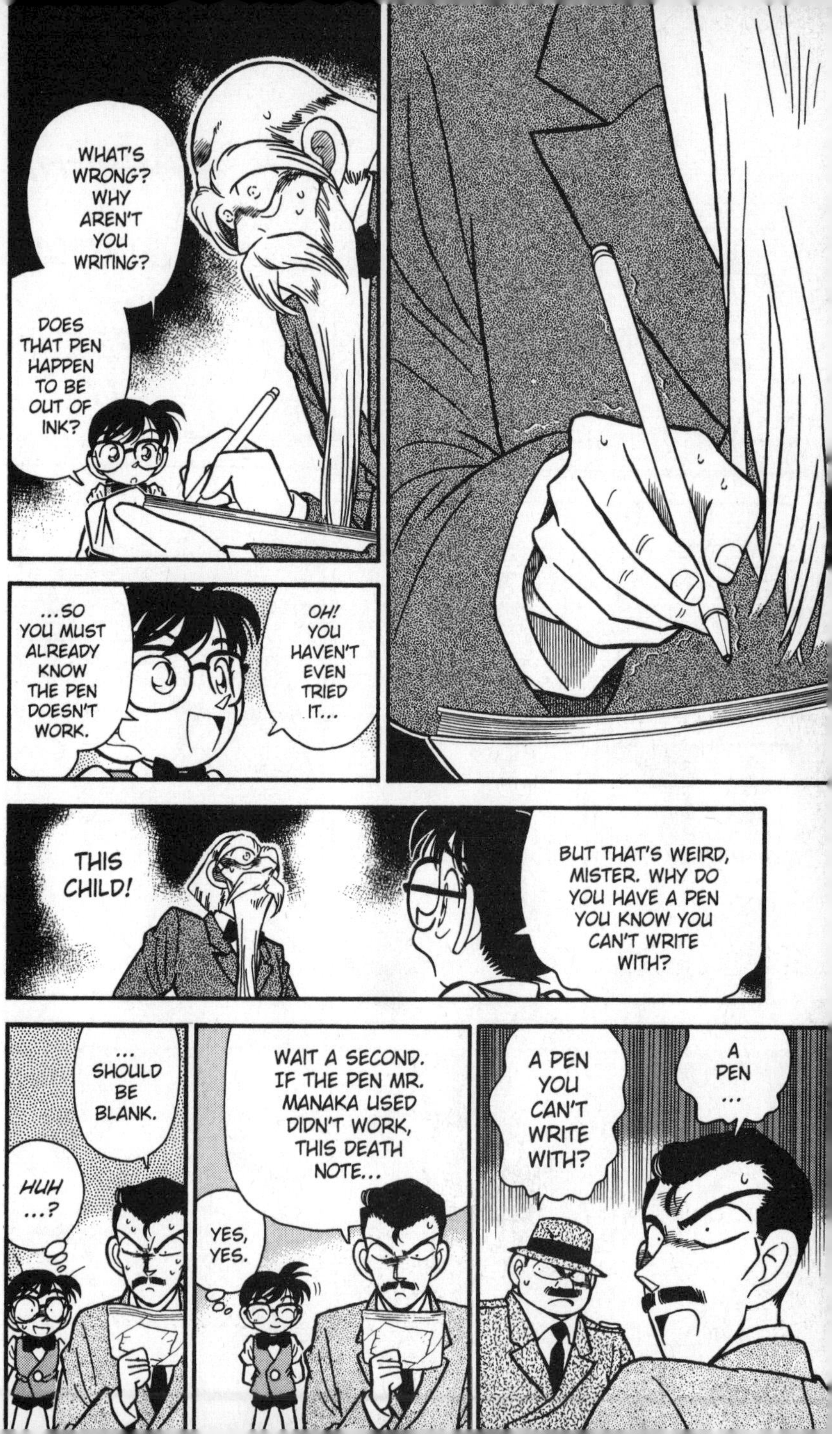
WHAT'S WRONG? WHY AREN'T YOU WRITING?
DOES THAT PEN HAPPEN TO BE OUT OF INK?
OH! YOU HAVEN'T EVEN TRIED IT...
...SO YOU MUST ALREADY KNOW THE PEN DOESN'T WORK.
BUT THAT'S WEIRD, MISTER. WHY DO YOU HAVE A PEN YOU KNOW YOU CAN'T WRITE WITH?
THIS CHILD!
A PEN ...
A PEN YOU CAN'T WRITE WITH?
WAIT A SECOND. IF THE PEN MR. MANAKA USED DIDN'T WORK, THIS DEATH NOTE...
YES, YES.
... SHOULD BE BLANK.
HUH ...?

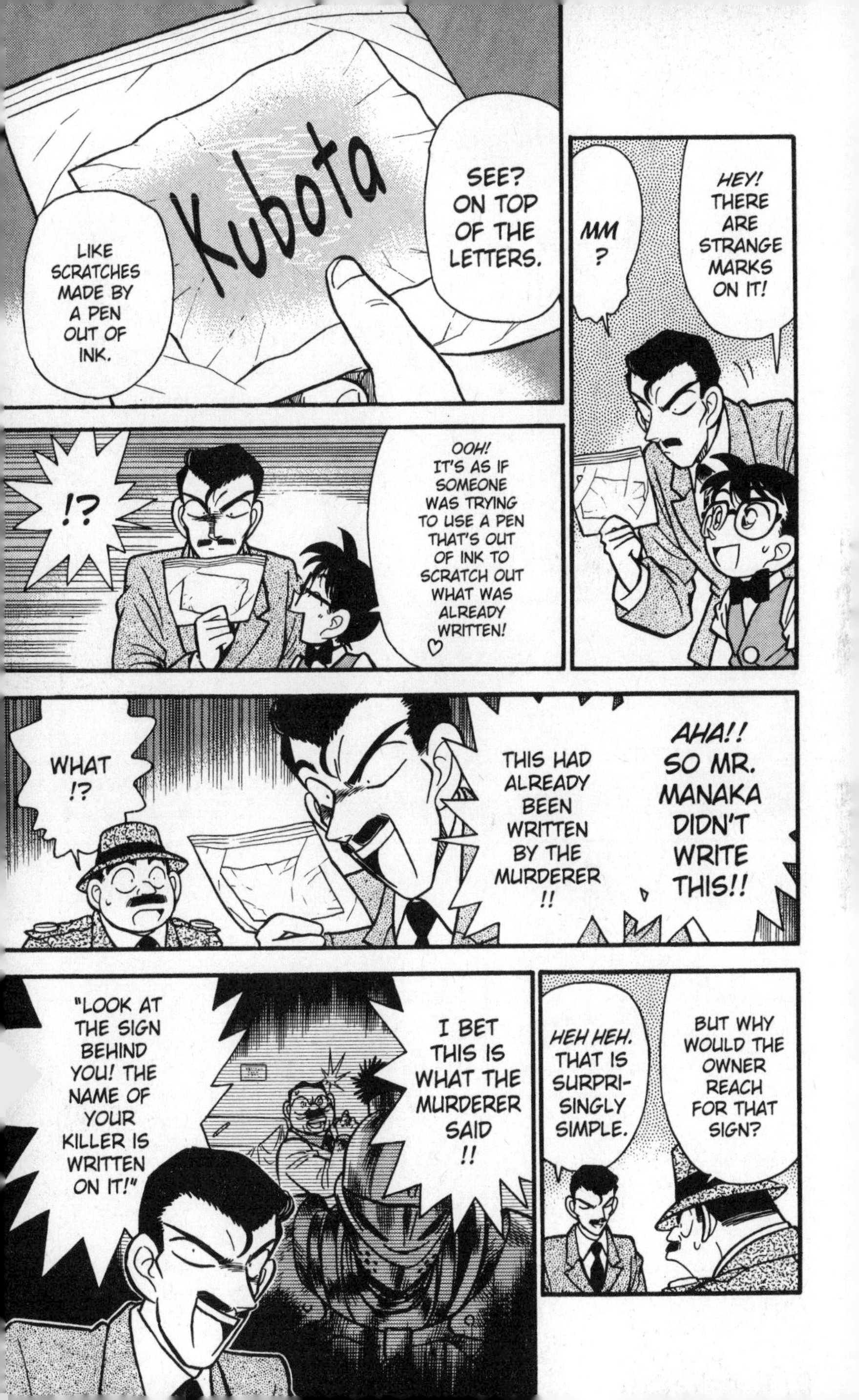
HEY! THERE ARE STRANGE MARKS ON IT!
MM ?
SEE? ON TOP OF THE LETTERS.
Kubota
LIKE SCRATCHES MADE BY A PEN OUT OF INK.
OOH! IT'S AS IF SOMEONE WAS TRYING TO USE A PEN THAT'S OUT OF INK TO SCRATCH OUT WHAT WAS ALREADY WRITTEN! ♡
!?
AHA!! SO MR. MANAKA DIDN'T WRITE THIS!!
THIS HAD ALREADY BEEN WRITTEN BY THE MURDERER !!
WHAT !?
BUT WHY WOULD THE OWNER REACH FOR THAT SIGN?
HEH HEH. THAT IS SURPRISINGLY SIMPLE.
I BET THIS IS WHAT THE MURDERER SAID !!
"LOOK AT THE SIGN BEHIND YOU! THE NAME OF YOUR KILLER IS WRITTEN ON IT!"

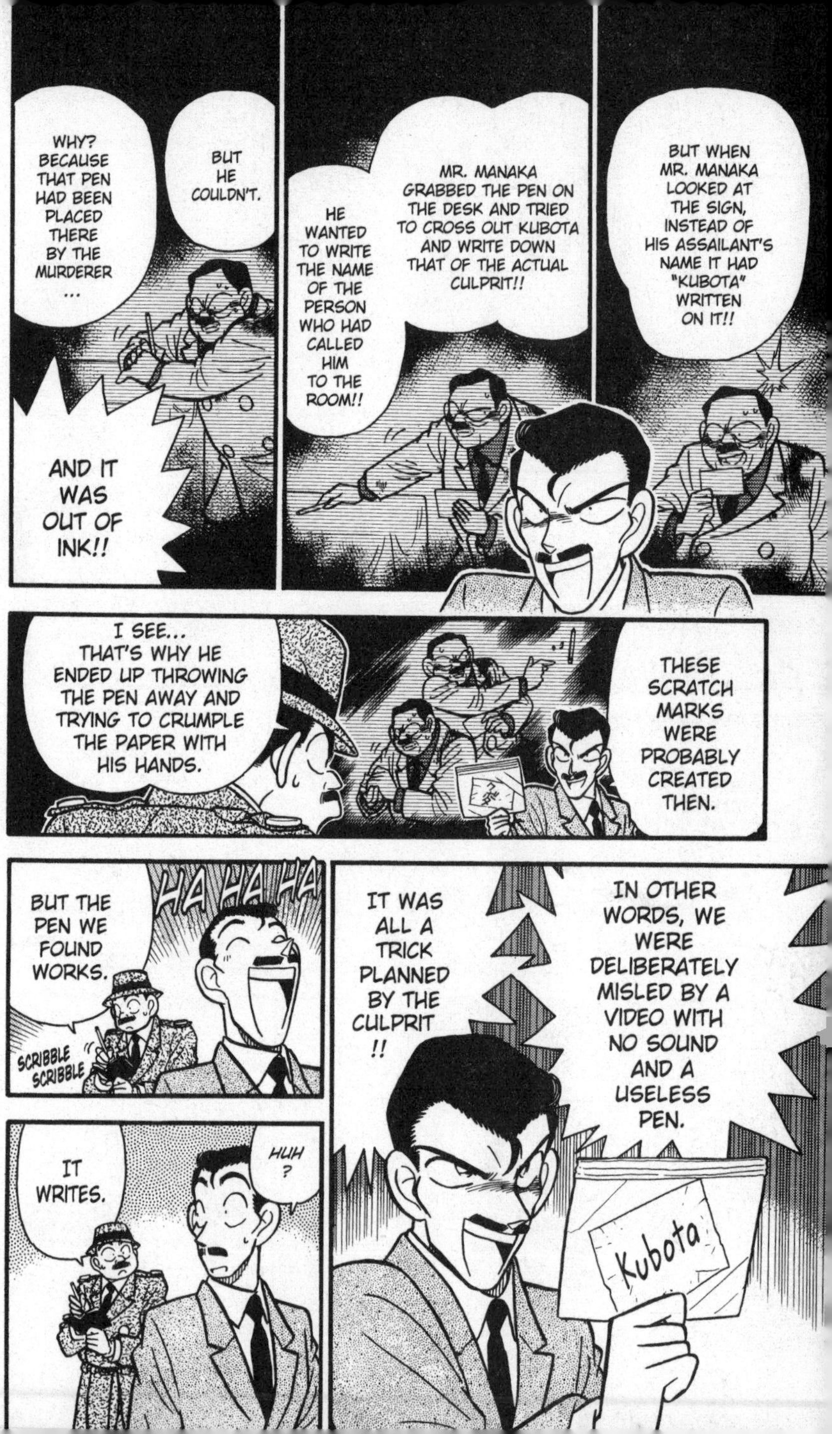
BUT WHEN MR. MANAKA LOOKED AT THE SIGN, INSTEAD OF HIS ASSAILANT'S NAME IT HAD "KUBOTA" WRITTEN ON IT!!
MR. MANAKA GRABBED THE PEN ON THE DESK AND TRIED TO CROSS OUT KUBOTA AND WRITE DOWN THAT OF THE ACTUAL CULPRIT!!
HE WANTED TO WRITE THE NAME OF THE PERSON WHO HAD CALLED HIM TO THE ROOM!!
BUT HE COULDN'T.
WHY? BECAUSE THAT PEN HAD BEEN PLACED THERE BY THE MURDERER ...
AND IT WAS OUT OF INK!!
THESE SCRATCH MARKS WERE PROBABLY CREATED THEN.
I SEE... THAT'S WHY HE ENDED UP THROWING THE PEN AWAY AND TRYING TO CRUMPLE THE PAPER WITH HIS HANDS.
IN OTHER WORDS, WE WERE DELIBERATELY MISLED BY A VIDEO WITH NO SOUND AND A USELESS PEN.
IT WAS ALL A TRICK PLANNED BY THE CULPRIT !!
Kubota
HA HA HA
BUT THE PEN WE FOUND WORKS.
SCRIBBLE SCRIBBLE
HUH ?
IT WRITES.

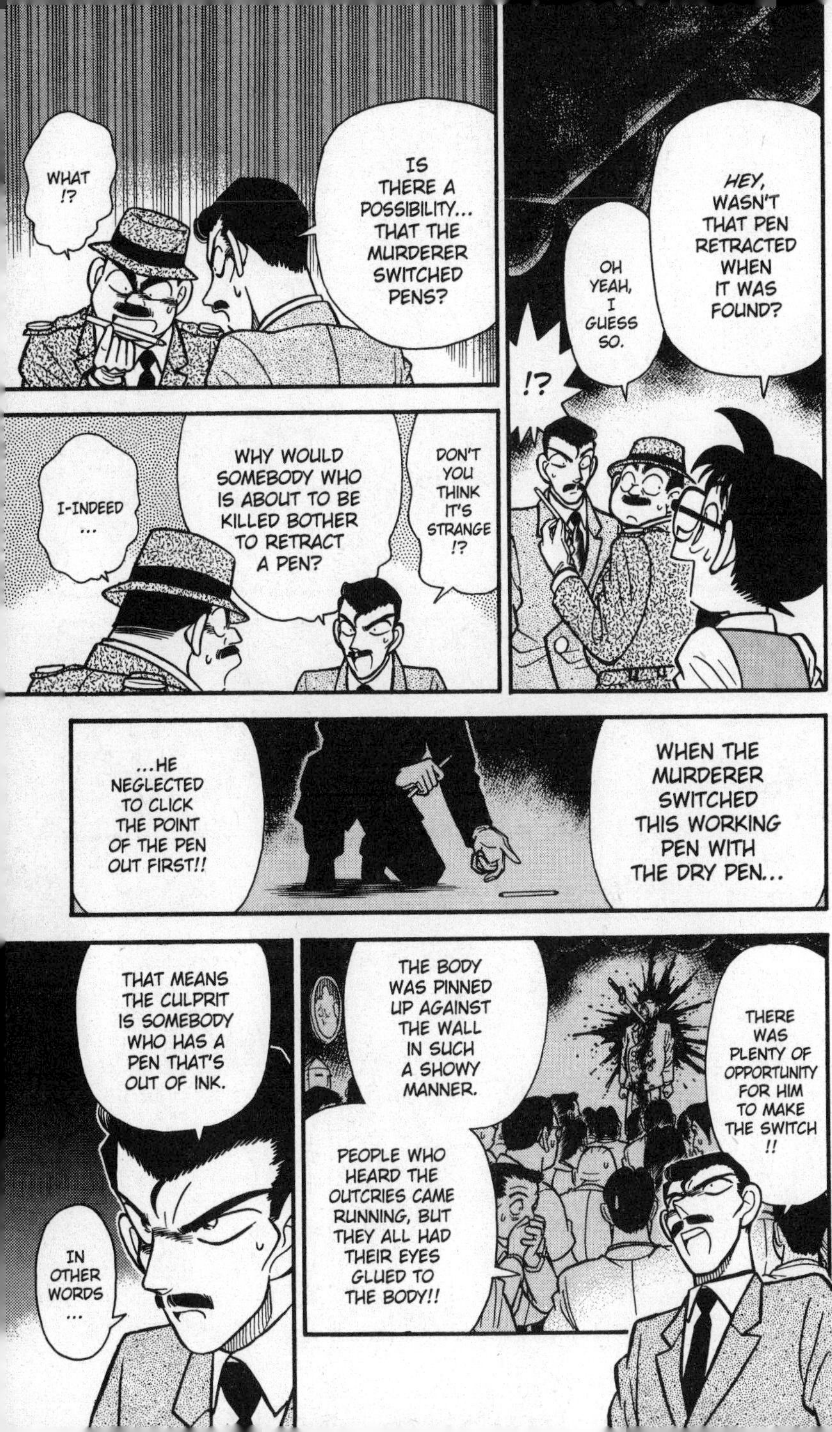
HEY, WASN'T THAT PEN RETRACTED WHEN IT WAS FOUND?
OH YEAH, I GUESS SO.
!?
IS THERE A POSSIBILITY... THAT THE MURDERER SWITCHED PENS?
WHAT !?
DON'T YOU THINK IT'S STRANGE !?
WHY WOULD SOMEBODY WHO IS ABOUT TO BE KILLED BOTHER TO RETRACT A PEN?
I-INDEED ...
WHEN THE MURDERER SWITCHED THIS WORKING PEN WITH THE DRY PEN...
...HE NEGLECTED TO CLICK THE POINT OF THE PEN OUT FIRST!!
THE BODY WAS PINNED UP AGAINST THE WALL IN SUCH A SHOWY MANNER.
PEOPLE WHO HEARD THE OUTCRIES CAME RUNNING, BUT THEY ALL HAD THEIR EYES GLUED TO THE BODY!!
THERE WAS PLENTY OF OPPORTUNITY FOR HIM TO MAKE THE SWITCH !!
THAT MEANS THE CULPRIT IS SOMEBODY WHO HAS A PEN THAT'S OUT OF INK.
IN OTHER WORDS ...

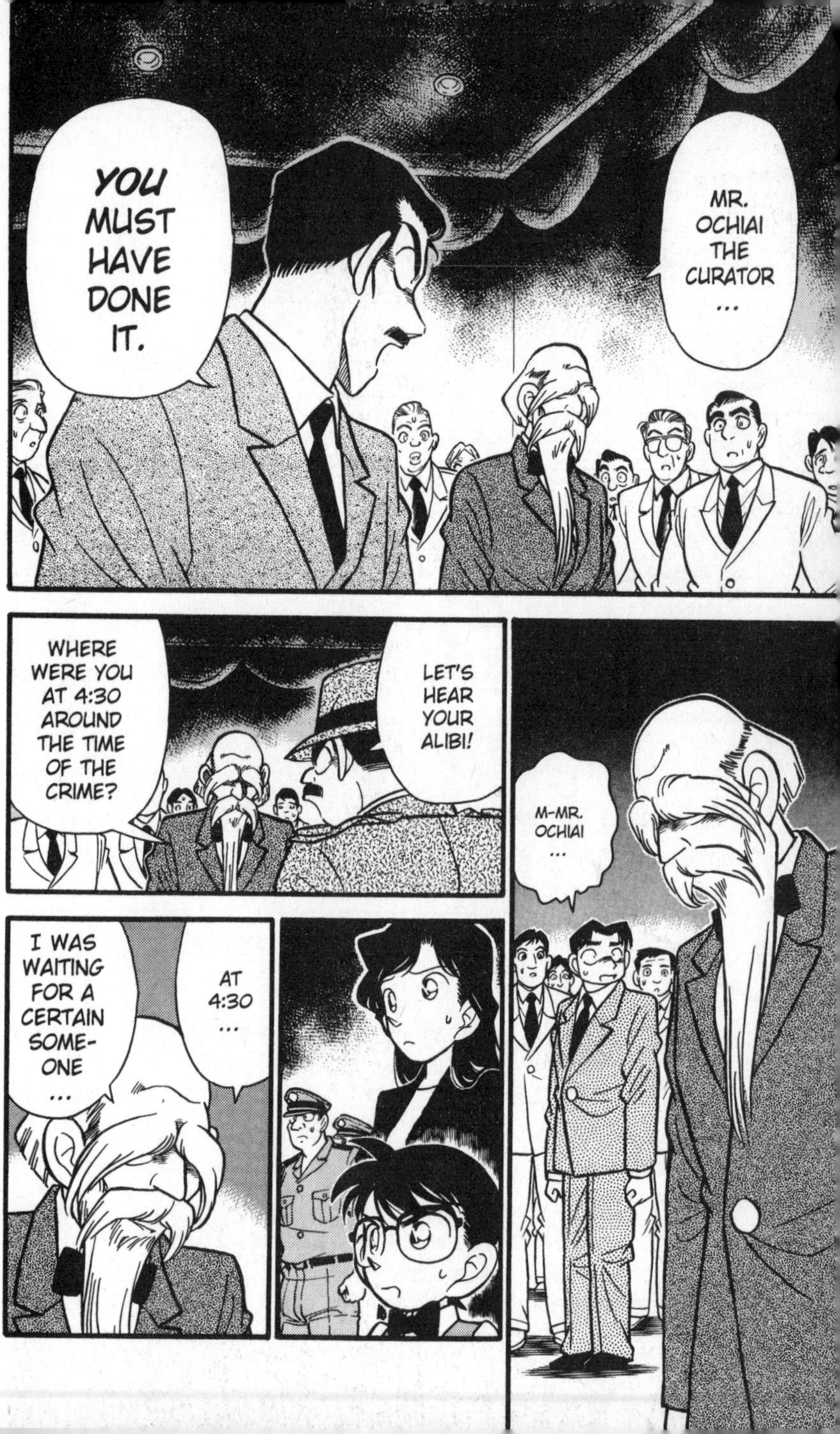
MR. OCHIAI THE CURATOR ...
YOU MUST HAVE DONE IT.
M-MR. OCHIAI ...
LET'S HEAR YOUR ALIBI!
WHERE WERE YOU AT 4:30 AROUND THE TIME OF THE CRIME?
AT 4:30 ...
I WAS WAITING FOR A CERTAIN SOME-ONE ...

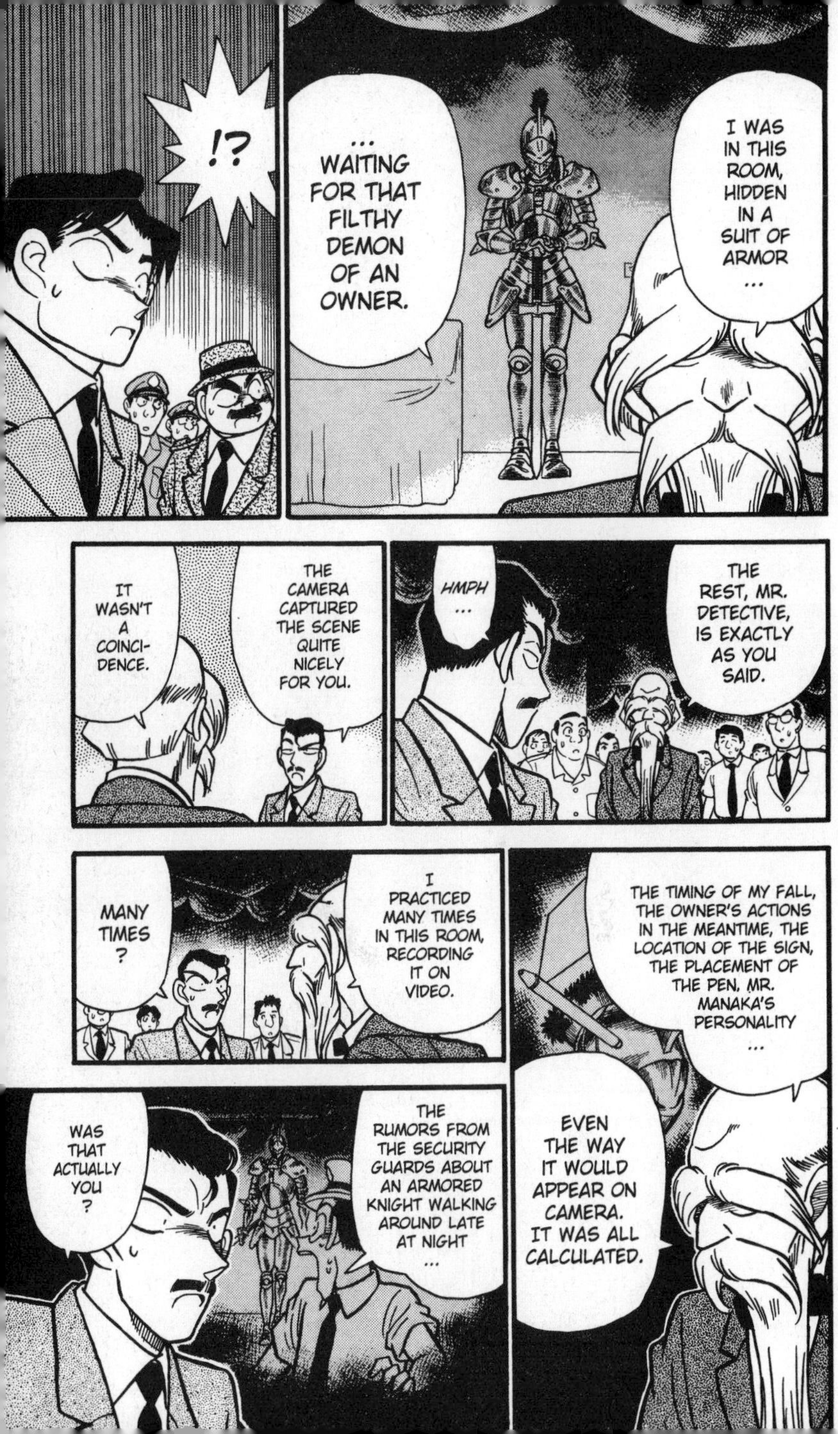
I WAS IN THIS ROOM, HIDDEN IN A SUIT OF ARMOR ...
... WAITING FOR THAT FILTHY DEMON OF AN OWNER.
!?
THE REST, MR. DETECTIVE, IS EXACTLY AS YOU SAID.
HMPH ...
THE CAMERA CAPTURED THE SCENE QUITE NICELY FOR YOU.
IT WASN'T A COINCI-DENCE.
THE TIMING OF MY FALL, THE OWNER'S ACTIONS IN THE MEANTIME, THE LOCATION OF THE SIGN, THE PLACEMENT OF THE PEN, MR. MANAKA'S PERSONALITY ...
EVEN THE WAY IT WOULD APPEAR ON CAMERA. IT WAS ALL CALCULATED.
I PRACTICED MANY TIMES IN THIS ROOM, RECORDING IT ON VIDEO.
MANY TIMES ?
THE RUMORS FROM THE SECURITY GUARDS ABOUT AN ARMORED KNIGHT WALKING AROUND LATE AT NIGHT ...
WAS THAT ACTUALLY YOU ?

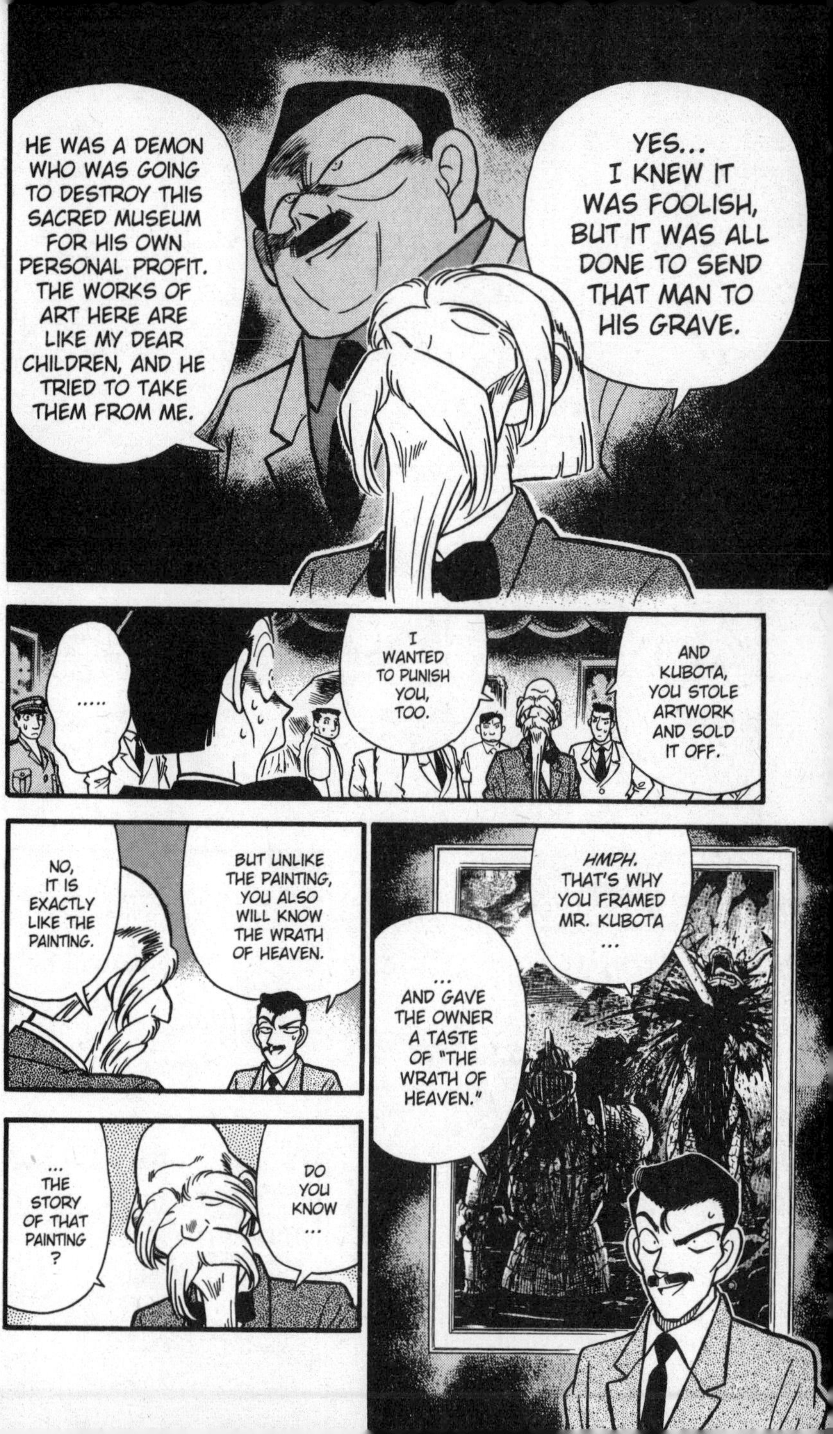
YES... I KNEW IT WAS FOOLISH, BUT IT WAS ALL DONE TO SEND THAT MAN TO HIS GRAVE.
HE WAS A DEMON WHO WAS GOING TO DESTROY THIS SACRED MUSEUM FOR HIS OWN PERSONAL PROFIT. THE WORKS OF ART HERE ARE LIKE MY DEAR CHILDREN, AND HE TRIED TO TAKE THEM FROM ME.
AND KUBOTA, YOU STOLE ARTWORK AND SOLD IT OFF.
I WANTED TO PUNISH YOU, TOO.
.....
HMPH. THAT'S WHY YOU FRAMED MR. KUBOTA ...
... AND GAVE THE OWNER A TASTE OF "THE WRATH OF HEAVEN."
BUT UNLIKE THE PAINTING, YOU ALSO WILL KNOW THE WRATH OF HEAVEN.
NO, IT IS EXACTLY LIKE THE PAINTING.
DO YOU KNOW ...
... THE STORY OF THAT PAINTING ?

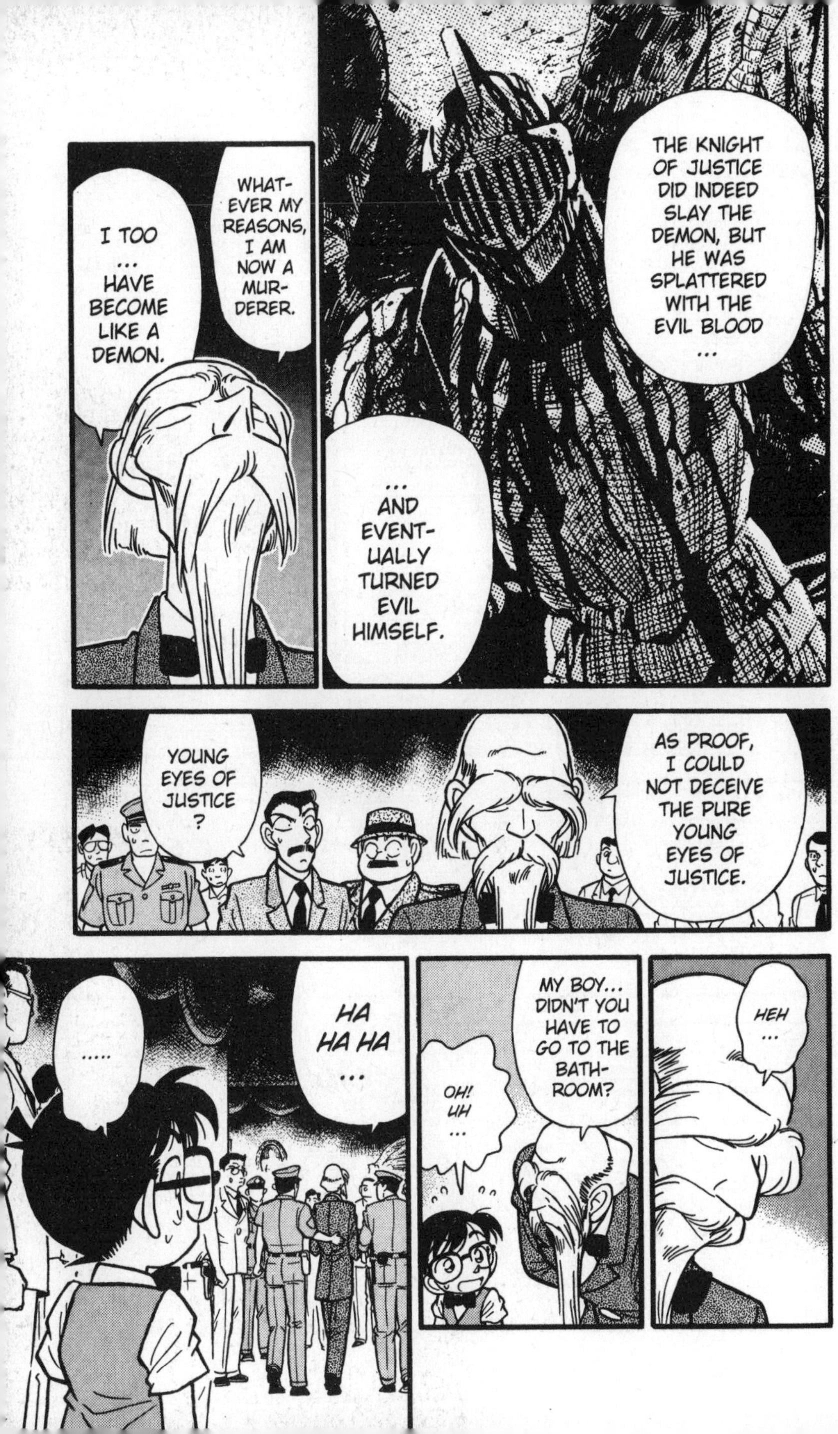
THE KNIGHT OF JUSTICE DID INDEED SLAY THE DEMON, BUT HE WAS SPLATTERED WITH THE EVIL BLOOD ...
... AND EVENT-UALLY TURNED EVIL HIMSELF.
WHAT-EVER MY REASONS, I AM NOW A MUR-DERER.
I TOO ... HAVE BECOME LIKE A DEMON.
AS PROOF, I COULD NOT DECEIVE THE PURE YOUNG EYES OF JUSTICE.
YOUNG EYES OF JUSTICE ?
HEH ...
MY BOY... DIDN'T YOU HAVE TO GO TO THE BATH-ROOM?
OH! UH ...
HA HA HA ...
.....

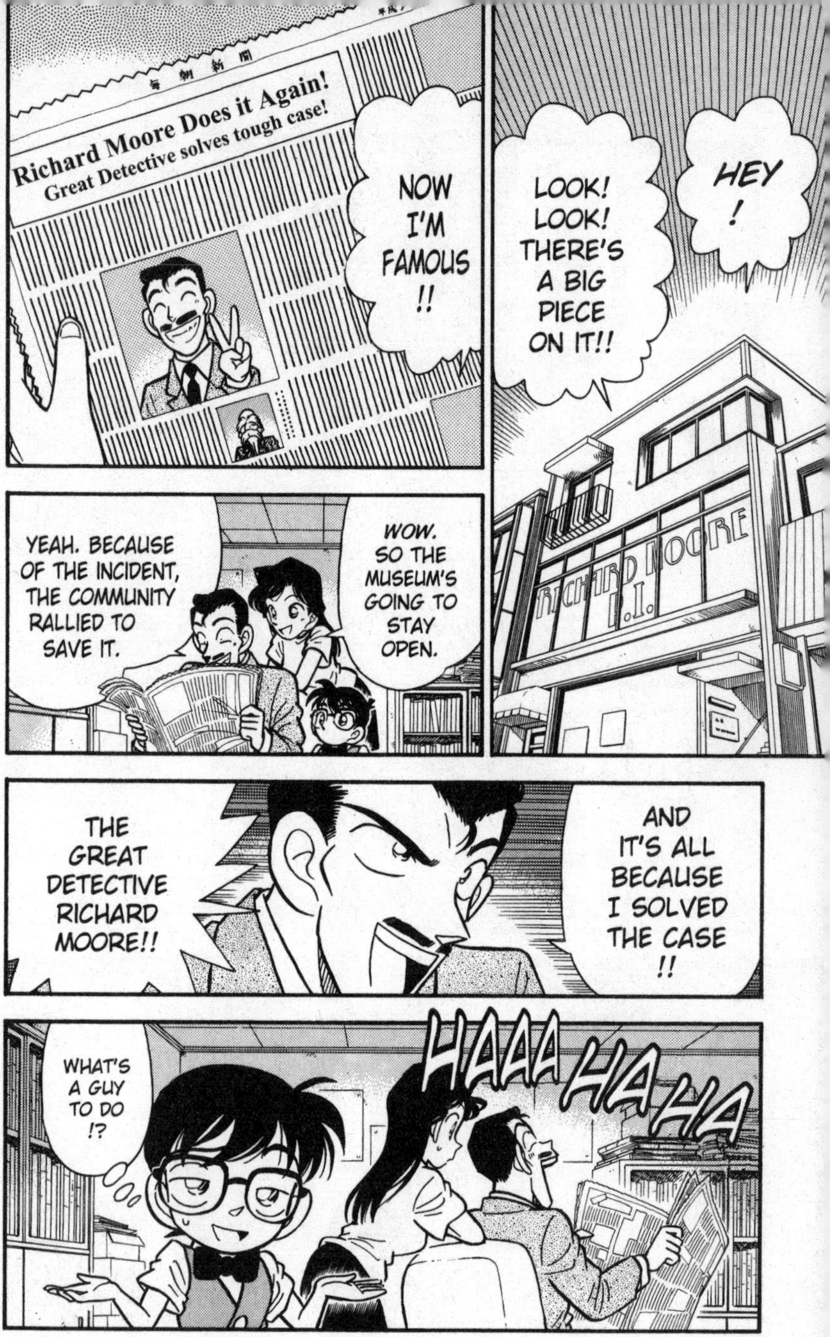
HEY!
LOOK! LOOK! THERE'S A BIG PIECE ON IT!!
RICHARD MOORE P.I.
NOW I'M FAMOUS!!
毎朝新聞
Richard Moore Does it Again!
Great Detective solves tough case!
WOW. SO THE MUSEUM'S GOING TO STAY OPEN.
YEAH. BECAUSE OF THE INCIDENT, THE COMMUNITY RALLIED TO SAVE IT.
AND IT'S ALL BECAUSE I SOLVED THE CASE!!
THE GREAT DETECTIVE RICHARD MOORE!!
HAAA HA HA
WHAT'S A GUY TO DO!?

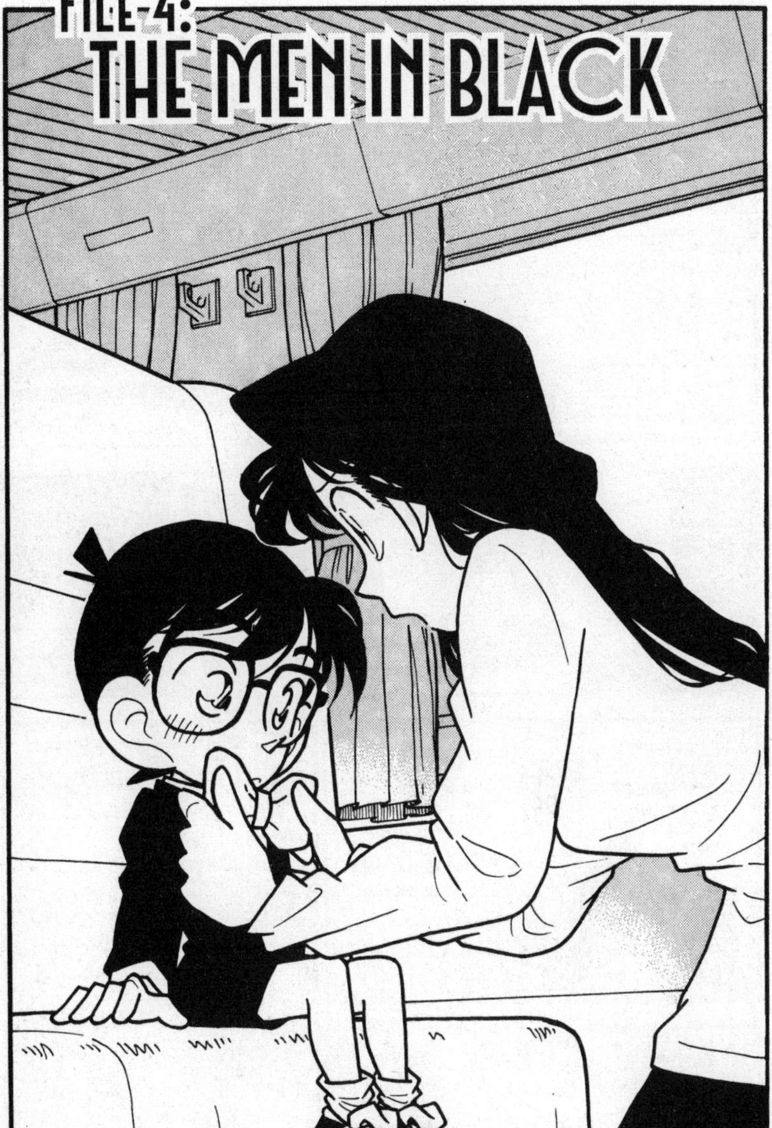
FILE 4:
THE MEN IN BLACK

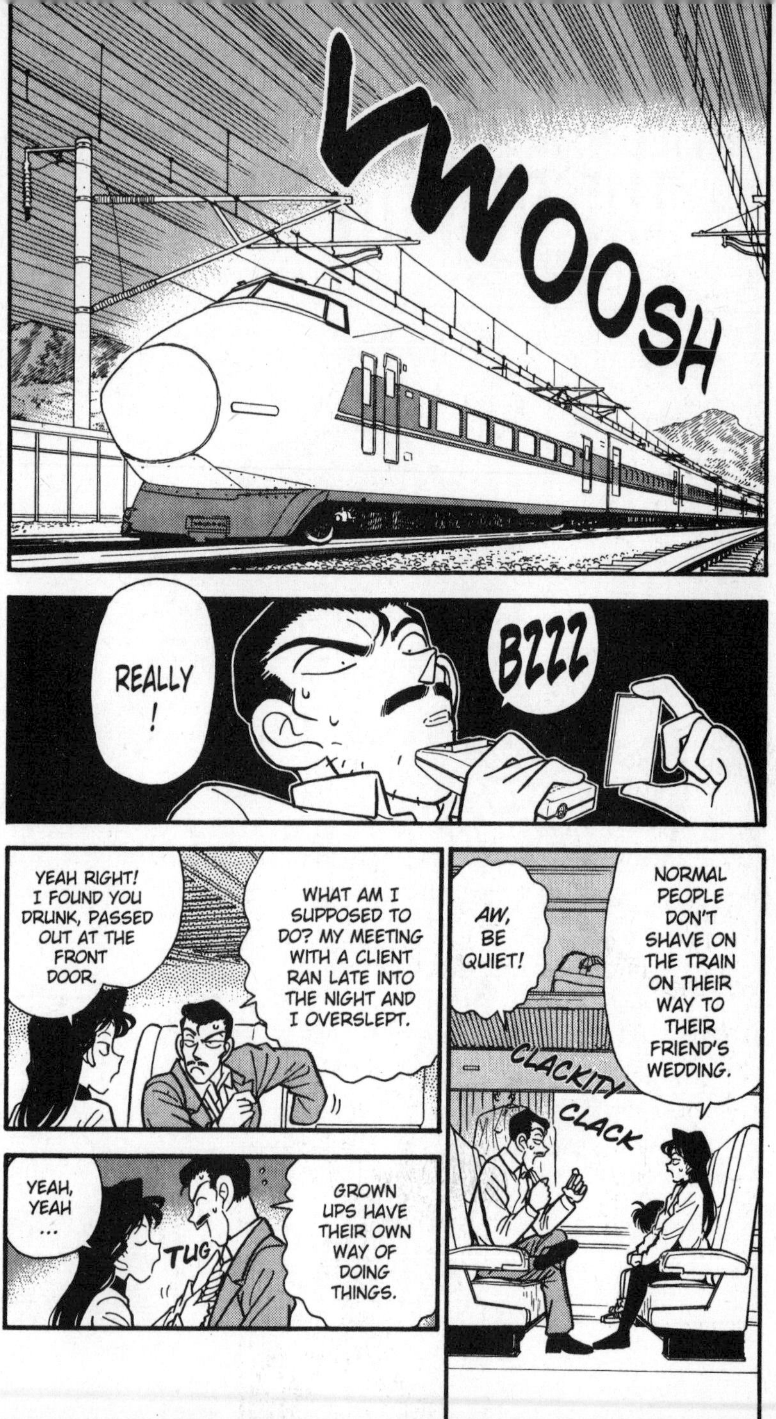
WOOSH
BZZZ
REALLY!
NORMAL PEOPLE DON'T SHAVE ON THE TRAIN ON THEIR WAY TO THEIR FRIEND'S WEDDING.
AW, BE QUIET!
CLACKITY CLACK
WHAT AM I SUPPOSED TO DO? MY MEETING WITH A CLIENT RAN LATE INTO THE NIGHT AND I OVERSLEPT.
YEAH RIGHT! I FOUND YOU DRUNK, PASSED OUT AT THE FRONT DOOR.
GROWN UPS HAVE THEIR OWN WAY OF DOING THINGS.
TUG
YEAH, YEAH ...

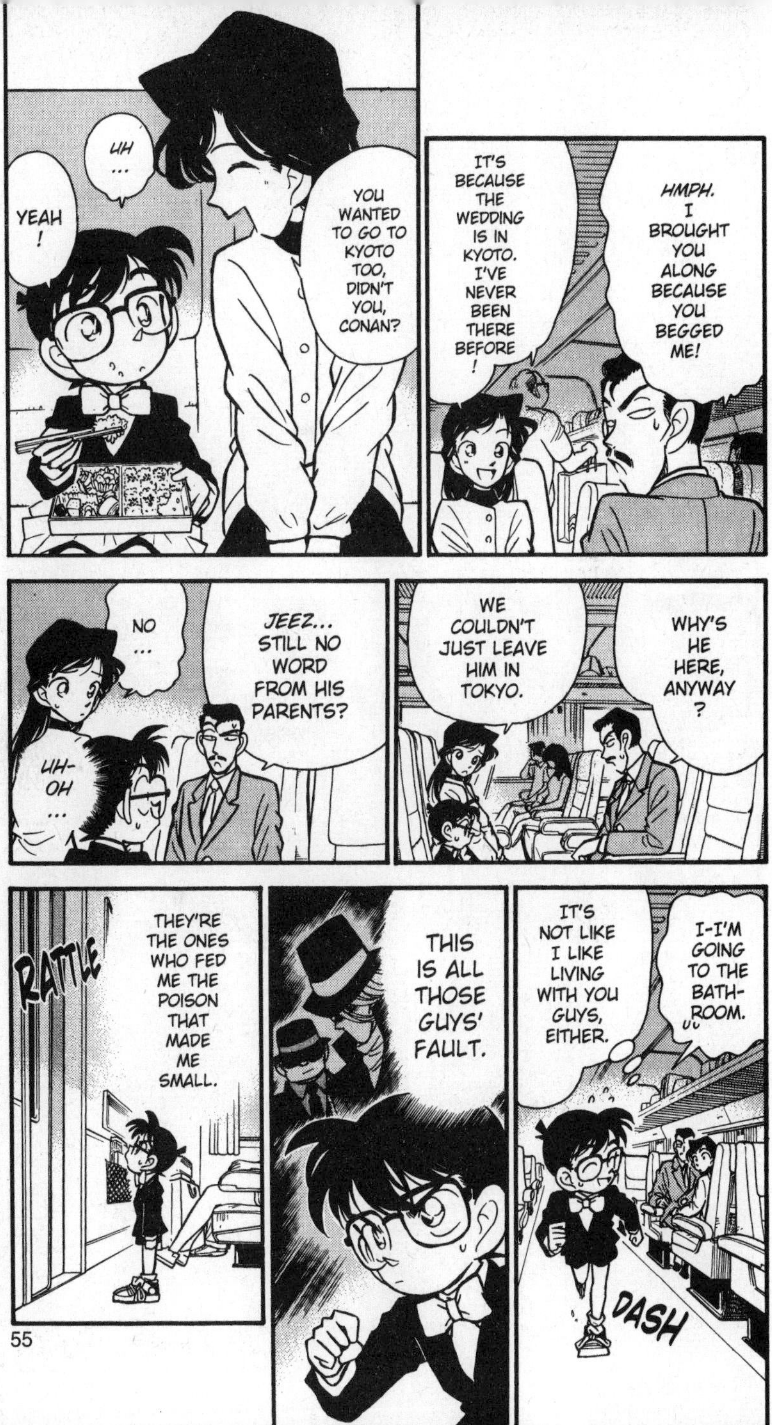
HMPH. I BROUGHT YOU ALONG BECAUSE YOU BEGGED ME!
IT'S BECAUSE THE WEDDING IS IN KYOTO. I'VE NEVER BEEN THERE BEFORE!
YOU WANTED TO GO TO KYOTO TOO, DIDN'T YOU, CONAN?
UH ...
YEAH!
WHY'S HE HERE, ANYWAY?
WE COULDN'T JUST LEAVE HIM IN TOKYO.
JEEZ... STILL NO WORD FROM HIS PARENTS?
NO ...
UH-OH ...
I-I'M GOING TO THE BATHROOM.
IT'S NOT LIKE I LIKE LIVING WITH YOU GUYS, EITHER.
DASH
THIS IS ALL THOSE GUYS' FAULT.
THEY'RE THE ONES WHO FED ME THE POISON THAT MADE ME SMALL.
RATTLE

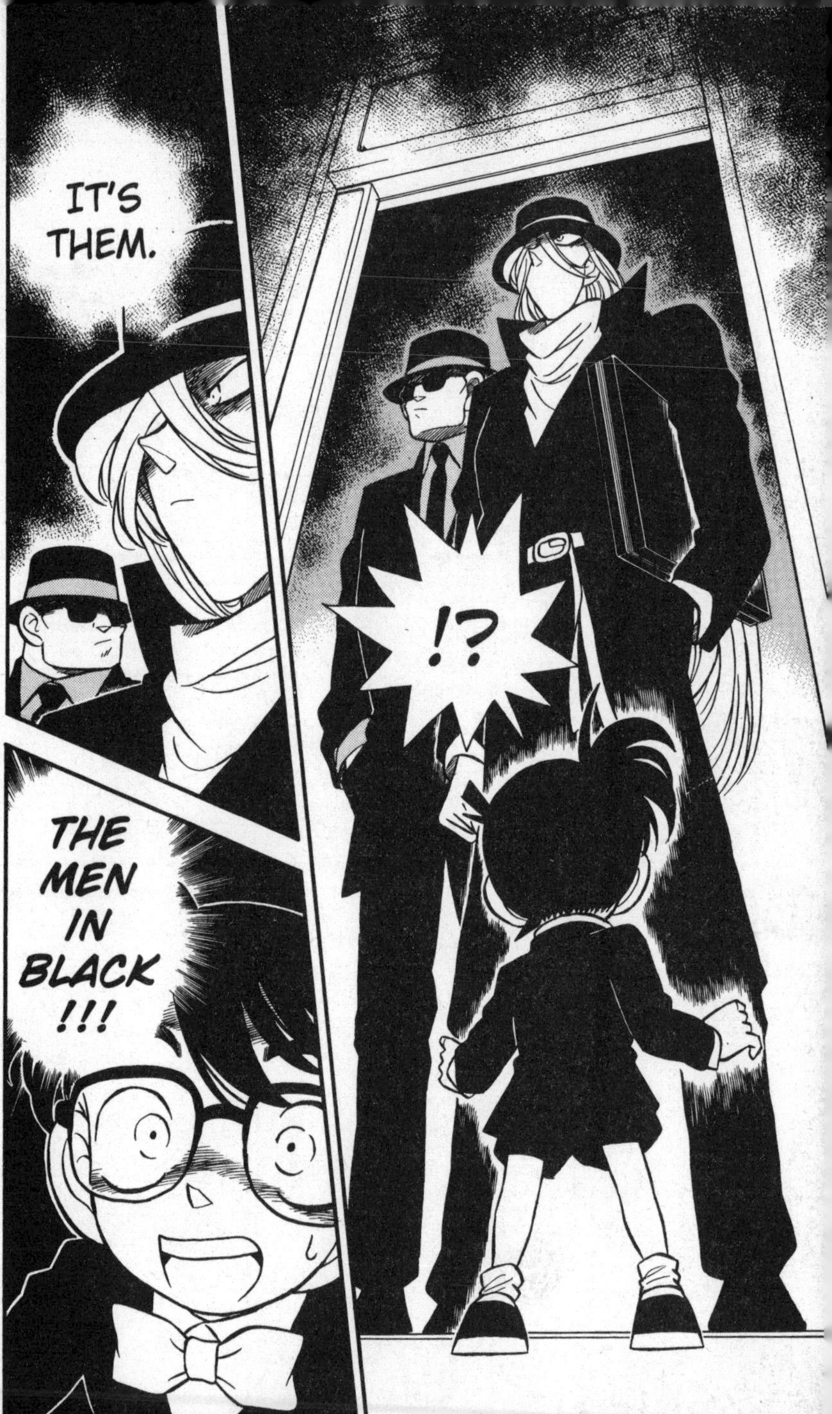
!?
IT'S THEM.
THE MEN IN BLACK!!!

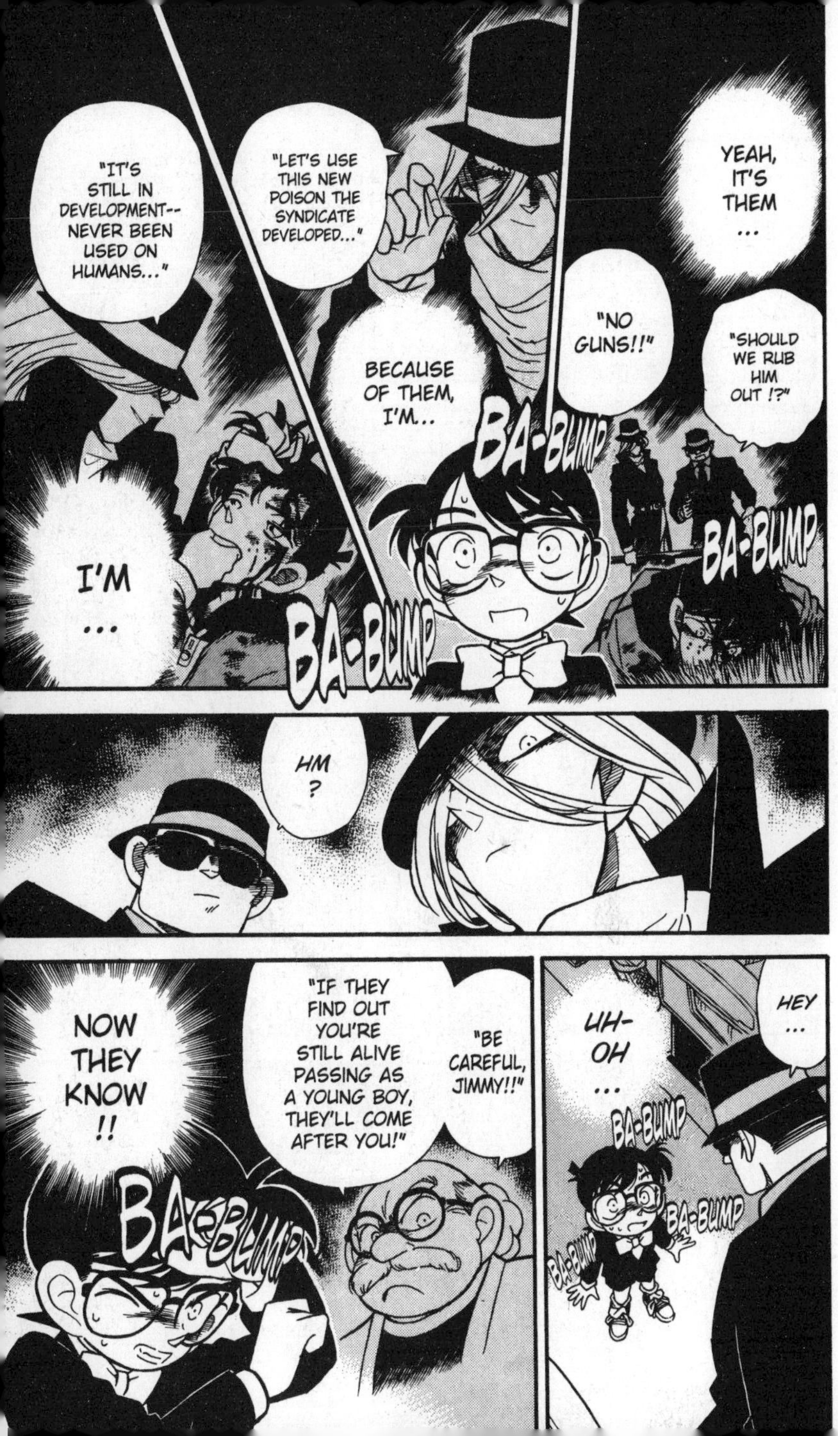
YEAH, IT'S THEM ...
"SHOULD WE RUB HIM OUT !?"
"NO GUNS!!"
BA-BUMP
"LET'S USE THIS NEW POISON THE SYNDICATE DEVELOPED..."
"IT'S STILL IN DEVELOPMENT-- NEVER BEEN USED ON HUMANS..."
BECAUSE OF THEM, I'M...
BA-BUMP
I'M ...
BA-BUMP
HM ?
HEY ...
UH-OH ...
BA-BUMP
BA-BUMP
BA-BUMP
"BE CAREFUL, JIMMY!!"
"IF THEY FIND OUT YOU'RE STILL ALIVE PASSING AS A YOUNG BOY, THEY'LL COME AFTER YOU!"
NOW THEY KNOW !!
BA-BUMP

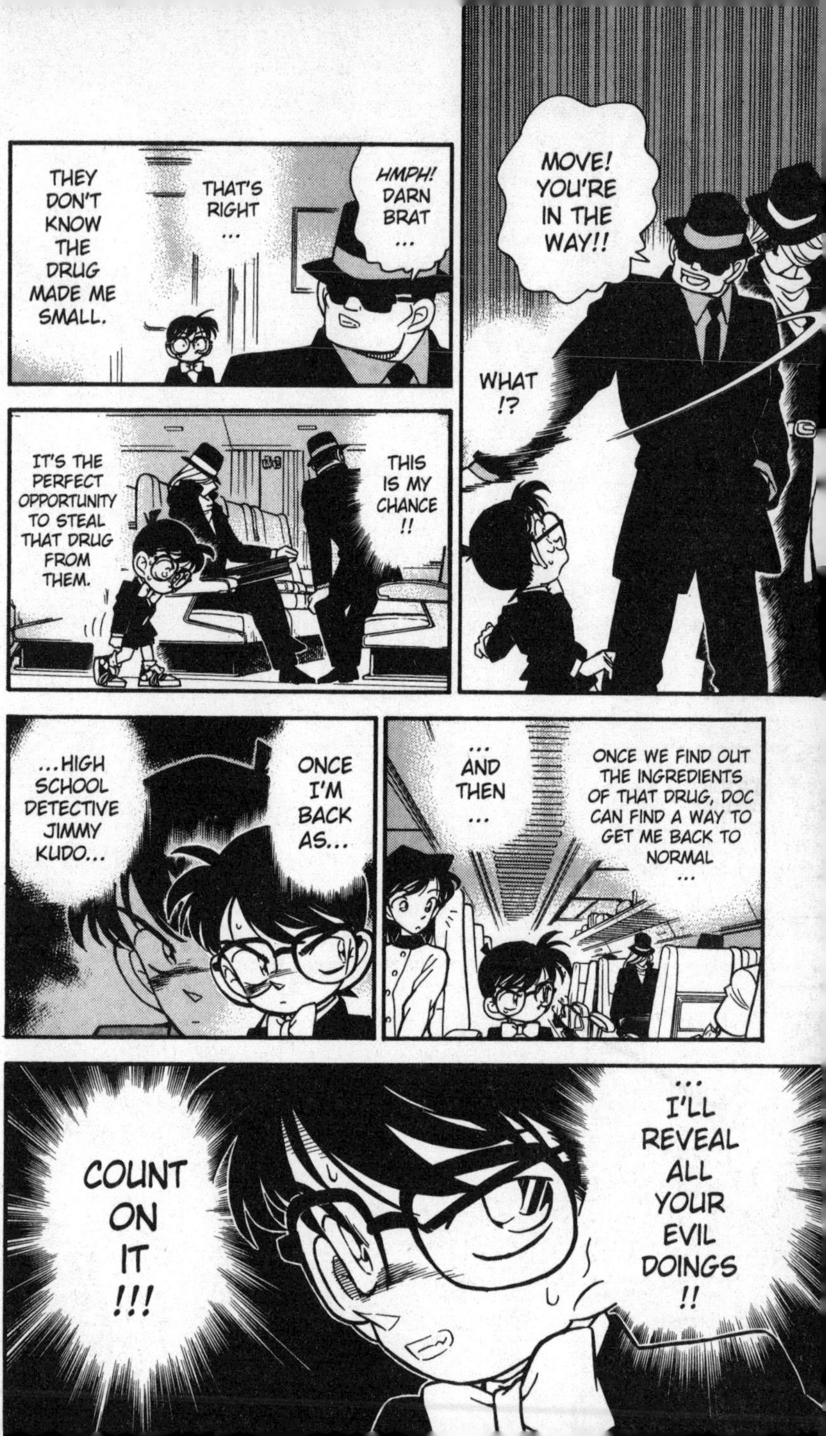
MOVE! YOU'RE IN THE WAY!!
WHAT !?
HMPH! DARN BRAT ...
THAT'S RIGHT ...
THEY DON'T KNOW THE DRUG MADE ME SMALL.
THIS IS MY CHANCE !!
IT'S THE PERFECT OPPORTUNITY TO STEAL THAT DRUG FROM THEM.
ONCE WE FIND OUT THE INGREDIENTS OF THAT DRUG, DOC CAN FIND A WAY TO GET ME BACK TO NORMAL ...
... AND THEN ...
ONCE I'M BACK AS...
...HIGH SCHOOL DETECTIVE JIMMY KUDO...
... I'LL REVEAL ALL YOUR EVIL DOINGS !!
COUNT ON IT !!!

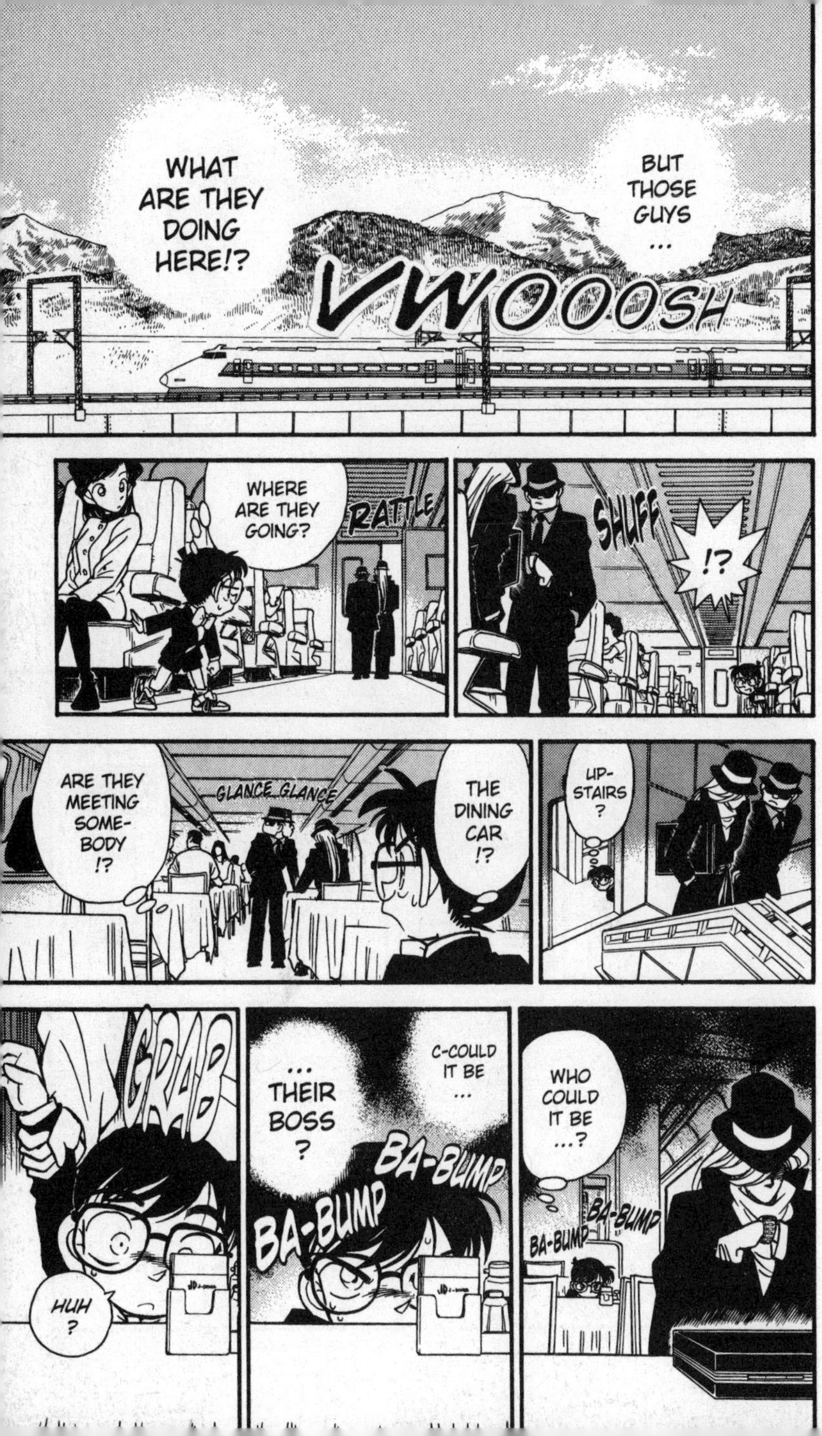
BUT THOSE GUYS ...
WHAT ARE THEY DOING HERE!?
VWOOOSH
SHUFF
!?
WHERE ARE THEY GOING?
RATTLE
UP-STAIRS ?
THE DINING CAR !?
GLANCE GLANCE
ARE THEY MEETING SOME-BODY !?
WHO COULD IT BE ...?
BA-BUMP
BA-BUMP
C-COULD IT BE ...
... THEIR BOSS ?
BA-BUMP
BA-BUMP
GRAB
HUH ?

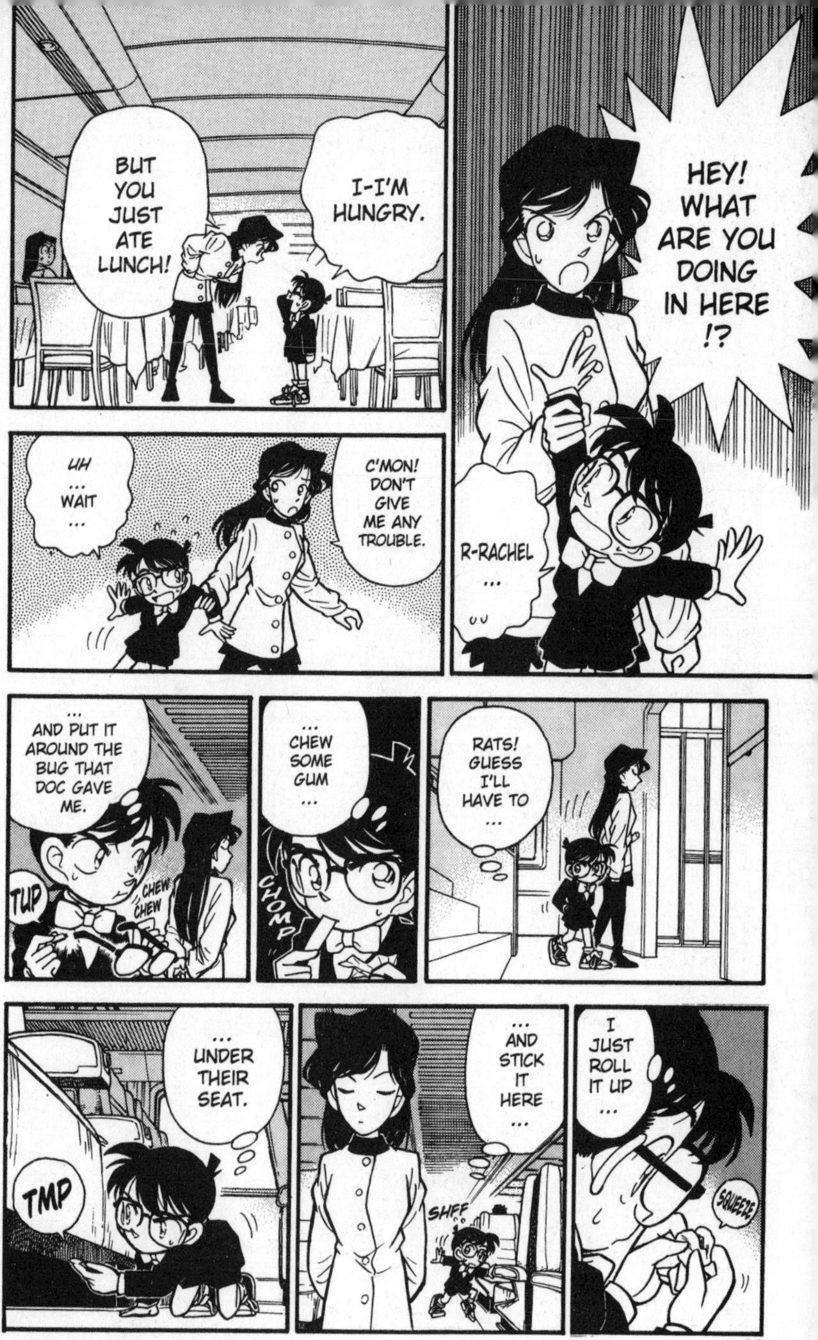
HEY! WHAT ARE YOU DOING IN HERE !?
R-RACHEL ...
I-I'M HUNGRY.
BUT YOU JUST ATE LUNCH!
C'MON! DON'T GIVE ME ANY TROUBLE.
UH ... WAIT ...
RATS! GUESS I'LL HAVE TO ...
... CHEW SOME GUM ...
CHOMP
... AND PUT IT AROUND THE BUG THAT DOC GAVE ME.
CHEW CHEW
TUP
I JUST ROLL IT UP ...
SQUEEZE
... AND STICK IT HERE ...
SHFF
... UNDER THEIR SEAT.
TMP

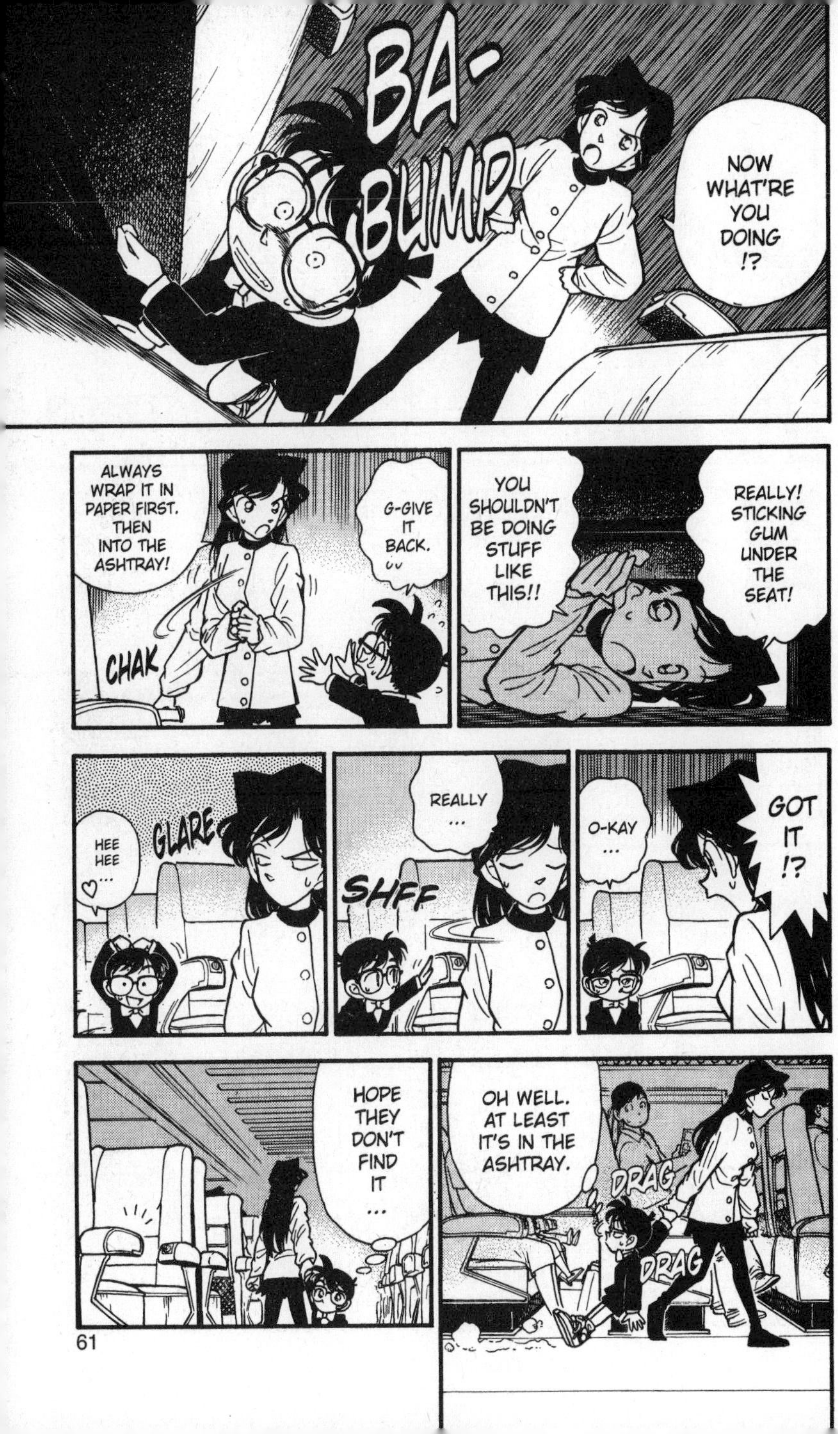
BA-BUMP
NOW WHAT'RE YOU DOING !?
REALLY! STICKING GUM UNDER THE SEAT!
YOU SHOULDN'T BE DOING STUFF LIKE THIS!!
G-GIVE IT BACK.
ALWAYS WRAP IT IN PAPER FIRST. THEN INTO THE ASHTRAY!
CHAK
GOT IT !?
O-KAY ...
REALLY ...
SHFF
GLARE
HEE HEE ♡...
OH WELL. AT LEAST IT'S IN THE ASHTRAY.
DRAG
DRAG
HOPE THEY DON'T FIND IT ...

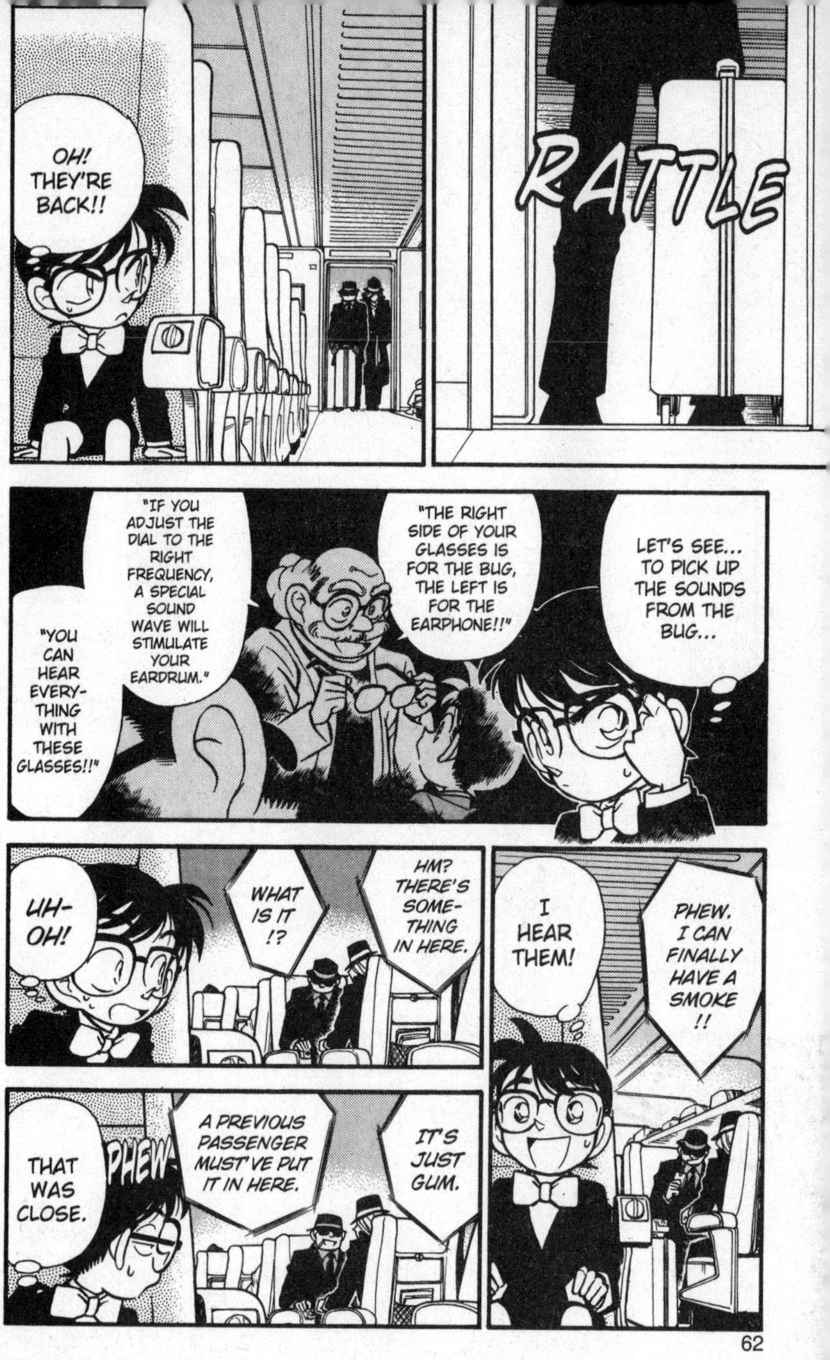
RATTLE
OH! THEY'RE BACK!!
LET'S SEE... TO PICK UP THE SOUNDS FROM THE BUG...
"THE RIGHT SIDE OF YOUR GLASSES IS FOR THE BUG, THE LEFT IS FOR THE EARPHONE!!"
"IF YOU ADJUST THE DIAL TO THE RIGHT FREQUENCY, A SPECIAL SOUND WAVE WILL STIMULATE YOUR EARDRUM."
"YOU CAN HEAR EVERY-THING WITH THESE GLASSES!!"
PHEW. I CAN FINALLY HAVE A SMOKE !!
I HEAR THEM!
HM? THERE'S SOME-THING IN HERE.
WHAT IS IT !?
UH-OH!
IT'S JUST GUM.
A PREVIOUS PASSENGER MUST'VE PUT IT IN HERE.
PHEW
THAT WAS CLOSE.

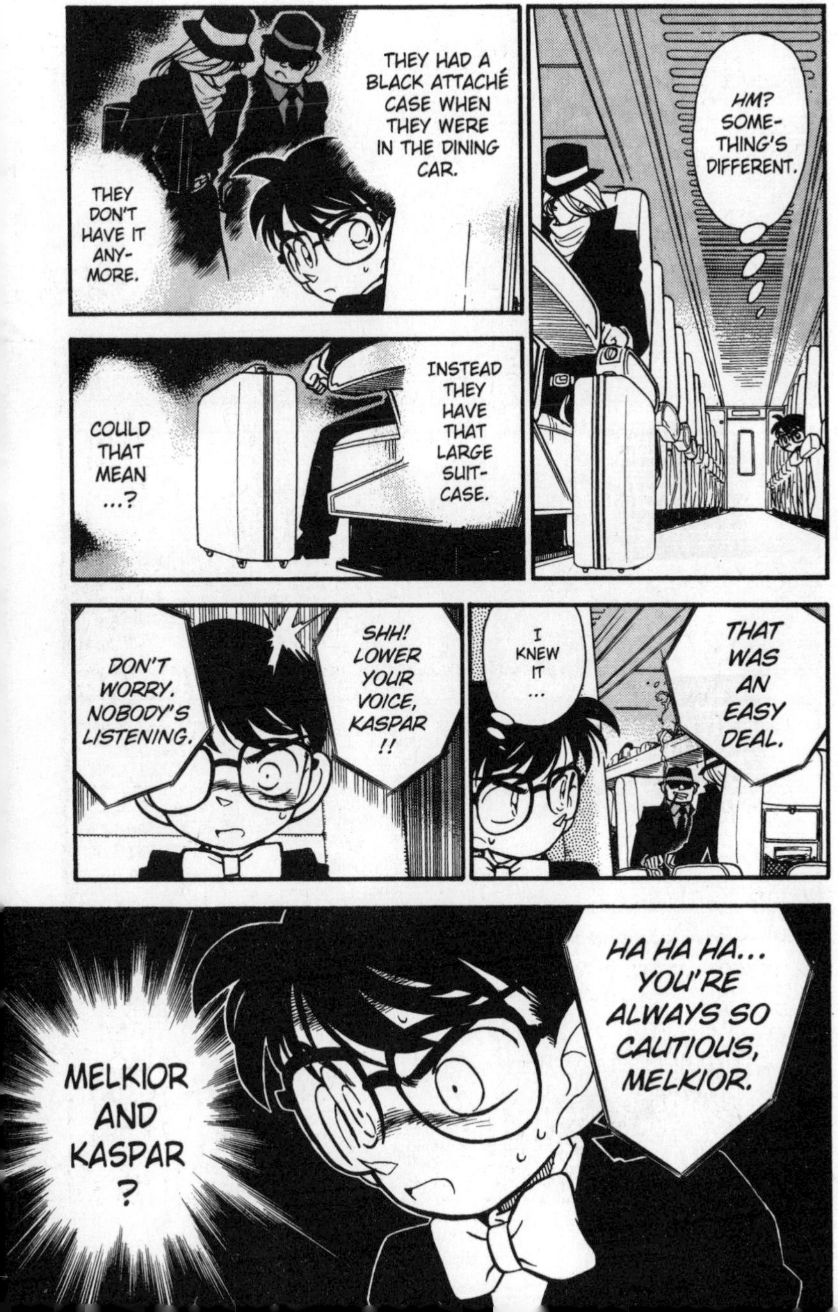
HM? SOME-THING'S DIFFERENT.
THEY HAD A BLACK ATTACHÉ CASE WHEN THEY WERE IN THE DINING CAR.
THEY DON'T HAVE IT ANY-MORE.
INSTEAD THEY HAVE THAT LARGE SUIT-CASE.
COULD THAT MEAN ...?
THAT WAS AN EASY DEAL.
I KNEW IT ...
SHH! LOWER YOUR VOICE, KASPAR !!
DON'T WORRY. NOBODY'S LISTENING.
HA HA HA... YOU'RE ALWAYS SO CAUTIOUS, MELKIOR.
MELKIOR AND KASPAR ?

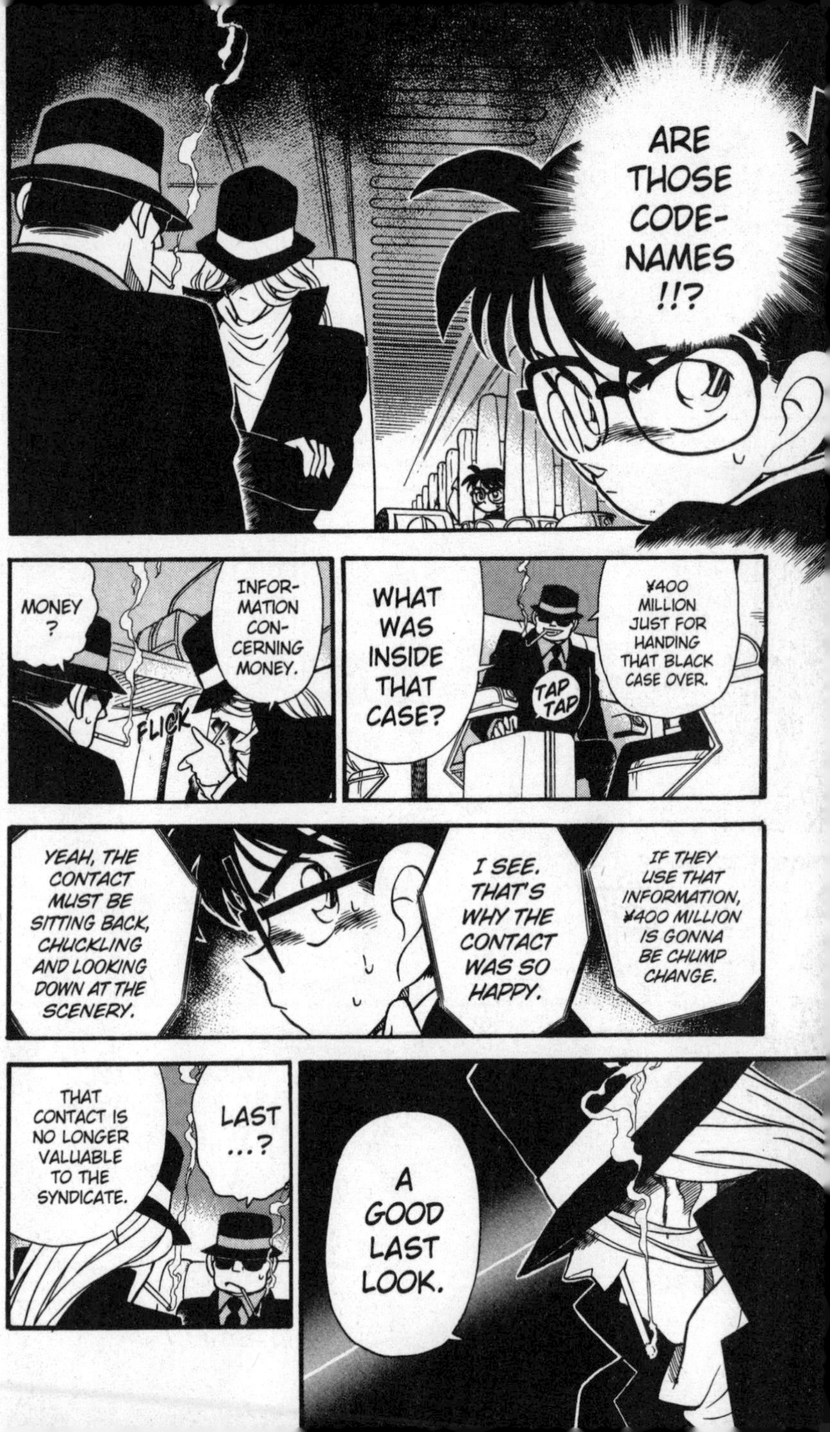
ARE THOSE CODE-NAMES !!?
¥400 MILLION JUST FOR HANDING THAT BLACK CASE OVER.
TAP TAP
WHAT WAS INSIDE THAT CASE?
INFORMATION CONCERNING MONEY.
MONEY ?
FLICK
IF THEY USE THAT INFORMATION, ¥400 MILLION IS GONNA BE CHUMP CHANGE.
I SEE. THAT'S WHY THE CONTACT WAS SO HAPPY.
YEAH, THE CONTACT MUST BE SITTING BACK, CHUCKLING AND LOOKING DOWN AT THE SCENERY.
A GOOD LAST LOOK.
LAST ...?
THAT CONTACT IS NO LONGER VALUABLE TO THE SYNDICATE.

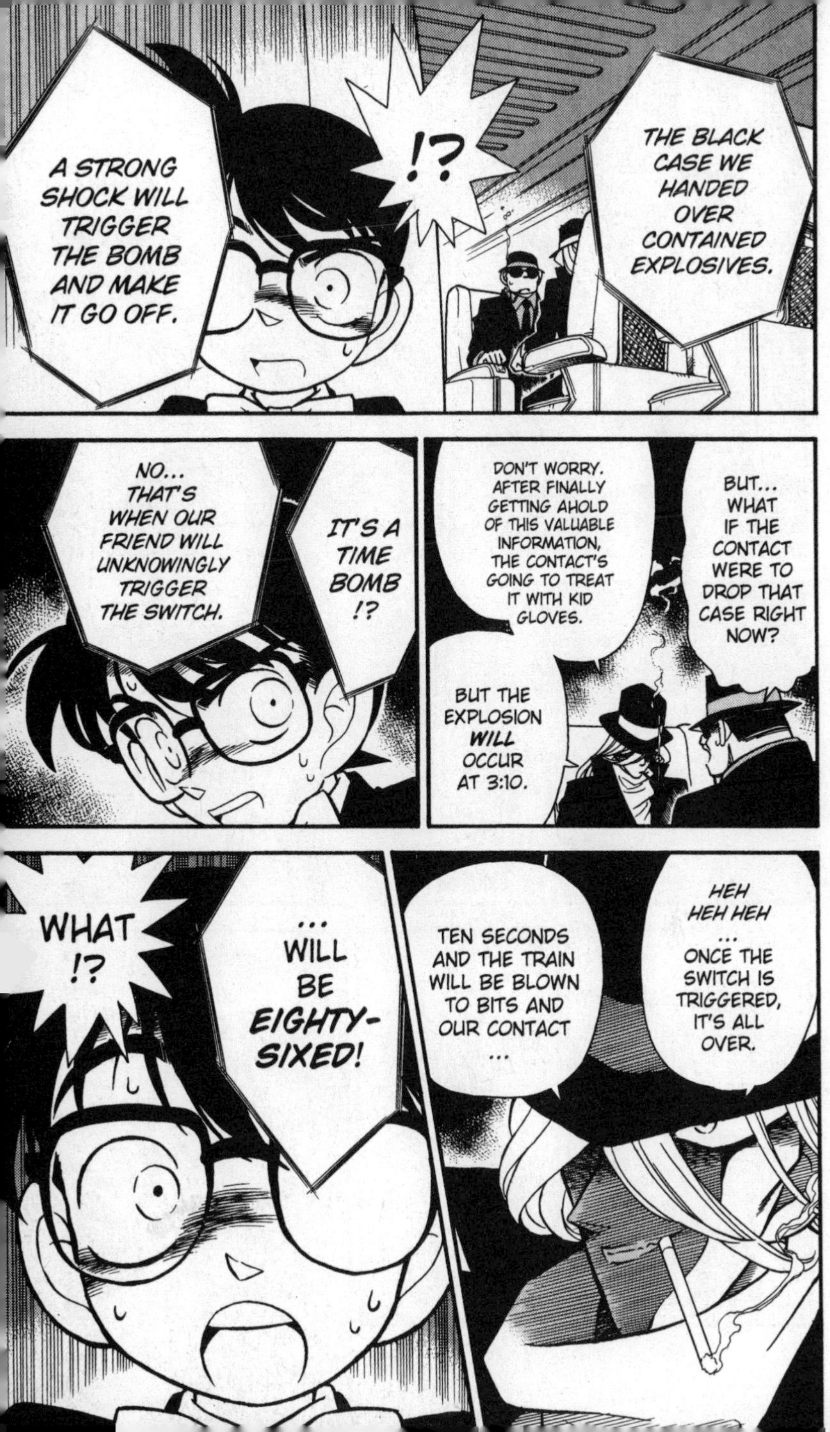
THE BLACK CASE WE HANDED OVER CONTAINED EXPLOSIVES.
!?
A STRONG SHOCK WILL TRIGGER THE BOMB AND MAKE IT GO OFF.
BUT... WHAT IF THE CONTACT WERE TO DROP THAT CASE RIGHT NOW?
DON'T WORRY. AFTER FINALLY GETTING AHOLD OF THIS VALUABLE INFORMATION, THE CONTACT'S GOING TO TREAT IT WITH KID GLOVES.
BUT THE EXPLOSION *WILL* OCCUR AT 3:10.
IT'S A TIME BOMB !?
NO... THAT'S WHEN OUR FRIEND WILL UNKNOWINGLY TRIGGER THE SWITCH.
HEH HEH HEH ... ONCE THE SWITCH IS TRIGGERED, IT'S ALL OVER.
TEN SECONDS AND THE TRAIN WILL BE BLOWN TO BITS AND OUR CONTACT ...
... WILL BE EIGHTY-SIXED!
WHAT !?

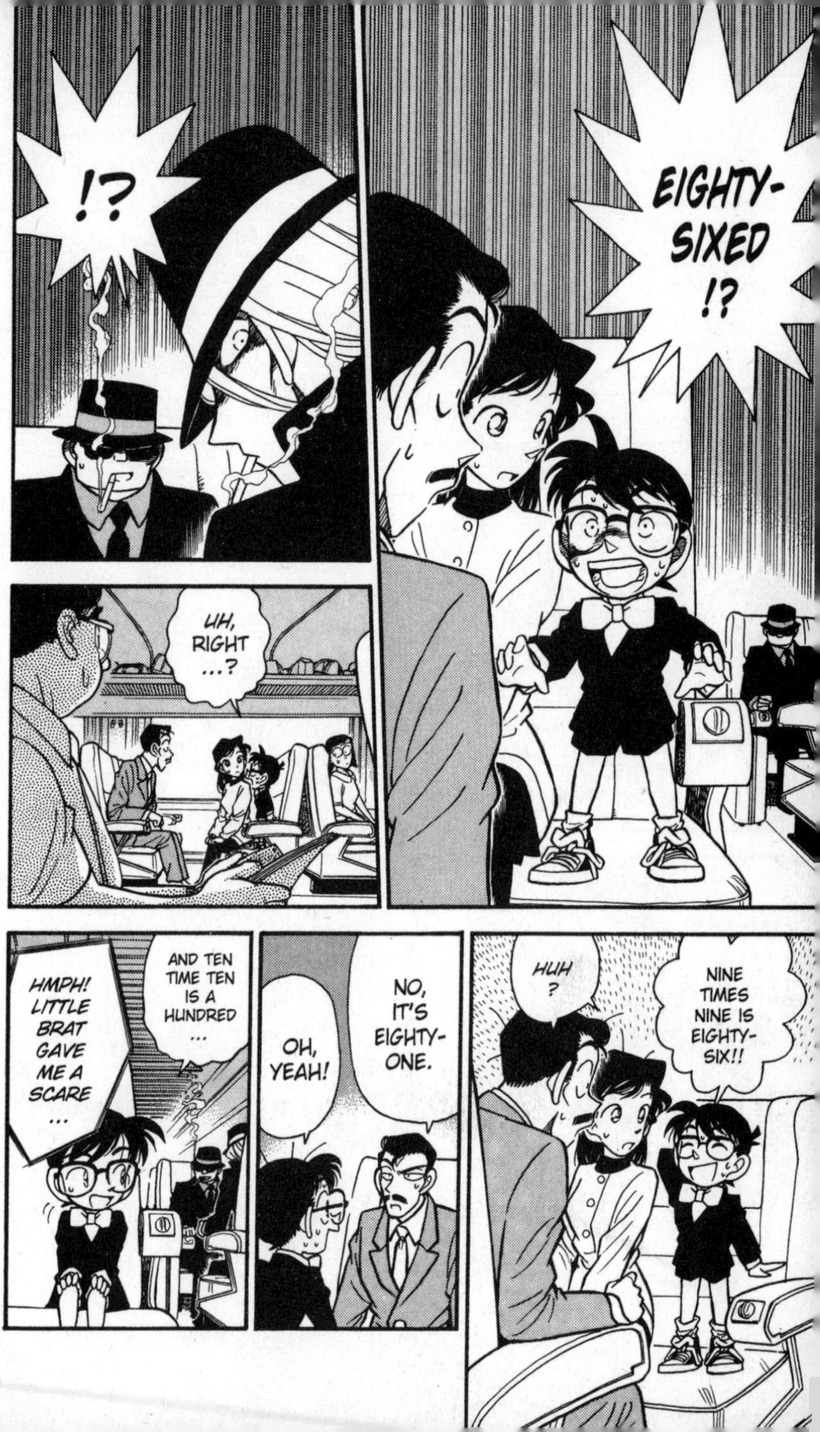
EIGHTY-SIXED !?
!?
UH, RIGHT ...?
NINE TIMES NINE IS EIGHTY-SIX!!
HUH?
NO, IT'S EIGHTY-ONE.
OH, YEAH!
AND TEN TIME TEN IS A HUNDRED ...
HMPH! LITTLE BRAT GAVE ME A SCARE ...

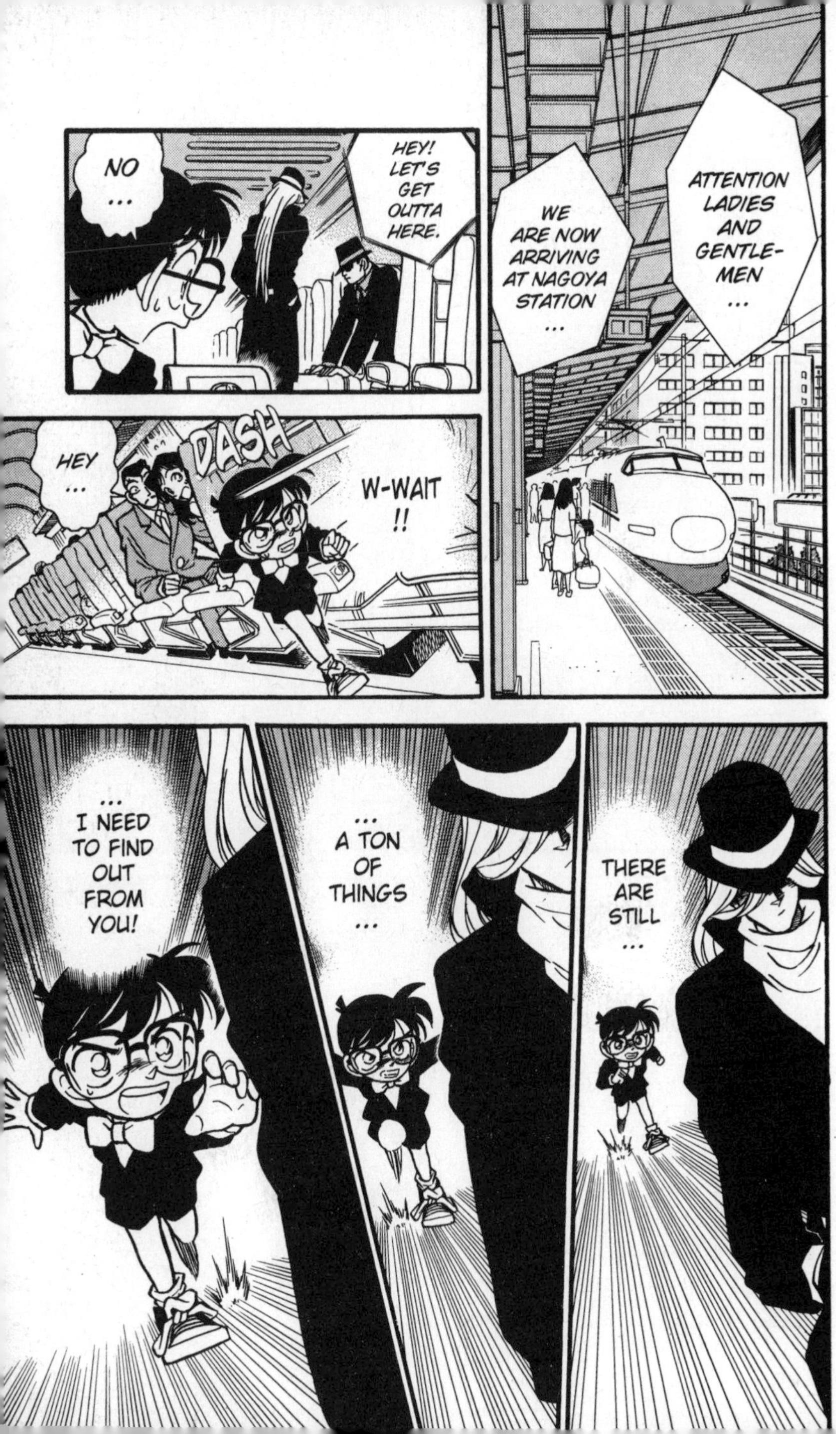
ATTENTION LADIES AND GENTLEMEN ...
WE ARE NOW ARRIVING AT NAGOYA STATION ...
HEY! LET'S GET OUTTA HERE.
NO ...
W-WAIT !!
DASH
HEY ...
THERE ARE STILL ...
... A TON OF THINGS ...
... I NEED TO FIND OUT FROM YOU!

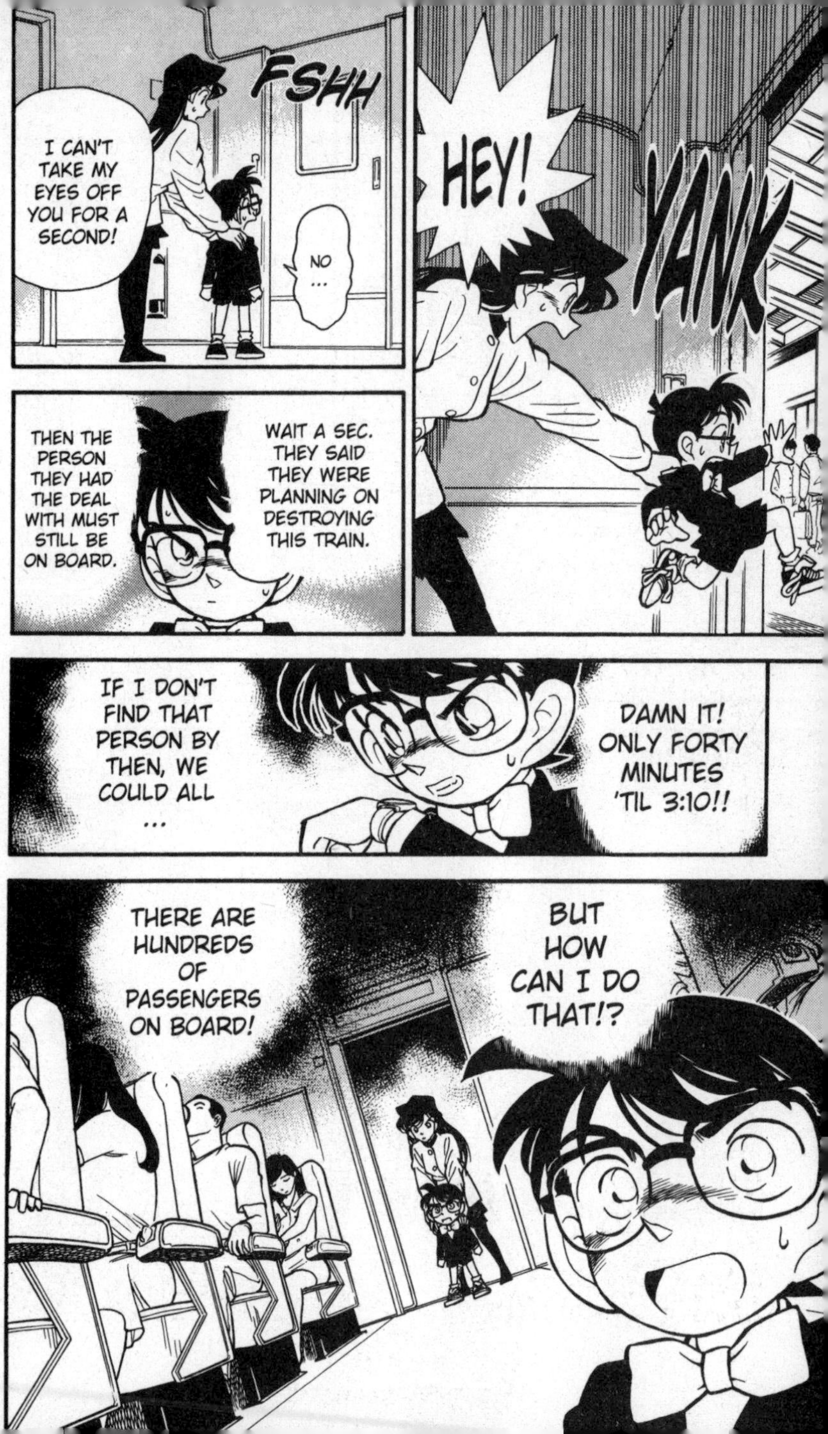
HEY!
YANK
FSHH
I CAN'T TAKE MY EYES OFF YOU FOR A SECOND!
NO ...
WAIT A SEC. THEY SAID THEY WERE PLANNING ON DESTROYING THIS TRAIN.
THEN THE PERSON THEY HAD THE DEAL WITH MUST STILL BE ON BOARD.
DAMN IT! ONLY FORTY MINUTES 'TIL 3:10!!
IF I DON'T FIND THAT PERSON BY THEN, WE COULD ALL ...
BUT HOW CAN I DO THAT!?
THERE ARE HUNDREDS OF PASSENGERS ON BOARD!

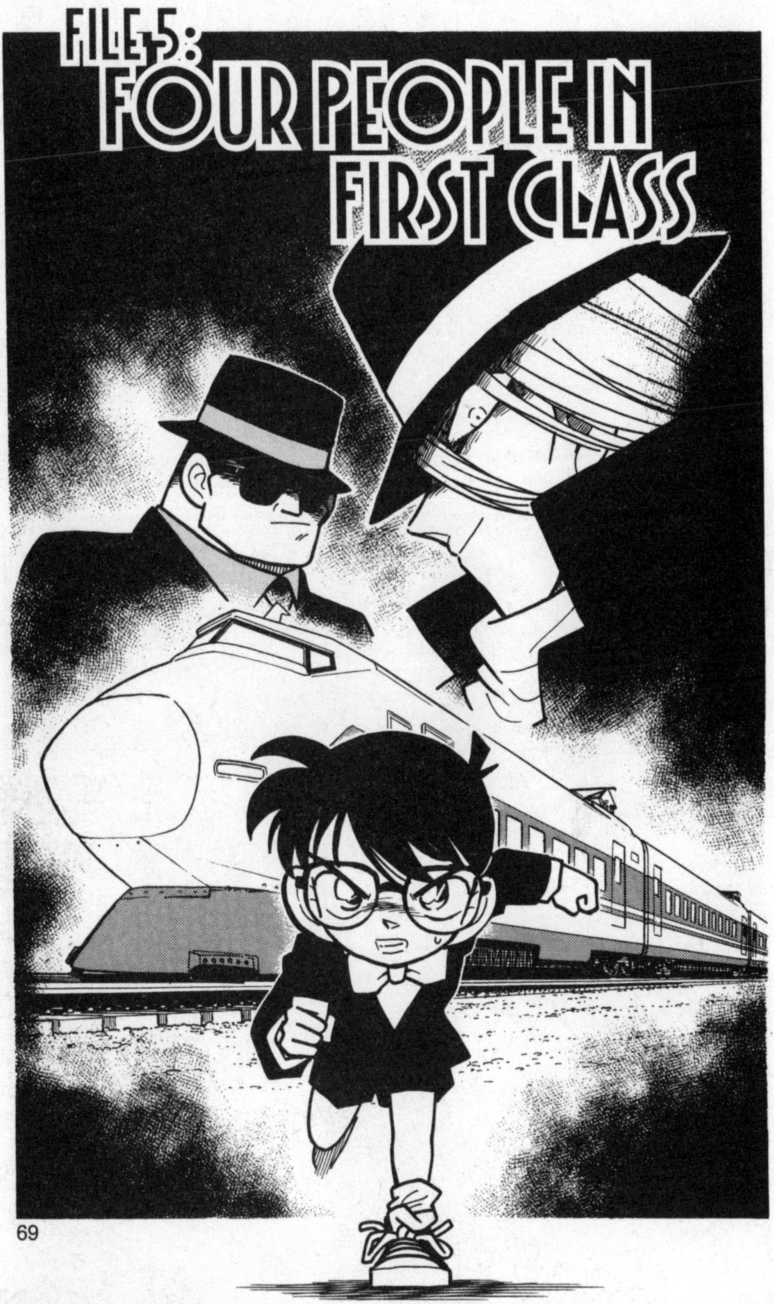
FILE 5:
FOUR PEOPLE IN FIRST CLASS

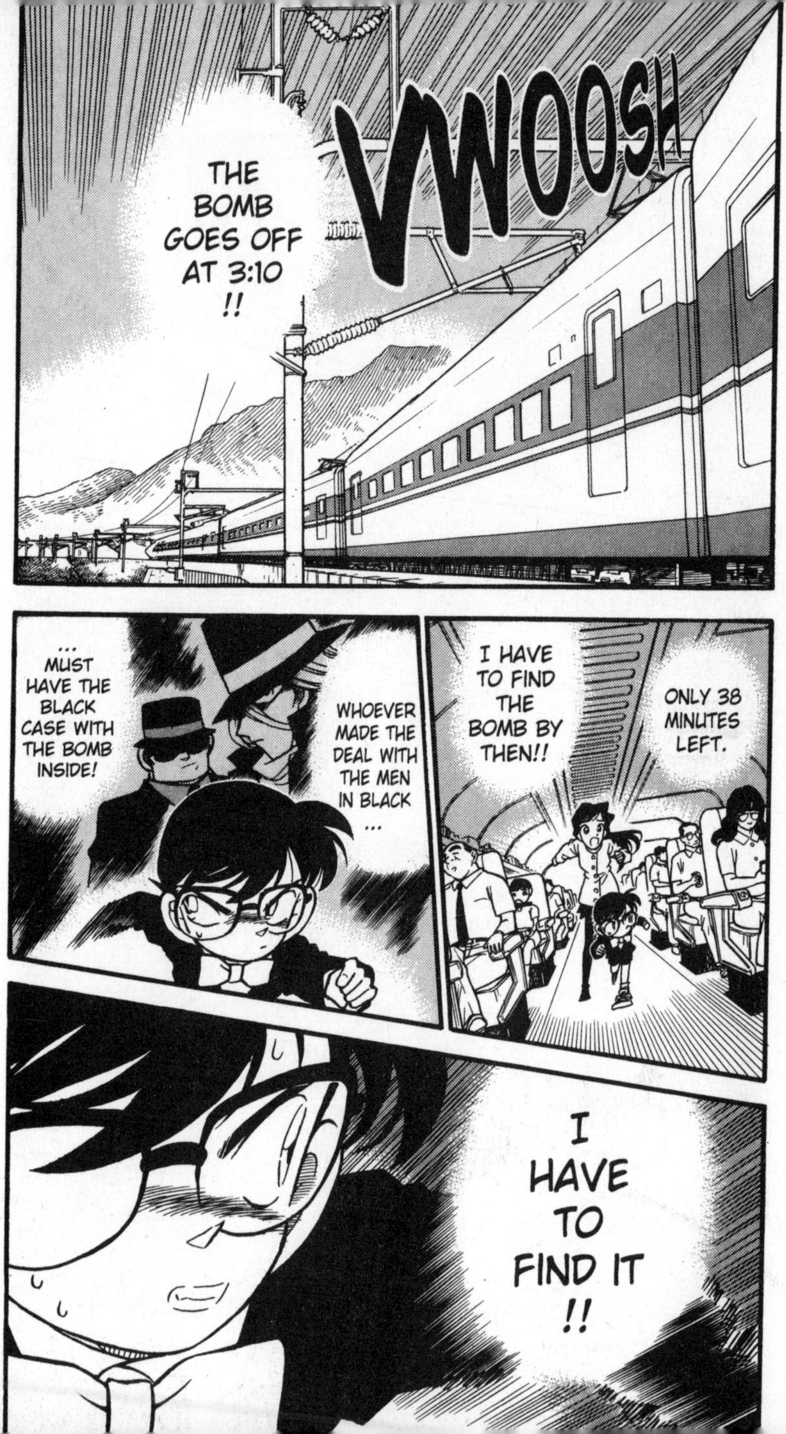
VWOOSH
THE BOMB GOES OFF AT 3:10 !!
ONLY 38 MINUTES LEFT.
I HAVE TO FIND THE BOMB BY THEN!!
WHOEVER MADE THE DEAL WITH THE MEN IN BLACK ...
... MUST HAVE THE BLACK CASE WITH THE BOMB INSIDE!
I HAVE TO FIND IT !!

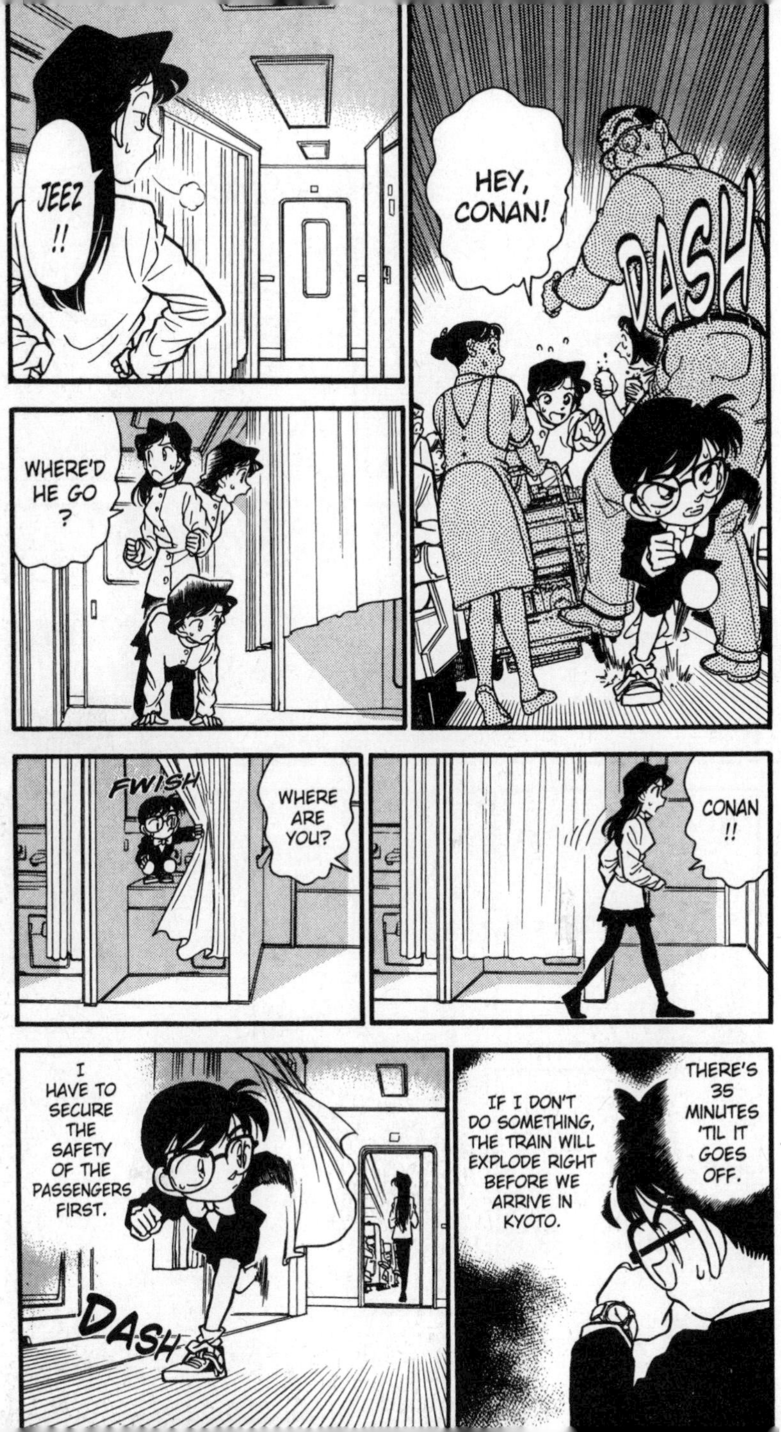
DASH
HEY, CONAN!
JEEZ !!
WHERE'D HE GO ?
CONAN !!
WHERE ARE YOU?
FWISH
THERE'S 35 MINUTES 'TIL IT GOES OFF.
IF I DON'T DO SOMETHING, THE TRAIN WILL EXPLODE RIGHT BEFORE WE ARRIVE IN KYOTO.
I HAVE TO SECURE THE SAFETY OF THE PASSENGERS FIRST.
DASH

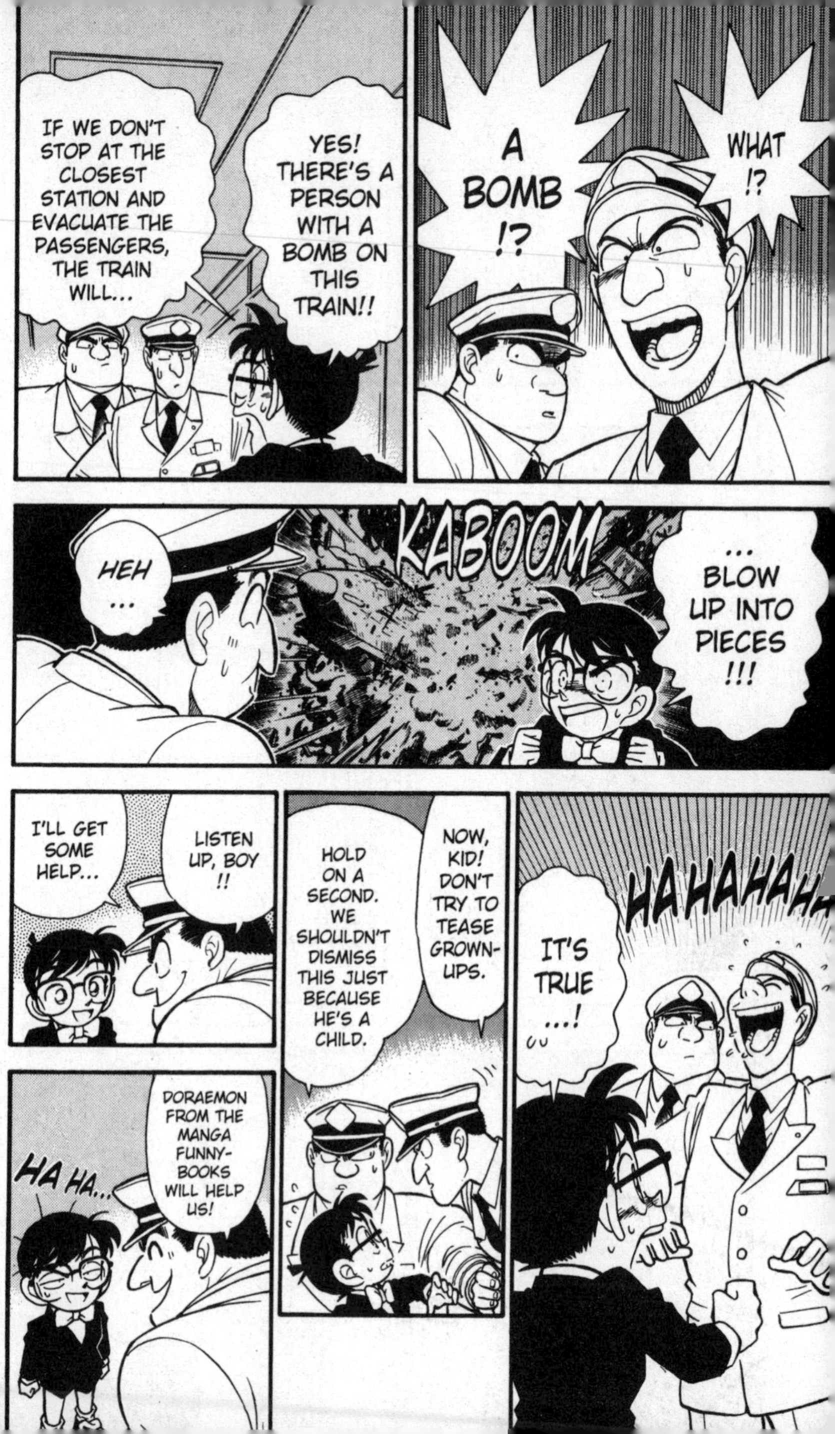
WHAT !?
A BOMB !?
YES! THERE'S A PERSON WITH A BOMB ON THIS TRAIN!!
IF WE DON'T STOP AT THE CLOSEST STATION AND EVACUATE THE PASSENGERS, THE TRAIN WILL...
... BLOW UP INTO PIECES !!!
KABOOM
HEH ...
HAHAHAHA
IT'S TRUE ...!
NOW, KID! DON'T TRY TO TEASE GROWN-UPS.
HOLD ON A SECOND. WE SHOULDN'T DISMISS THIS JUST BECAUSE HE'S A CHILD.
LISTEN UP, BOY !!
I'LL GET SOME HELP...
DORAEMON FROM THE MANGA FUNNY-BOOKS WILL HELP US!
HA HA...

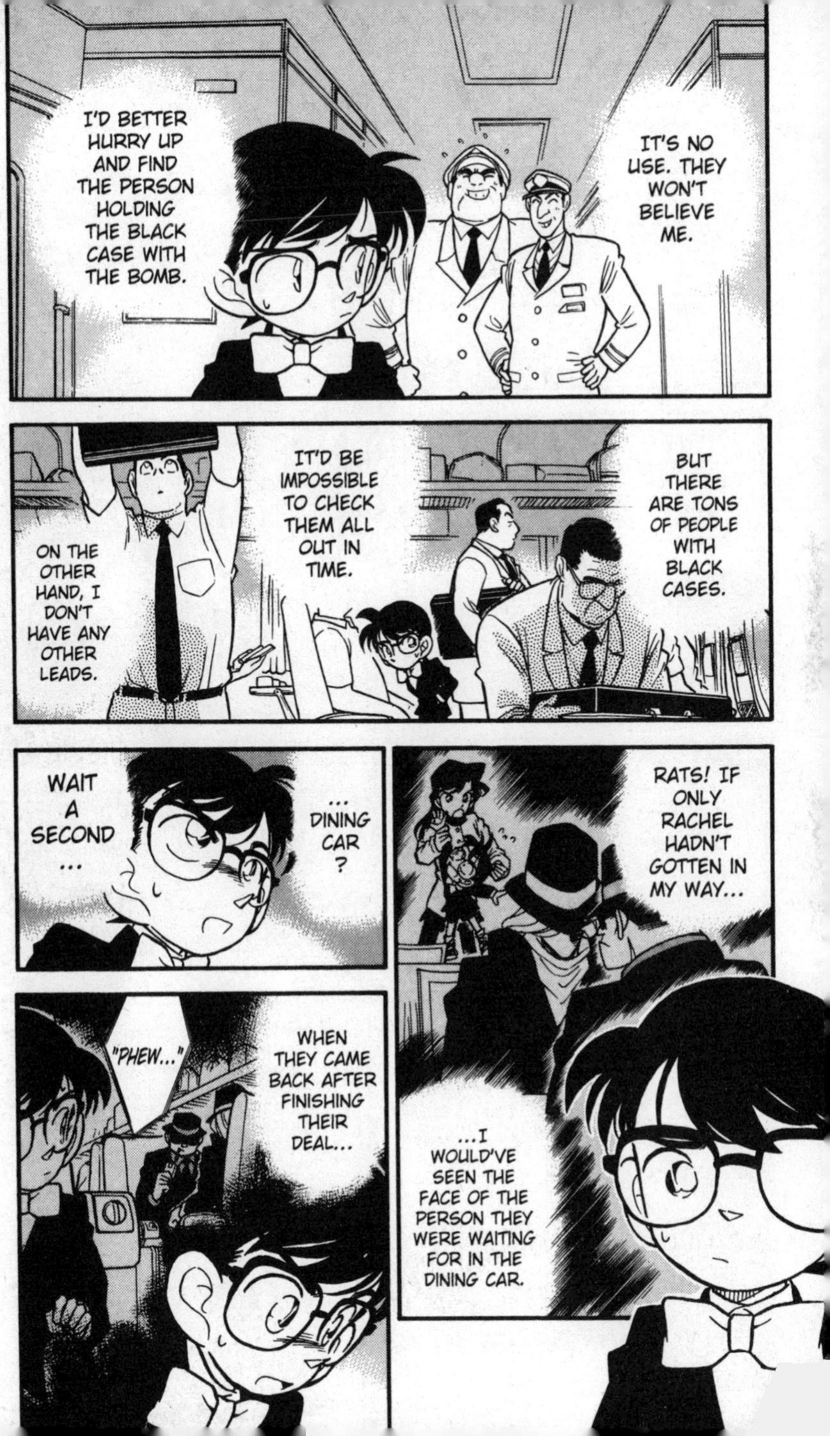
IT'S NO USE. THEY WON'T BELIEVE ME.
I'D BETTER HURRY UP AND FIND THE PERSON HOLDING THE BLACK CASE WITH THE BOMB.
BUT THERE ARE TONS OF PEOPLE WITH BLACK CASES.
IT'D BE IMPOSSIBLE TO CHECK THEM ALL OUT IN TIME.
ON THE OTHER HAND, I DON'T HAVE ANY OTHER LEADS.
RATS! IF ONLY RACHEL HADN'T GOTTEN IN MY WAY...
...I WOULD'VE SEEN THE FACE OF THE PERSON THEY WERE WAITING FOR IN THE DINING CAR.
WAIT A SECOND ...
... DINING CAR ?
WHEN THEY CAME BACK AFTER FINISHING THEIR DEAL...
"PHEW..."

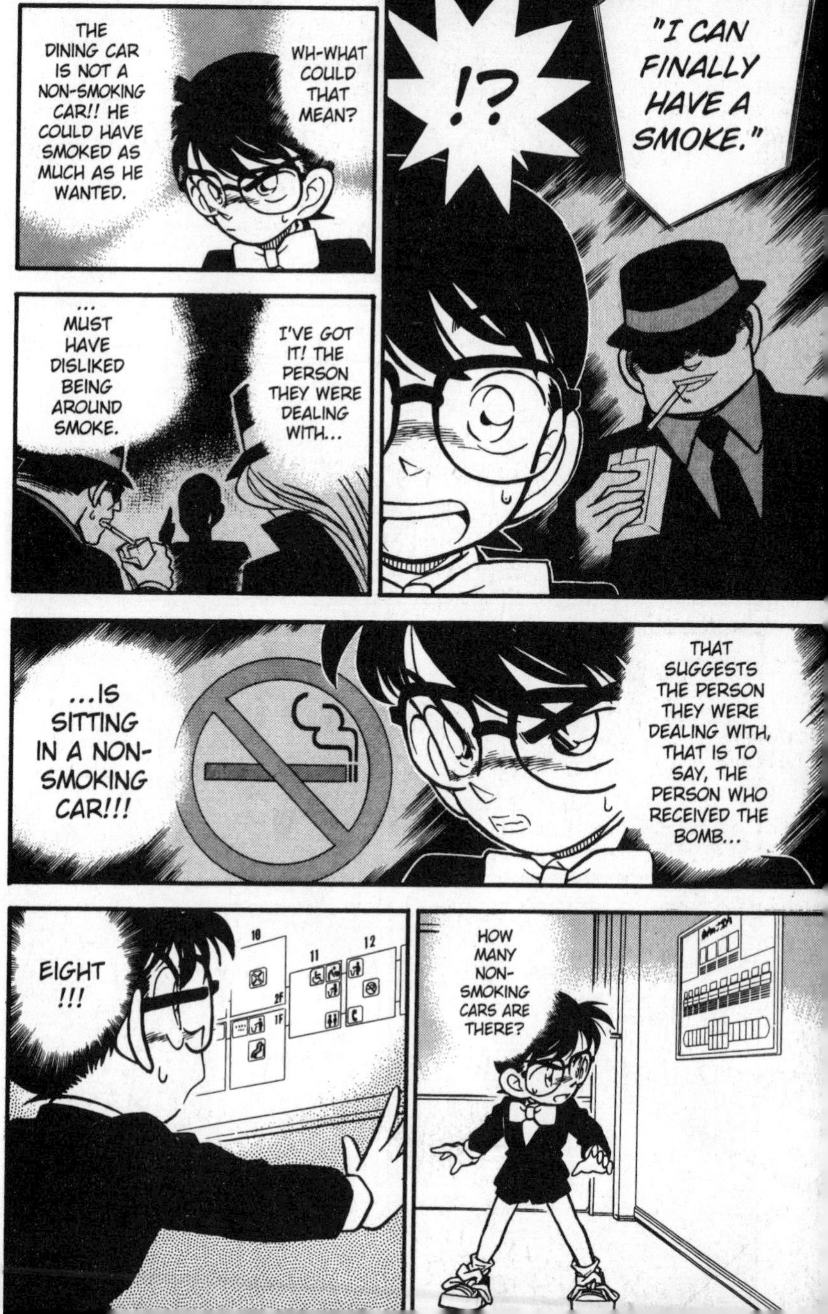
"I CAN FINALLY HAVE A SMOKE."
!?
WH-WHAT COULD THAT MEAN?
THE DINING CAR IS NOT A NON-SMOKING CAR!! HE COULD HAVE SMOKED AS MUCH AS HE WANTED.
I'VE GOT IT! THE PERSON THEY WERE DEALING WITH...
... MUST HAVE DISLIKED BEING AROUND SMOKE.
THAT SUGGESTS THE PERSON THEY WERE DEALING WITH, THAT IS TO SAY, THE PERSON WHO RECEIVED THE BOMB...
...IS SITTING IN A NON-SMOKING CAR!!!
HOW MANY NON-SMOKING CARS ARE THERE?
EIGHT !!!

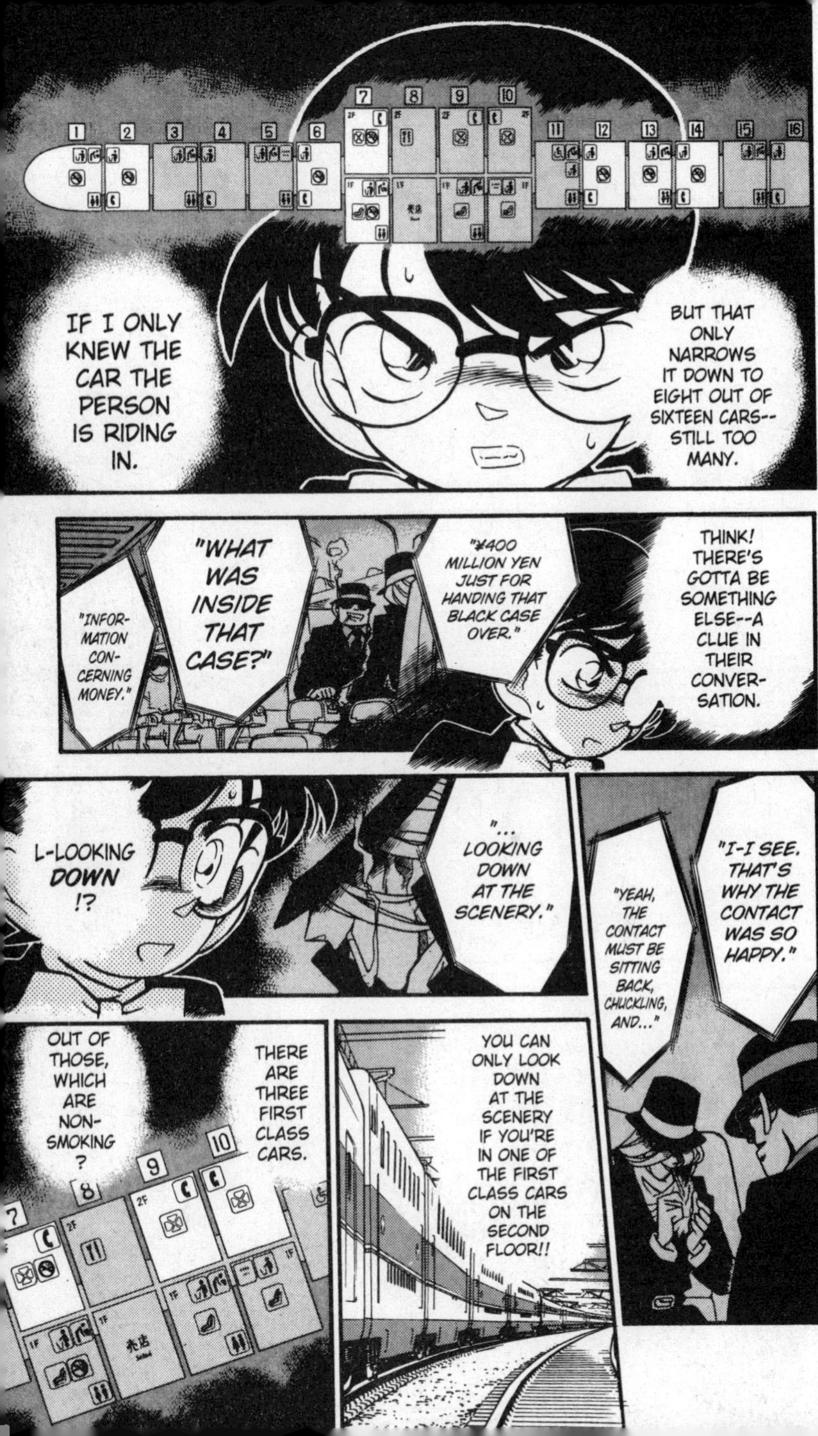
1 2 3 4 5 6 7 8 9 10 11 12 13 14 15 16
BUT THAT ONLY NARROWS IT DOWN TO EIGHT OUT OF SIXTEEN CARS-- STILL TOO MANY.
IF I ONLY KNEW THE CAR THE PERSON IS RIDING IN.
THINK! THERE'S GOTTA BE SOMETHING ELSE--A CLUE IN THEIR CONVER-SATION.
"¥400 MILLION YEN JUST FOR HANDING THAT BLACK CASE OVER."
"WHAT WAS INSIDE THAT CASE?"
"INFOR-MATION CON-CERNING MONEY."
"I-I SEE. THAT'S WHY THE CONTACT WAS SO HAPPY."
"YEAH, THE CONTACT MUST BE SITTING BACK, CHUCKLING, AND..."
"... LOOKING DOWN AT THE SCENERY."
L-LOOKING DOWN !?
YOU CAN ONLY LOOK DOWN AT THE SCENERY IF YOU'RE IN ONE OF THE FIRST CLASS CARS ON THE SECOND FLOOR!!
THERE ARE THREE FIRST CLASS CARS.
OUT OF THOSE, WHICH ARE NON-SMOKING ?
7 8 9 10

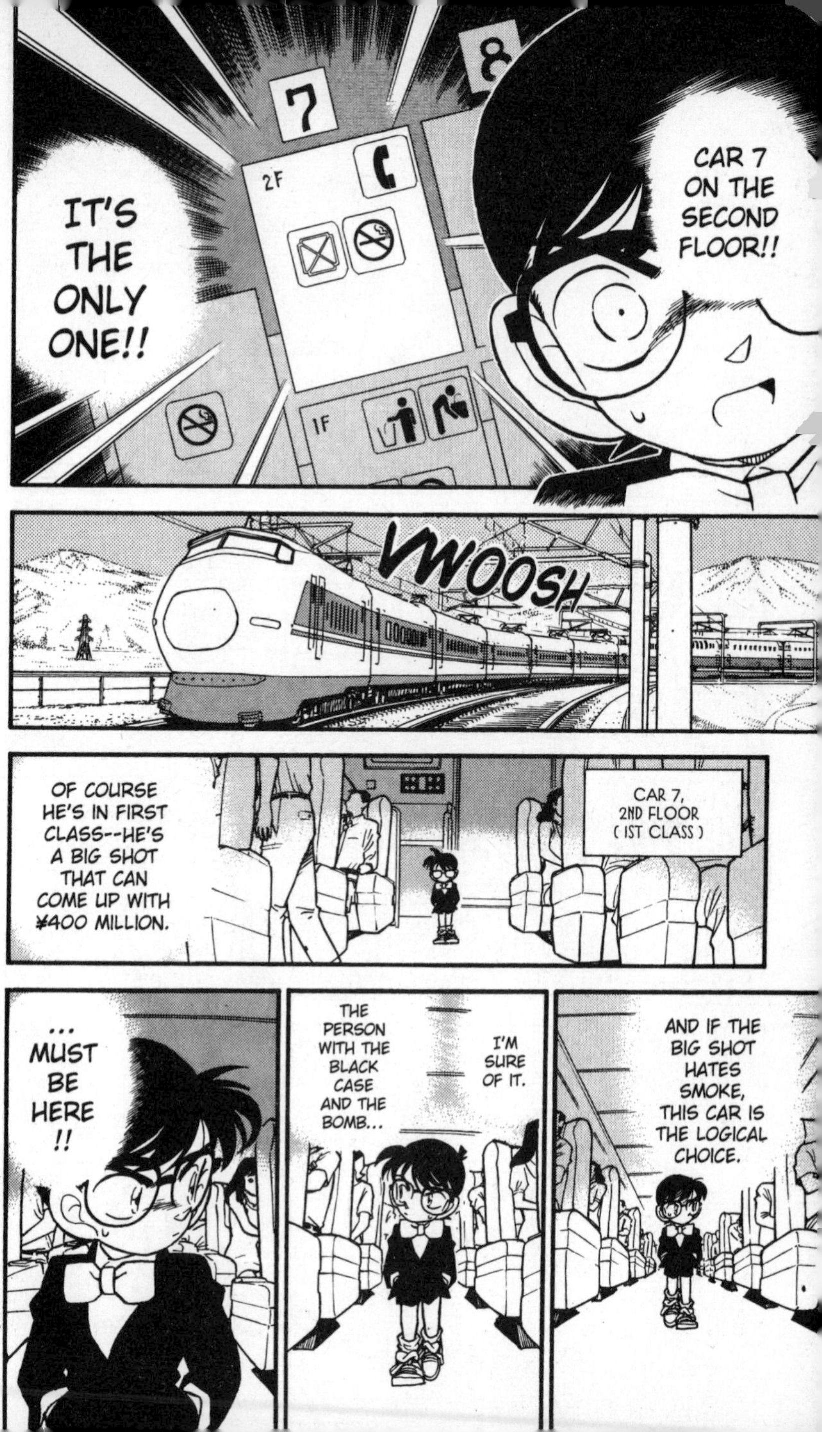
CAR 7 ON THE SECOND FLOOR!!
IT'S THE ONLY ONE!!
VWOOSH
CAR 7, 2ND FLOOR (1ST CLASS)
OF COURSE HE'S IN FIRST CLASS--HE'S A BIG SHOT THAT CAN COME UP WITH ¥400 MILLION.
AND IF THE BIG SHOT HATES SMOKE, THIS CAR IS THE LOGICAL CHOICE.
I'M SURE OF IT.
THE PERSON WITH THE BLACK CASE AND THE BOMB...
...MUST BE HERE!!

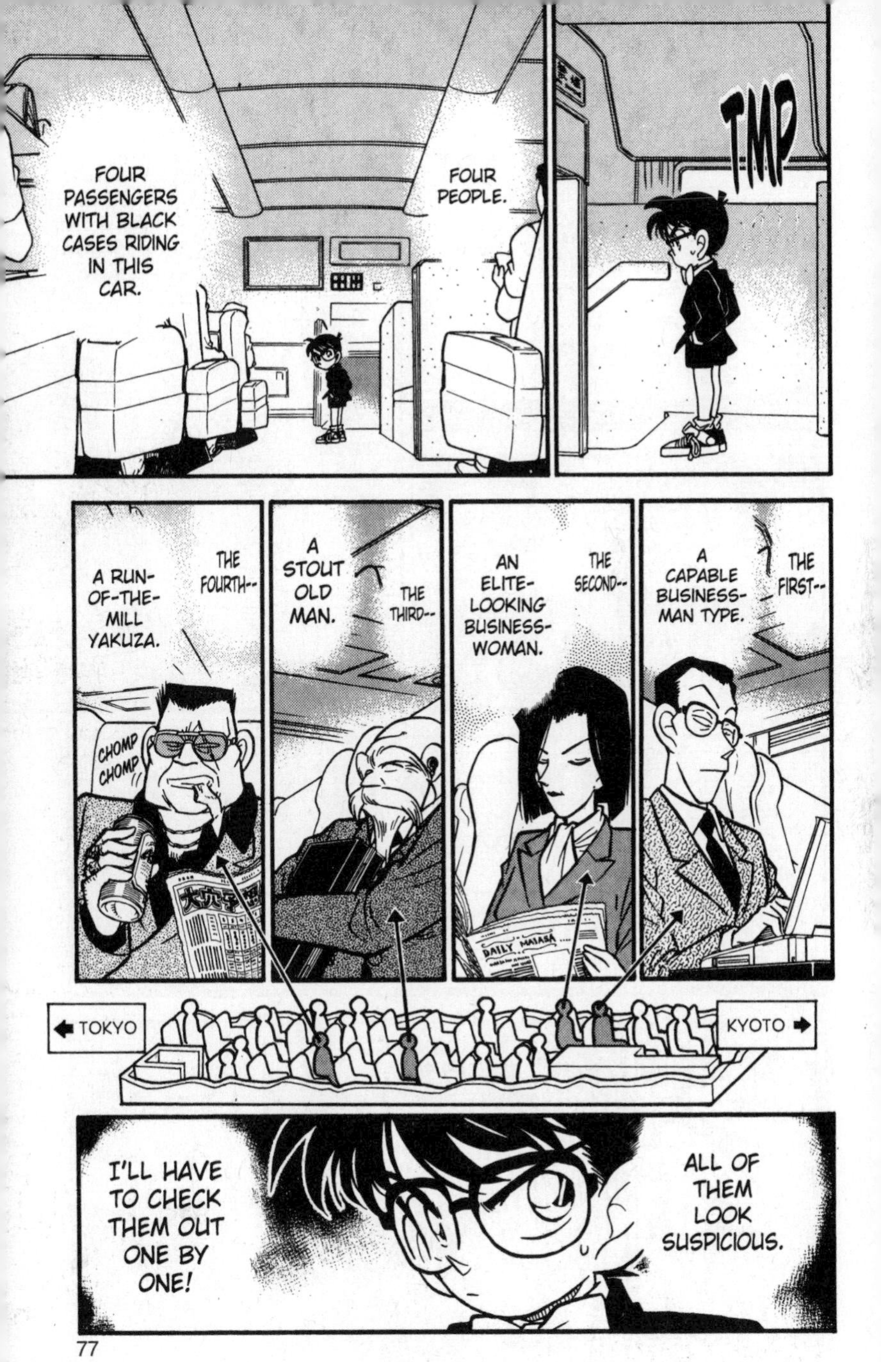
TMP
FOUR PEOPLE.
FOUR PASSENGERS WITH BLACK CASES RIDING IN THIS CAR.
THE FIRST--
A CAPABLE BUSINESS-MAN TYPE.
THE SECOND--
AN ELITE-LOOKING BUSINESS-WOMAN.
DAILY MAIASA
THE THIRD--
A STOUT OLD MAN.
THE FOURTH--
A RUN-OF-THE-MILL YAKUZA.
CHOMP CHOMP
KYOTO
TOKYO
ALL OF THEM LOOK SUSPICIOUS.
I'LL HAVE TO CHECK THEM OUT ONE BY ONE!

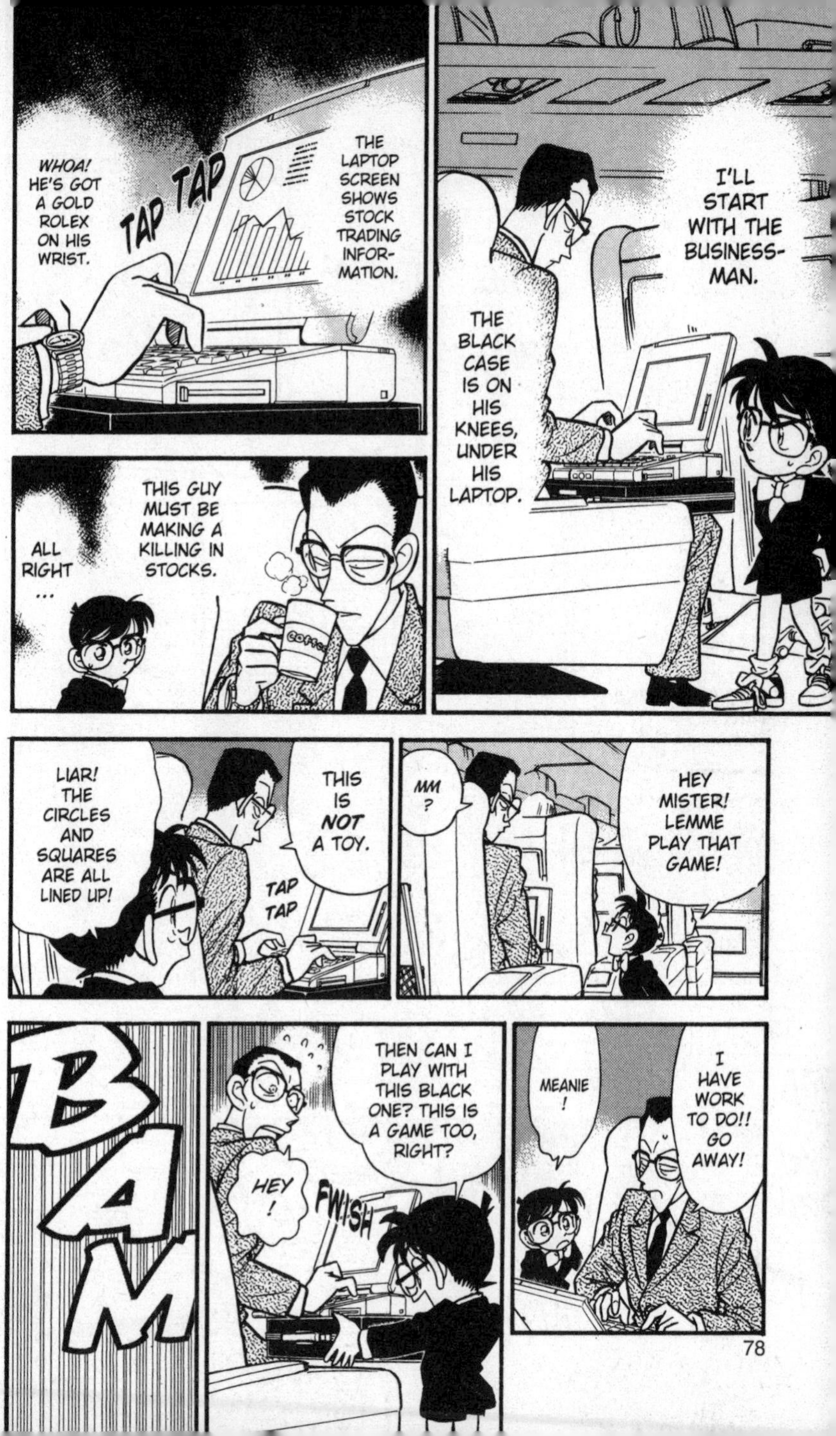
I'LL START WITH THE BUSINESS-MAN.
THE BLACK CASE IS ON HIS KNEES, UNDER HIS LAPTOP.
THE LAPTOP SCREEN SHOWS STOCK TRADING INFOR-MATION.
TAP TAP
WHOA! HE'S GOT A GOLD ROLEX ON HIS WRIST.
THIS GUY MUST BE MAKING A KILLING IN STOCKS.
ALL RIGHT ...
HEY MISTER! LEMME PLAY THAT GAME!
MM ?
THIS IS NOT A TOY.
TAP TAP
LIAR! THE CIRCLES AND SQUARES ARE ALL LINED UP!
I HAVE WORK TO DO!! GO AWAY!
MEANIE !
THEN CAN I PLAY WITH THIS BLACK ONE? THIS IS A GAME TOO, RIGHT?
FWISH
HEY !
BAM

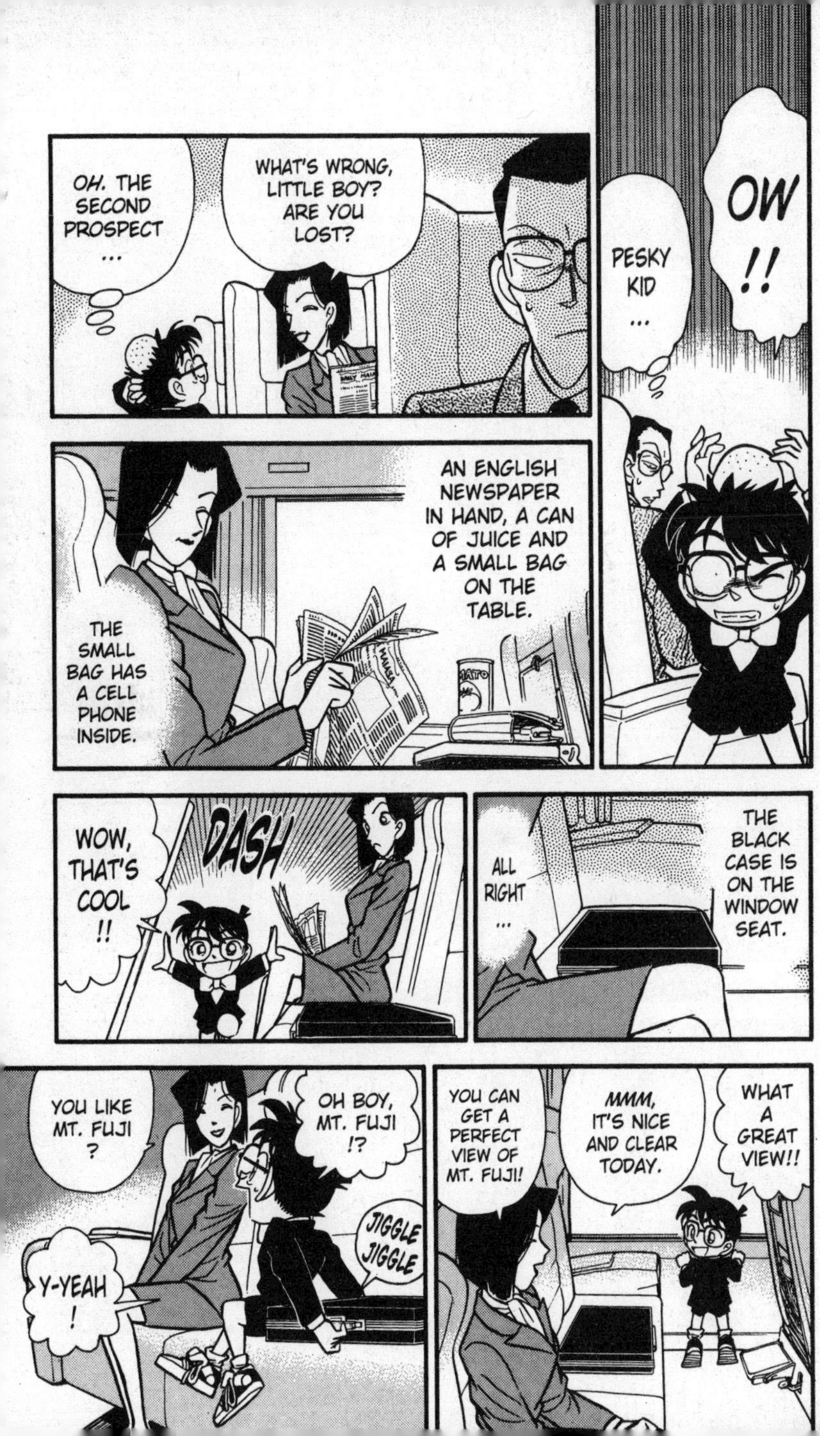
OW !!
PESKY KID ...
WHAT'S WRONG, LITTLE BOY? ARE YOU LOST?
OH. THE SECOND PROSPECT ...
AN ENGLISH NEWSPAPER IN HAND, A CAN OF JUICE AND A SMALL BAG ON THE TABLE.
THE SMALL BAG HAS A CELL PHONE INSIDE.
THE BLACK CASE IS ON THE WINDOW SEAT.
ALL RIGHT ...
DASH
WOW, THAT'S COOL !!
WHAT A GREAT VIEW!!
MMM, IT'S NICE AND CLEAR TODAY.
YOU CAN GET A PERFECT VIEW OF MT. FUJI!
OH BOY, MT. FUJI !?
YOU LIKE MT. FUJI ?
JIGGLE JIGGLE
Y-YEAH !

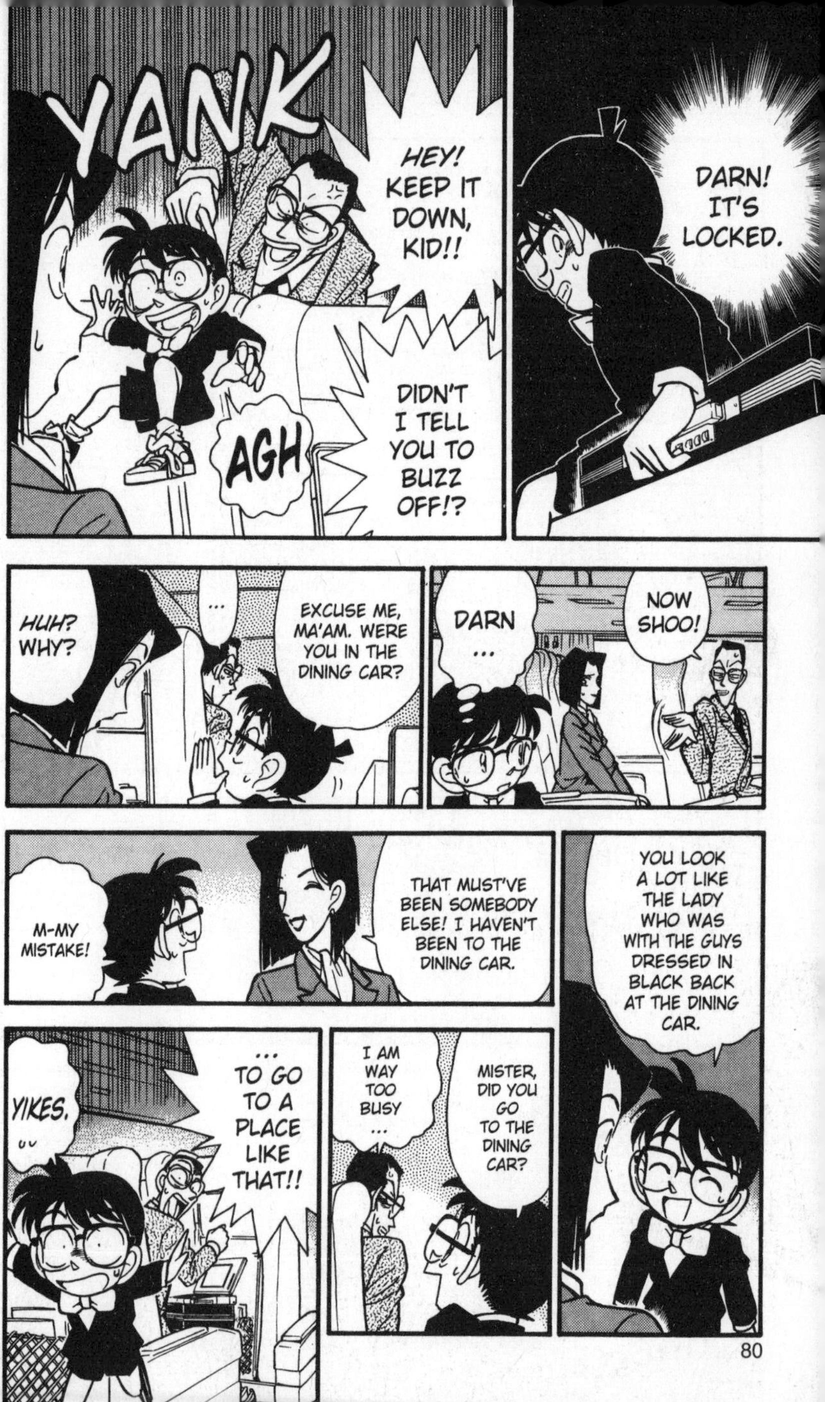
DARN! IT'S LOCKED.
HEY! KEEP IT DOWN, KID!!
YANK
DIDN'T I TELL YOU TO BUZZ OFF!?
AGH
NOW SHOO!
DARN ...
EXCUSE ME, MA'AM. WERE YOU IN THE DINING CAR?
...
HUH? WHY?
YOU LOOK A LOT LIKE THE LADY WHO WAS WITH THE GUYS DRESSED IN BLACK BACK AT THE DINING CAR.
THAT MUST'VE BEEN SOMEBODY ELSE! I HAVEN'T BEEN TO THE DINING CAR.
M-MY MISTAKE!
MISTER, DID YOU GO TO THE DINING CAR?
I AM WAY TOO BUSY ...
... TO GO TO A PLACE LIKE THAT!!
YIKES.

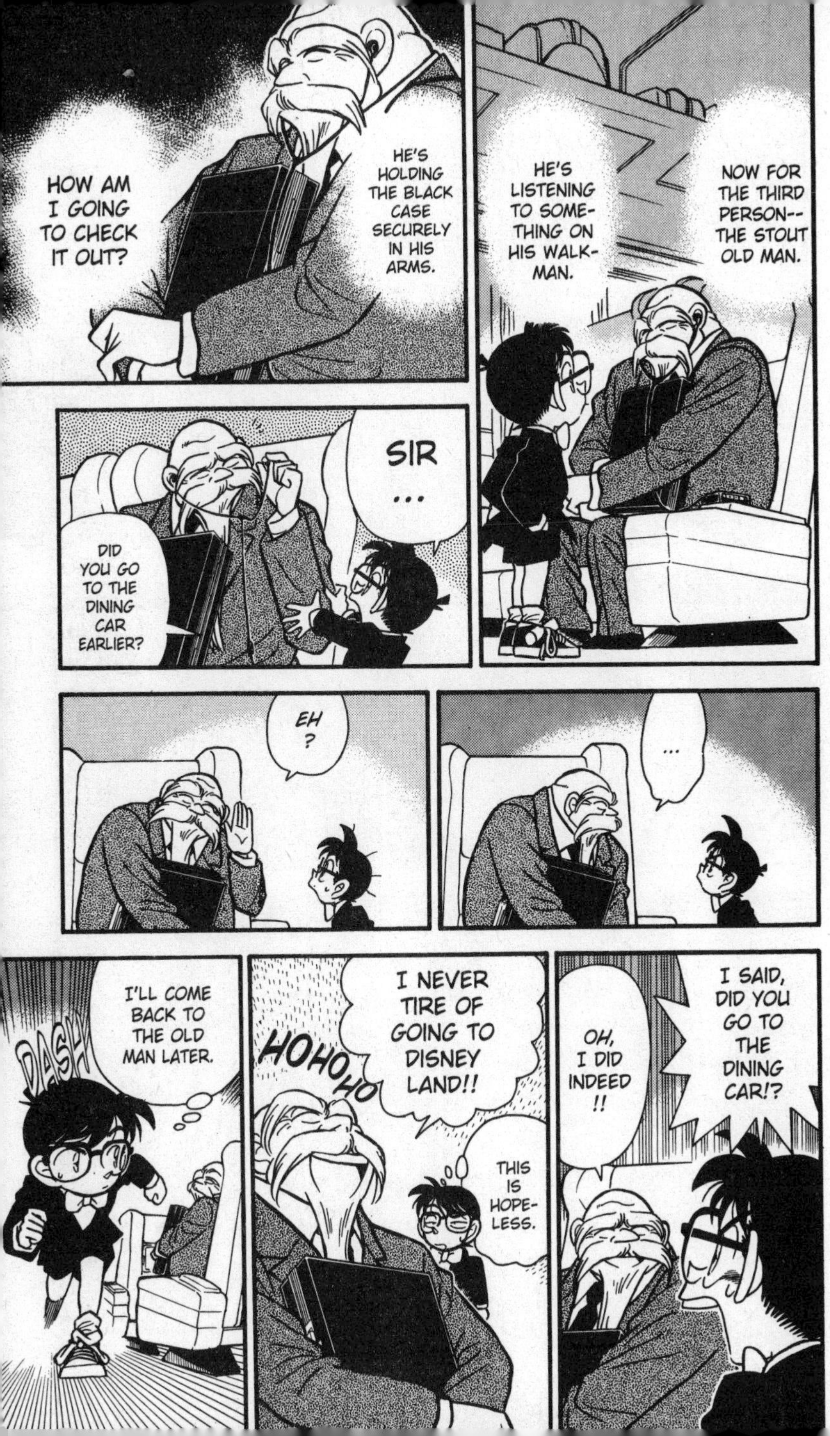
NOW FOR THE THIRD PERSON-- THE STOUT OLD MAN.
HE'S LISTENING TO SOMETHING ON HIS WALKMAN.
HE'S HOLDING THE BLACK CASE SECURELY IN HIS ARMS.
HOW AM I GOING TO CHECK IT OUT?
SIR ...
DID YOU GO TO THE DINING CAR EARLIER?
...
EH ?
I SAID, DID YOU GO TO THE DINING CAR!?
OH, I DID INDEED !!
I NEVER TIRE OF GOING TO DISNEY LAND!!
HOHOHO
THIS IS HOPELESS.
I'LL COME BACK TO THE OLD MAN LATER.
DASH

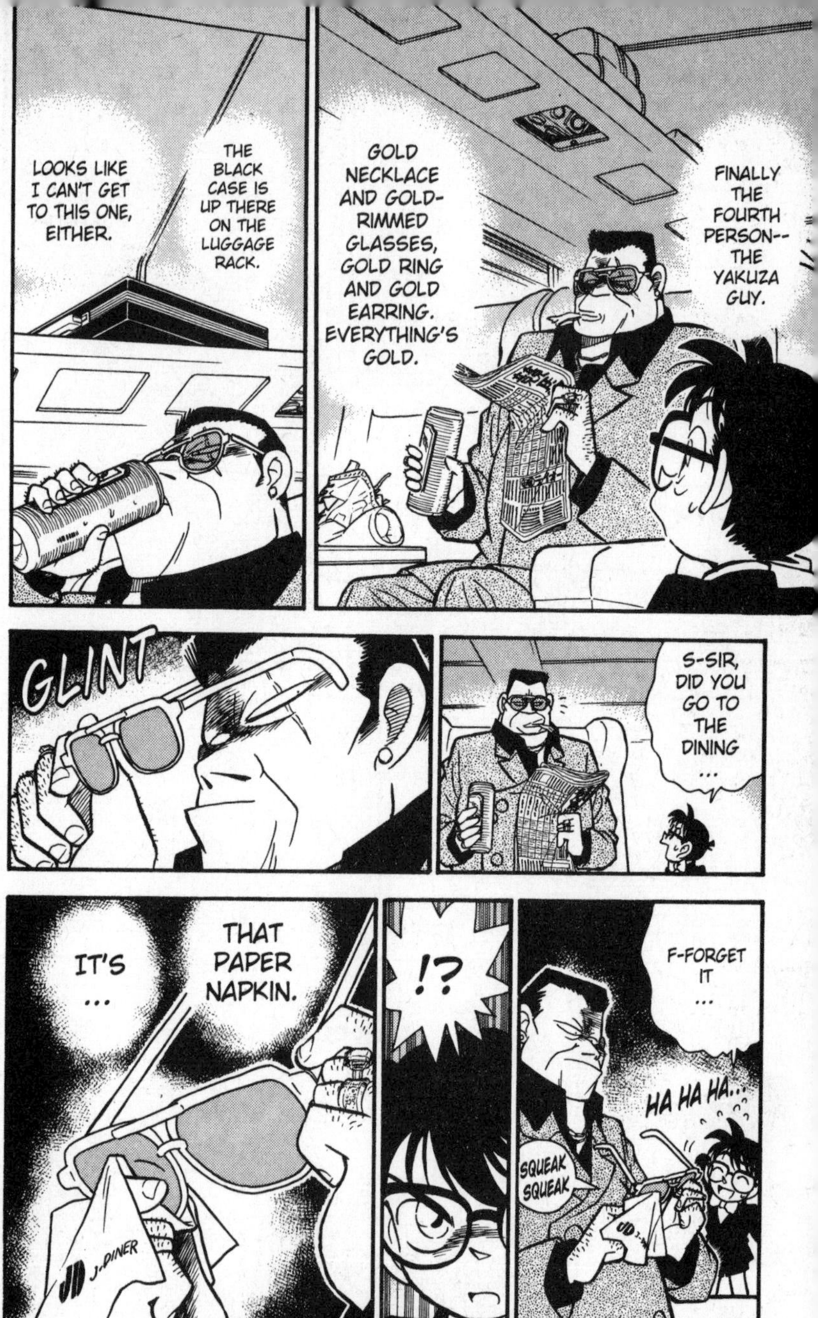
FINALLY THE FOURTH PERSON--THE YAKUZA GUY.
GOLD NECKLACE AND GOLD-RIMMED GLASSES, GOLD RING AND GOLD EARRING. EVERYTHING'S GOLD.
THE BLACK CASE IS UP THERE ON THE LUGGAGE RACK.
LOOKS LIKE I CAN'T GET TO THIS ONE, EITHER.
S-SIR, DID YOU GO TO THE DINING ...
GLINT
F-FORGET IT ...
HA HA HA...
SQUEAK SQUEAK
!?
THAT PAPER NAPKIN.
IT'S ...
J. DINER

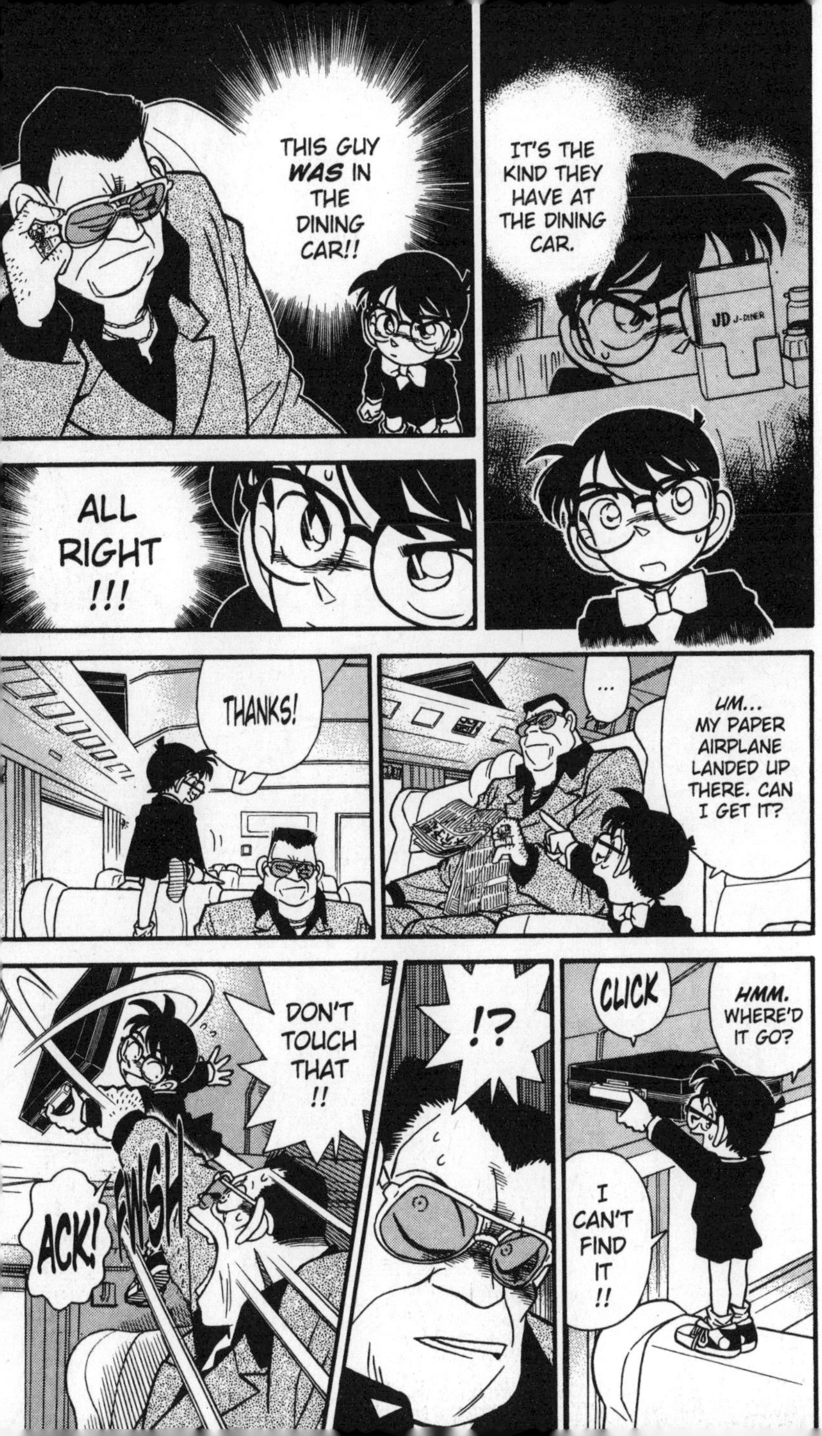
IT'S THE KIND THEY HAVE AT THE DINING CAR.
JD J-DINER
THIS GUY *WAS* IN THE DINING CAR!!
ALL RIGHT !!!
...
UM... MY PAPER AIRPLANE LANDED UP THERE. CAN I GET IT?
THANKS!
HMM. WHERE'D IT GO?
CLICK
I CAN'T FIND IT !!
!?
DON'T TOUCH THAT !!
FWSH
ACK!

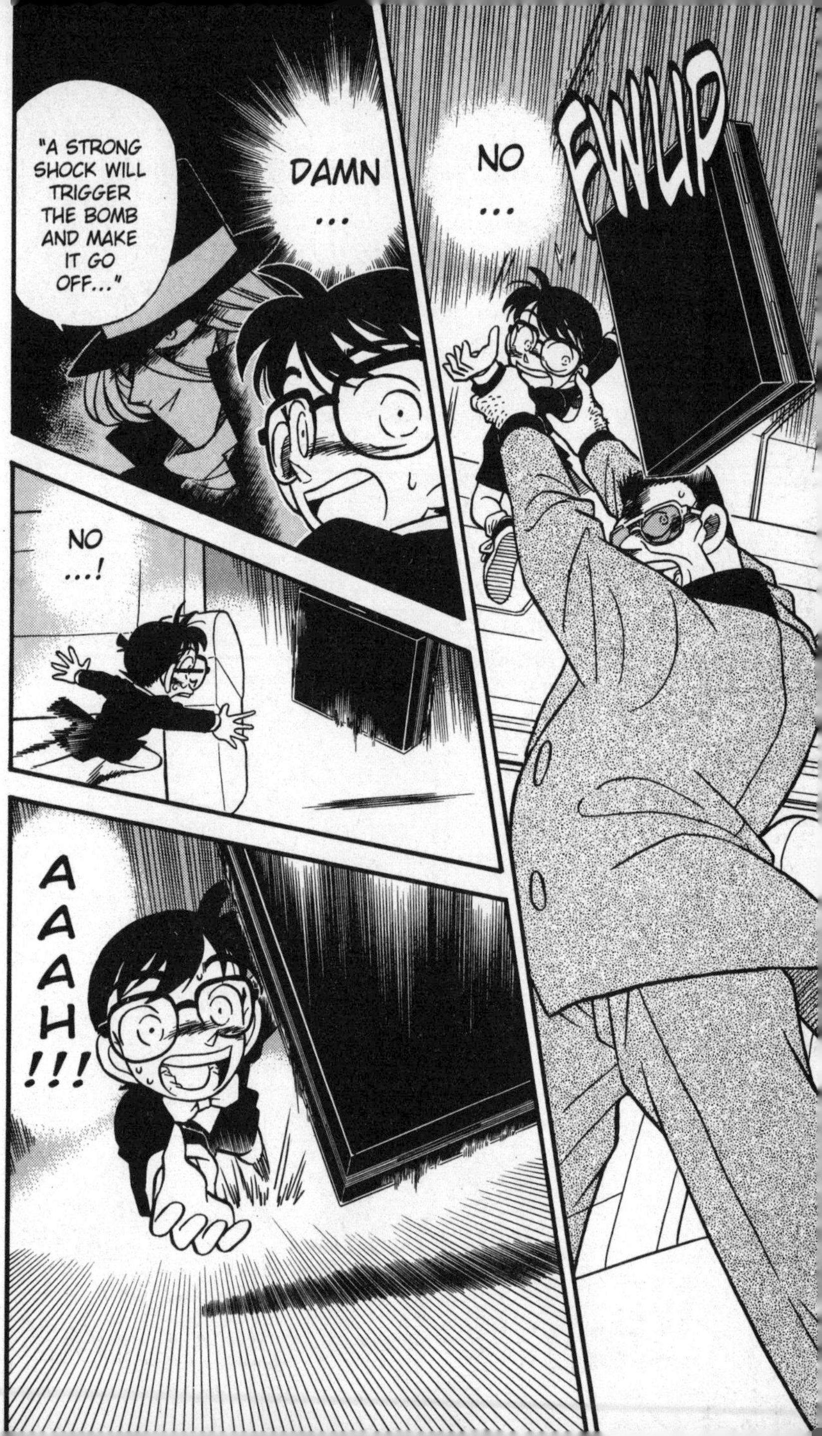

FWUP
NO ...
DAMN ...
"A STRONG SHOCK WILL TRIGGER THE BOMB AND MAKE IT GO OFF..."
NO ...!
AAAH!!!

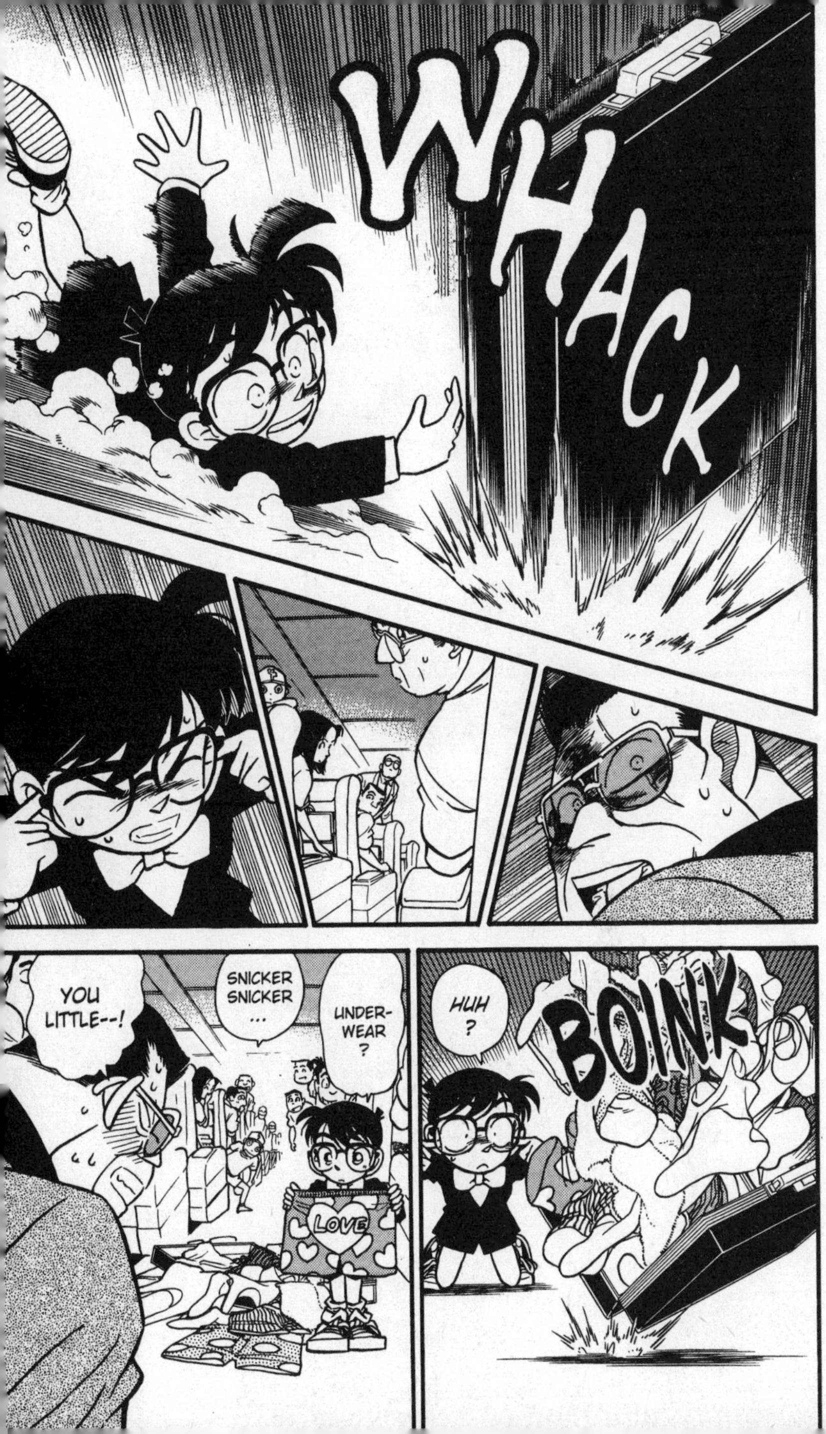
WHACK
BOINK
HUH ?
UNDER-WEAR ?
SNICKER SNICKER ...
YOU LITTLE--!

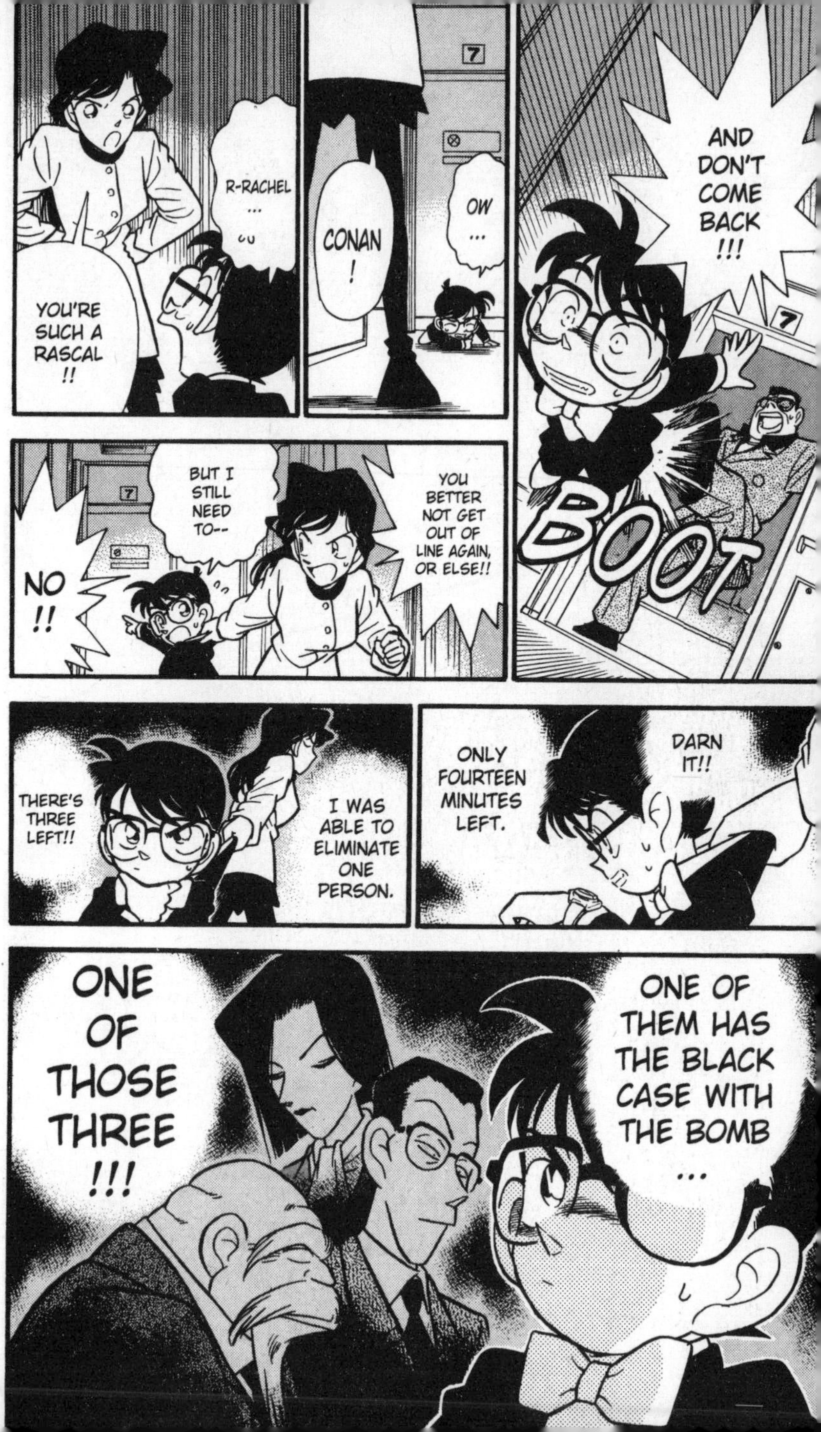
AND DON'T COME BACK!!!
BOOT
OW...
CONAN!
R-RACHEL...
YOU'RE SUCH A RASCAL!!
YOU BETTER NOT GET OUT OF LINE AGAIN, OR ELSE!!
BUT I STILL NEED TO--
NO!!
DARN IT!!
ONLY FOURTEEN MINUTES LEFT.
I WAS ABLE TO ELIMINATE ONE PERSON.
THERE'S THREE LEFT!!
ONE OF THEM HAS THE BLACK CASE WITH THE BOMB...
ONE OF THOSE THREE!!!

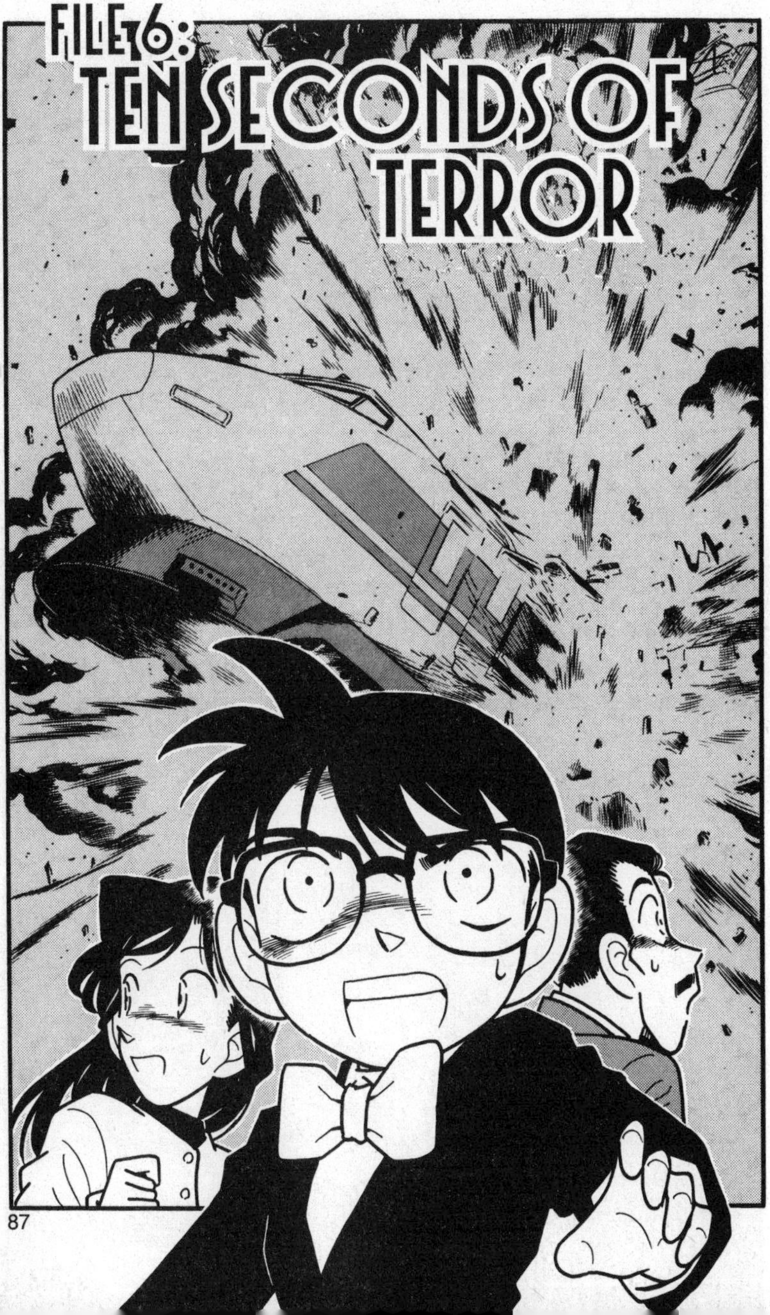
FILE 6:
TEN SECONDS OF TERROR

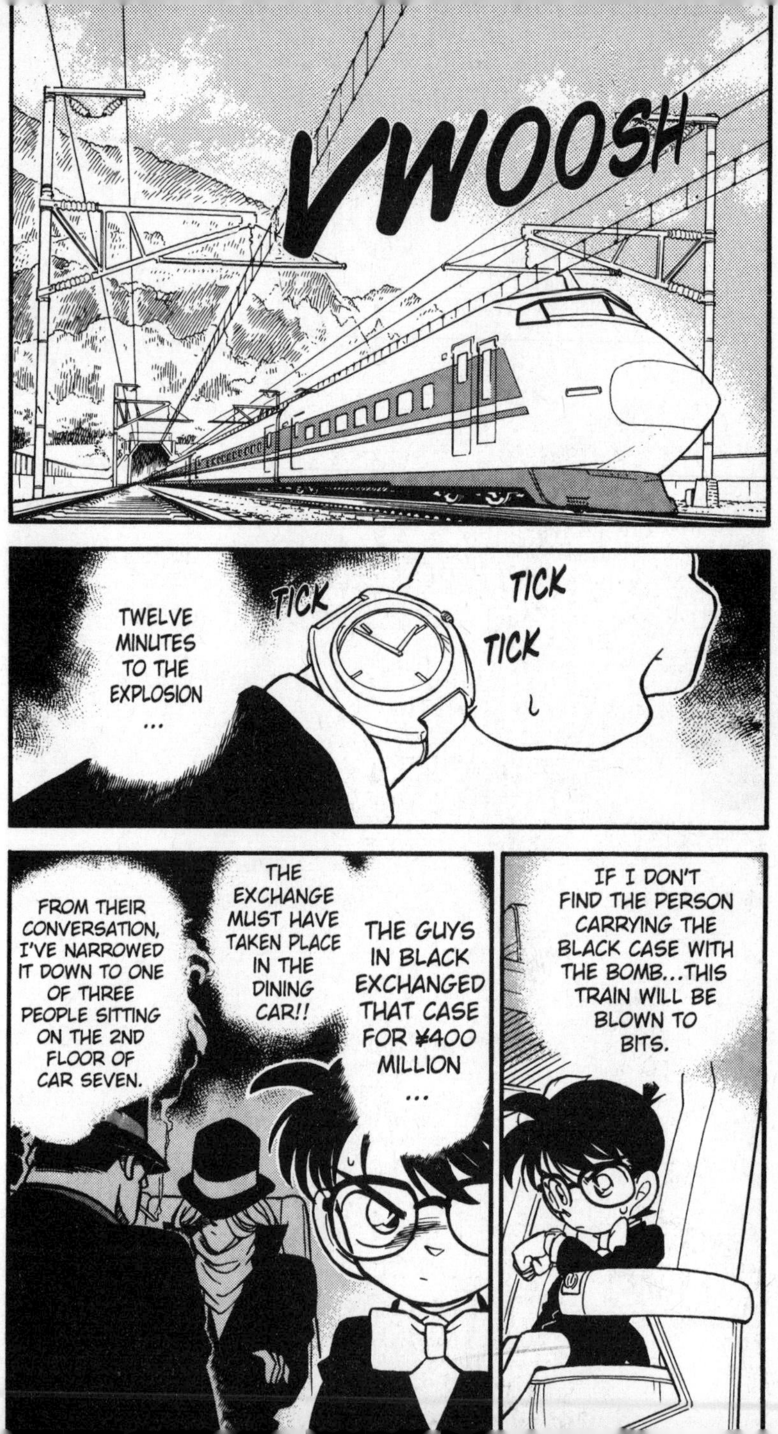
VWOOSH
TICK
TICK
TICK
TWELVE MINUTES TO THE EXPLOSION ...
IF I DON'T FIND THE PERSON CARRYING THE BLACK CASE WITH THE BOMB...THIS TRAIN WILL BE BLOWN TO BITS.
THE GUYS IN BLACK EXCHANGED THAT CASE FOR ¥400 MILLION ...
THE EXCHANGE MUST HAVE TAKEN PLACE IN THE DINING CAR!!
FROM THEIR CONVERSATION, I'VE NARROWED IT DOWN TO ONE OF THREE PEOPLE SITTING ON THE 2ND FLOOR OF CAR SEVEN.

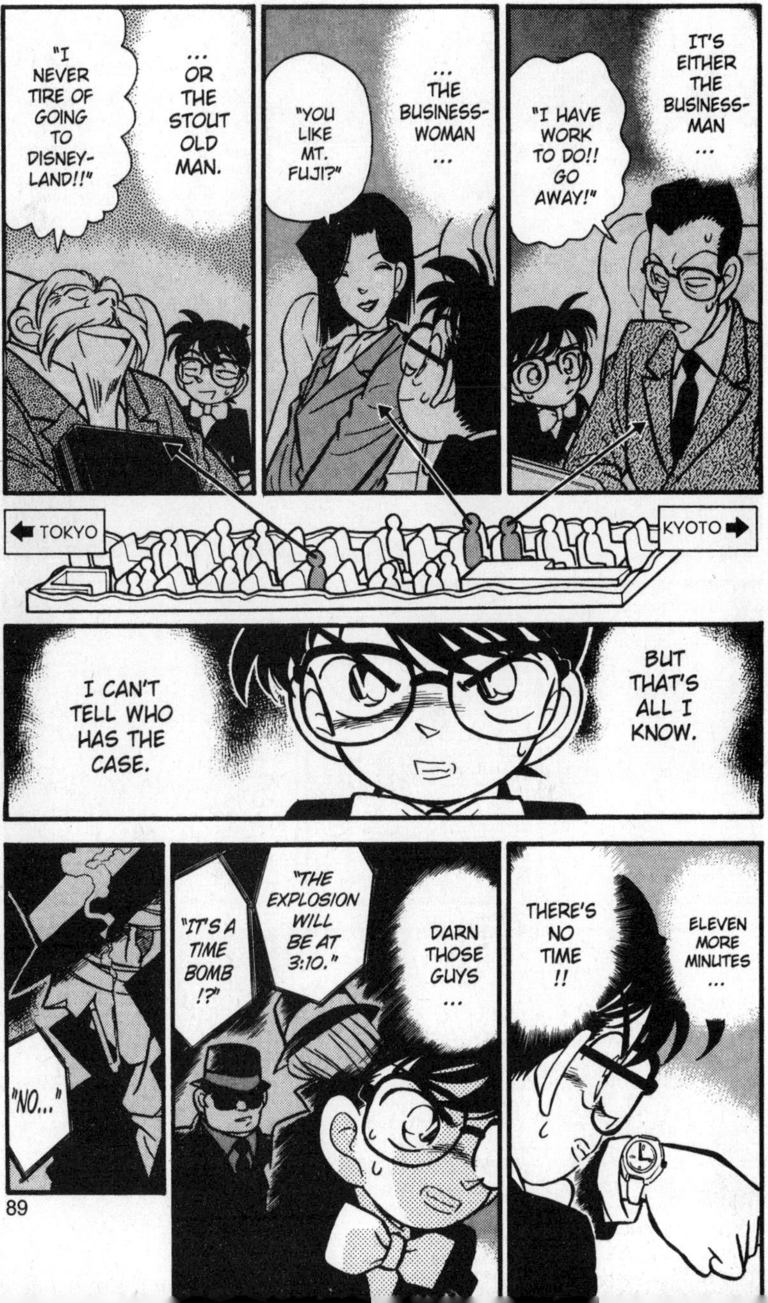
IT'S EITHER THE BUSINESS-MAN ...
"I HAVE WORK TO DO!! GO AWAY!"
... THE BUSINESS-WOMAN ...
"YOU LIKE MT. FUJI?"
... OR THE STOUT OLD MAN.
"I NEVER TIRE OF GOING TO DISNEY-LAND!!"
KYOTO
TOKYO
BUT THAT'S ALL I KNOW.
I CAN'T TELL WHO HAS THE CASE.
ELEVEN MORE MINUTES ...
THERE'S NO TIME !!
DARN THOSE GUYS ...
"THE EXPLOSION WILL BE AT 3:10."
"IT'S A TIME BOMB !?"
"NO..."

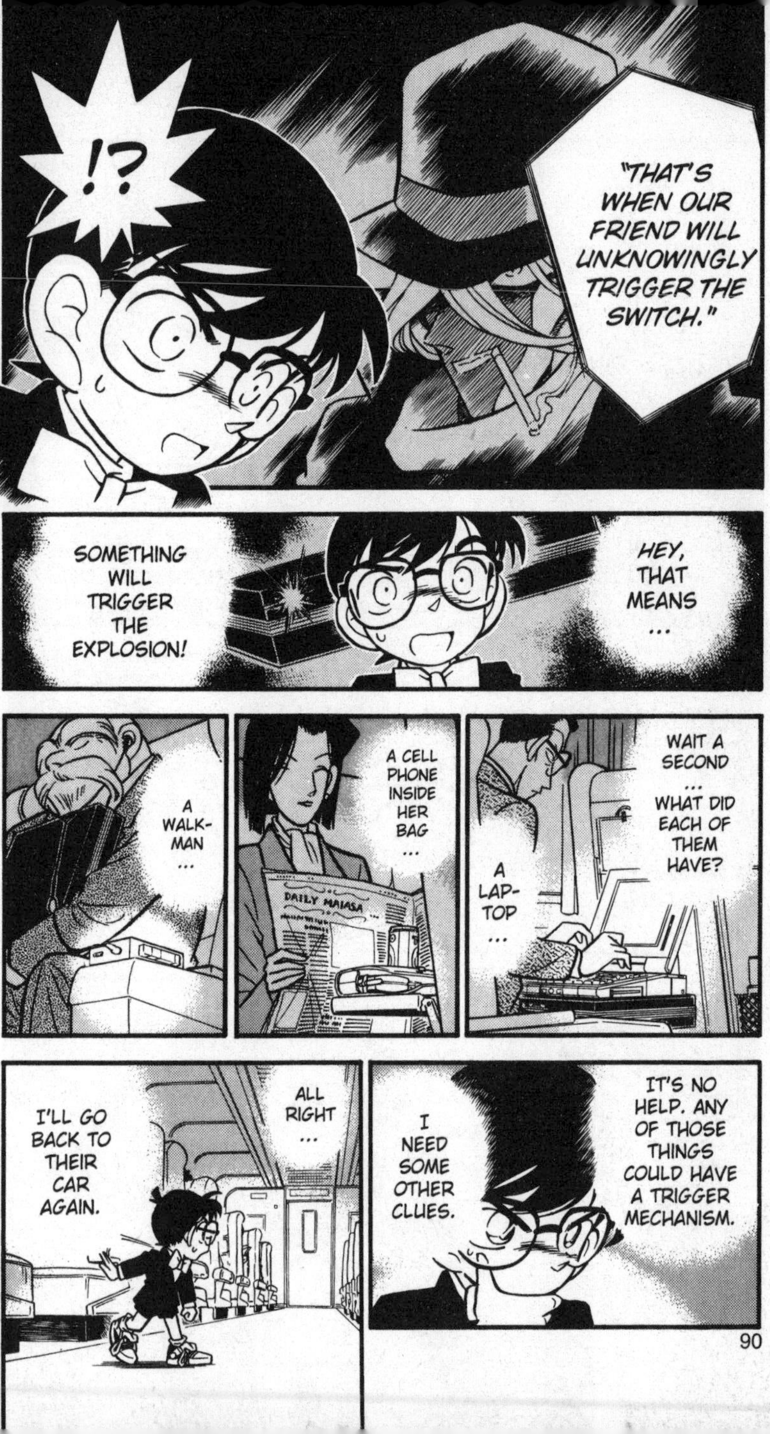
"THAT'S WHEN OUR FRIEND WILL UNKNOWINGLY TRIGGER THE SWITCH."
!?
HEY, THAT MEANS ...
SOMETHING WILL TRIGGER THE EXPLOSION!
WAIT A SECOND ... WHAT DID EACH OF THEM HAVE?
A LAPTOP ...
A CELL PHONE INSIDE HER BAG ...
DAILY MAIASA
A WALKMAN ...
IT'S NO HELP. ANY OF THOSE THINGS COULD HAVE A TRIGGER MECHANISM.
I NEED SOME OTHER CLUES.
ALL RIGHT ...
I'LL GO BACK TO THEIR CAR AGAIN.

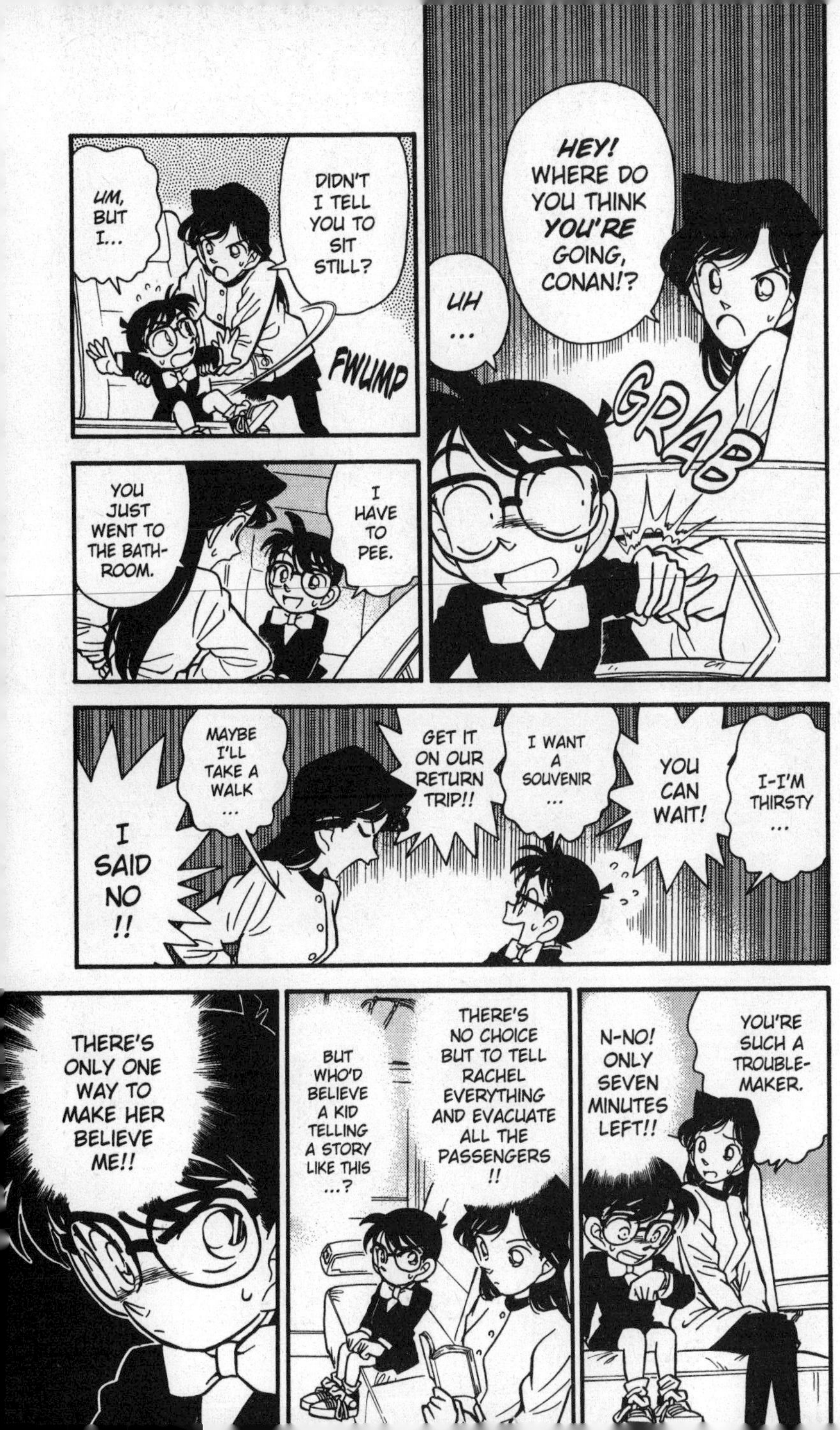
HEY! WHERE DO YOU THINK YOU'RE GOING, CONAN!?
UH ...
GRAB
DIDN'T I TELL YOU TO SIT STILL?
UM, BUT I...
FWUMP
I HAVE TO PEE.
YOU JUST WENT TO THE BATH-ROOM.
I-I'M THIRSTY ...
YOU CAN WAIT!
I WANT A SOUVENIR ...
GET IT ON OUR RETURN TRIP!!
MAYBE I'LL TAKE A WALK ...
I SAID NO !!
YOU'RE SUCH A TROUBLE-MAKER.
N-NO! ONLY SEVEN MINUTES LEFT!!
THERE'S NO CHOICE BUT TO TELL RACHEL EVERYTHING AND EVACUATE ALL THE PASSENGERS !!
BUT WHO'D BELIEVE A KID TELLING A STORY LIKE THIS ...?
THERE'S ONLY ONE WAY TO MAKE HER BELIEVE ME!!

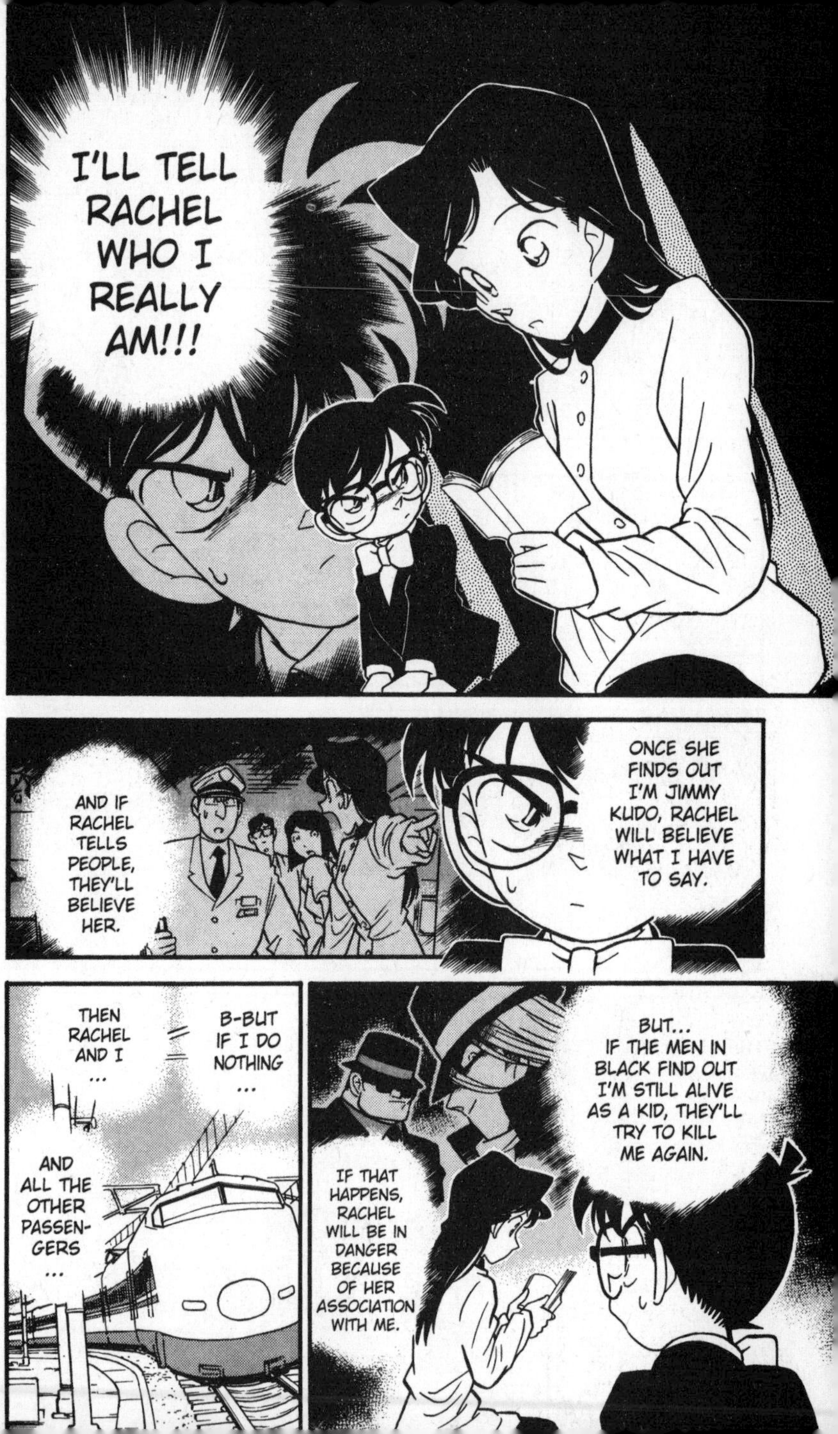
I'LL TELL RACHEL WHO I REALLY AM!!!
ONCE SHE FINDS OUT I'M JIMMY KUDO, RACHEL WILL BELIEVE WHAT I HAVE TO SAY.
AND IF RACHEL TELLS PEOPLE, THEY'LL BELIEVE HER.
BUT... IF THE MEN IN BLACK FIND OUT I'M STILL ALIVE AS A KID, THEY'LL TRY TO KILL ME AGAIN.
IF THAT HAPPENS, RACHEL WILL BE IN DANGER BECAUSE OF HER ASSOCIATION WITH ME.
B-BUT IF I DO NOTHING ...
THEN RACHEL AND I ...
AND ALL THE OTHER PASSENGERS ...

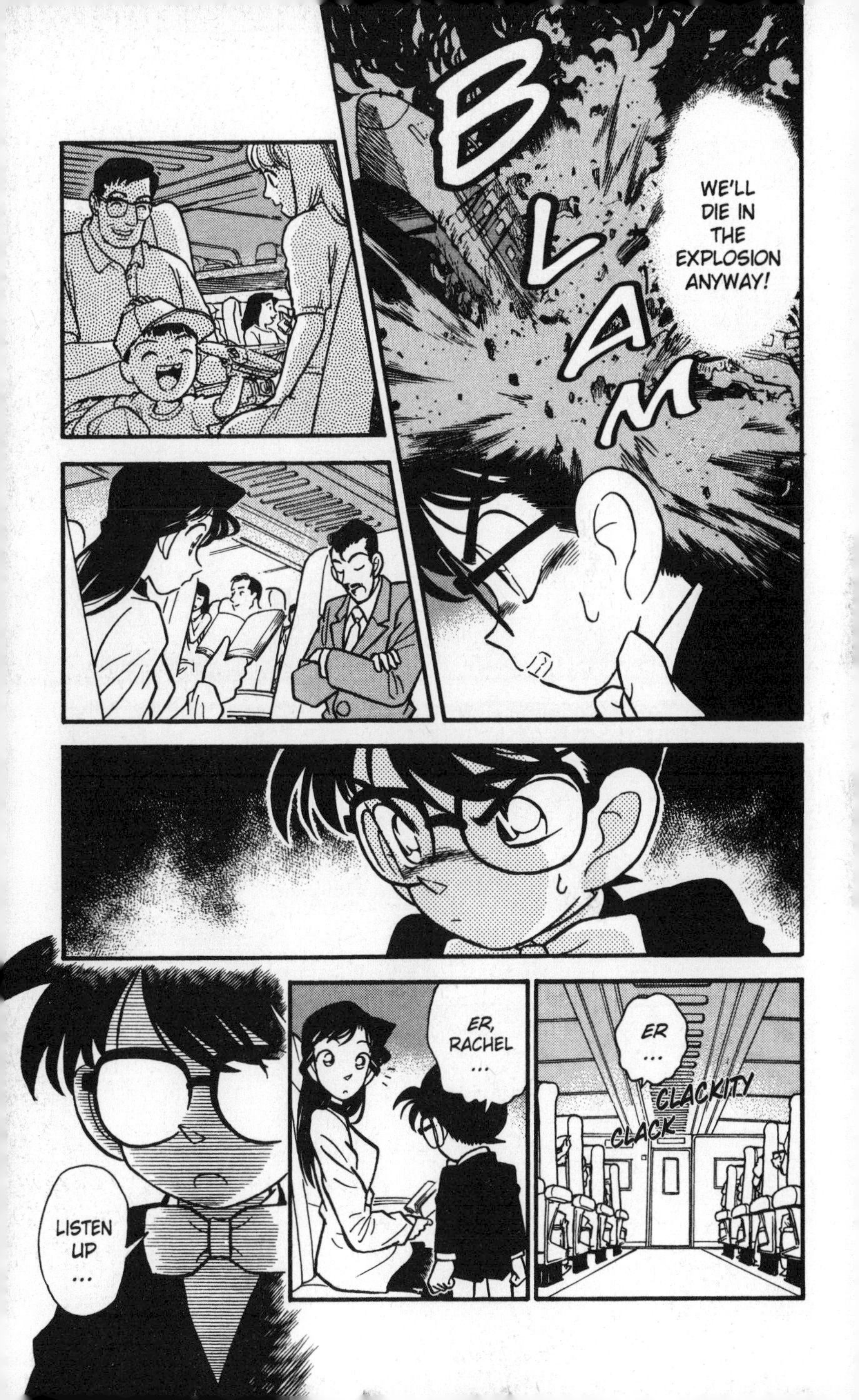
BLAM
WE'LL DIE IN THE EXPLOSION ANYWAY!
ER ...
CLACKITY
CLACK
ER, RACHEL ...
LISTEN UP ...

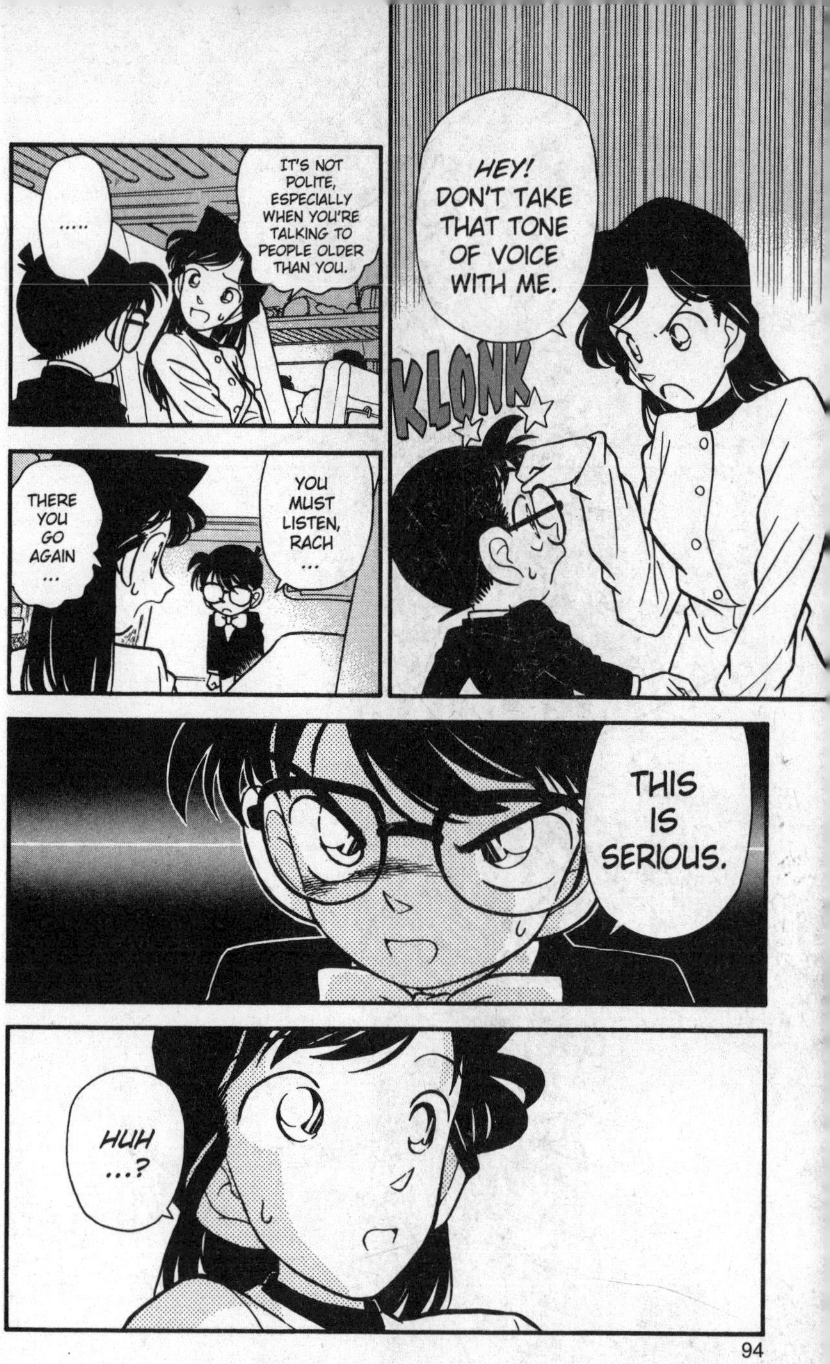
HEY! DON'T TAKE THAT TONE OF VOICE WITH ME.
KLONK
IT'S NOT POLITE, ESPECIALLY WHEN YOU'RE TALKING TO PEOPLE OLDER THAN YOU.
.....
YOU MUST LISTEN, RACH ...
THERE YOU GO AGAIN ...
THIS IS SERIOUS.
HUH ...?

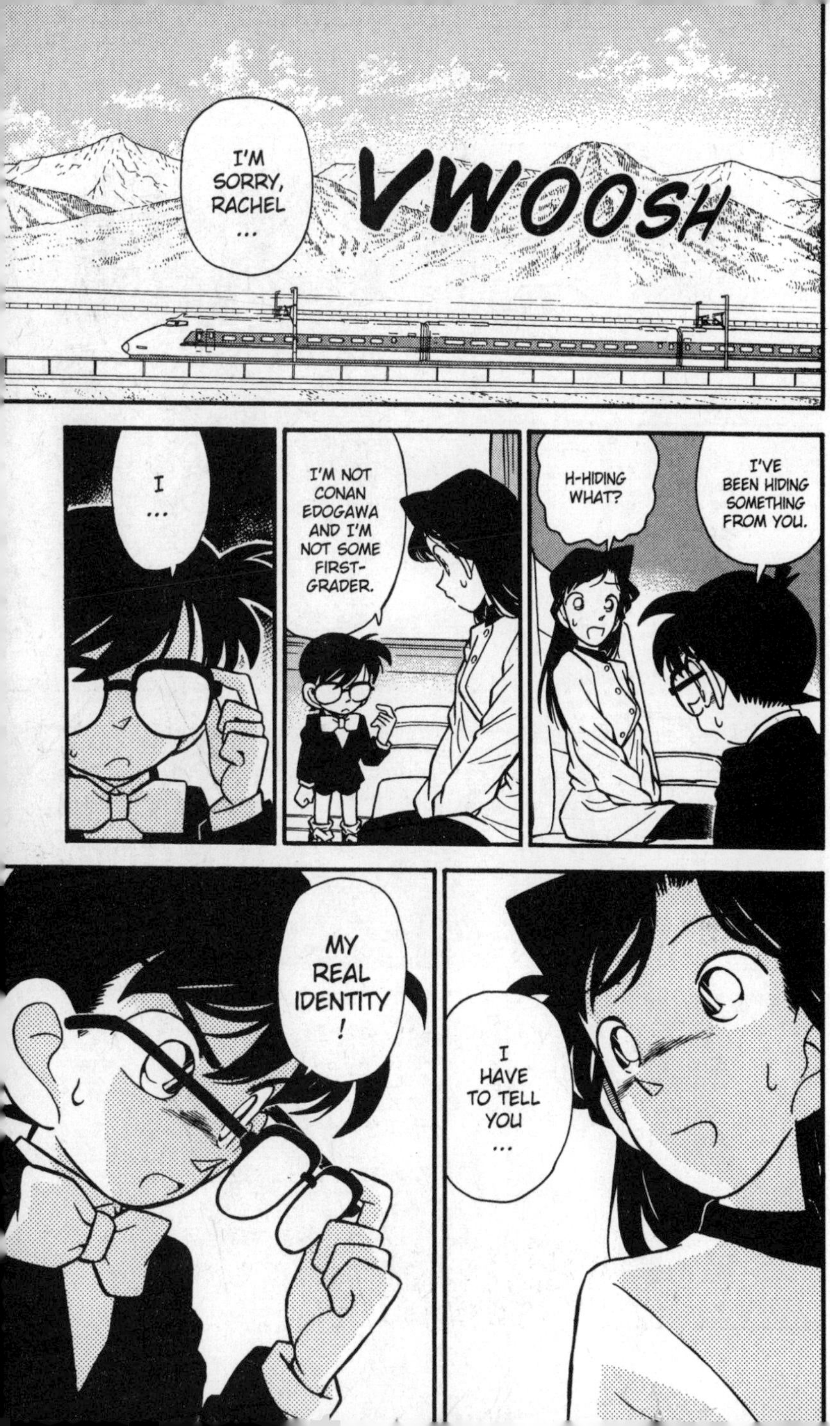
I'M SORRY, RACHEL ...
VWOOSH
I'VE BEEN HIDING SOMETHING FROM YOU.
H-HIDING WHAT?
I'M NOT CONAN EDOGAWA AND I'M NOT SOME FIRST-GRADER.
I ...
I HAVE TO TELL YOU ...
MY REAL IDENTITY!

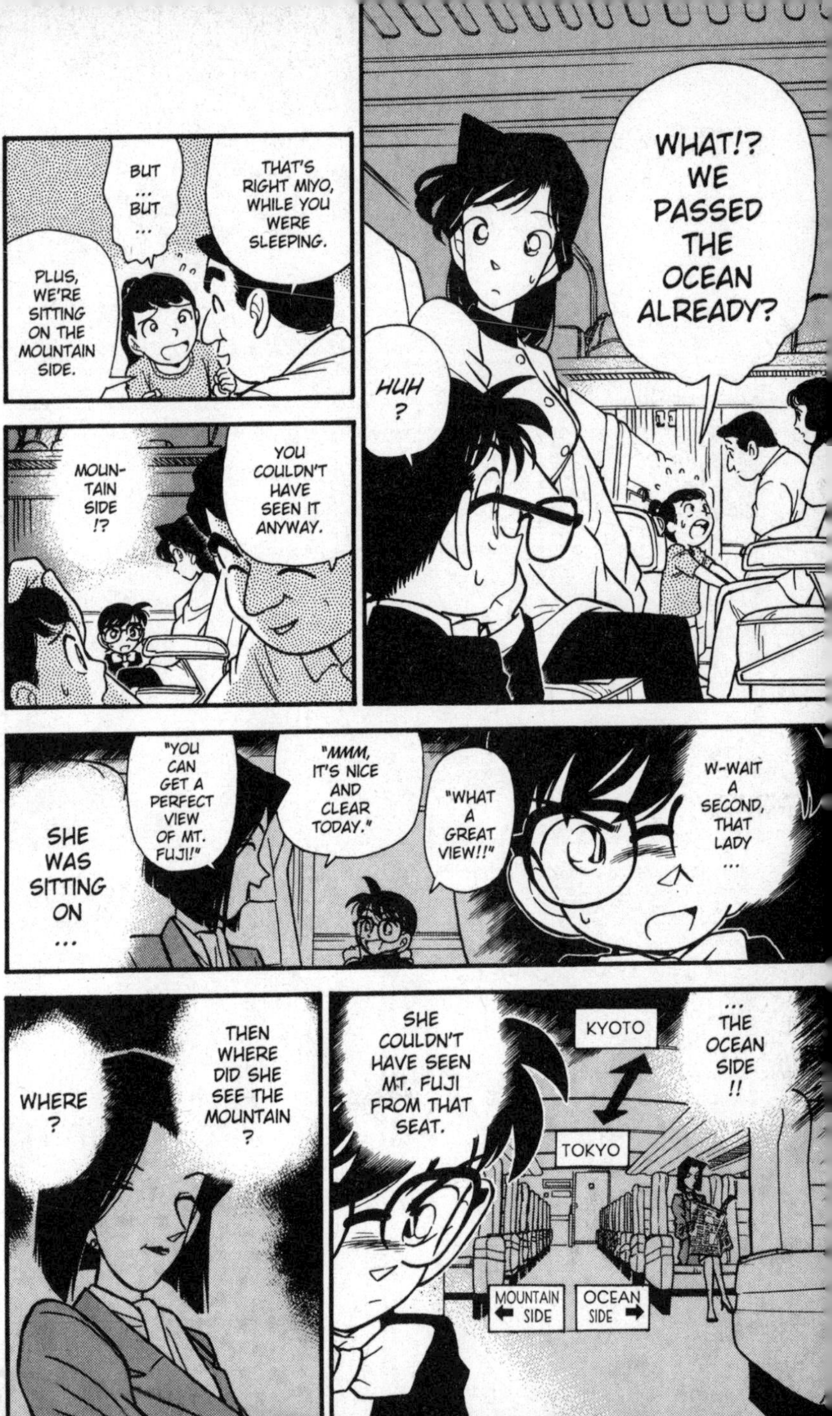
WHAT!? WE PASSED THE OCEAN ALREADY?
HUH?
THAT'S RIGHT MIYO, WHILE YOU WERE SLEEPING.
BUT ... BUT ...
PLUS, WE'RE SITTING ON THE MOUNTAIN SIDE.
YOU COULDN'T HAVE SEEN IT ANYWAY.
MOUN-TAIN SIDE !?
W-WAIT A SECOND, THAT LADY ...
"WHAT A GREAT VIEW!!"
"MMM, IT'S NICE AND CLEAR TODAY."
"YOU CAN GET A PERFECT VIEW OF MT. FUJI!"
SHE WAS SITTING ON ...
... THE OCEAN SIDE !!
KYOTO
SHE COULDN'T HAVE SEEN MT. FUJI FROM THAT SEAT.
TOKYO
MOUNTAIN SIDE
OCEAN SIDE
THEN WHERE DID SHE SEE THE MOUNTAIN ?
WHERE ?

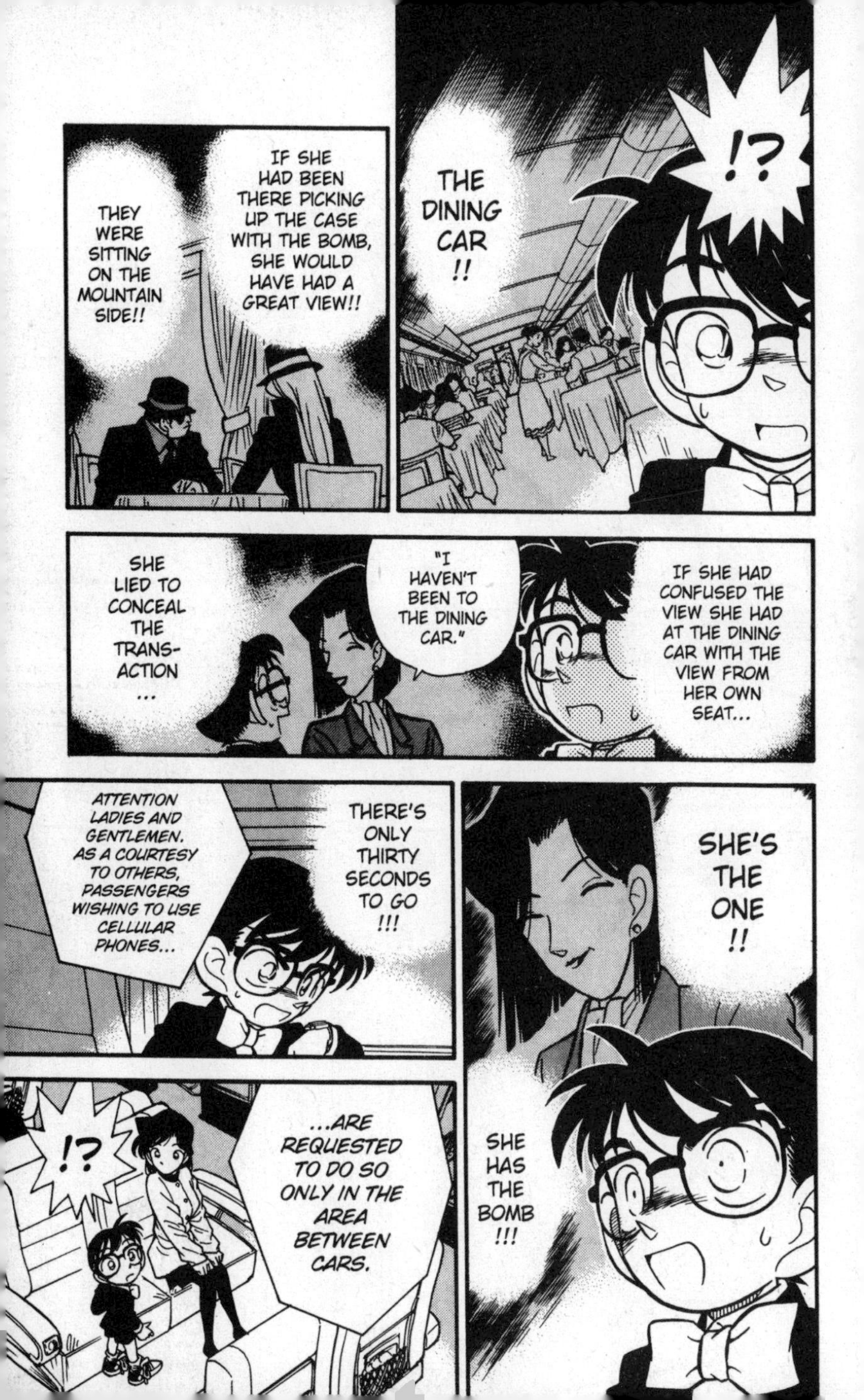
!?
THE DINING CAR !!
IF SHE HAD BEEN THERE PICKING UP THE CASE WITH THE BOMB, SHE WOULD HAVE HAD A GREAT VIEW!!
THEY WERE SITTING ON THE MOUNTAIN SIDE!!
IF SHE HAD CONFUSED THE VIEW SHE HAD AT THE DINING CAR WITH THE VIEW FROM HER OWN SEAT...
"I HAVEN'T BEEN TO THE DINING CAR."
SHE LIED TO CONCEAL THE TRANS-ACTION ...
SHE'S THE ONE !!
SHE HAS THE BOMB !!!
THERE'S ONLY THIRTY SECONDS TO GO !!!
ATTENTION LADIES AND GENTLEMEN. AS A COURTESY TO OTHERS, PASSENGERS WISHING TO USE CELLULAR PHONES...
...ARE REQUESTED TO DO SO ONLY IN THE AREA BETWEEN CARS.
!?

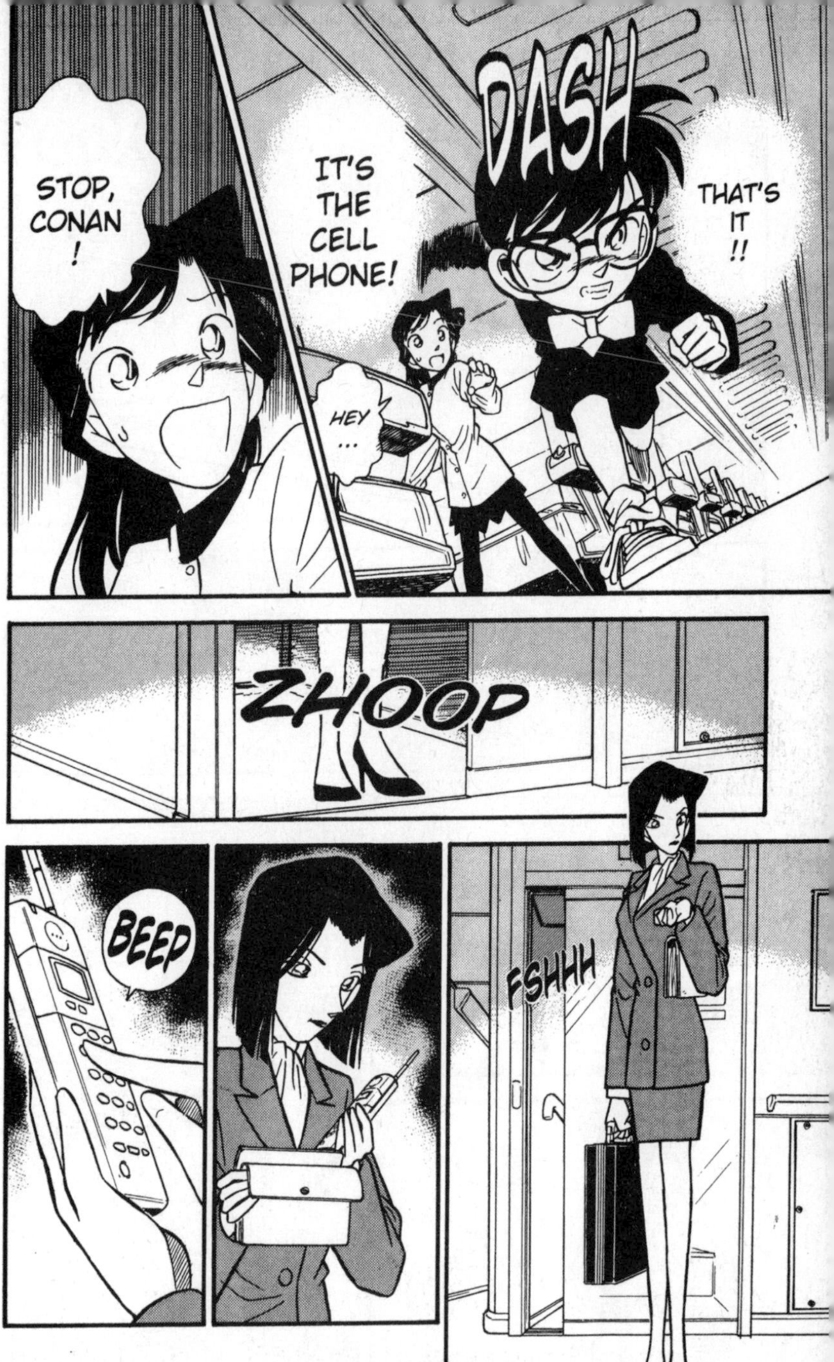
DASH
THAT'S IT !!
IT'S THE CELL PHONE!
HEY ...
STOP, CONAN !
ZHOOP
FSHHH
BEEP

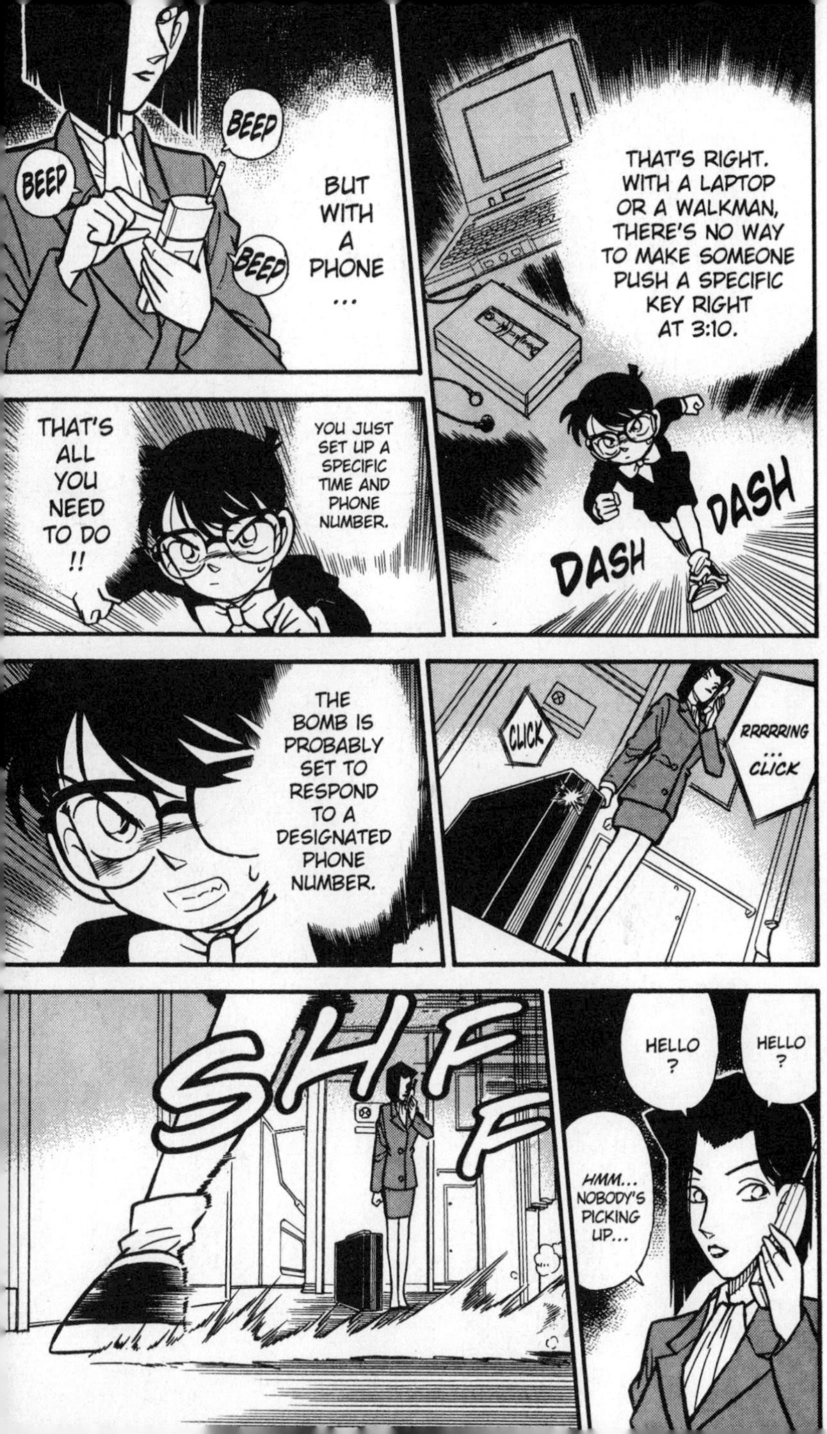
THAT'S RIGHT. WITH A LAPTOP OR A WALKMAN, THERE'S NO WAY TO MAKE SOMEONE PUSH A SPECIFIC KEY RIGHT AT 3:10.
DASH
DASH
BEEP
BEEP
BEEP
BUT WITH A PHONE...
YOU JUST SET UP A SPECIFIC TIME AND PHONE NUMBER.
THAT'S ALL YOU NEED TO DO!!
RRRRRING... CLICK
CLICK
THE BOMB IS PROBABLY SET TO RESPOND TO A DESIGNATED PHONE NUMBER.
HELLO?
HELLO?
HMM... NOBODY'S PICKING UP...
SHFF

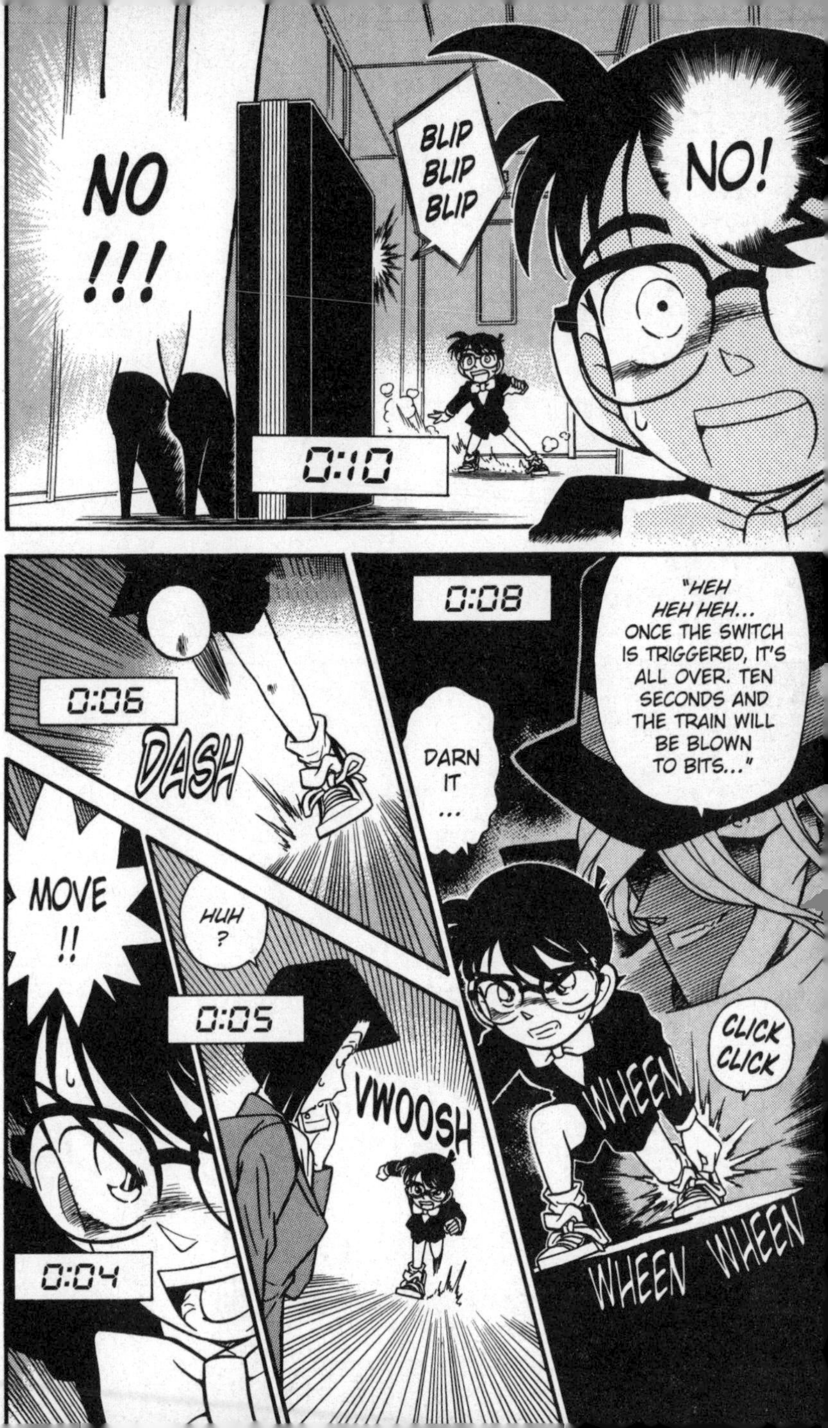
NO!
BLIP BLIP BLIP
0:10
NO !!!
0:08
"HEH HEH HEH... ONCE THE SWITCH IS TRIGGERED, IT'S ALL OVER. TEN SECONDS AND THE TRAIN WILL BE BLOWN TO BITS..."
DARN IT ...
CLICK CLICK
WHEEN
WHEEN WHEEN
0:06
DASH
HUH ?
0:05
VWOOSH
MOVE !!
0:04

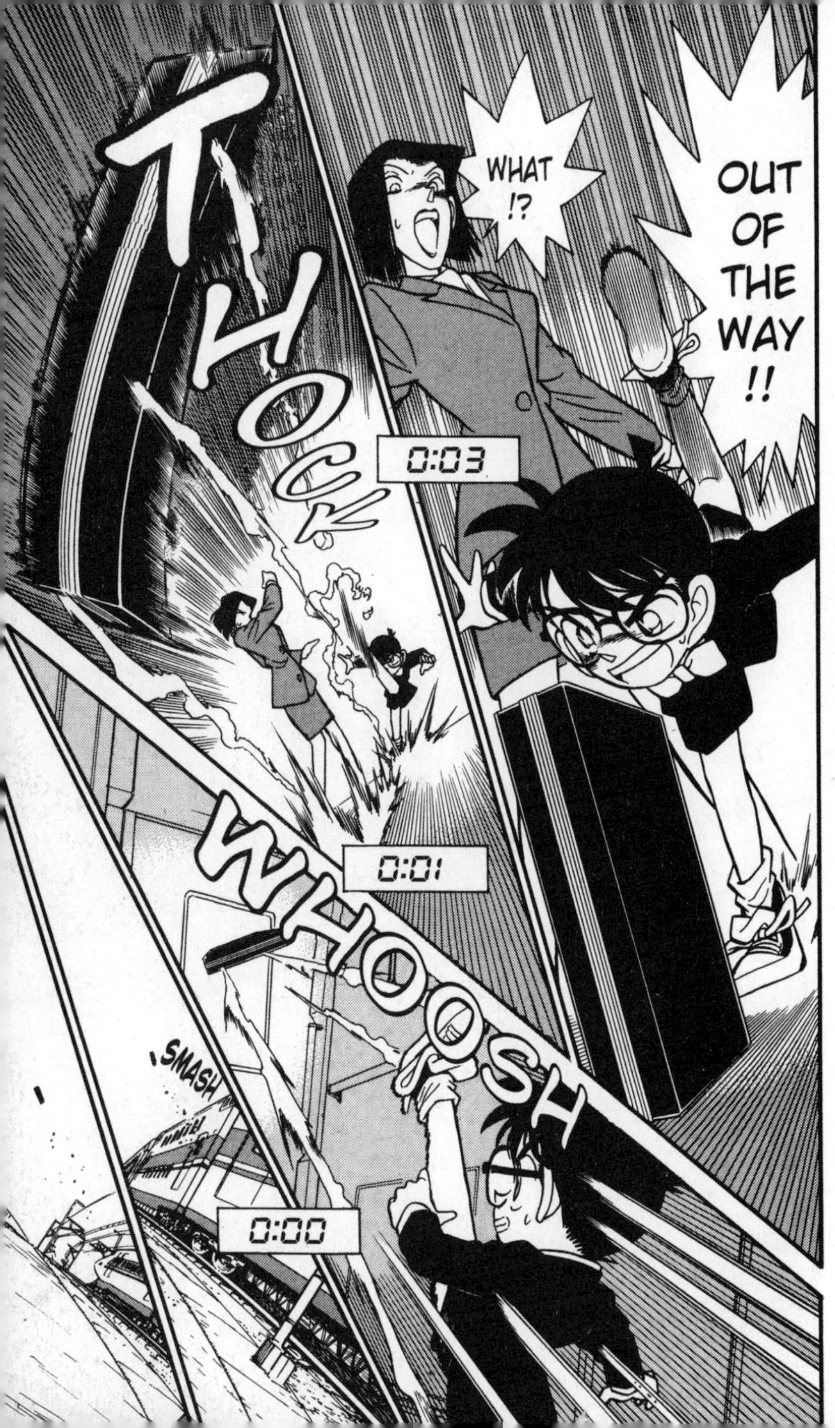
OUT OF THE WAY !!
WHAT !?
THOCK
0:03
WHOOSH
0:01
SMASH
0:00

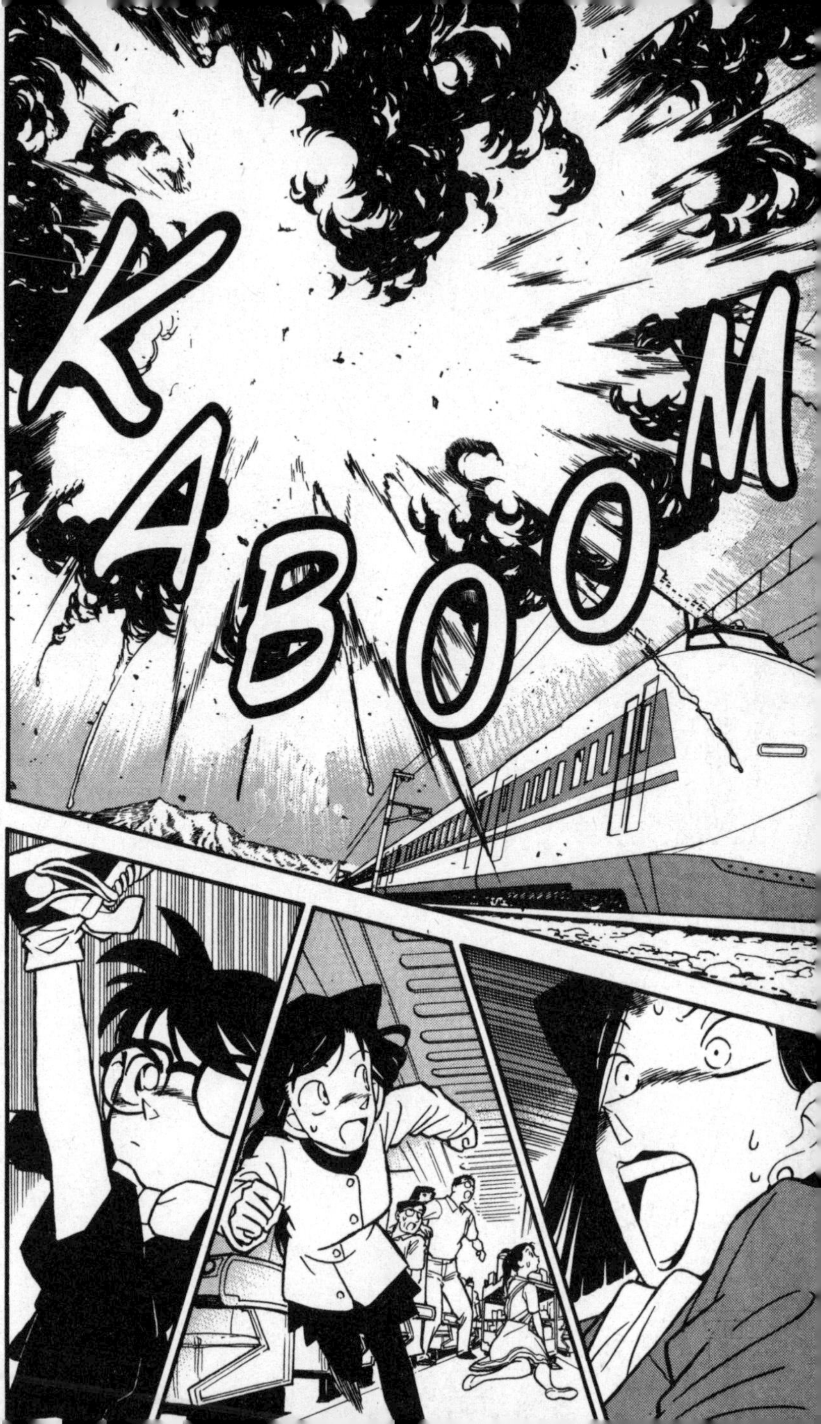
KABOOM

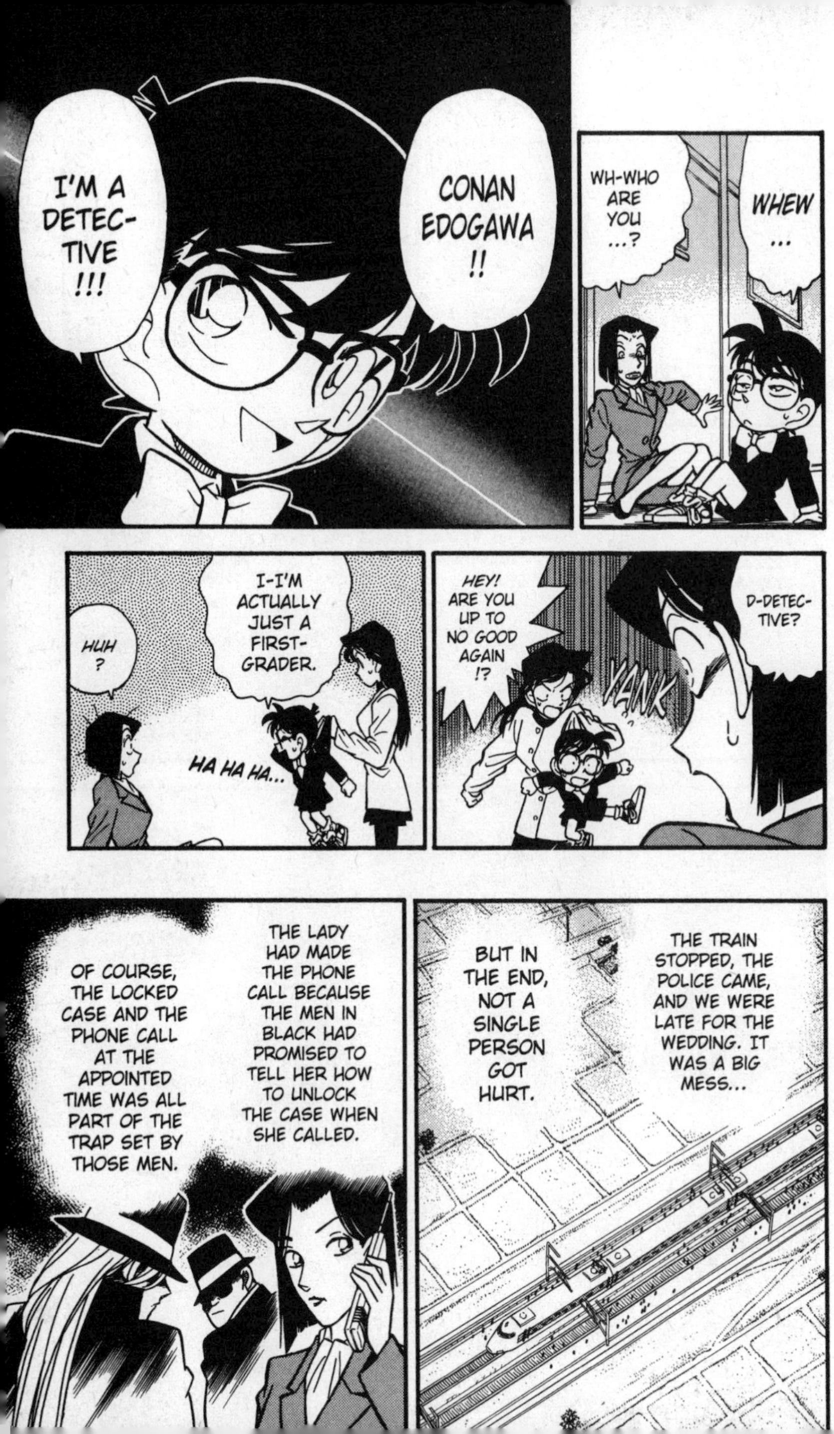
WHEW ...
WH-WHO ARE YOU ...?
CONAN EDOGAWA !!
I'M A DETEC-TIVE !!!
D-DETEC-TIVE?
HEY! ARE YOU UP TO NO GOOD AGAIN !?
YANK
I-I'M ACTUALLY JUST A FIRST-GRADER.
HUH ?
HA HA HA...
THE TRAIN STOPPED, THE POLICE CAME, AND WE WERE LATE FOR THE WEDDING. IT WAS A BIG MESS...
BUT IN THE END, NOT A SINGLE PERSON GOT HURT.
THE LADY HAD MADE THE PHONE CALL BECAUSE THE MEN IN BLACK HAD PROMISED TO TELL HER HOW TO UNLOCK THE CASE WHEN SHE CALLED.
OF COURSE, THE LOCKED CASE AND THE PHONE CALL AT THE APPOINTED TIME WAS ALL PART OF THE TRAP SET BY THOSE MEN.

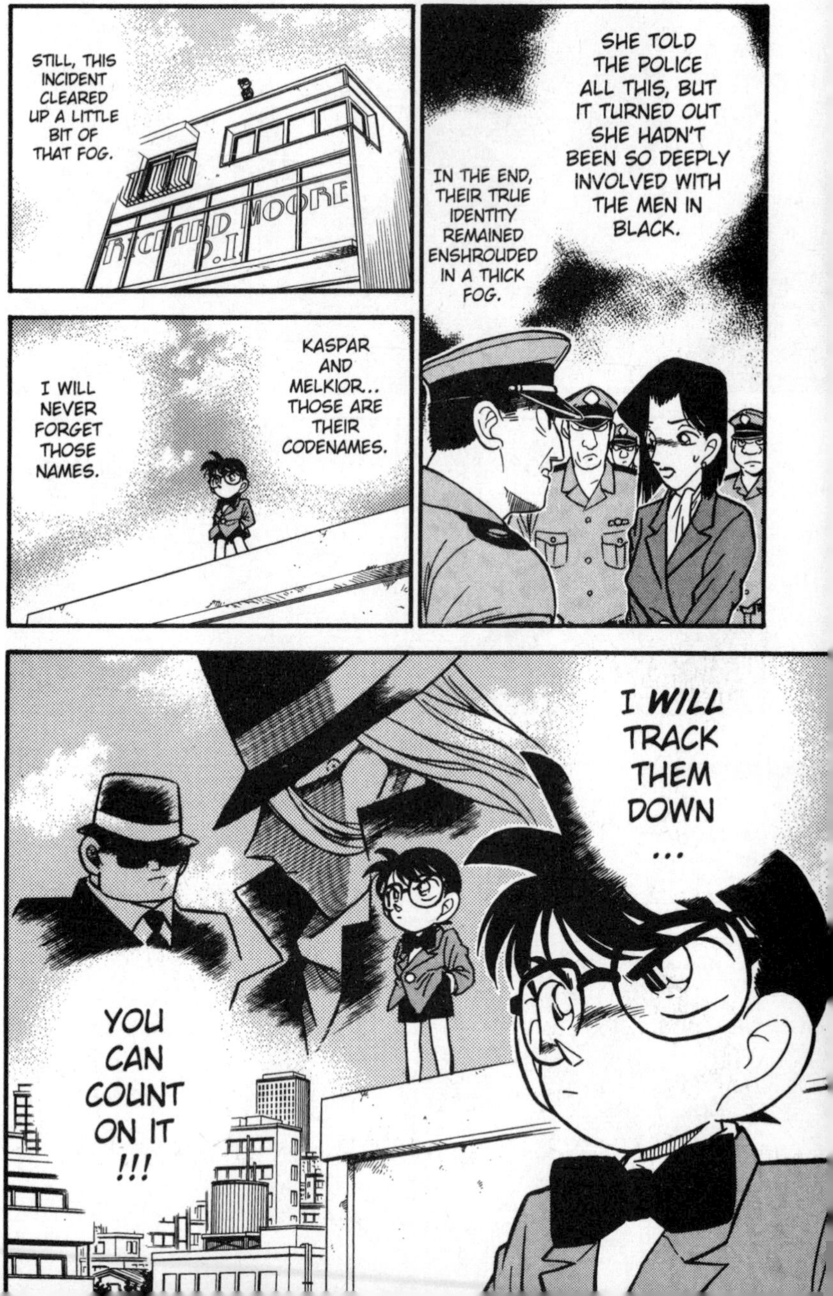
SHE TOLD THE POLICE ALL THIS, BUT IT TURNED OUT SHE HADN'T BEEN SO DEEPLY INVOLVED WITH THE MEN IN BLACK.
IN THE END, THEIR TRUE IDENTITY REMAINED ENSHROUDED IN A THICK FOG.
STILL, THIS INCIDENT CLEARED UP A LITTLE BIT OF THAT FOG.
RICHARD MOORE P.I.
KASPAR AND MELKIOR.. THOSE ARE THEIR CODENAMES.
I WILL NEVER FORGET THOSE NAMES.
I *WILL* TRACK THEM DOWN ...
YOU CAN COUNT ON IT !!!

FILE 7:
GET THE CODE!!

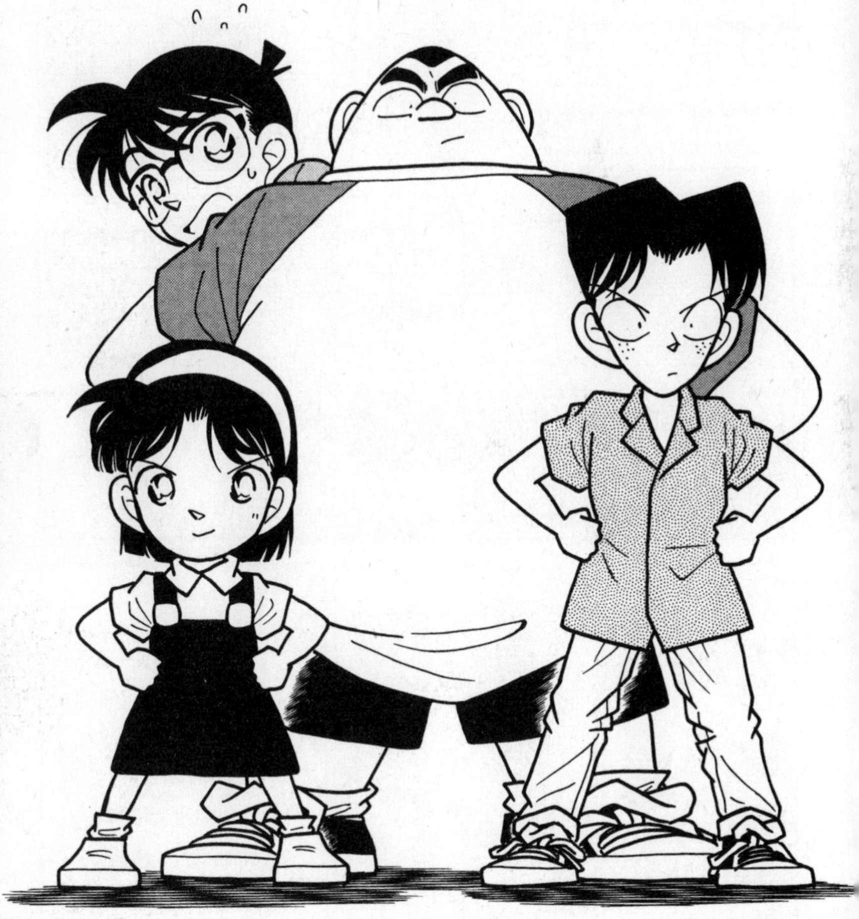

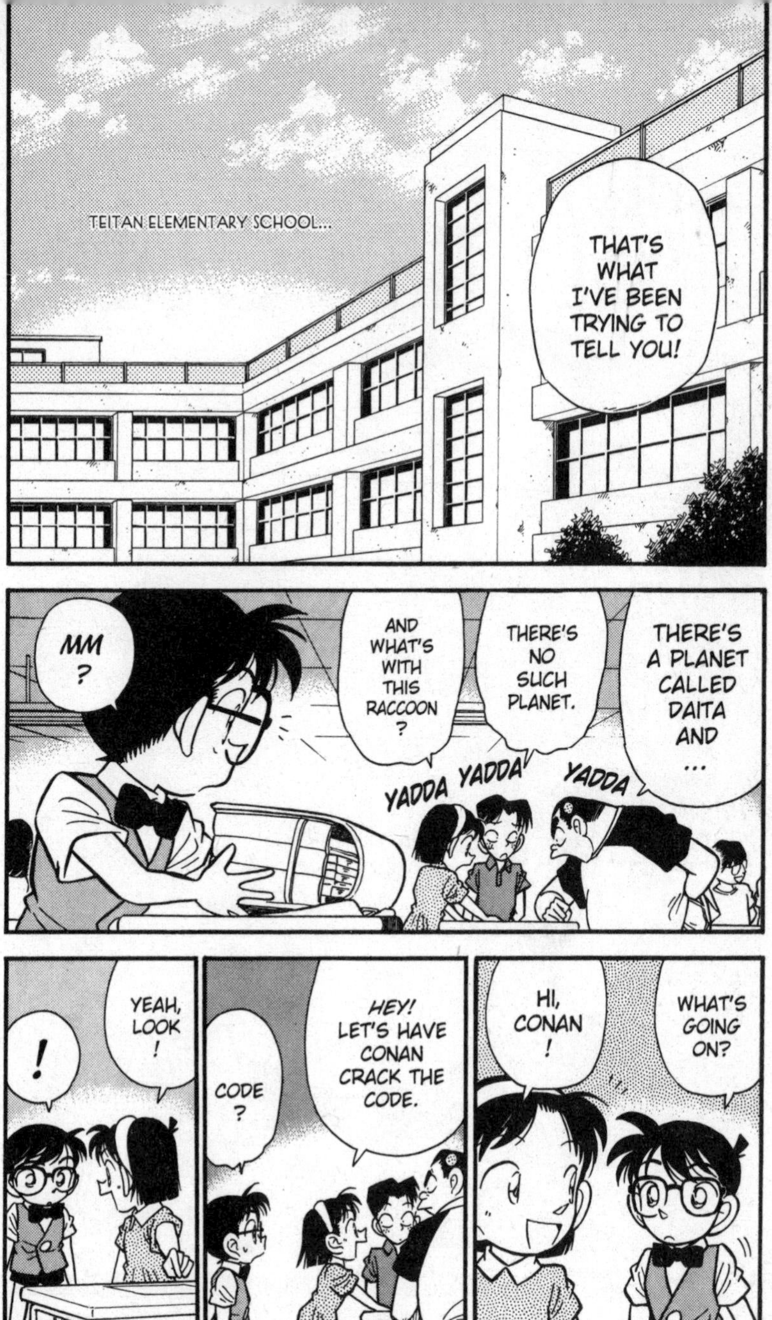
THAT'S WHAT I'VE BEEN TRYING TO TELL YOU!
TEITAN ELEMENTARY SCHOOL...
THERE'S A PLANET CALLED DAITA AND ...
YADDA
THERE'S NO SUCH PLANET.
YADDA
AND WHAT'S WITH THIS RACCOON?
YADDA
MM?
WHAT'S GOING ON?
HI, CONAN!
HEY! LET'S HAVE CONAN CRACK THE CODE.
CODE?
YEAH, LOOK!
!

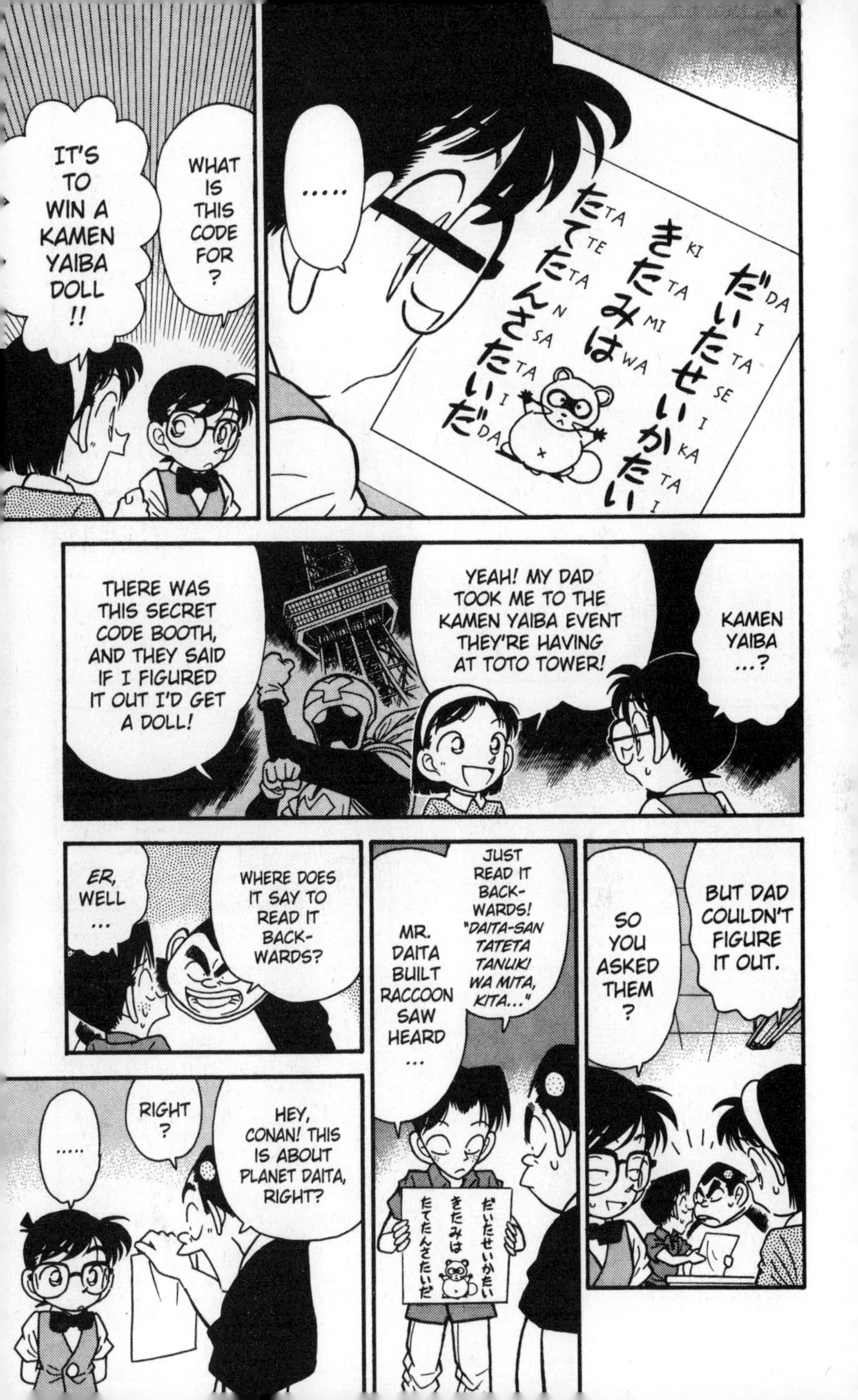
.....
だいたせいかたい
DA I TA SE I KA TA I
きたみは
KI TA MI WA
たてたんさたいだ
TA TE TA N SA TA I DA
WHAT IS THIS CODE FOR?
IT'S TO WIN A KAMEN YAIBA DOLL!!
KAMEN YAIBA...?
YEAH! MY DAD TOOK ME TO THE KAMEN YAIBA EVENT THEY'RE HAVING AT TOTO TOWER!
THERE WAS THIS SECRET CODE BOOTH, AND THEY SAID IF I FIGURED IT OUT I'D GET A DOLL!
BUT DAD COULDN'T FIGURE IT OUT.
SO YOU ASKED THEM?
JUST READ IT BACKWARDS! "DAITA-SAN TATETA TANUKI WA MITA, KITA..."
MR. DAITA BUILT RACCOON SAW HEARD...
WHERE DOES IT SAY TO READ IT BACKWARDS?
ER, WELL...
だいたせいかたい
きたみは
たてたんさたいだ
HEY, CONAN! THIS IS ABOUT PLANET DAITA, RIGHT?
RIGHT?
.....

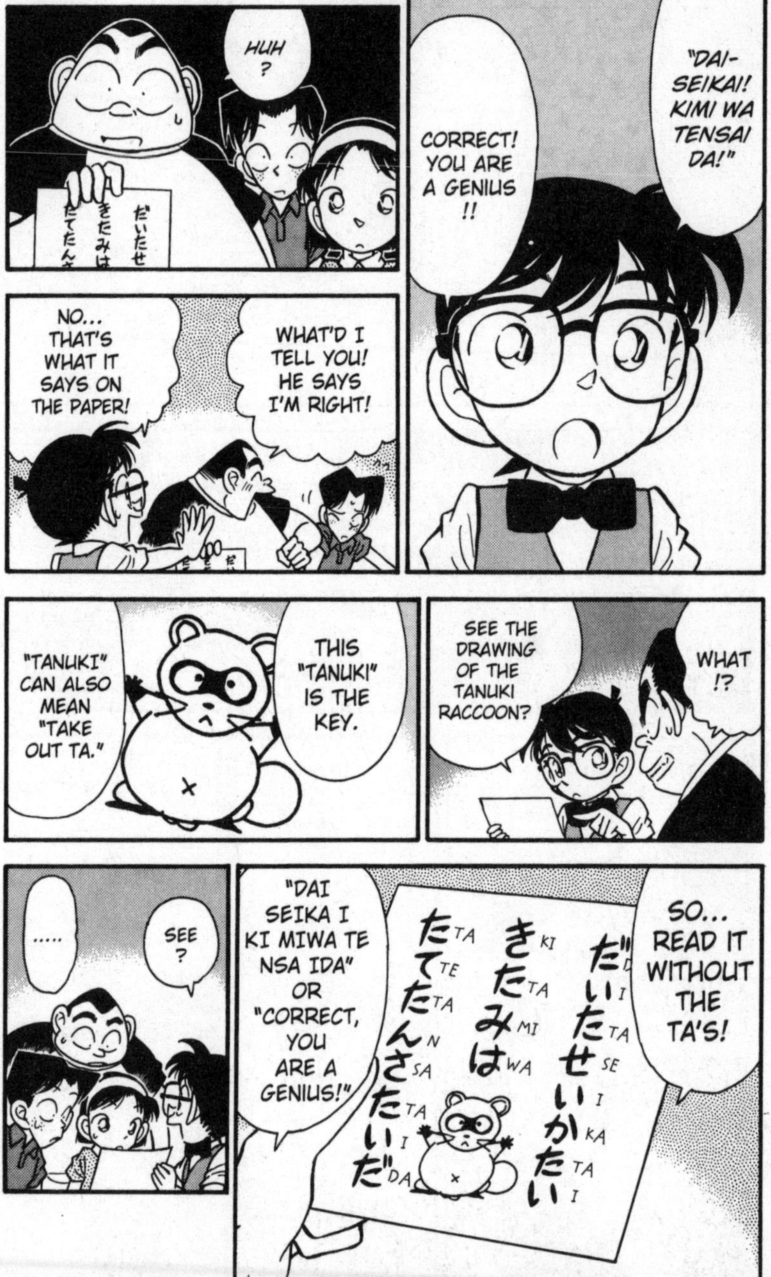
"DAI-SEIKAI! KIMI WA TENSAI DA!"
CORRECT! YOU ARE A GENIUS !!
HUH ?
だいたせ
きたみは
WHAT'D I TELL YOU! HE SAYS I'M RIGHT!
NO... THAT'S WHAT IT SAYS ON THE PAPER!
WHAT !?
SEE THE DRAWING OF THE TANUKI RACCOON?
THIS "TANUKI" IS THE KEY.
"TANUKI" CAN ALSO MEAN "TAKE OUT TA."
SO... READ IT WITHOUT THE TA'S!
だいたせいかたい
DA I TA SE I KA TA I
きたみは
KI TA MI WA
たてたんさたいだ
TA TE TA N SA TA I DA
"DAI SEIKA I KI MIWA TE NSA IDA" OR "CORRECT, YOU ARE A GENIUS!"
SEE ?
.....

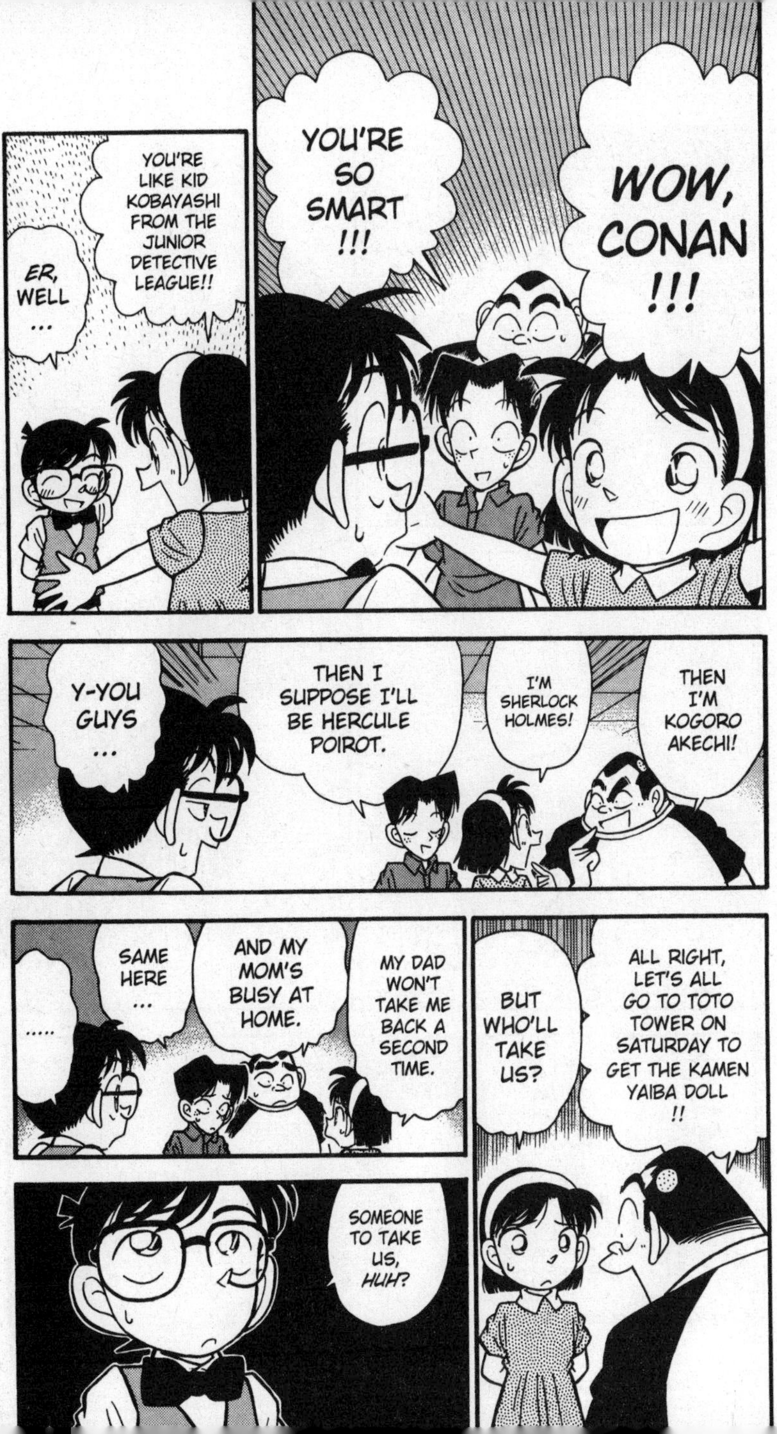
WOW, CONAN!!!
YOU'RE SO SMART!!!
YOU'RE LIKE KID KOBAYASHI FROM THE JUNIOR DETECTIVE LEAGUE!!
ER, WELL...
THEN I'M KOGORO AKECHI!
I'M SHERLOCK HOLMES!
THEN I SUPPOSE I'LL BE HERCULE POIROT.
Y-YOU GUYS...
ALL RIGHT, LET'S ALL GO TO TOTO TOWER ON SATURDAY TO GET THE KAMEN YAIBA DOLL!!
BUT WHO'LL TAKE US?
MY DAD WON'T TAKE ME BACK A SECOND TIME.
AND MY MOM'S BUSY AT HOME.
SAME HERE...
......
SOMEONE TO TAKE US, HUH?

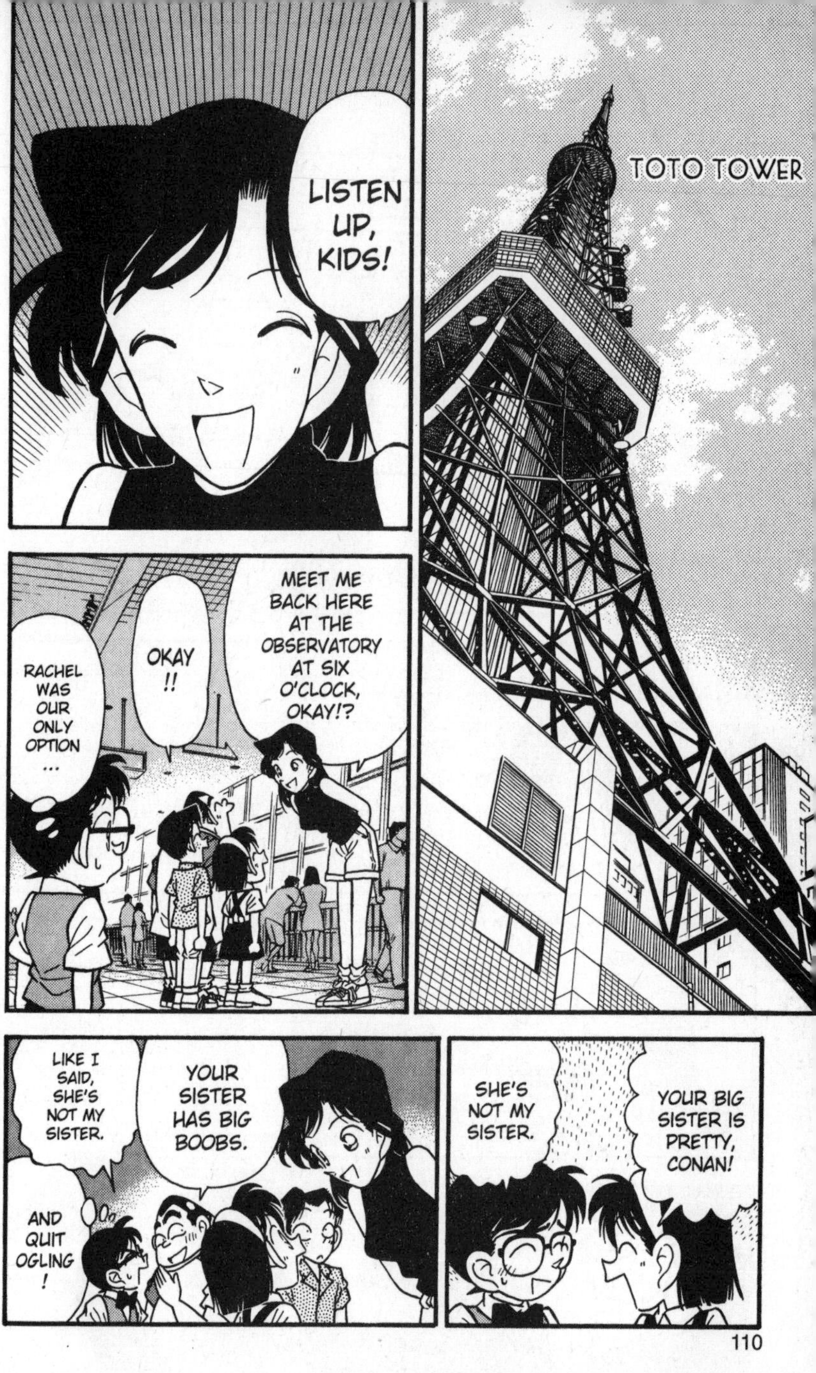
TOTO TOWER
LISTEN UP, KIDS!
MEET ME BACK HERE AT THE OBSERVATORY AT SIX O'CLOCK, OKAY!?
OKAY !!
RACHEL WAS OUR ONLY OPTION ...
YOUR BIG SISTER IS PRETTY, CONAN!
SHE'S NOT MY SISTER.
YOUR SISTER HAS BIG BOOBS.
LIKE I SAID, SHE'S NOT MY SISTER.
AND QUIT OGLING !

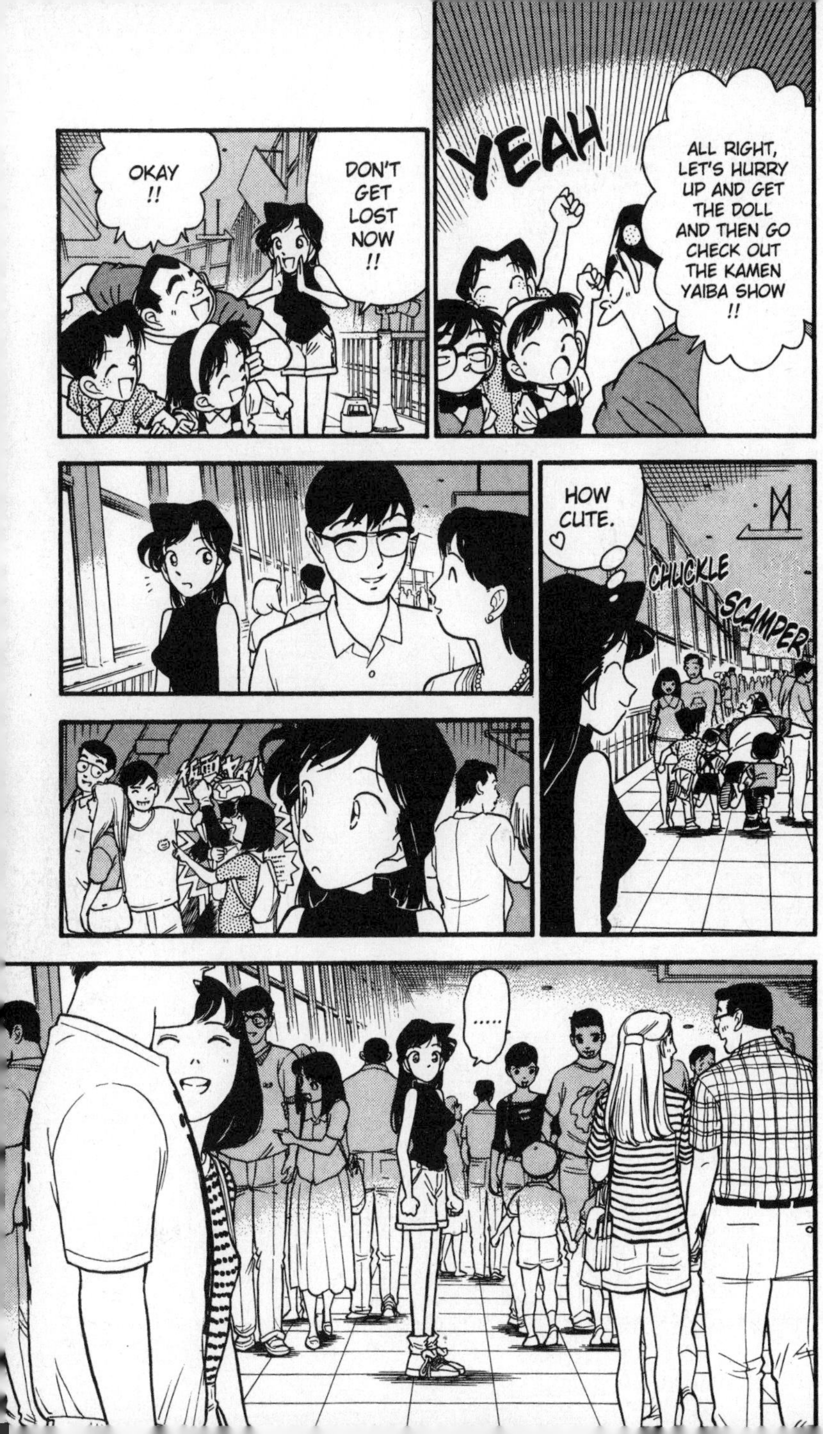
YEAH
ALL RIGHT, LET'S HURRY UP AND GET THE DOLL AND THEN GO CHECK OUT THE KAMEN YAIBA SHOW !!
DON'T GET LOST NOW !!
OKAY !!
HOW CUTE. ♥
CHUCKLE
SCAMPER
......

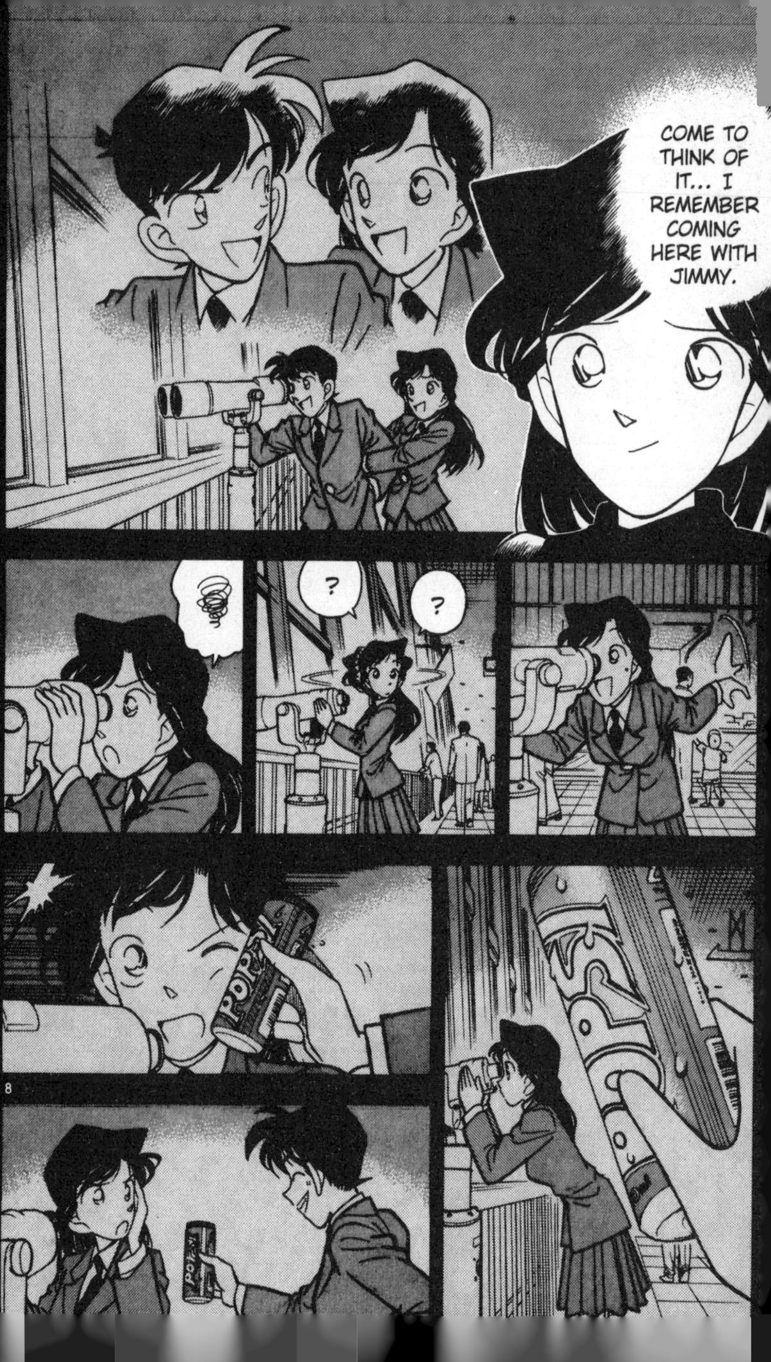
COME TO THINK OF IT... I REMEMBER COMING HERE WITH JIMMY.
?
?

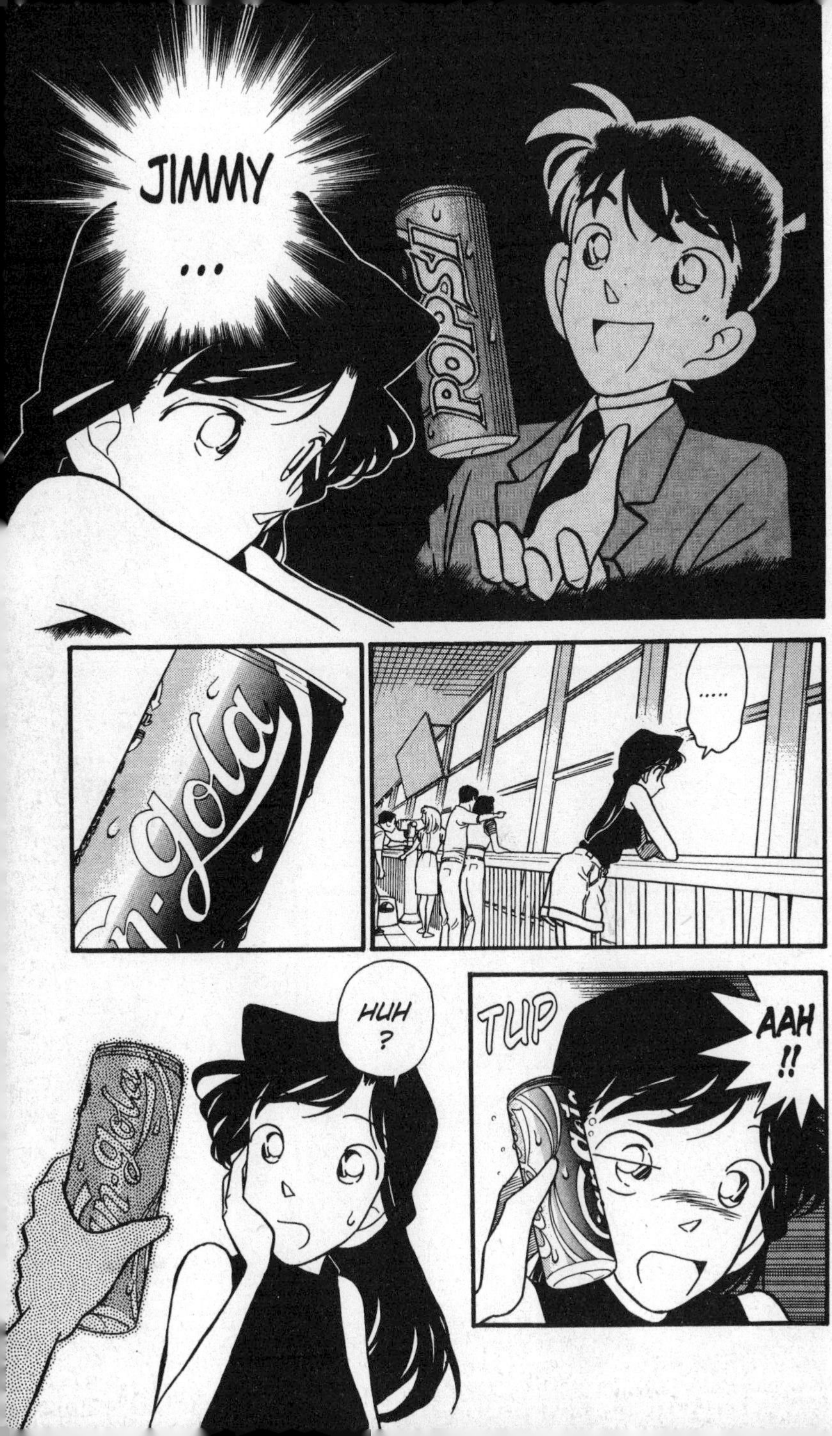
JIMMY ...
.....
TUP
AAH !!
HUH ?

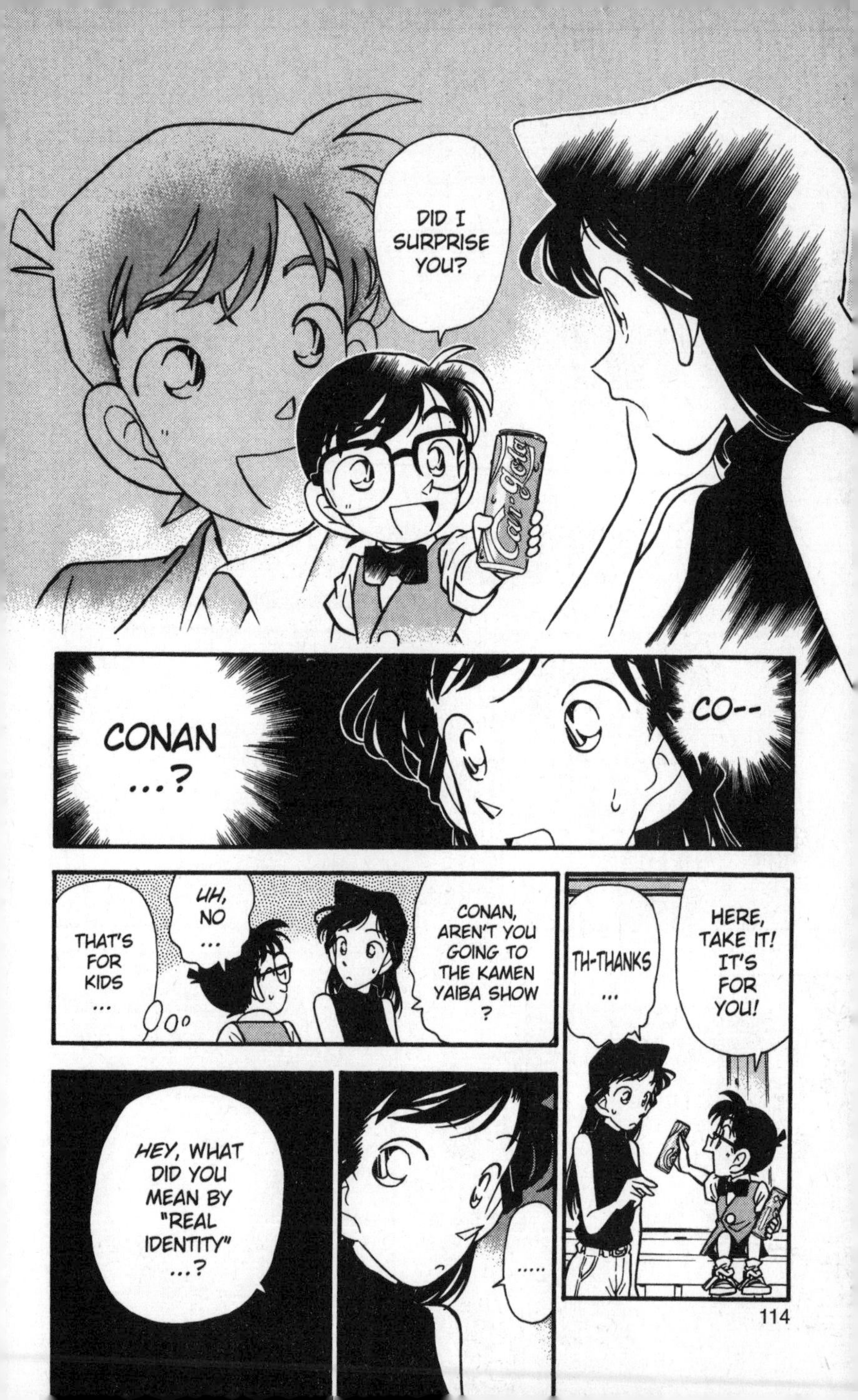
DID I SURPRISE YOU?
CO--
CONAN ...?
HERE, TAKE IT! IT'S FOR YOU!
TH-THANKS ...
CONAN, AREN'T YOU GOING TO THE KAMEN YAIBA SHOW ?
UH, NO ...
THAT'S FOR KIDS ...
.....
HEY, WHAT DID YOU MEAN BY "REAL IDENTITY" ...?

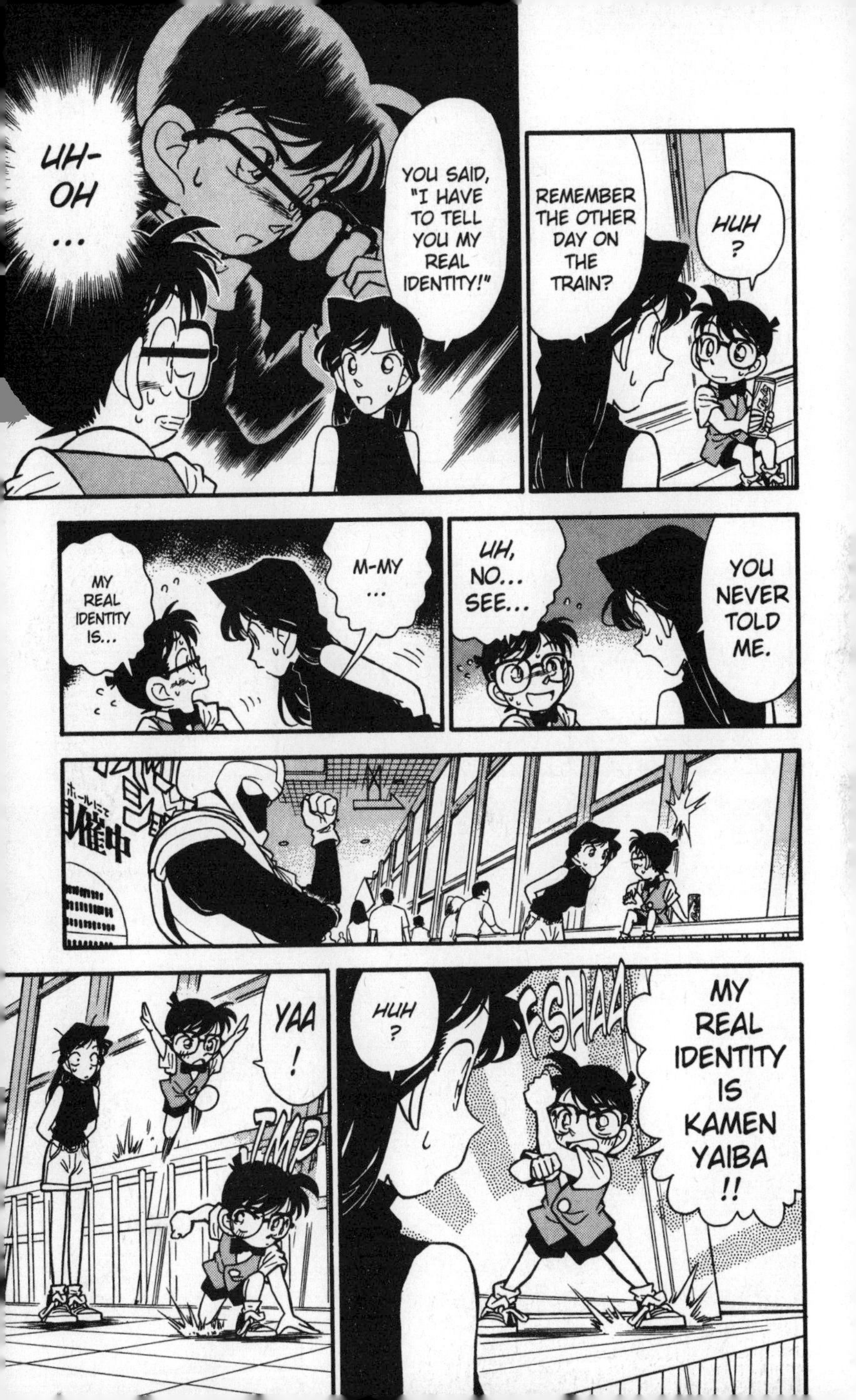
HUH ?
REMEMBER THE OTHER DAY ON THE TRAIN?
YOU SAID, "I HAVE TO TELL YOU MY REAL IDENTITY!"
UH-OH ...
YOU NEVER TOLD ME.
UH, NO... SEE...
M-MY ...
MY REAL IDENTITY IS...
ホールにて
MY REAL IDENTITY IS KAMEN YAIBA !!
SHAA
HUH ?
YAA !
TMP

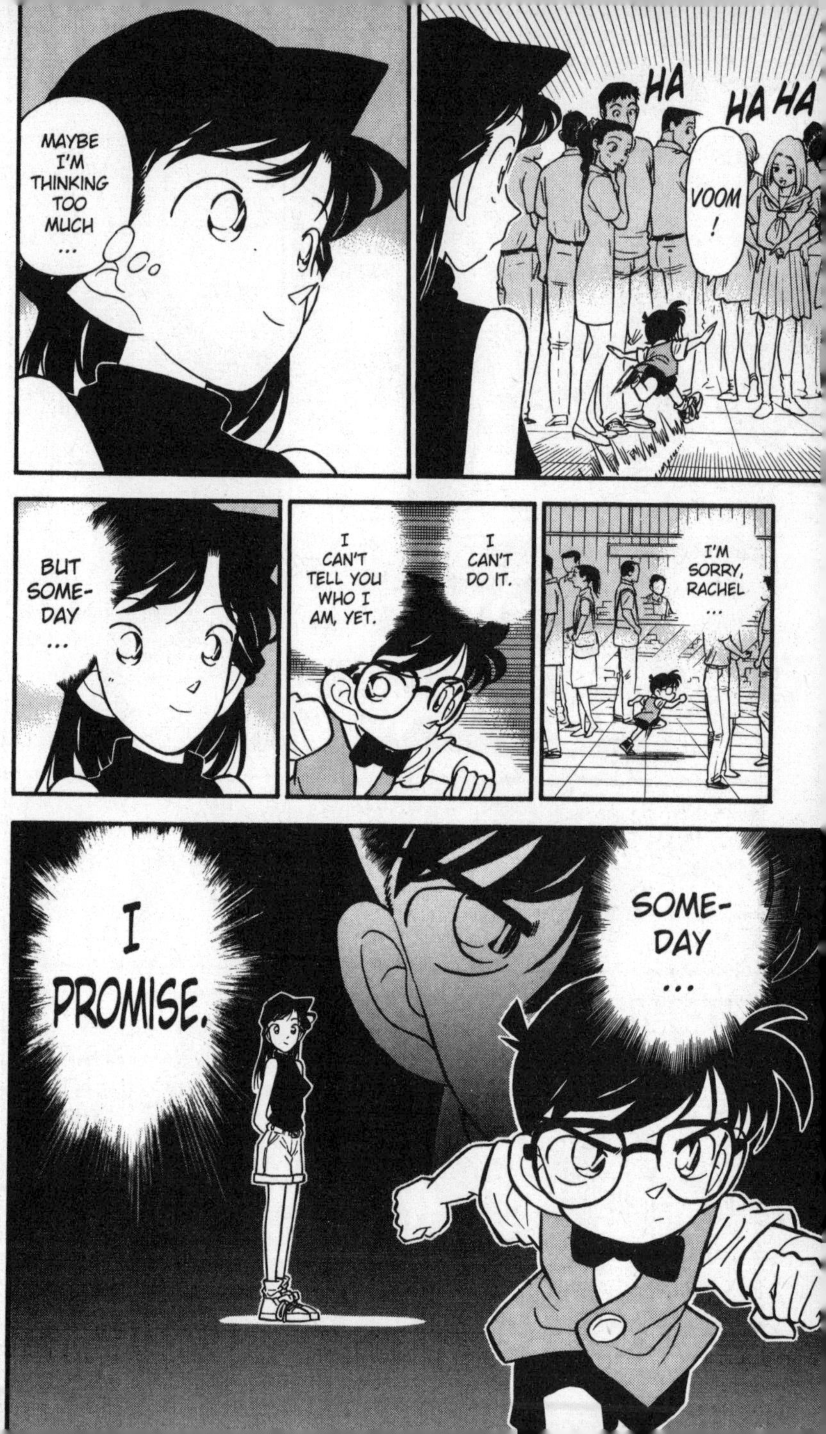
HA
HA HA
VOOM!
MAYBE I'M THINKING TOO MUCH ...
I'M SORRY, RACHEL ...
I CAN'T DO IT.
I CAN'T TELL YOU WHO I AM, YET.
BUT SOME-DAY ...
SOME-DAY ...
I PROMISE.

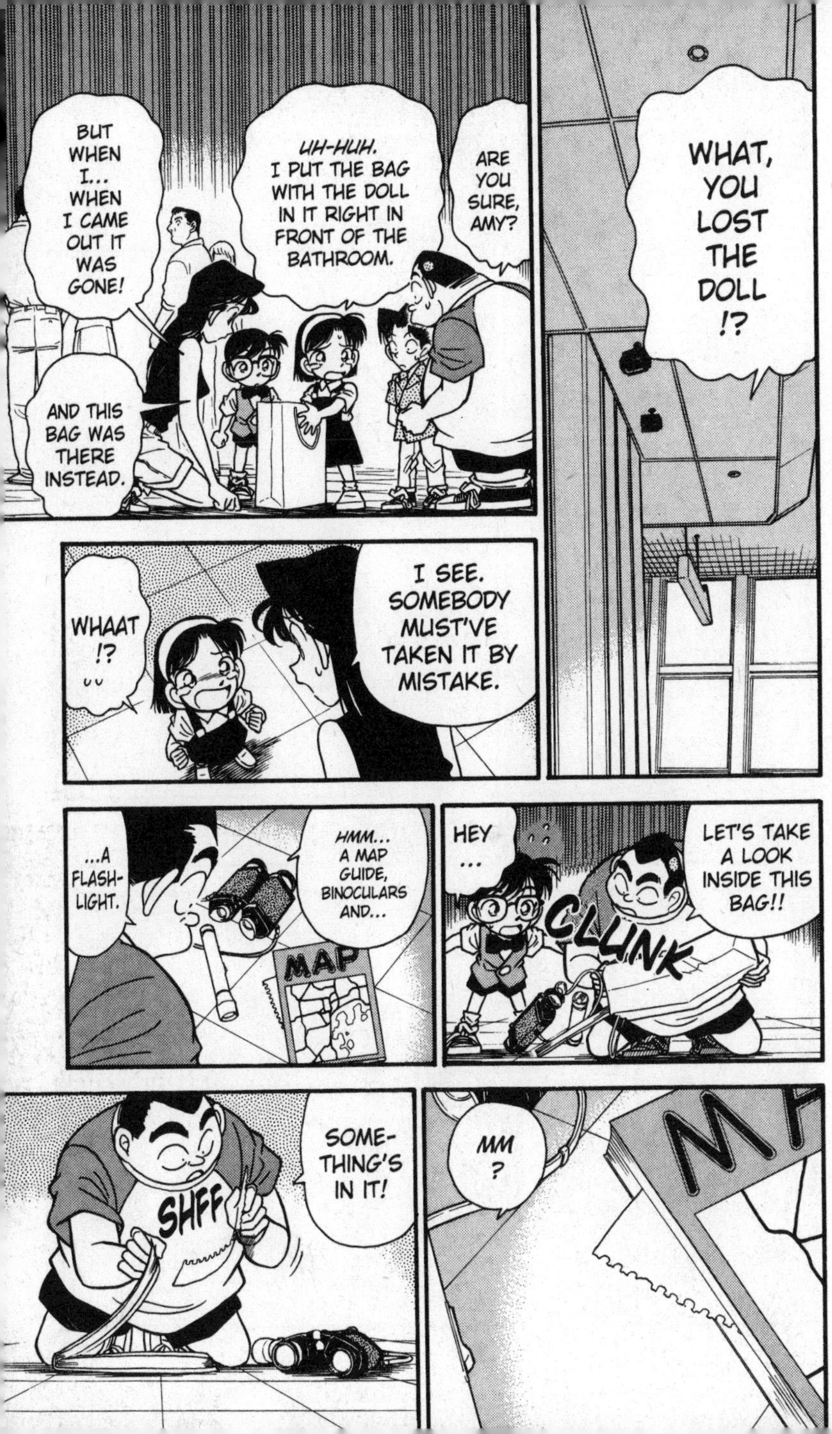
WHAT, YOU LOST THE DOLL!?
ARE YOU SURE, AMY?
UH-HUH. I PUT THE BAG WITH THE DOLL IN IT RIGHT IN FRONT OF THE BATHROOM.
BUT WHEN I... WHEN I CAME OUT IT WAS GONE!
AND THIS BAG WAS THERE INSTEAD.
I SEE. SOMEBODY MUST'VE TAKEN IT BY MISTAKE.
WHAAT!?
LET'S TAKE A LOOK INSIDE THIS BAG!!
CLUNK
HEY ...
HMM... A MAP GUIDE, BINOCULARS AND...
...A FLASHLIGHT.
MAP
MM ?
SOME-THING'S IN IT!
SHFF

UM...

WHAT'S THIS?

←ORO

OH, SO IT'S YOURS.

HEY! THAT'S MY BAG!!

.....

I'M SORRY TO HAVE TROUBLED YOU.

NO PROBLEM.

I'M SORRY. I WAS IN A RUSH. I MUST HAVE MISTAKEN HER BAG FOR MINE.

THERE YOU ARE, KAMEN YAIBA!!

I WANT SUSHI!!

REALLY? I WANT GRILLED EEL!!

I'LL TREAT YOU GUYS TO A SNACK!

HOW ABOUT A FRENCH RESTAURANT?

SHALL WE GET A BITE TO EAT?

BOY, I'M STARVING!

UM...

I SAID A SNACK, DIDN'T I!?

OH...

PAPER?

WAS THERE A SMALL PIECE OF PAPER INSIDE THAT BAG?

SORRY TO TROUBLE YOU AGAIN.

WHAT IS IT NOW?

HEY...

LET ME CHECK...

VWSH

NO...

BUT IT MUST HAVE BEEN IN THERE...

HUH?

RIGHT!?

WE HAVEN'T SEEN IT!!

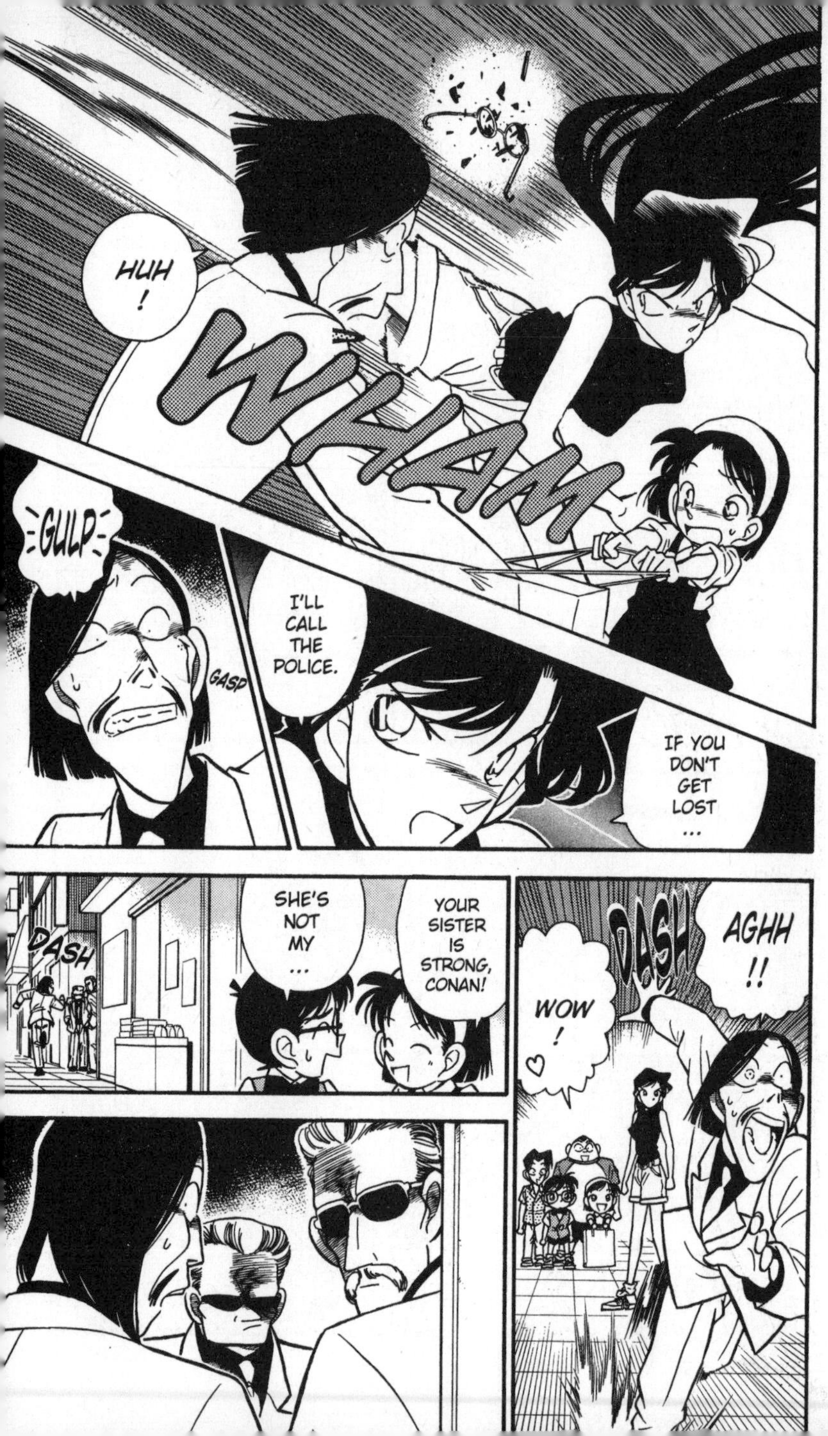
HUH!
WHAM
IF YOU DON'T GET LOST ...
I'LL CALL THE POLICE.
GULP
GASP
AGHH!!
DASH
WOW!
YOUR SISTER IS STRONG, CONAN!
SHE'S NOT MY ...
DASH

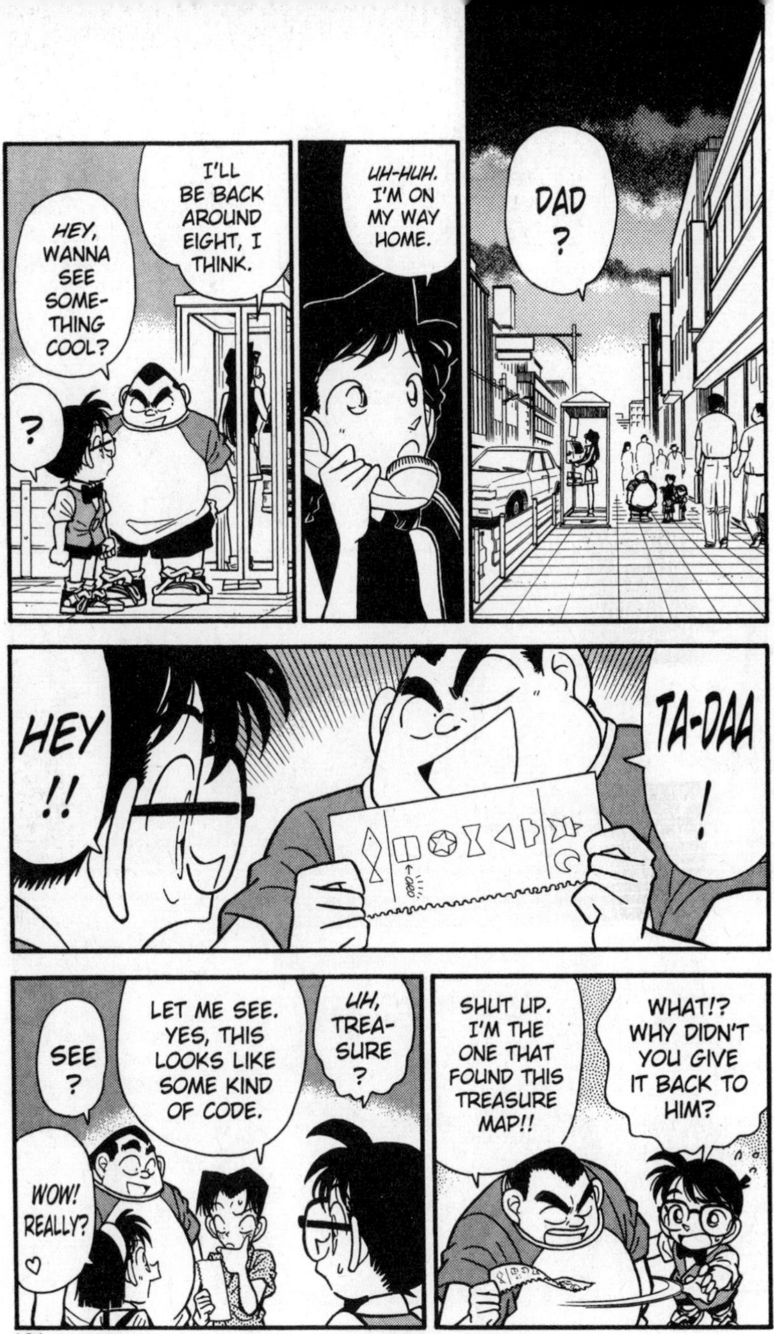
DAD ?
UH-HUH. I'M ON MY WAY HOME.
I'LL BE BACK AROUND EIGHT, I THINK.
HEY, WANNA SEE SOME-THING COOL?
?
TA-DAA !
HEY !!
WHAT!? WHY DIDN'T YOU GIVE IT BACK TO HIM?
SHUT UP. I'M THE ONE THAT FOUND THIS TREASURE MAP!!
UH, TREA-SURE ?
LET ME SEE. YES, THIS LOOKS LIKE SOME KIND OF CODE.
SEE ?
WOW! REALLY? ♡

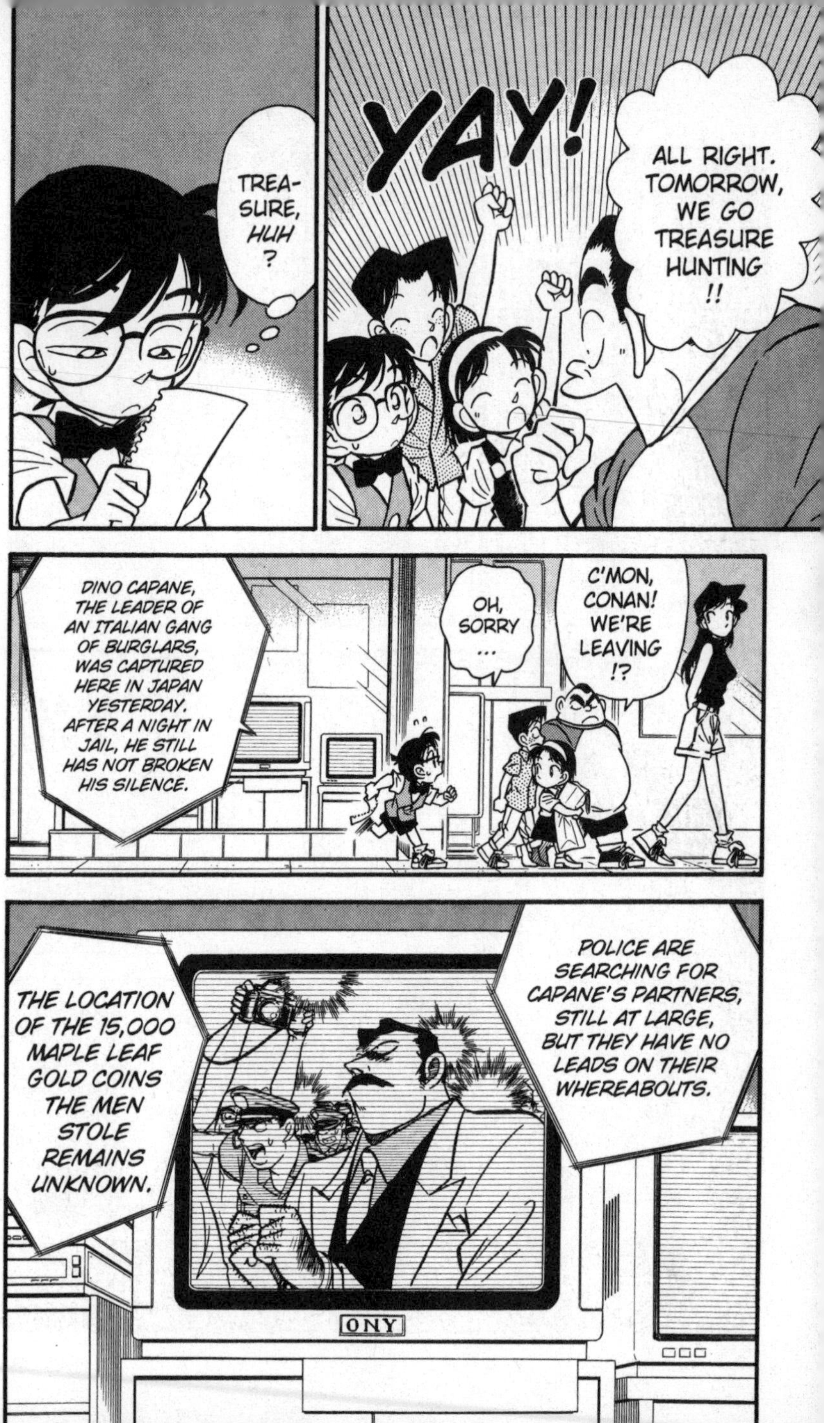
ALL RIGHT. TOMORROW, WE GO TREASURE HUNTING!!
YAY!
TREA-SURE, HUH?
C'MON, CONAN! WE'RE LEAVING!?
OH, SORRY...
DINO CAPANE, THE LEADER OF AN ITALIAN GANG OF BURGLARS, WAS CAPTURED HERE IN JAPAN YESTERDAY. AFTER A NIGHT IN JAIL, HE STILL HAS NOT BROKEN HIS SILENCE.
POLICE ARE SEARCHING FOR CAPANE'S PARTNERS, STILL AT LARGE, BUT THEY HAVE NO LEADS ON THEIR WHEREABOUTS.
THE LOCATION OF THE 15,000 MAPLE LEAF GOLD COINS THE MEN STOLE REMAINS UNKNOWN.
ONY

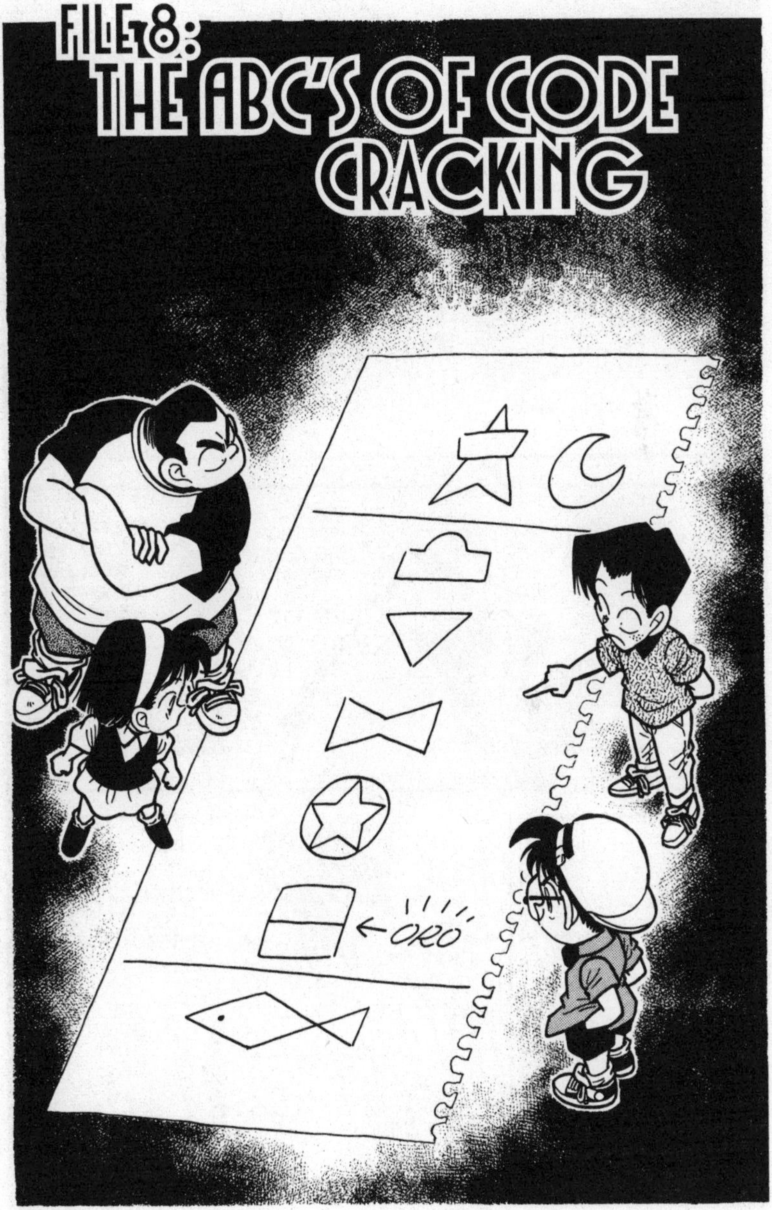
FILE 8:
THE ABC'S OF CODE CRACKING
ORO

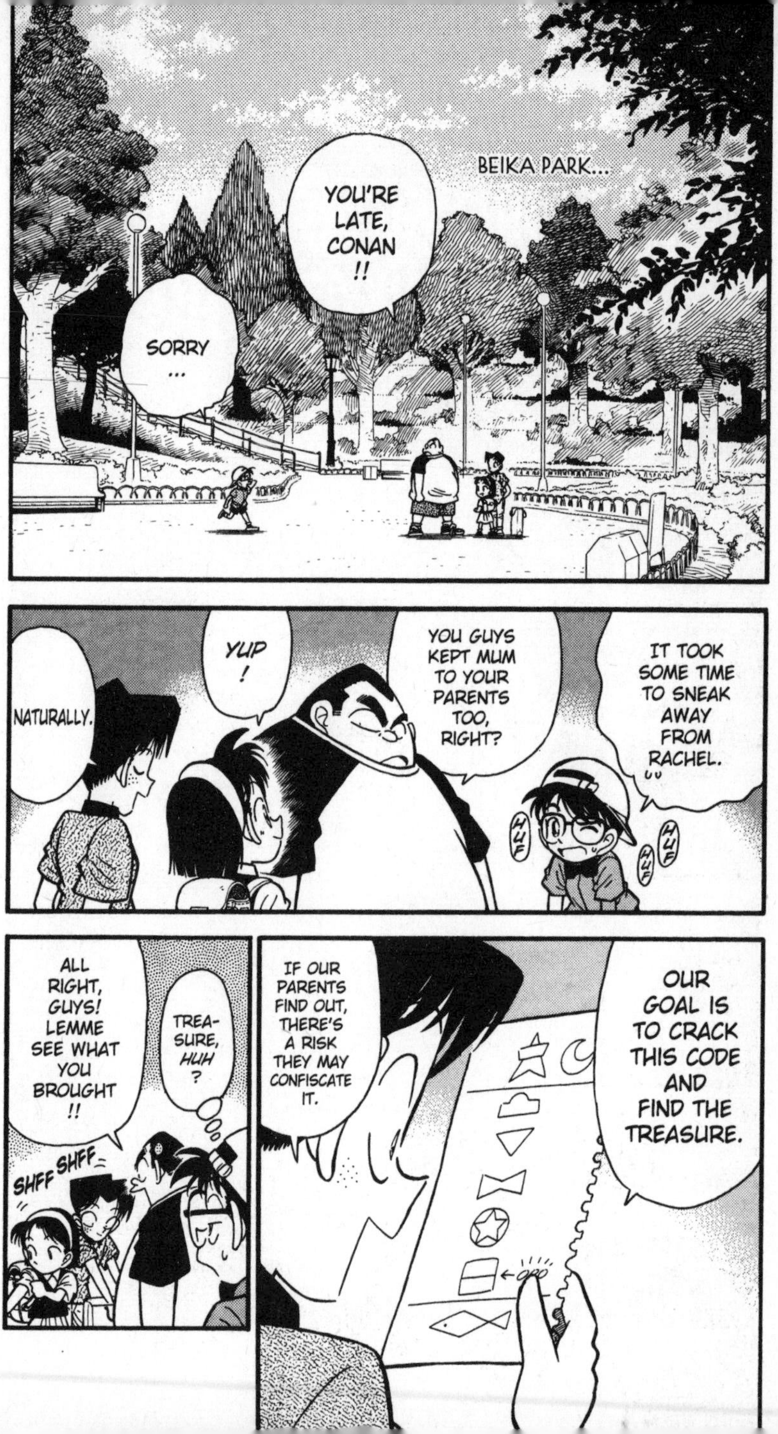
BEIKA PARK...
YOU'RE LATE, CONAN !!
SORRY ...
IT TOOK SOME TIME TO SNEAK AWAY FROM RACHEL.
HUF HUF
HUF
YOU GUYS KEPT MUM TO YOUR PARENTS TOO, RIGHT?
YUP!
NATURALLY.
OUR GOAL IS TO CRACK THIS CODE AND FIND THE TREASURE.
IF OUR PARENTS FIND OUT, THERE'S A RISK THEY MAY CONFISCATE IT.
TREA-SURE, HUH?
ALL RIGHT, GUYS! LEMME SEE WHAT YOU BROUGHT !!
SHFF SHFF

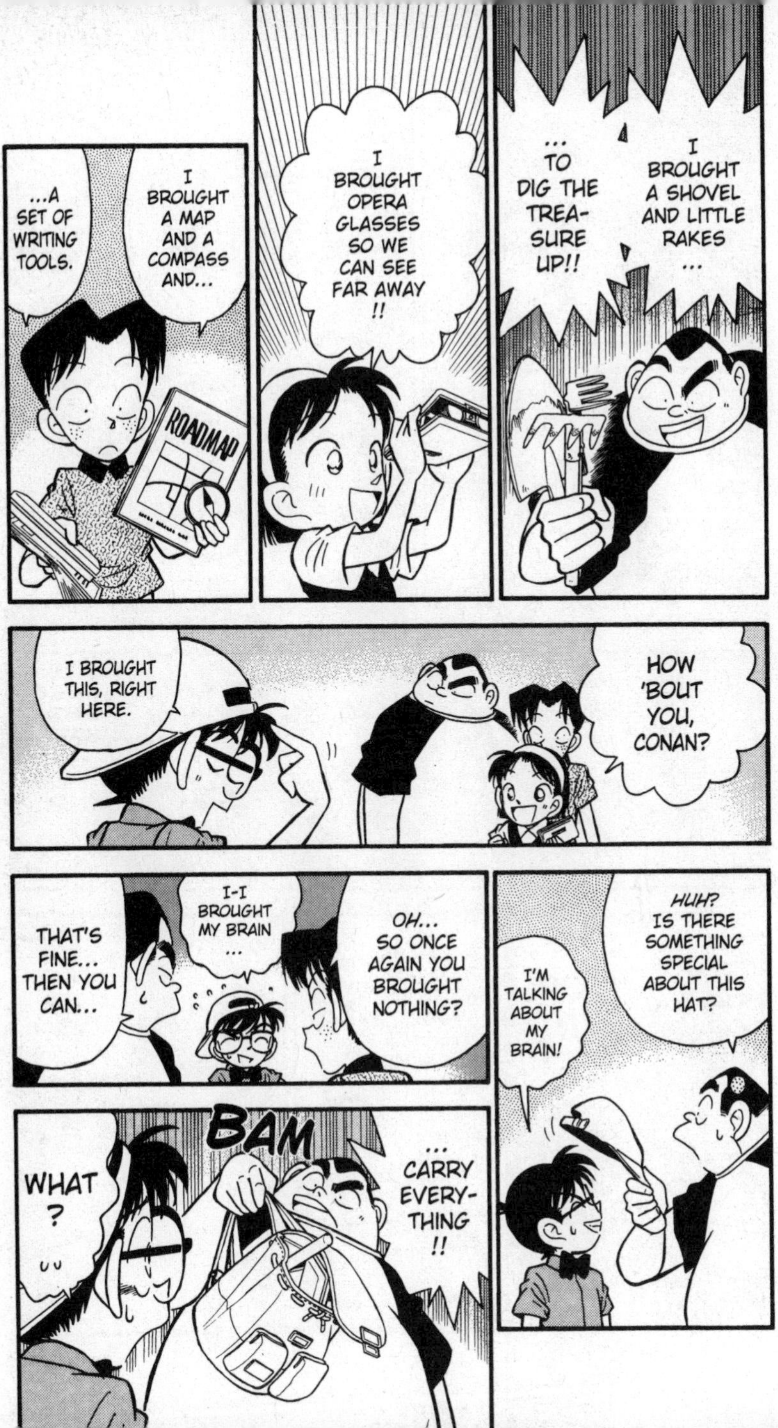
I BROUGHT A SHOVEL AND LITTLE RAKES ...
... TO DIG THE TREA-SURE UP!!
I BROUGHT OPERA GLASSES SO WE CAN SEE FAR AWAY !!
I BROUGHT A MAP AND A COMPASS AND...
...A SET OF WRITING TOOLS.
ROADMAP
HOW 'BOUT YOU, CONAN?
I BROUGHT THIS, RIGHT HERE.
HUH? IS THERE SOMETHING SPECIAL ABOUT THIS HAT?
I'M TALKING ABOUT MY BRAIN!
OH... SO ONCE AGAIN YOU BROUGHT NOTHING?
I-I BROUGHT MY BRAIN ...
THAT'S FINE... THEN YOU CAN...
... CARRY EVERY-THING !!
BAM
WHAT ?

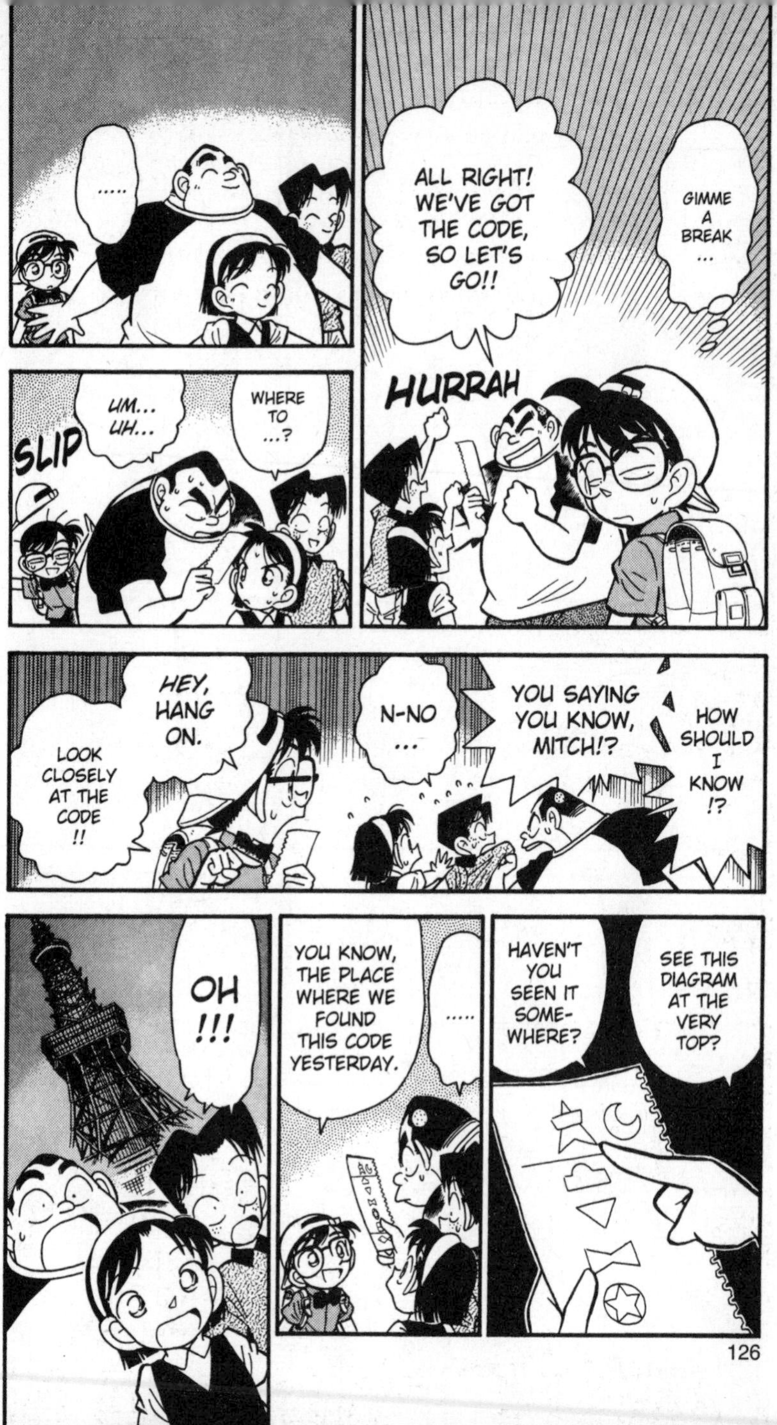
ALL RIGHT! WE'VE GOT THE CODE, SO LET'S GO!!
HURRAH
GIMME A BREAK ...
.....
WHERE TO ...?
UM... UH...
SLIP
HOW SHOULD I KNOW !?
YOU SAYING YOU KNOW, MITCH!?
N-NO ...
HEY, HANG ON.
LOOK CLOSELY AT THE CODE !!
SEE THIS DIAGRAM AT THE VERY TOP?
HAVEN'T YOU SEEN IT SOME-WHERE?
.....
YOU KNOW, THE PLACE WHERE WE FOUND THIS CODE YESTERDAY.
OH !!!

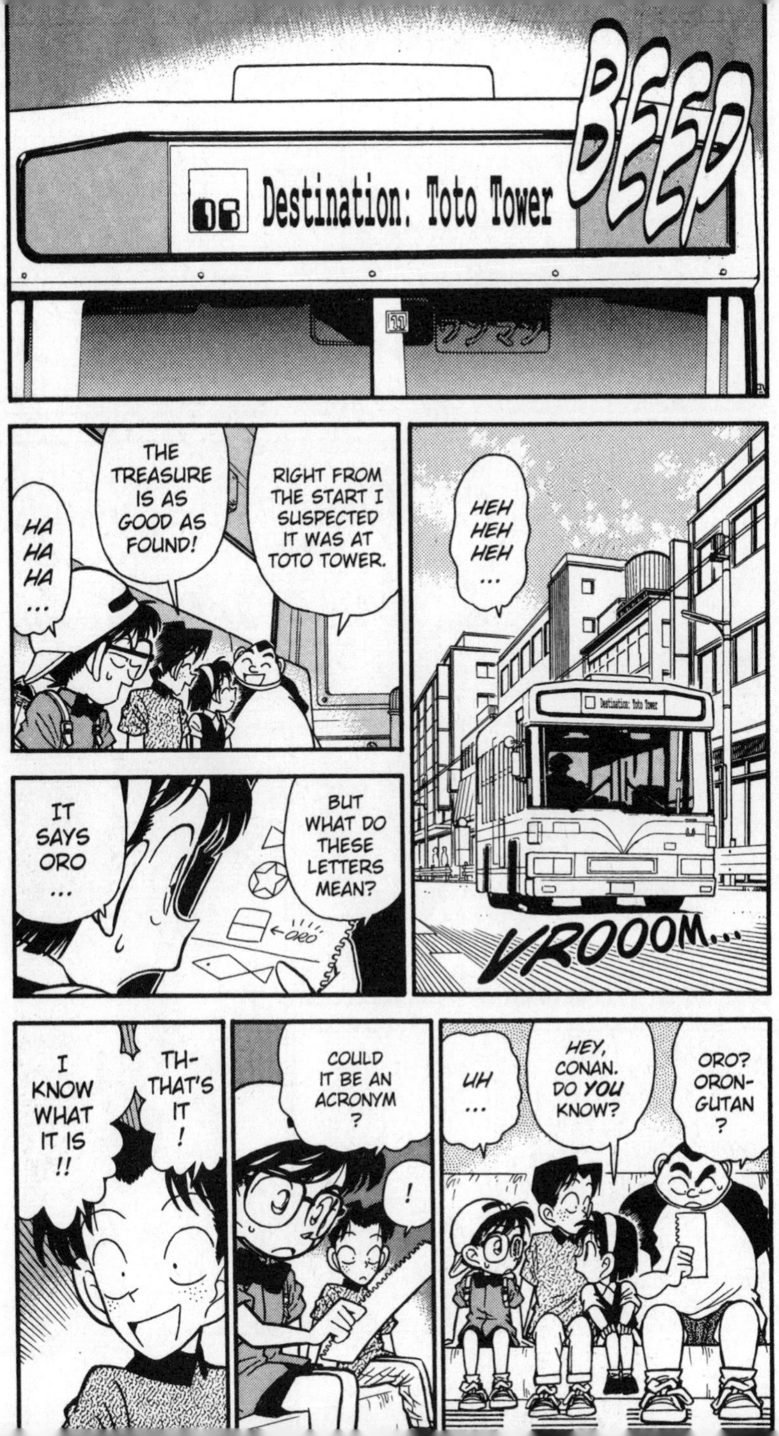
16 Destination: Toto Tower
BEEP
ワンマン
HEH HEH HEH ...
Destination: Toto Tower
VROOOM...
RIGHT FROM THE START I SUSPECTED IT WAS AT TOTO TOWER.
THE TREASURE IS AS GOOD AS FOUND!
HA HA HA ...
BUT WHAT DO THESE LETTERS MEAN?
IT SAYS ORO ...
←ORO
ORO? ORON-GUTAN ?
HEY, CONAN. DO YOU KNOW?
UH ...
!
COULD IT BE AN ACRONYM ?
TH-THAT'S IT !
I KNOW WHAT IT IS !!

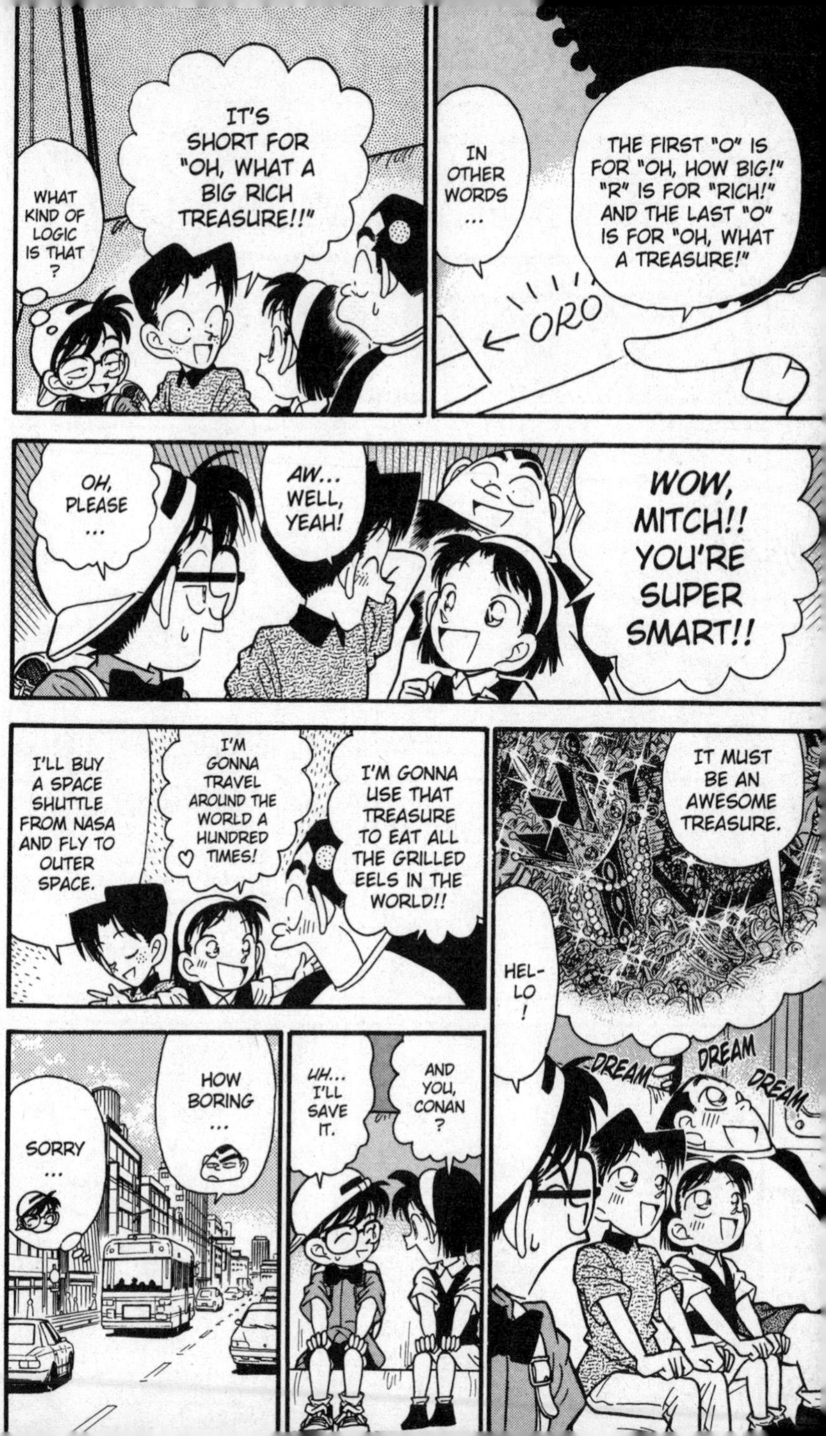
THE FIRST "O" IS FOR "OH, HOW BIG!" "R" IS FOR "RICH!" AND THE LAST "O" IS FOR "OH, WHAT A TREASURE!"
ORO
IN OTHER WORDS ...
IT'S SHORT FOR "OH, WHAT A BIG RICH TREASURE!!"
WHAT KIND OF LOGIC IS THAT ?
WOW, MITCH!! YOU'RE SUPER SMART!!
AW... WELL, YEAH!
OH, PLEASE ...
IT MUST BE AN AWESOME TREASURE.
HEL-LO !
DREAM
DREAM
DREAM
I'M GONNA USE THAT TREASURE TO EAT ALL THE GRILLED EELS IN THE WORLD!!
I'M GONNA TRAVEL AROUND THE WORLD A HUNDRED TIMES!
I'LL BUY A SPACE SHUTTLE FROM NASA AND FLY TO OUTER SPACE.
AND YOU, CONAN ?
UH... I'LL SAVE IT.
HOW BORING ...
SORRY ...

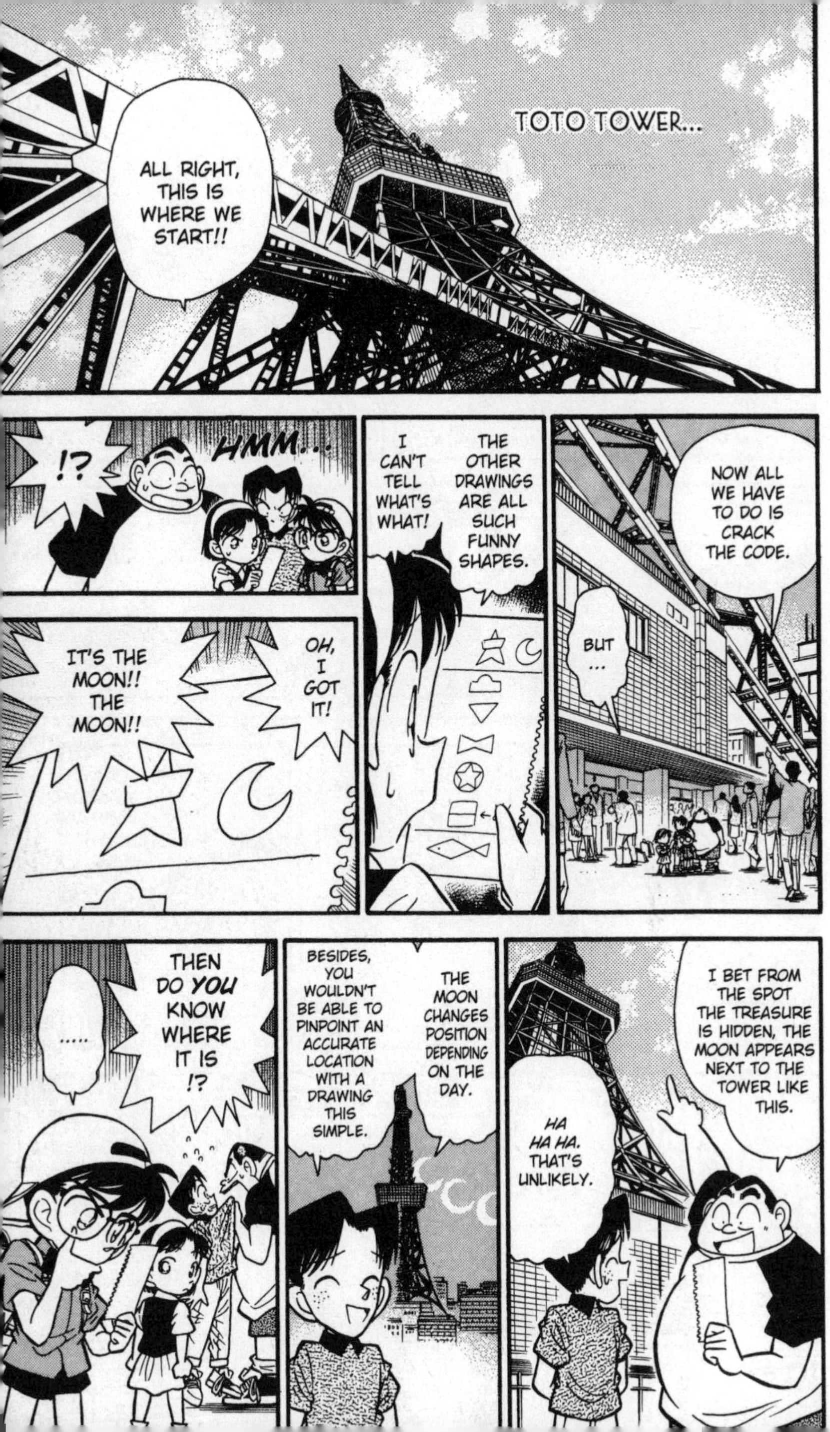
TOTO TOWER...
ALL RIGHT, THIS IS WHERE WE START!!
NOW ALL WE HAVE TO DO IS CRACK THE CODE.
BUT ...
THE OTHER DRAWINGS ARE ALL SUCH FUNNY SHAPES.
I CAN'T TELL WHAT'S WHAT!
HMM...
!?
OH, I GOT IT!
IT'S THE MOON!! THE MOON!!
I BET FROM THE SPOT THE TREASURE IS HIDDEN, THE MOON APPEARS NEXT TO THE TOWER LIKE THIS.
HA HA HA. THAT'S UNLIKELY.
THE MOON CHANGES POSITION DEPENDING ON THE DAY.
BESIDES, YOU WOULDN'T BE ABLE TO PINPOINT AN ACCURATE LOCATION WITH A DRAWING THIS SIMPLE.
THEN DO YOU KNOW WHERE IT IS !?
.....

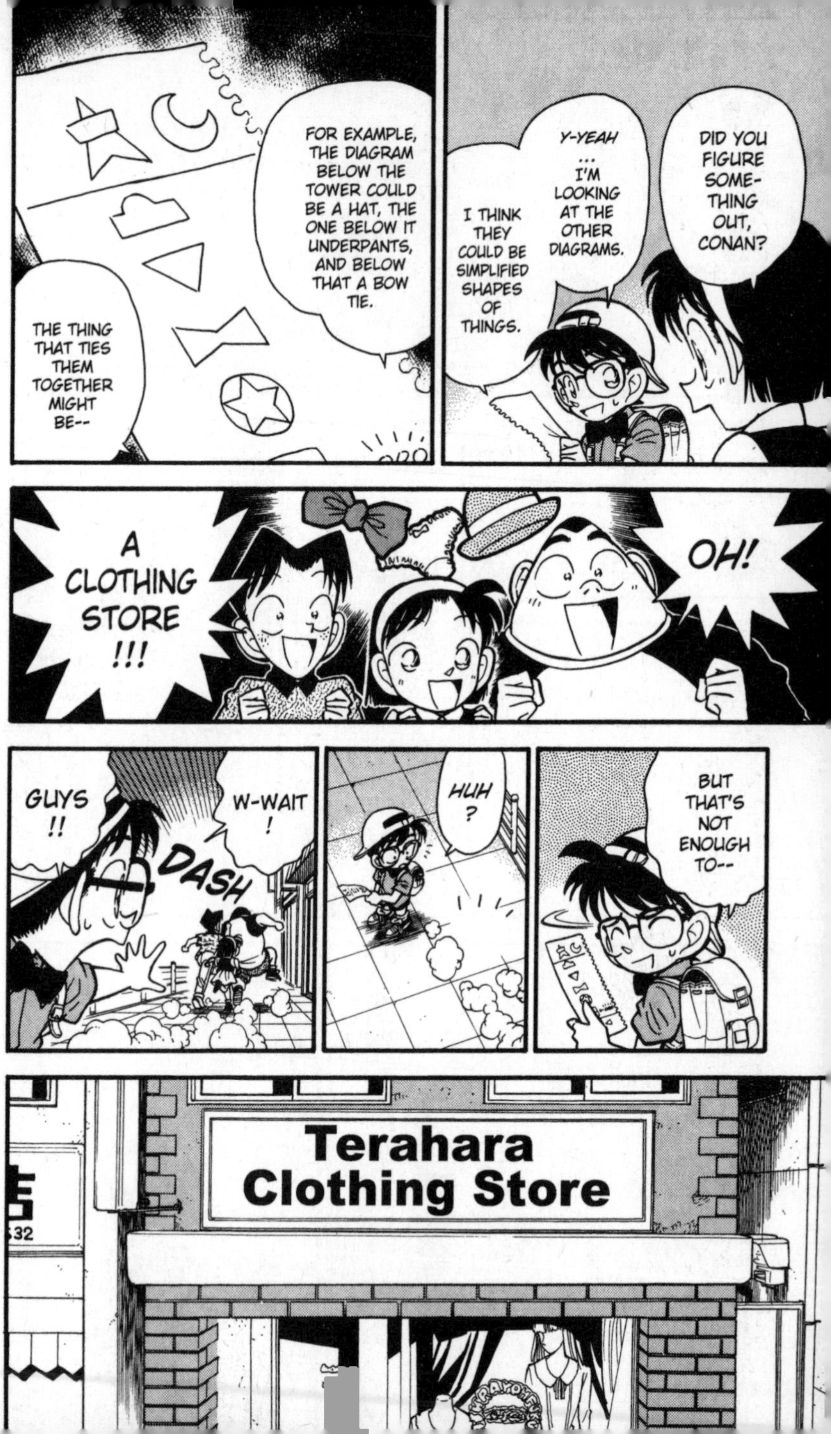
DID YOU FIGURE SOME-THING OUT, CONAN?
Y-YEAH... I'M LOOKING AT THE OTHER DIAGRAMS.
I THINK THEY COULD BE SIMPLIFIED SHAPES OF THINGS.
FOR EXAMPLE, THE DIAGRAM BELOW THE TOWER COULD BE A HAT, THE ONE BELOW IT UNDERPANTS, AND BELOW THAT A BOW TIE.
THE THING THAT TIES THEM TOGETHER MIGHT BE--
OH!
A CLOTHING STORE!!!
BUT THAT'S NOT ENOUGH TO--
HUH?
W-WAIT!
GUYS!!
DASH
Terahara Clothing Store

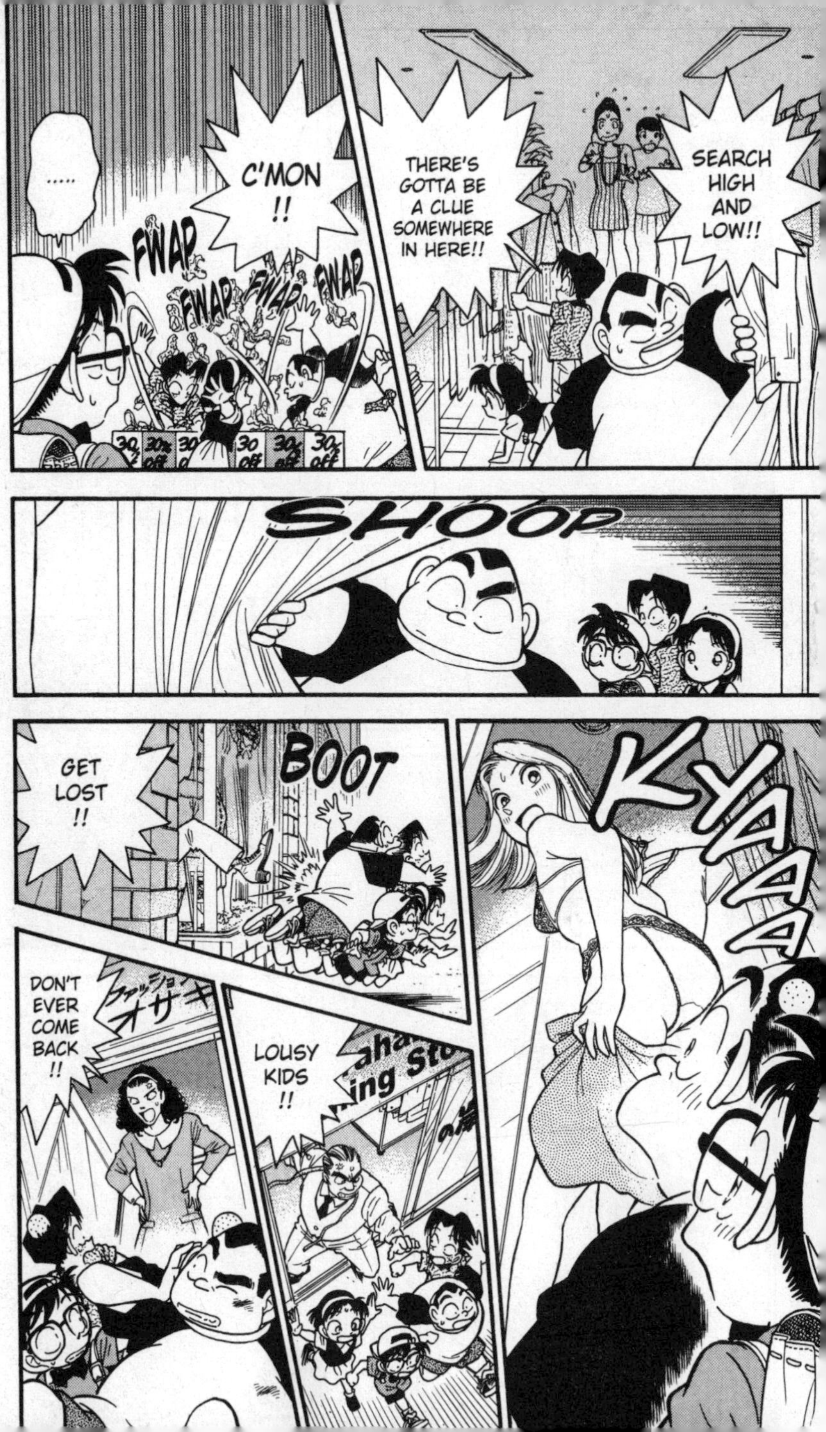
SEARCH HIGH AND LOW!!
THERE'S GOTTA BE A CLUE SOMEWHERE IN HERE!!
C'MON !!
FWAP
FWAP
FWAP
FWAP
......
SHOOP
KYAAAA
GET LOST !!
BOOT
LOUSY KIDS !!
DON'T EVER COME BACK !!
オサキ

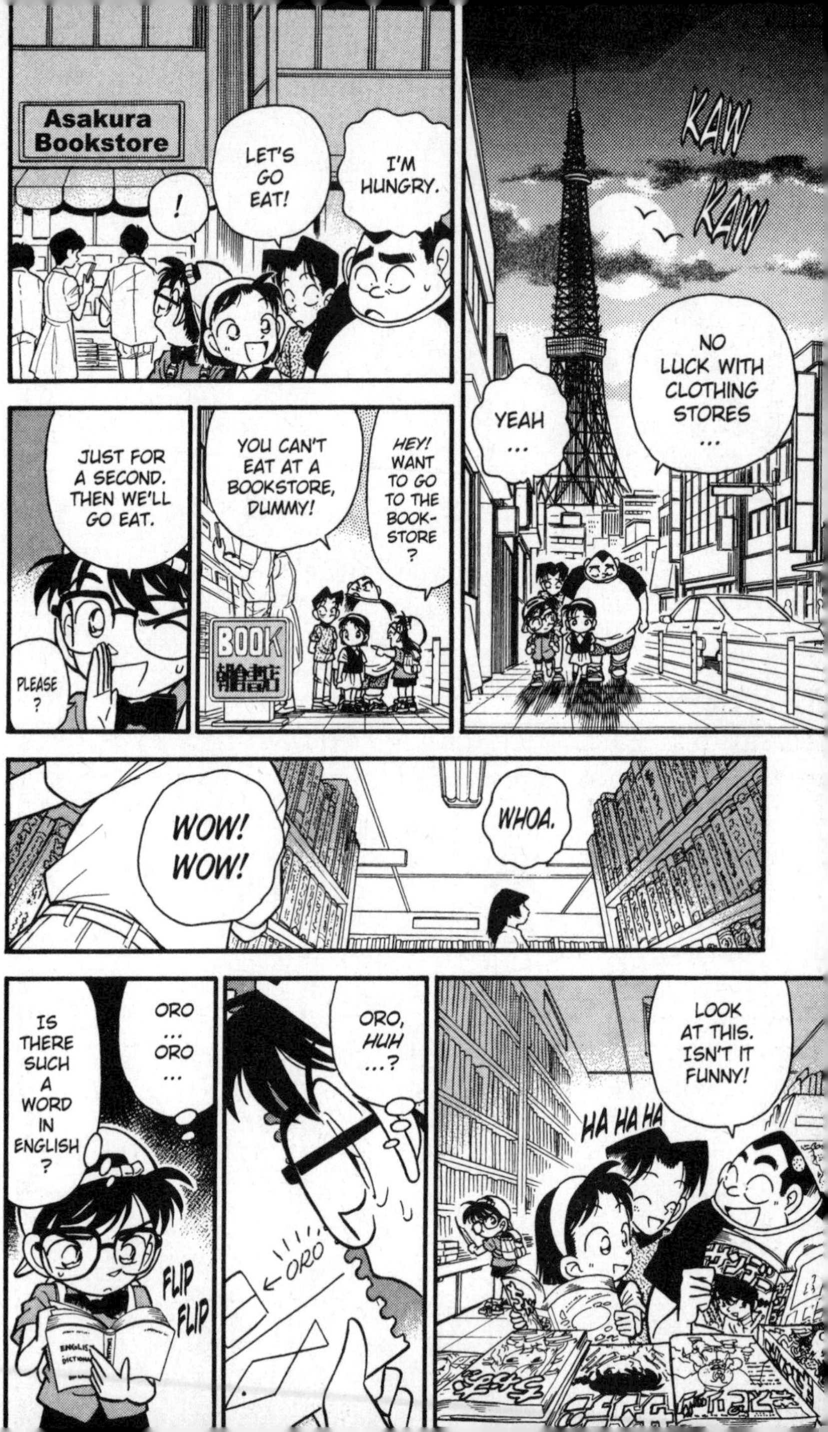
KAW
KAW
NO LUCK WITH CLOTHING STORES ...
YEAH ...
Asakura Bookstore
I'M HUNGRY.
LET'S GO EAT!
!
HEY! WANT TO GO TO THE BOOKSTORE?
YOU CAN'T EAT AT A BOOKSTORE, DUMMY!
BOOK
JUST FOR A SECOND. THEN WE'LL GO EAT.
PLEASE?
WHOA.
WOW! WOW!
LOOK AT THIS. ISN'T IT FUNNY!
HA HA HA
ORO, HUH ...?
← ORO
ORO ... ORO ...
IS THERE SUCH A WORD IN ENGLISH?
FLIP
FLIP

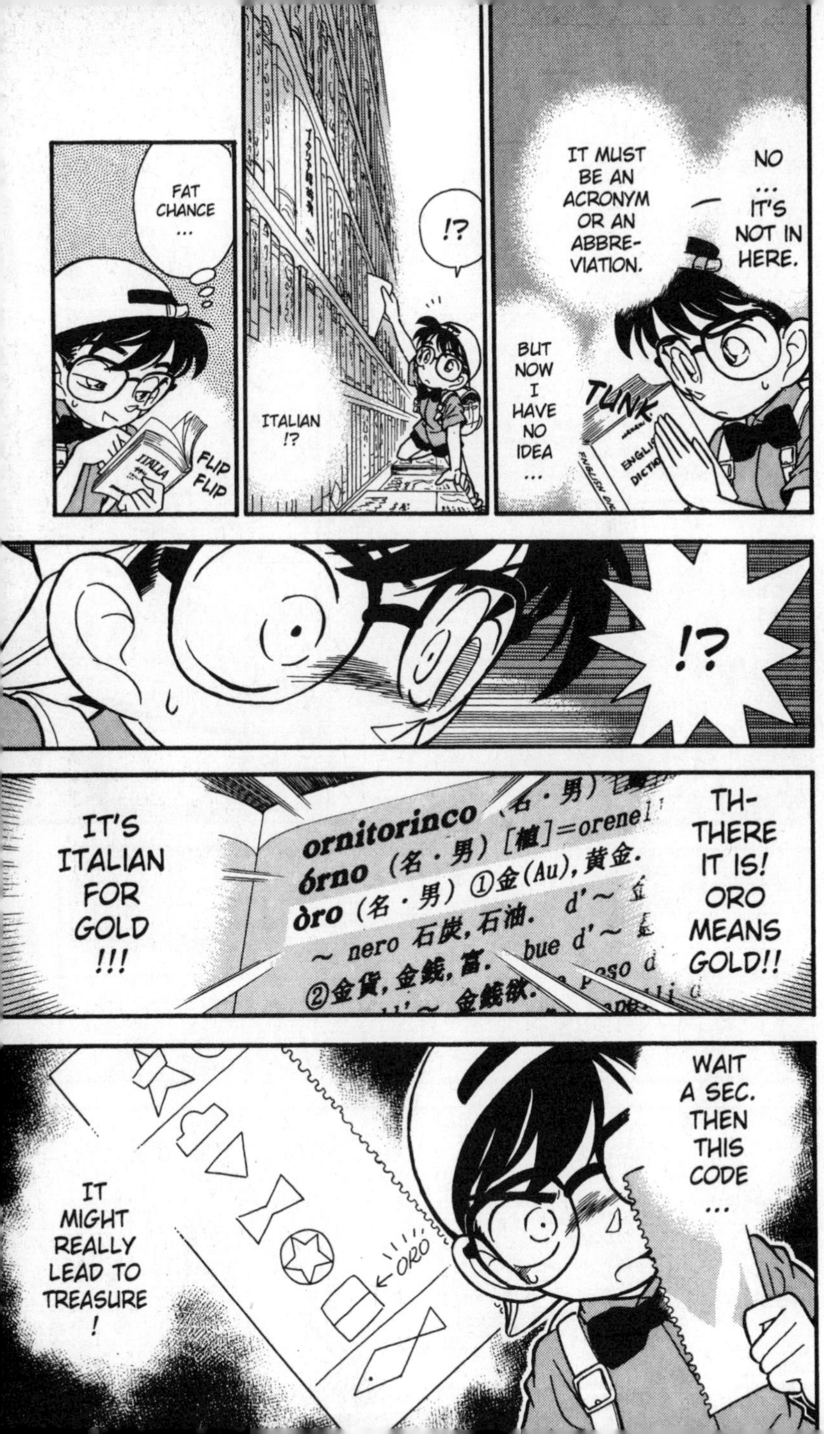
NO ... IT'S NOT IN HERE.
IT MUST BE AN ACRONYM OR AN ABBREVIATION.
TUNK
ENGLISH DICTIONARY
BUT NOW I HAVE NO IDEA ...
!?
ITALIAN !?
FAT CHANCE ...
ITALIA
FLIP FLIP
!?
TH-THERE IT IS! ORO MEANS GOLD!!
ornitorinco (名・男)
órno (名・男) [植]=ornel
òro (名・男) ①金(Au), 黄金.
~ nero 石炭, 石油. d'~
bue d'~
②金貨, 金銭, 富.
金銭欲
IT'S ITALIAN FOR GOLD !!!
WAIT A SEC. THEN THIS CODE ...
ORO
IT MIGHT REALLY LEAD TO TREASURE !

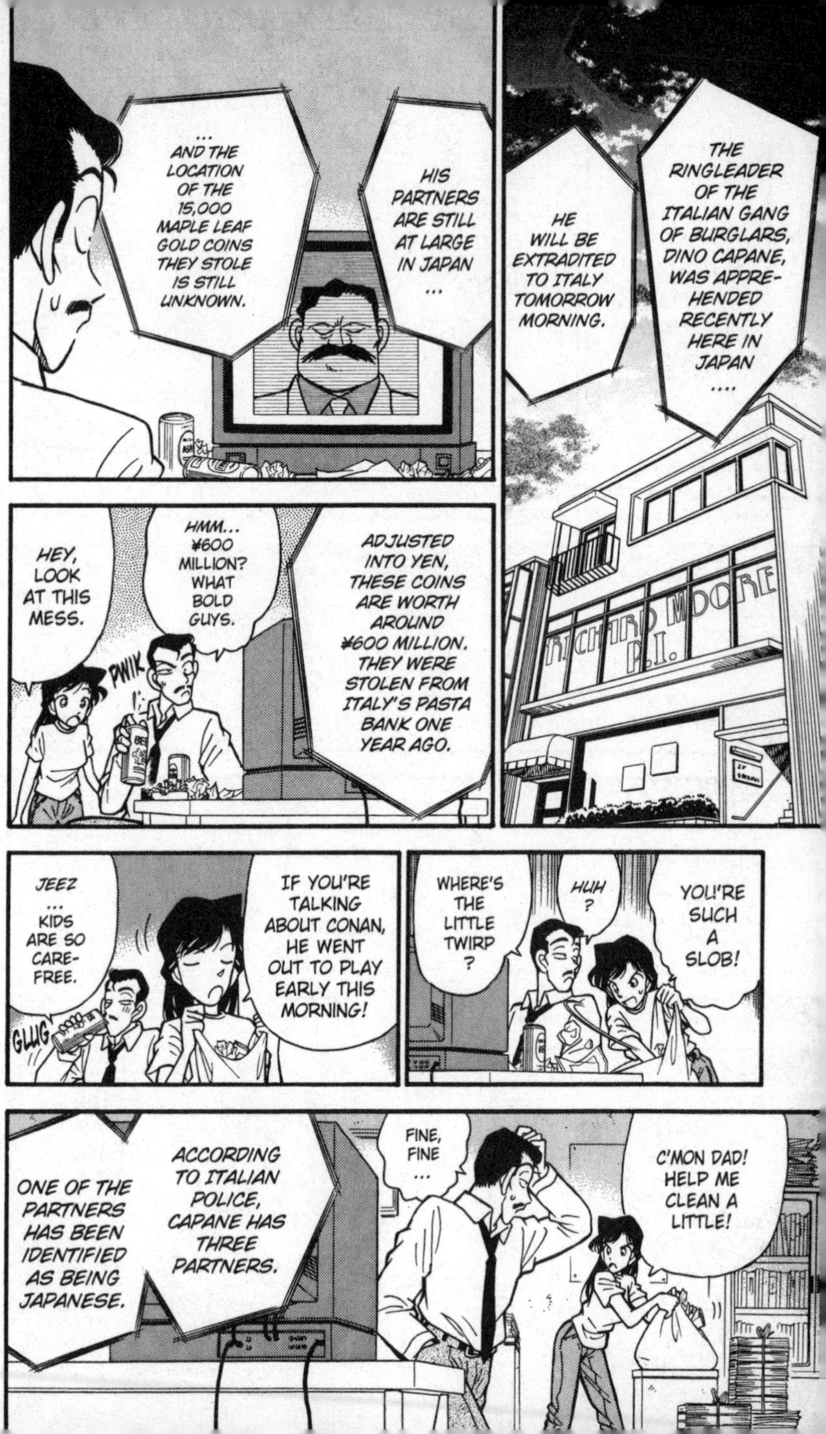
THE RINGLEADER OF THE ITALIAN GANG OF BURGLARS, DINO CAPANE, WAS APPREHENDED RECENTLY HERE IN JAPAN ....
HE WILL BE EXTRADITED TO ITALY TOMORROW MORNING.
RICHARD MOORE P.I.
HIS PARTNERS ARE STILL AT LARGE IN JAPAN ...
... AND THE LOCATION OF THE 15,000 MAPLE LEAF GOLD COINS THEY STOLE IS STILL UNKNOWN.
ADJUSTED INTO YEN, THESE COINS ARE WORTH AROUND ¥600 MILLION. THEY WERE STOLEN FROM ITALY'S PASTA BANK ONE YEAR AGO.
HMM... ¥600 MILLION? WHAT BOLD GUYS.
PWIK
HEY, LOOK AT THIS MESS.
YOU'RE SUCH A SLOB!
HUH ?
WHERE'S THE LITTLE TWIRP ?
IF YOU'RE TALKING ABOUT CONAN, HE WENT OUT TO PLAY EARLY THIS MORNING!
JEEZ ... KIDS ARE SO CAREFREE.
GLUG
C'MON DAD! HELP ME CLEAN A LITTLE!
FINE, FINE ...
ACCORDING TO ITALIAN POLICE, CAPANE HAS THREE PARTNERS.
ONE OF THE PARTNERS HAS BEEN IDENTIFIED AS BEING JAPANESE.

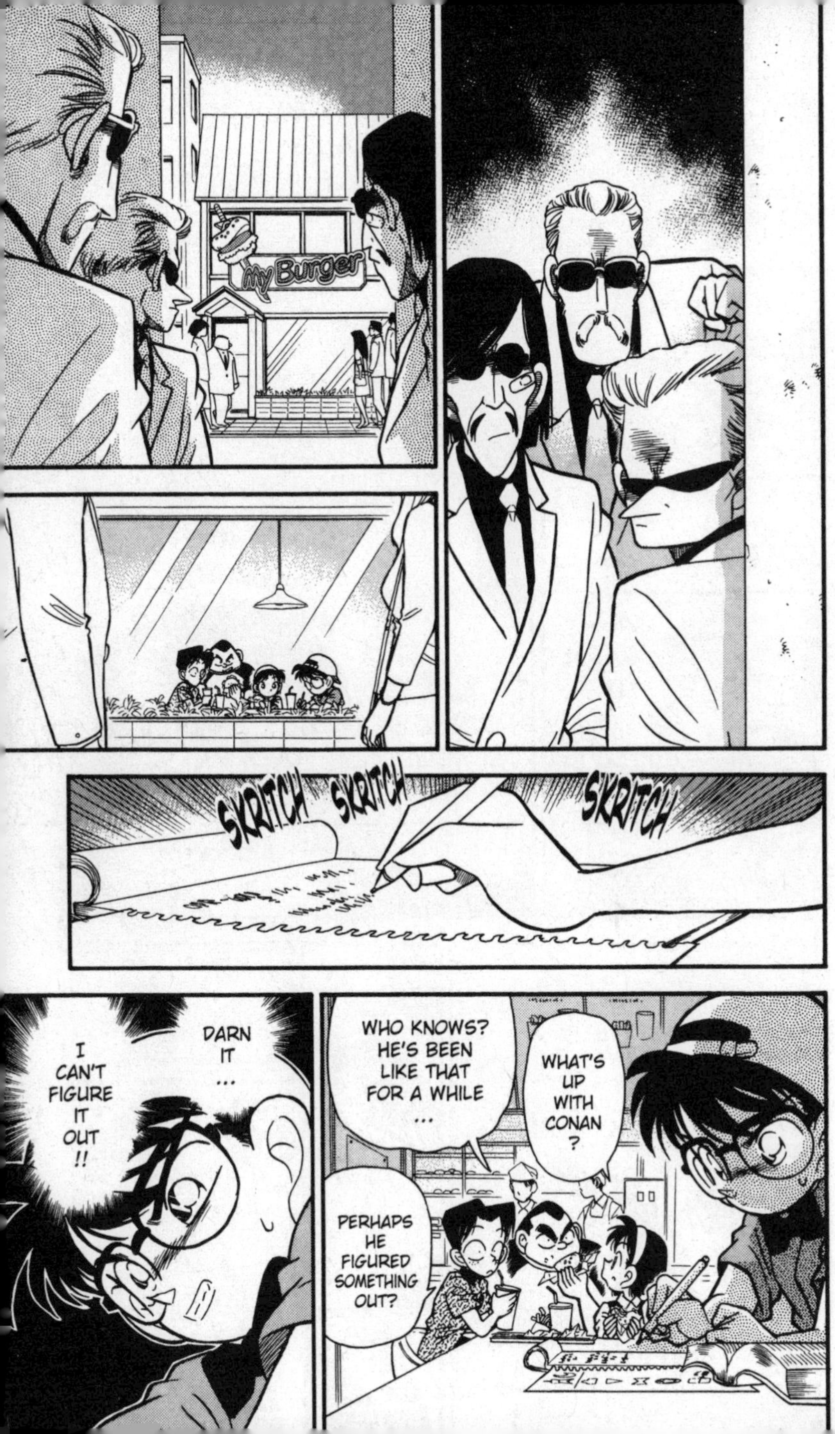
My Burger
SKRITCH
SKRITCH
SKRITCH
WHAT'S UP WITH CONAN?
WHO KNOWS? HE'S BEEN LIKE THAT FOR A WHILE ...
PERHAPS HE FIGURED SOMETHING OUT?
DARN IT ...
I CAN'T FIGURE IT OUT !!

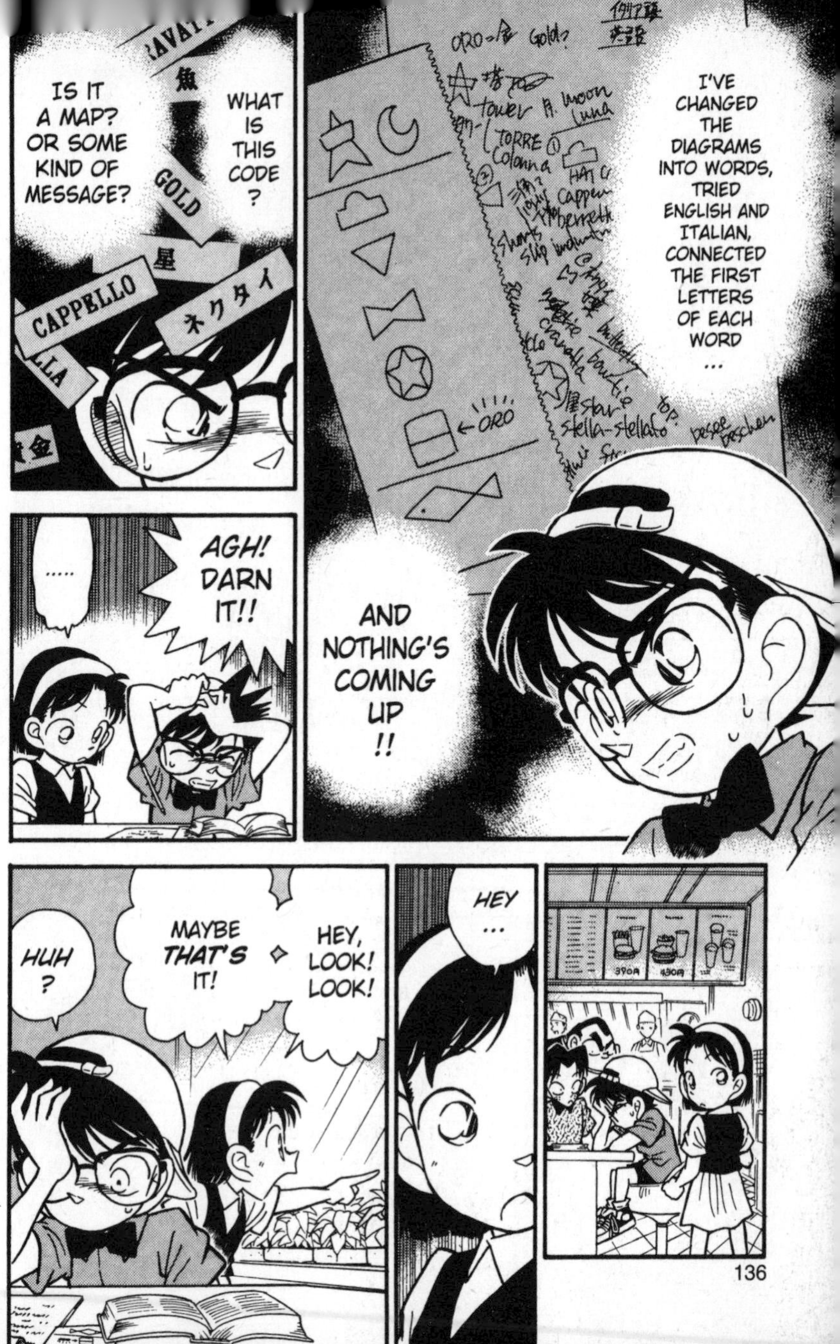
←ORO
I'VE CHANGED THE DIAGRAMS INTO WORDS, TRIED ENGLISH AND ITALIAN, CONNECTED THE FIRST LETTERS OF EACH WORD ...
AND NOTHING'S COMING UP !!
魚
GOLD
星
CAPPELLO
ネクタイ
WHAT IS THIS CODE ?
IS IT A MAP? OR SOME KIND OF MESSAGE?
AGH! DARN IT!!
......
HEY ...
HEY, LOOK! LOOK!
MAYBE THAT'S IT!
HUH ?

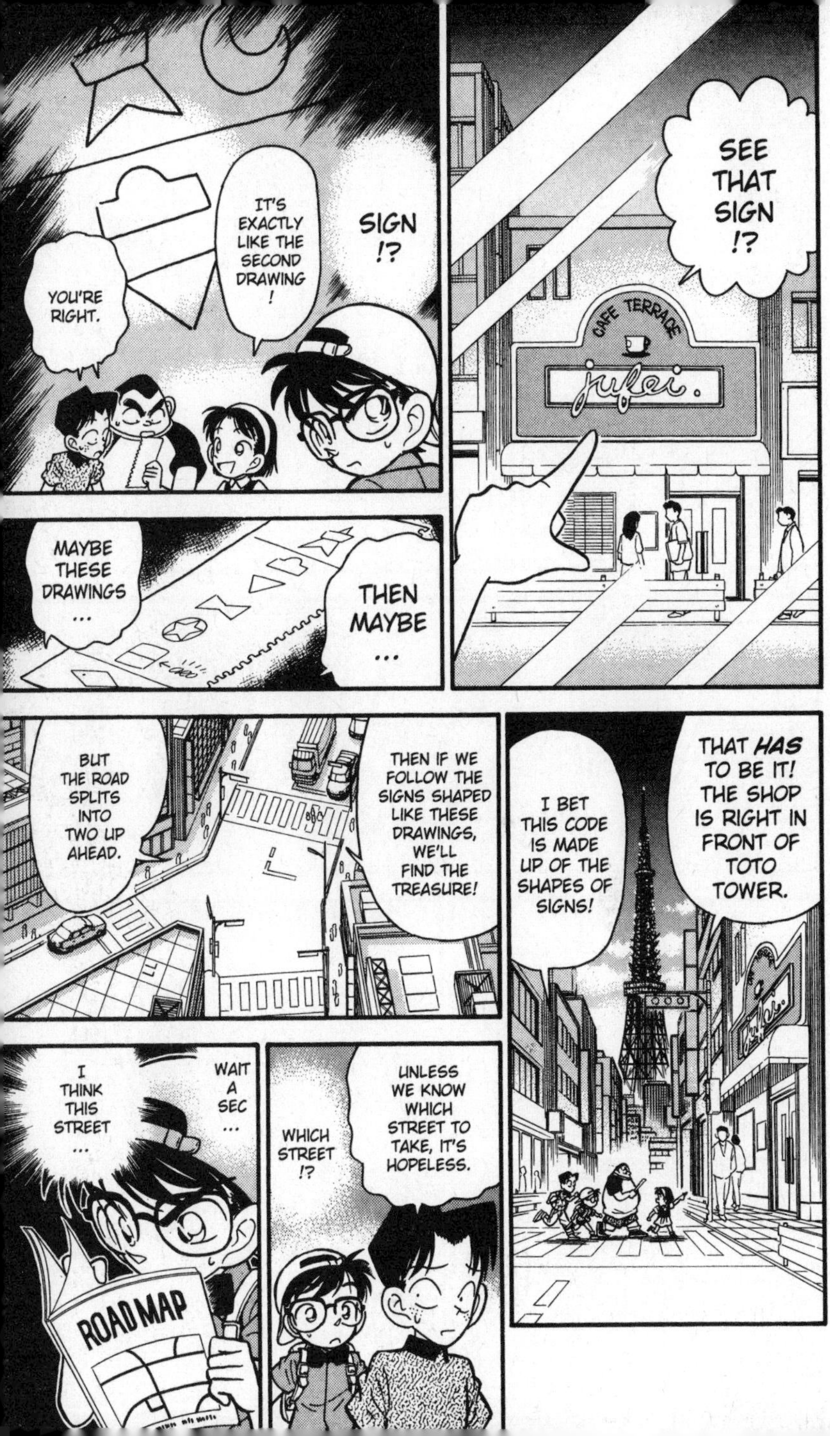
SEE THAT SIGN !?
CAFE TERRACE
jufei.
SIGN !?
IT'S EXACTLY LIKE THE SECOND DRAWING !
YOU'RE RIGHT.
THEN MAYBE ...
MAYBE THESE DRAWINGS ...
THAT HAS TO BE IT! THE SHOP IS RIGHT IN FRONT OF TOTO TOWER.
I BET THIS CODE IS MADE UP OF THE SHAPES OF SIGNS!
THEN IF WE FOLLOW THE SIGNS SHAPED LIKE THESE DRAWINGS, WE'LL FIND THE TREASURE!
BUT THE ROAD SPLITS INTO TWO UP AHEAD.
UNLESS WE KNOW WHICH STREET TO TAKE, IT'S HOPELESS.
WHICH STREET !?
WAIT A SEC ...
I THINK THIS STREET ...
ROAD MAP

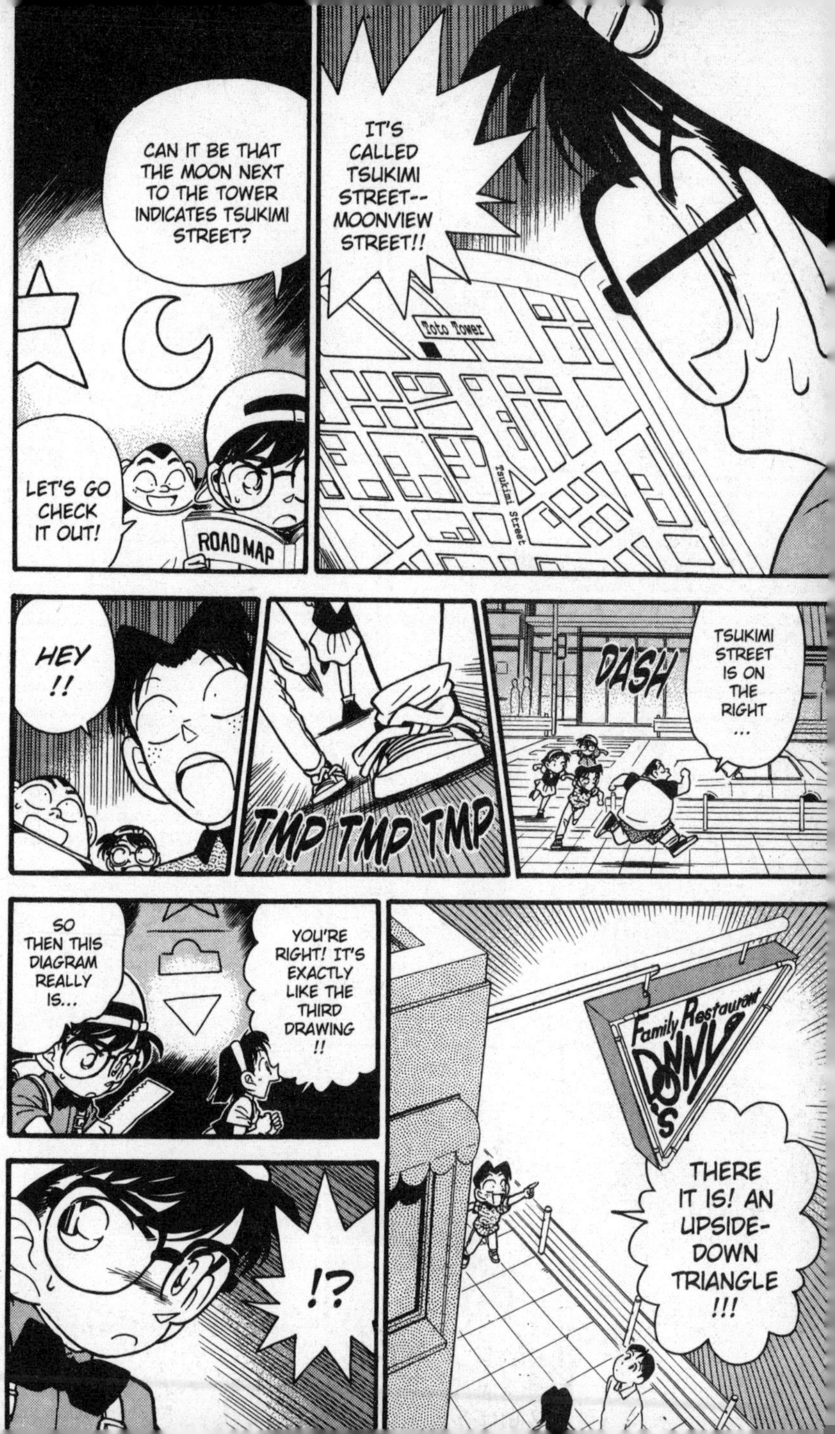
IT'S CALLED TSUKIMI STREET-- MOONVIEW STREET!!
Toto Tower
Tsukimi Street
CAN IT BE THAT THE MOON NEXT TO THE TOWER INDICATES TSUKIMI STREET?
LET'S GO CHECK IT OUT!
ROAD MAP
TSUKIMI STREET IS ON THE RIGHT ...
DASH
TMP TMP TMP
HEY !!
Family Restaurant
THERE IT IS! AN UPSIDE-DOWN TRIANGLE !!!
SO THEN THIS DIAGRAM REALLY IS...
YOU'RE RIGHT! IT'S EXACTLY LIKE THE THIRD DRAWING !!
!?

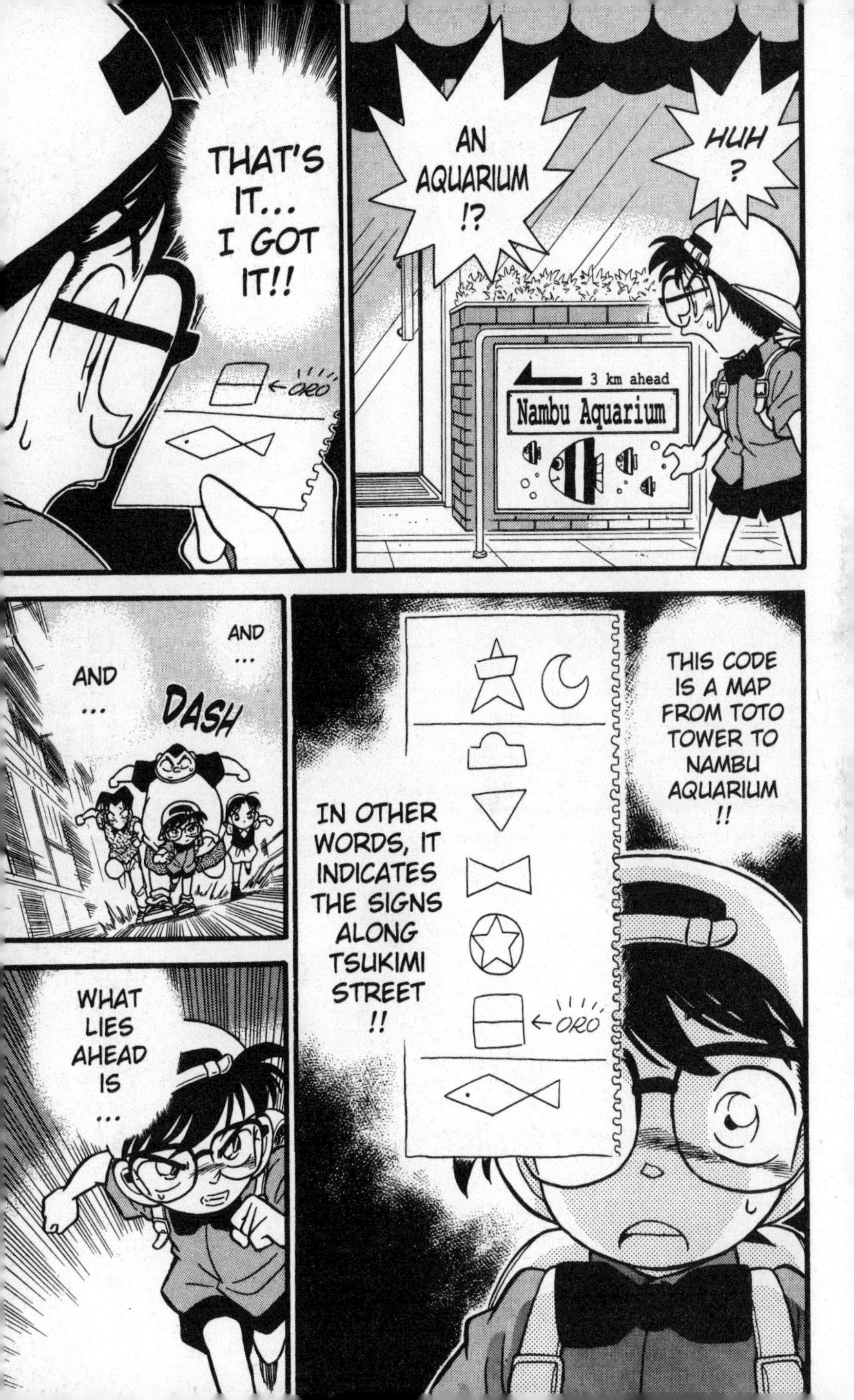
HUH ?
AN AQUARIUM !?
3 km ahead
Nambu Aquarium
THAT'S IT... I GOT IT!!
ORO
THIS CODE IS A MAP FROM TOTO TOWER TO NAMBU AQUARIUM !!
IN OTHER WORDS, IT INDICATES THE SIGNS ALONG TSUKIMI STREET !!
ORO
AND ...
AND ...
DASH
WHAT LIES AHEAD IS ...

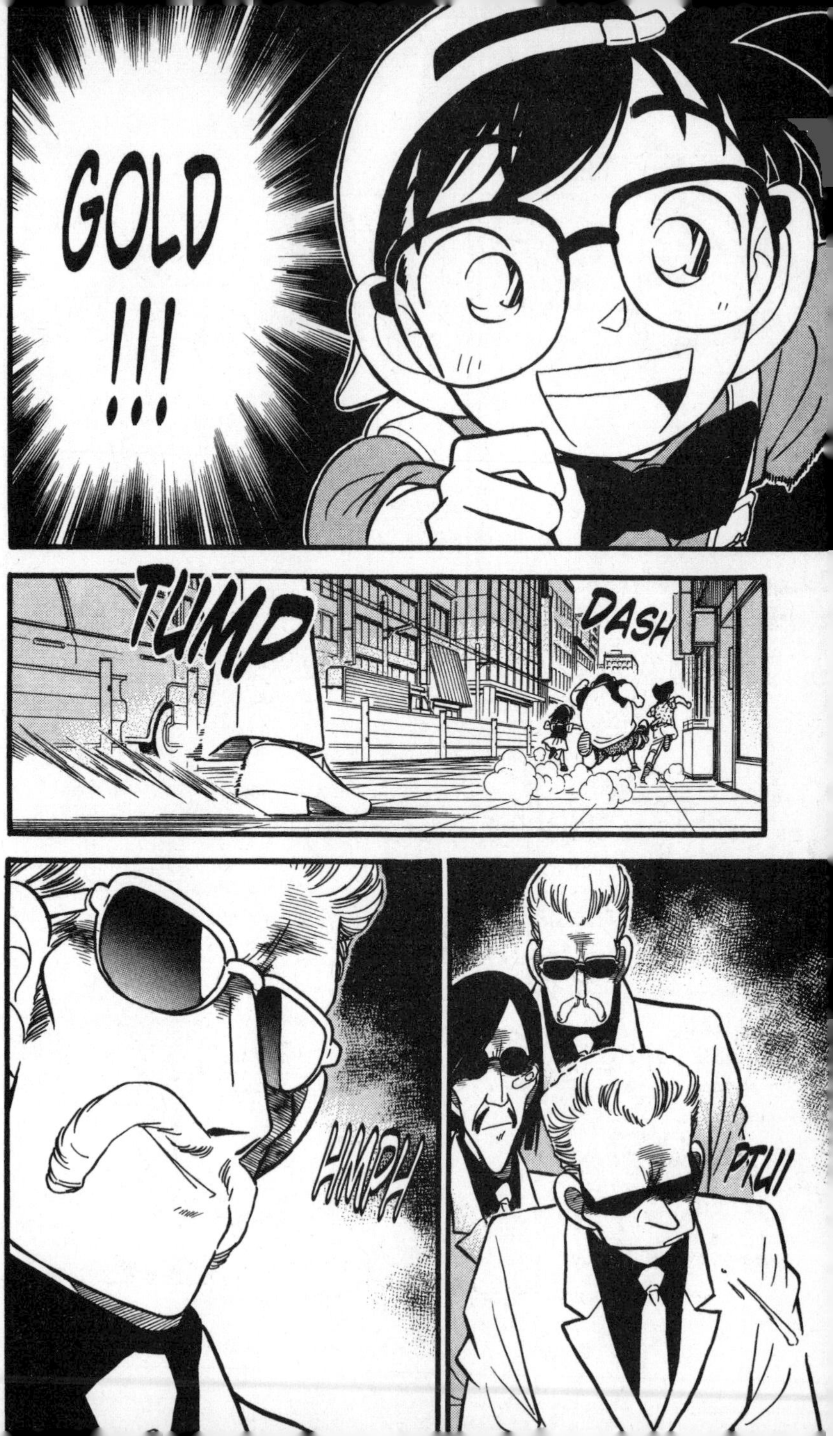
GOLD !!!
DASH
TUMP
PTUI
HMPH

FILE 9: THE ANSWER AND ANOTHER ANSWER

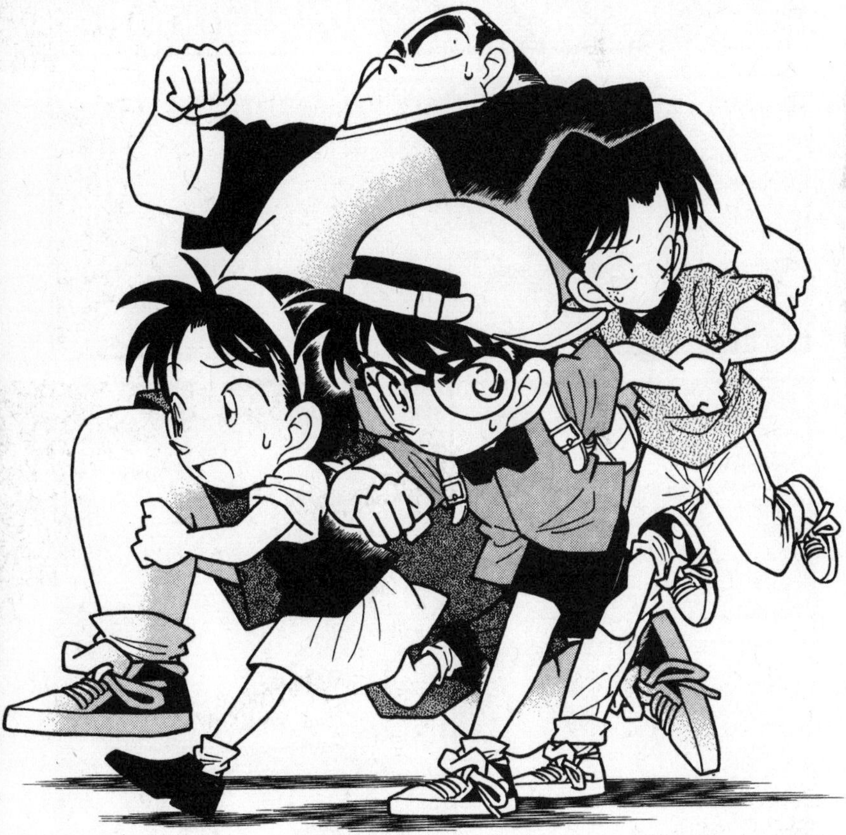

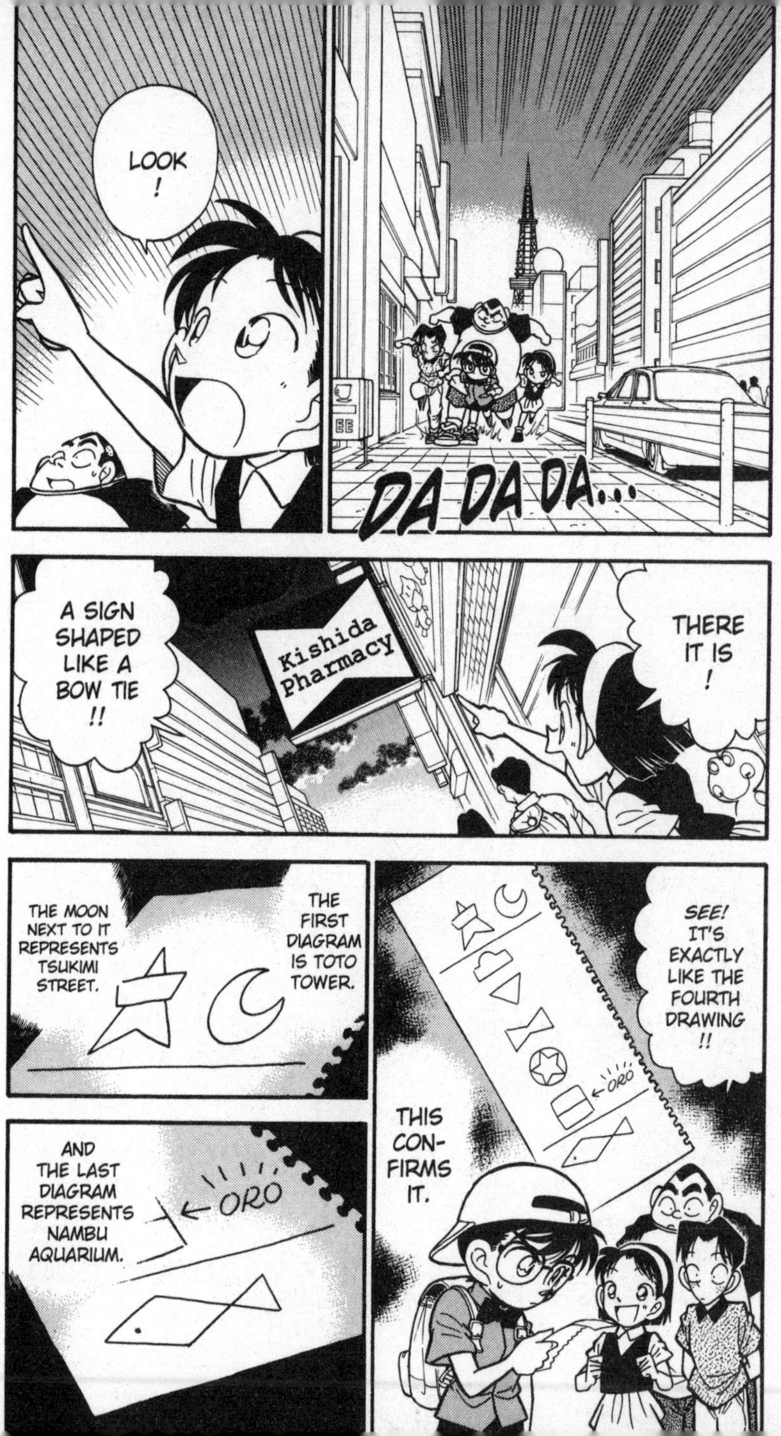

DA DA DA...
LOOK!
THERE IT IS!
Kishida Pharmacy
A SIGN SHAPED LIKE A BOW TIE!!
SEE! IT'S EXACTLY LIKE THE FOURTH DRAWING!!
ORO
THIS CON-FIRMS IT.
THE FIRST DIAGRAM IS TOTO TOWER.
THE MOON NEXT TO IT REPRESENTS TSUKIMI STREET.
AND THE LAST DIAGRAM REPRESENTS NAMBU AQUARIUM.
ORO

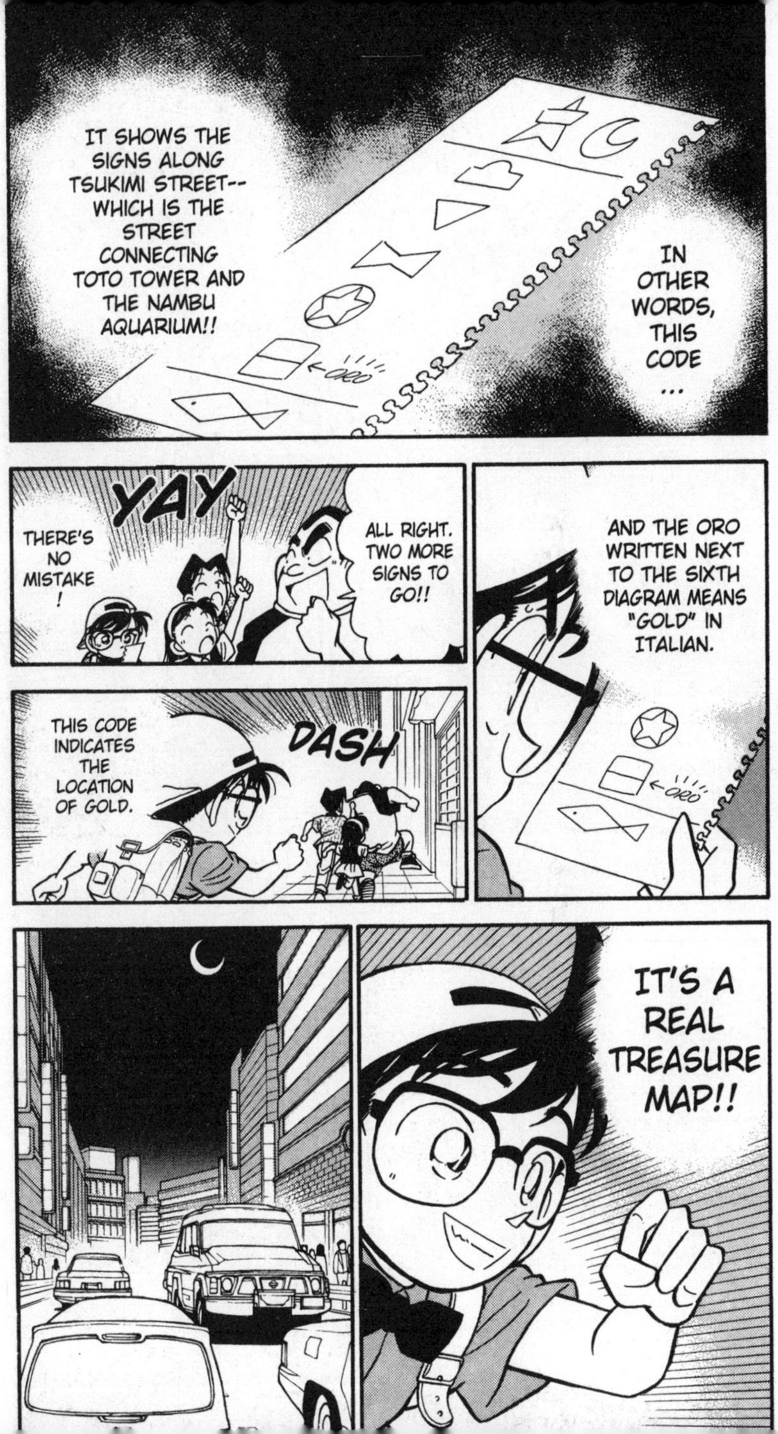
IT SHOWS THE SIGNS ALONG TSUKIMI STREET-- WHICH IS THE STREET CONNECTING TOTO TOWER AND THE NAMBU AQUARIUM!!
ORO
IN OTHER WORDS, THIS CODE ...
YAY
THERE'S NO MISTAKE !
ALL RIGHT. TWO MORE SIGNS TO GO!!
THIS CODE INDICATES THE LOCATION OF GOLD.
DASH
AND THE ORO WRITTEN NEXT TO THE SIXTH DIAGRAM MEANS "GOLD" IN ITALIAN.
ORO
IT'S A REAL TREASURE MAP!!

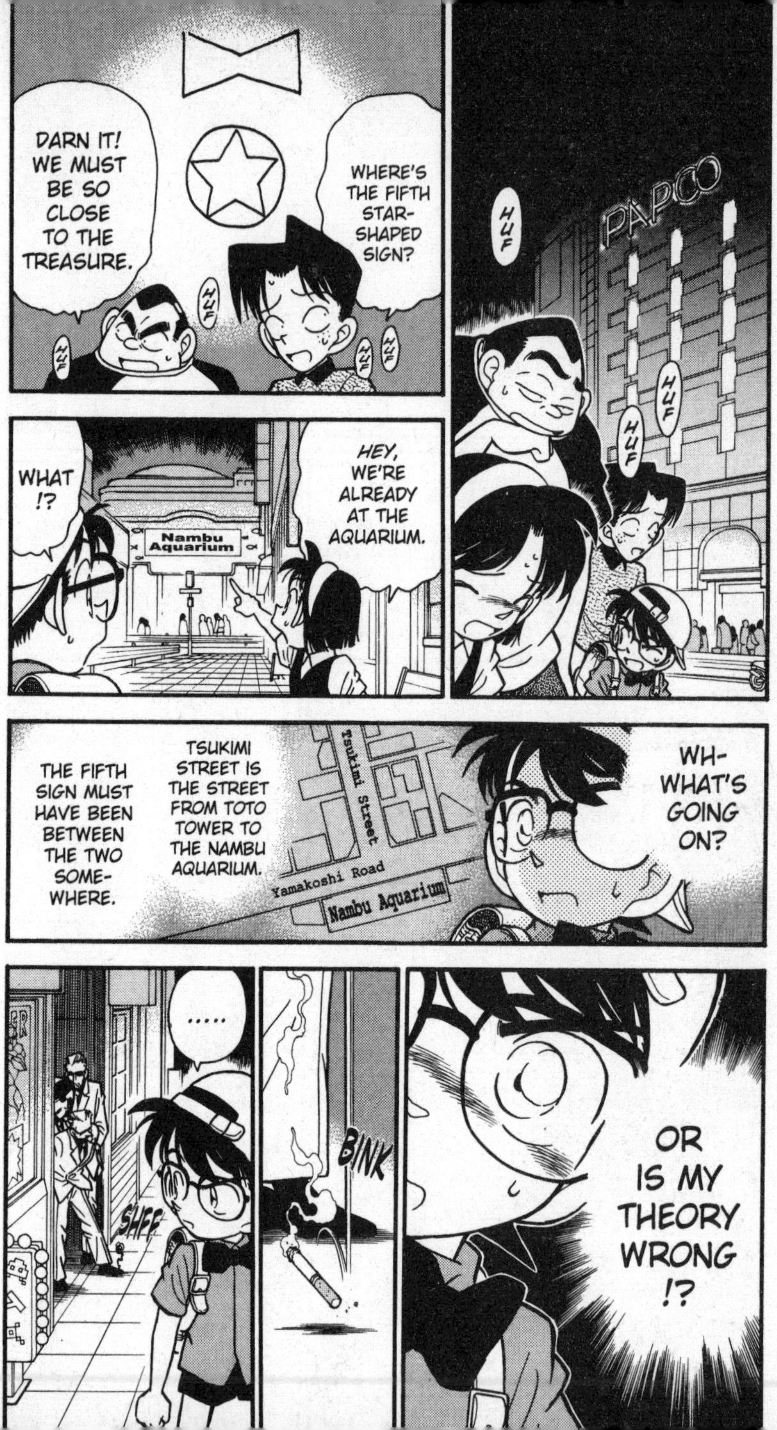
HUF
PARCO
HUF
HUF
WHERE'S THE FIFTH STAR-SHAPED SIGN?
DARN IT! WE MUST BE SO CLOSE TO THE TREASURE.
HUF
HUF
HUF
HUF
HEY, WE'RE ALREADY AT THE AQUARIUM.
WHAT !?
Nambu Aquarium
WH-WHAT'S GOING ON?
Tsukimi Street
Yamakoshi Road
Nambu Aquarium
TSUKIMI STREET IS THE STREET FROM TOTO TOWER TO THE NAMBU AQUARIUM.
THE FIFTH SIGN MUST HAVE BEEN BETWEEN THE TWO SOME-WHERE.
OR IS MY THEORY WRONG !?
BINK
.....
SHFF

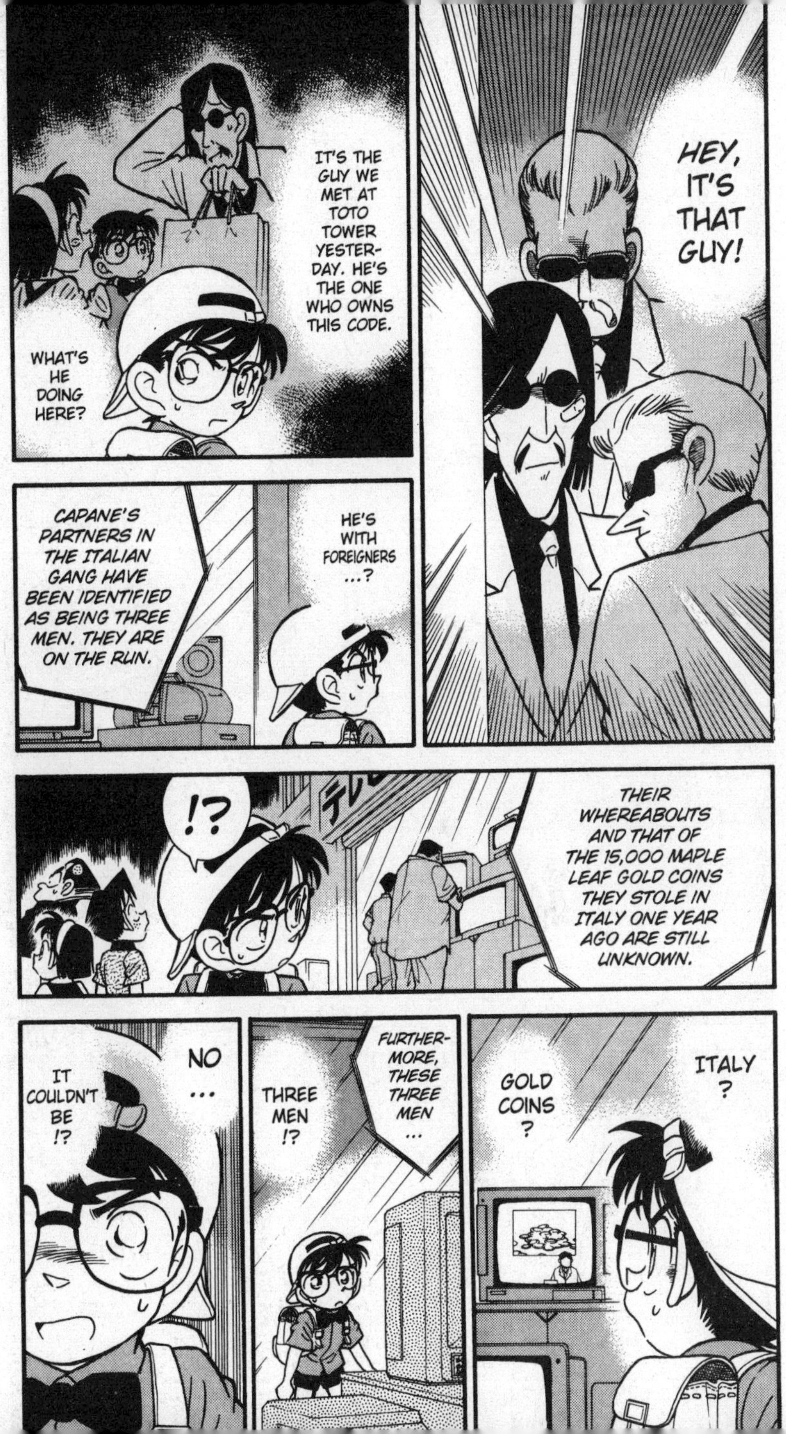
HEY, IT'S THAT GUY!
IT'S THE GUY WE MET AT TOTO TOWER YESTER-DAY. HE'S THE ONE WHO OWNS THIS CODE.
WHAT'S HE DOING HERE?
HE'S WITH FOREIGNERS ...?
CAPANE'S PARTNERS IN THE ITALIAN GANG HAVE BEEN IDENTIFIED AS BEING THREE MEN. THEY ARE ON THE RUN.
THEIR WHEREABOUTS AND THAT OF THE 15,000 MAPLE LEAF GOLD COINS THEY STOLE IN ITALY ONE YEAR AGO ARE STILL UNKNOWN.
!?
ITALY ?
GOLD COINS ?
FURTHER-MORE, THESE THREE MEN ...
THREE MEN !?
NO ...
IT COULDN'T BE !?

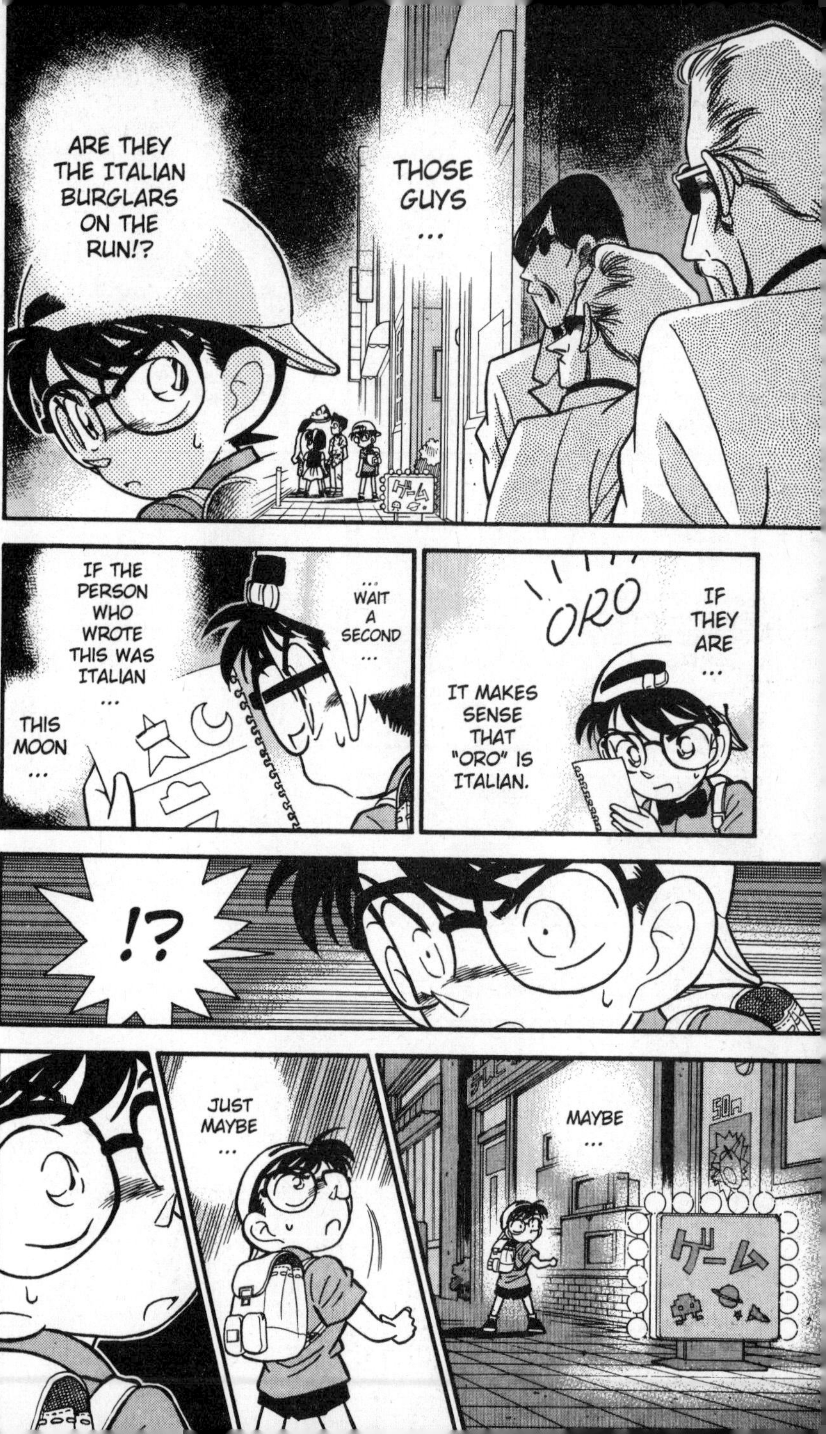
THOSE GUYS ...
ARE THEY THE ITALIAN BURGLARS ON THE RUN!?
ゲーム
ORO
IF THEY ARE ...
IT MAKES SENSE THAT "ORO" IS ITALIAN.
... WAIT A SECOND ...
IF THE PERSON WHO WROTE THIS WAS ITALIAN ...
THIS MOON ...
!?
MAYBE ...
ゲーム
JUST MAYBE ...

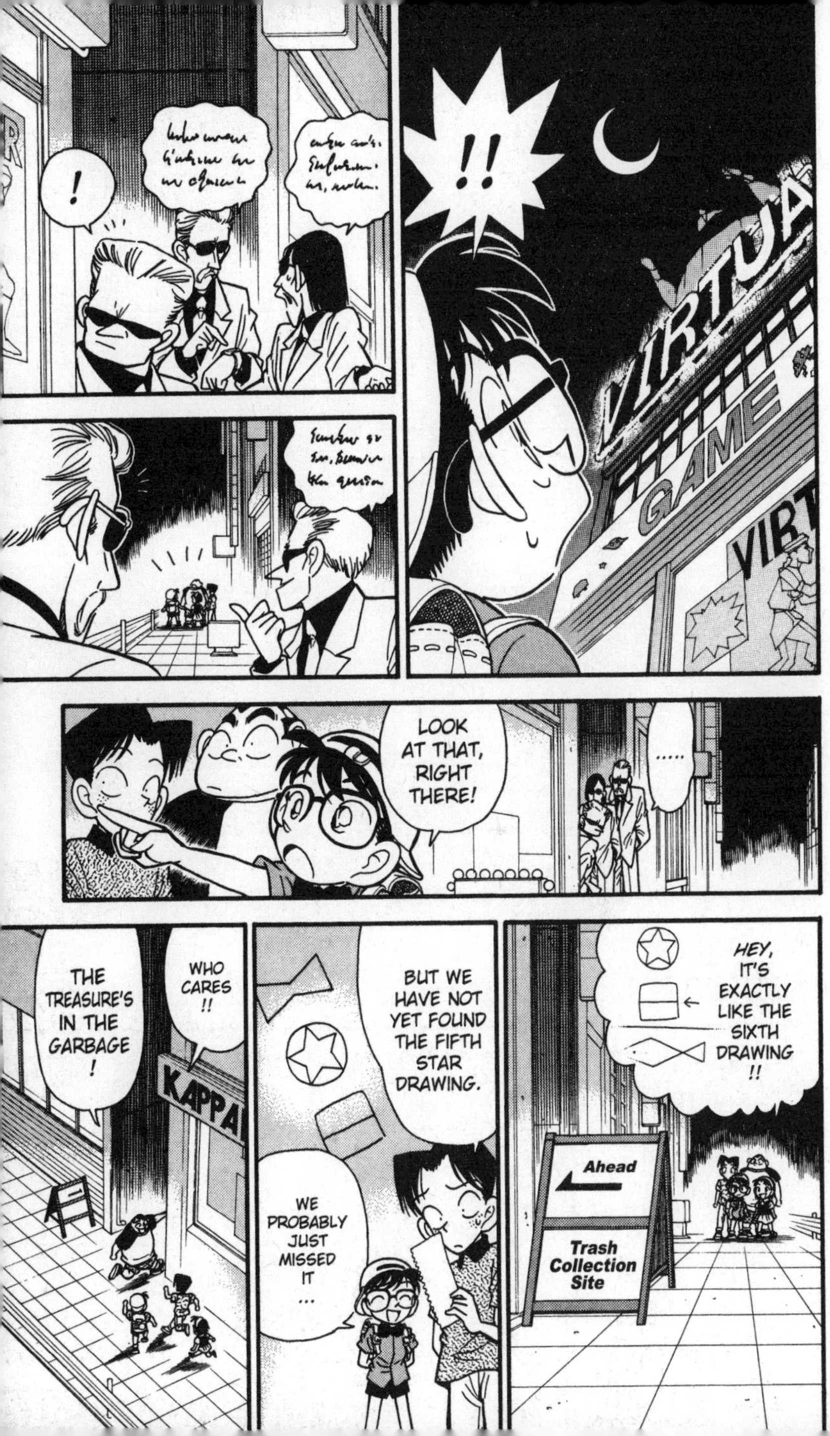
!!
GAME
!
.....
LOOK AT THAT, RIGHT THERE!
HEY, IT'S EXACTLY LIKE THE SIXTH DRAWING !!
Ahead
Trash Collection Site
BUT WE HAVE NOT YET FOUND THE FIFTH STAR DRAWING.
WE PROBABLY JUST MISSED IT ...
WHO CARES !!
THE TREASURE'S IN THE GARBAGE !

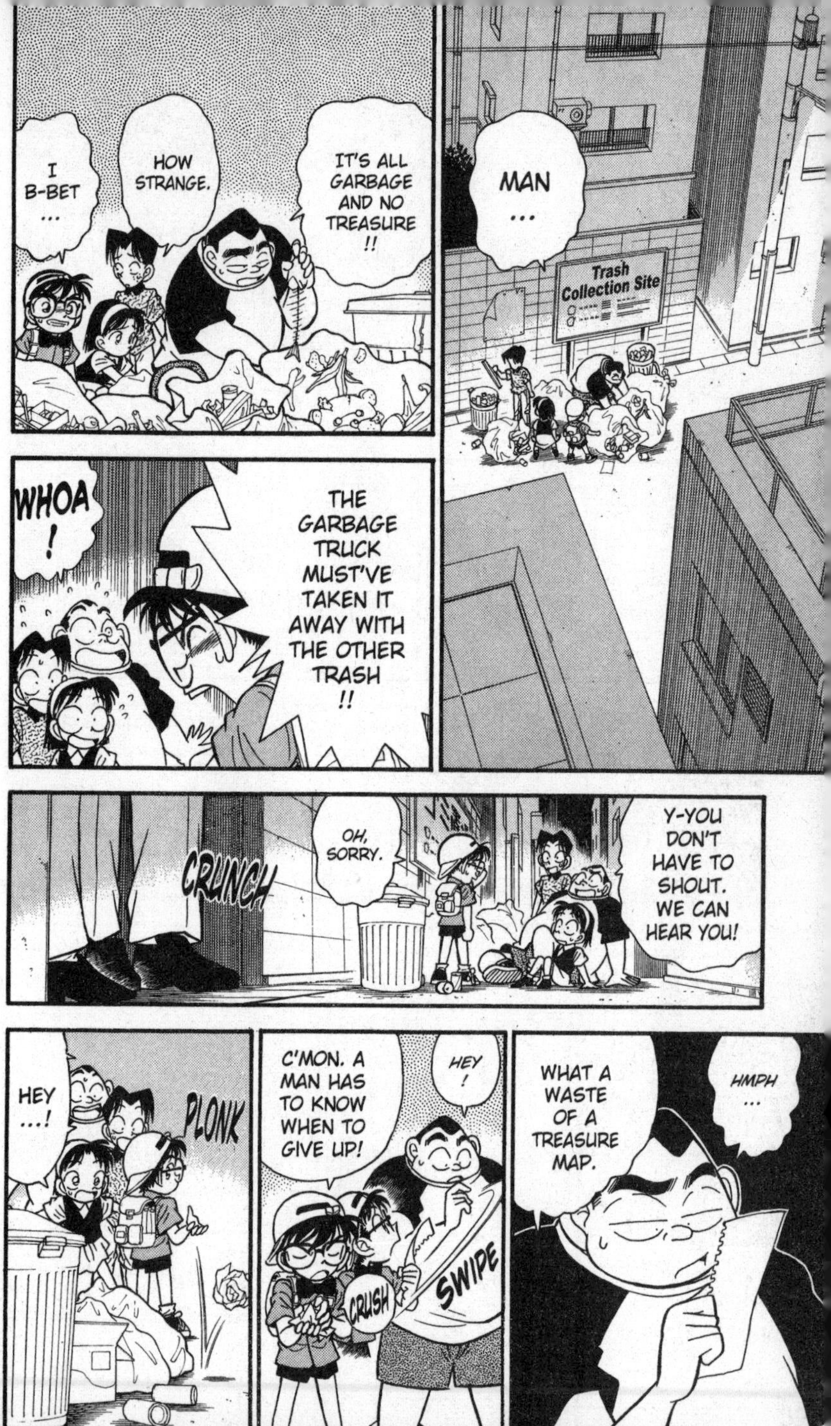
MAN ...
Trash Collection Site
IT'S ALL GARBAGE AND NO TREASURE !!
HOW STRANGE.
I B-BET ...
THE GARBAGE TRUCK MUST'VE TAKEN IT AWAY WITH THE OTHER TRASH !!
WHOA !
Y-YOU DON'T HAVE TO SHOUT. WE CAN HEAR YOU!
OH, SORRY.
CRUNCH
HMPH ...
WHAT A WASTE OF A TREASURE MAP.
HEY !
C'MON. A MAN HAS TO KNOW WHEN TO GIVE UP!
SWIPE
CRUSH
PLONK
HEY ...!

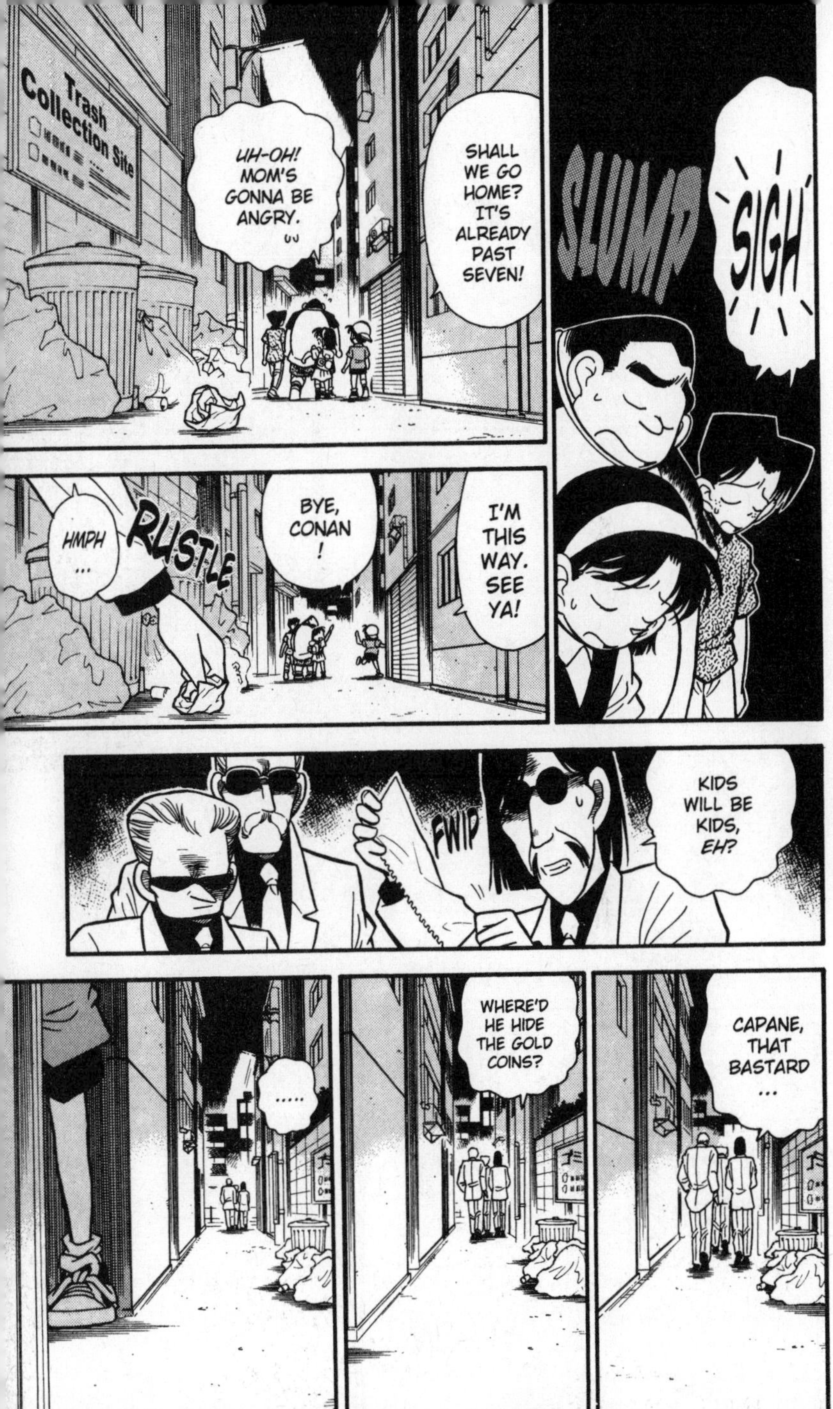
SLUMP
SIGH
SHALL WE GO HOME? IT'S ALREADY PAST SEVEN!
UH-OH! MOM'S GONNA BE ANGRY.
Trash Collection Site
I'M THIS WAY. SEE YA!
BYE, CONAN!
RUSTLE
HMPH ...
KIDS WILL BE KIDS, EH?
FWIP
CAPANE, THAT BASTARD ...
WHERE'D HE HIDE THE GOLD COINS?
......

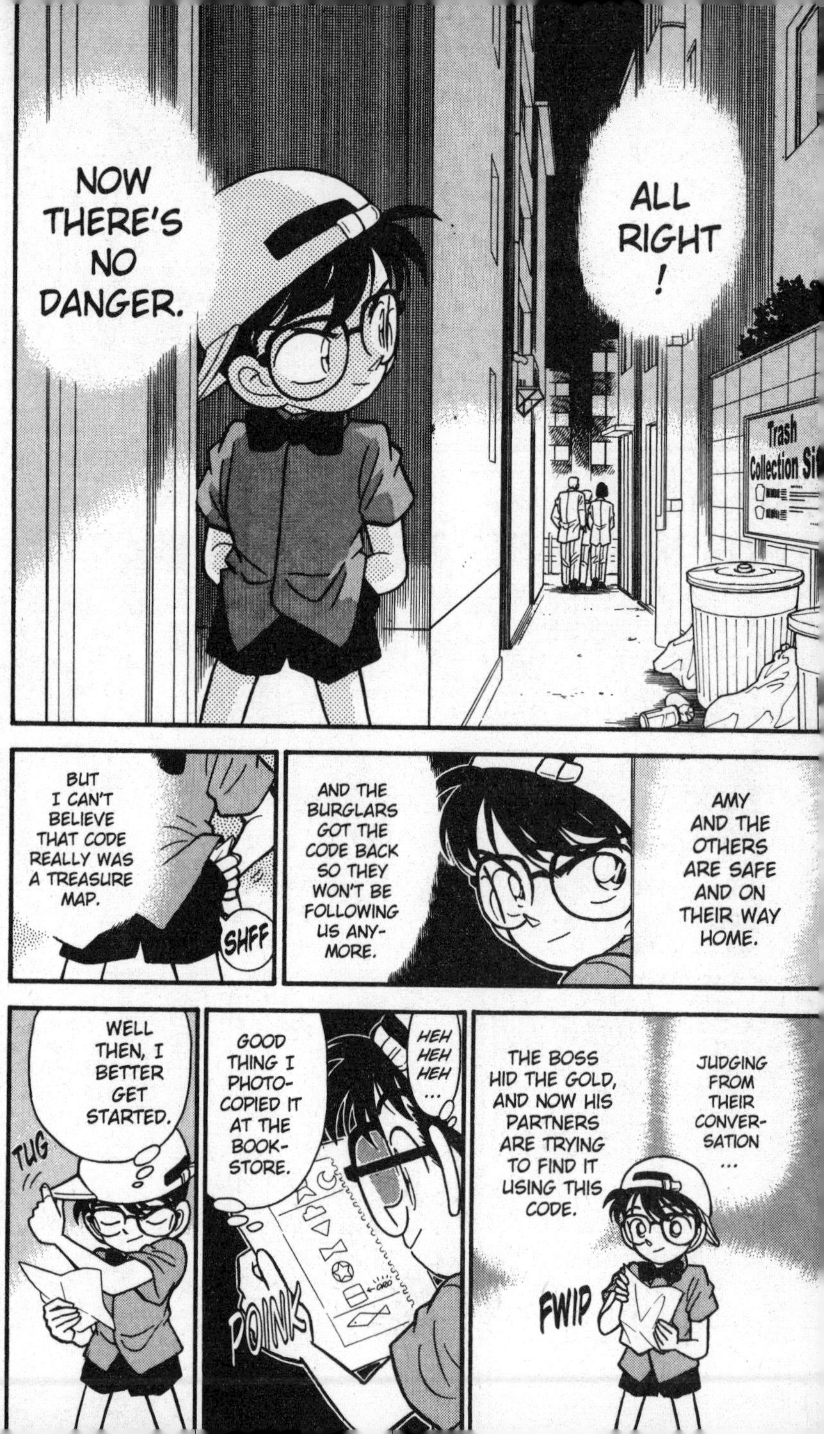
ALL RIGHT!
NOW THERE'S NO DANGER.
Trash Collection Si
AMY AND THE OTHERS ARE SAFE AND ON THEIR WAY HOME.
AND THE BURGLARS GOT THE CODE BACK SO THEY WON'T BE FOLLOWING US ANY-MORE.
BUT I CAN'T BELIEVE THAT CODE REALLY WAS A TREASURE MAP.
SHFF
JUDGING FROM THEIR CONVER-SATION...
THE BOSS HID THE GOLD, AND NOW HIS PARTNERS ARE TRYING TO FIND IT USING THIS CODE.
FWIP
HEH HEH HEH...
GOOD THING I PHOTO-COPIED IT AT THE BOOK-STORE.
POINK
WELL THEN, I BETTER GET STARTED.
TUG

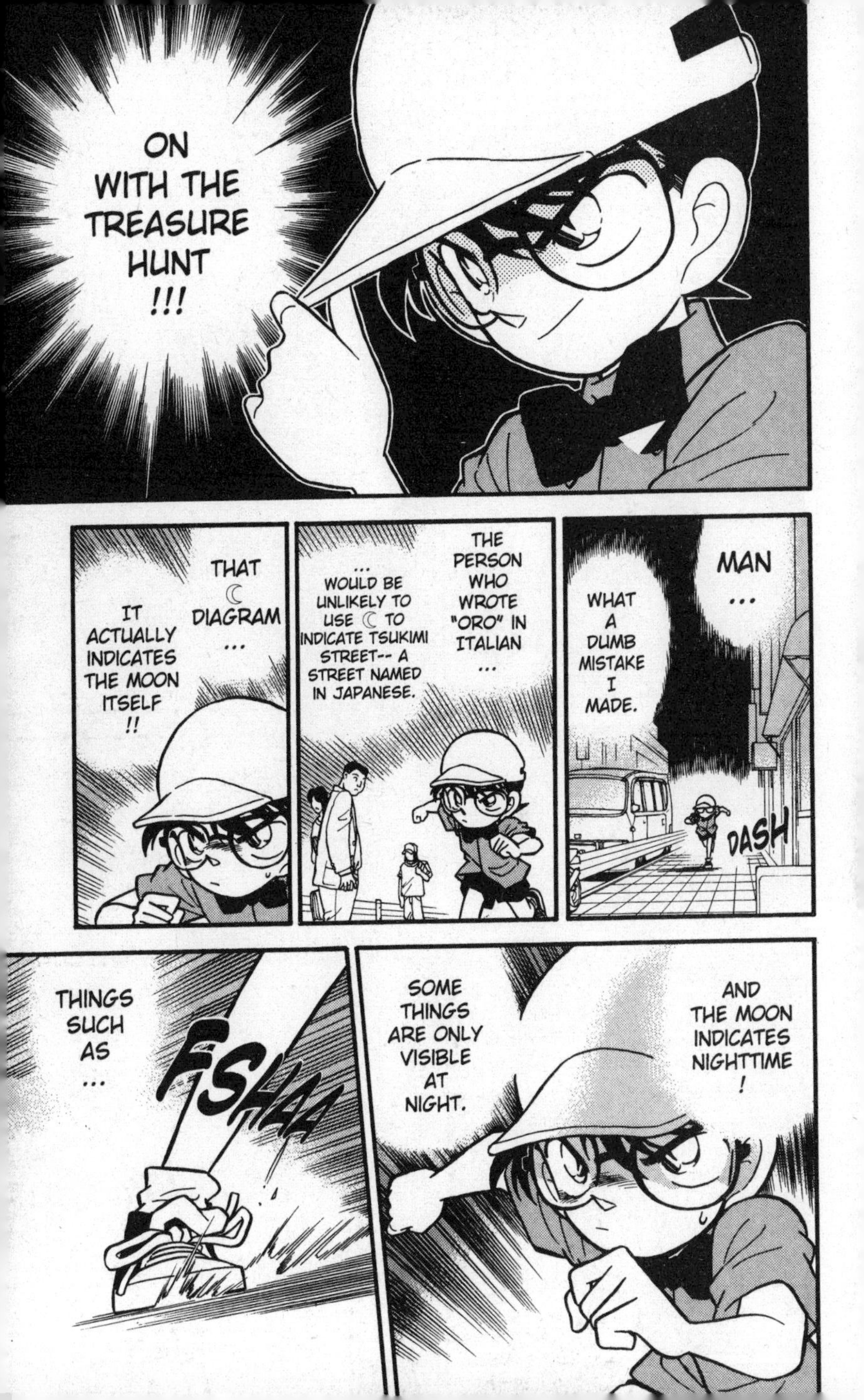
ON WITH THE TREASURE HUNT !!!
MAN ...
WHAT A DUMB MISTAKE I MADE.
DASH
THE PERSON WHO WROTE "ORO" IN ITALIAN ...
... WOULD BE UNLIKELY TO USE ☾ TO INDICATE TSUKIMI STREET-- A STREET NAMED IN JAPANESE.
THAT ☾ DIAGRAM ...
IT ACTUALLY INDICATES THE MOON ITSELF !!
AND THE MOON INDICATES NIGHTTIME !
SOME THINGS ARE ONLY VISIBLE AT NIGHT.
THINGS SUCH AS ...
FSHAA

NEON SIGNS !!

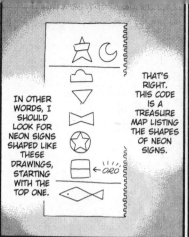

THAT'S RIGHT. THIS CODE IS A TREASURE MAP LISTING THE SHAPES OF NEON SIGNS.

IN OTHER WORDS, I SHOULD LOOK FOR NEON SIGNS SHAPED LIKE THESE DRAWINGS, STARTING WITH THE TOP ONE.

←ORO

FROM EACH SIGN, I'LL GO TO THE NEXT ONE THAT CAN BE SEEN FROM THERE.

ピッグカメラ

THAT SHOULD LEAD ME TO WHERE THE GOLD COINS ARE HIDDEN.

LOOKS LIKE I'M RIGHT THIS TIME.

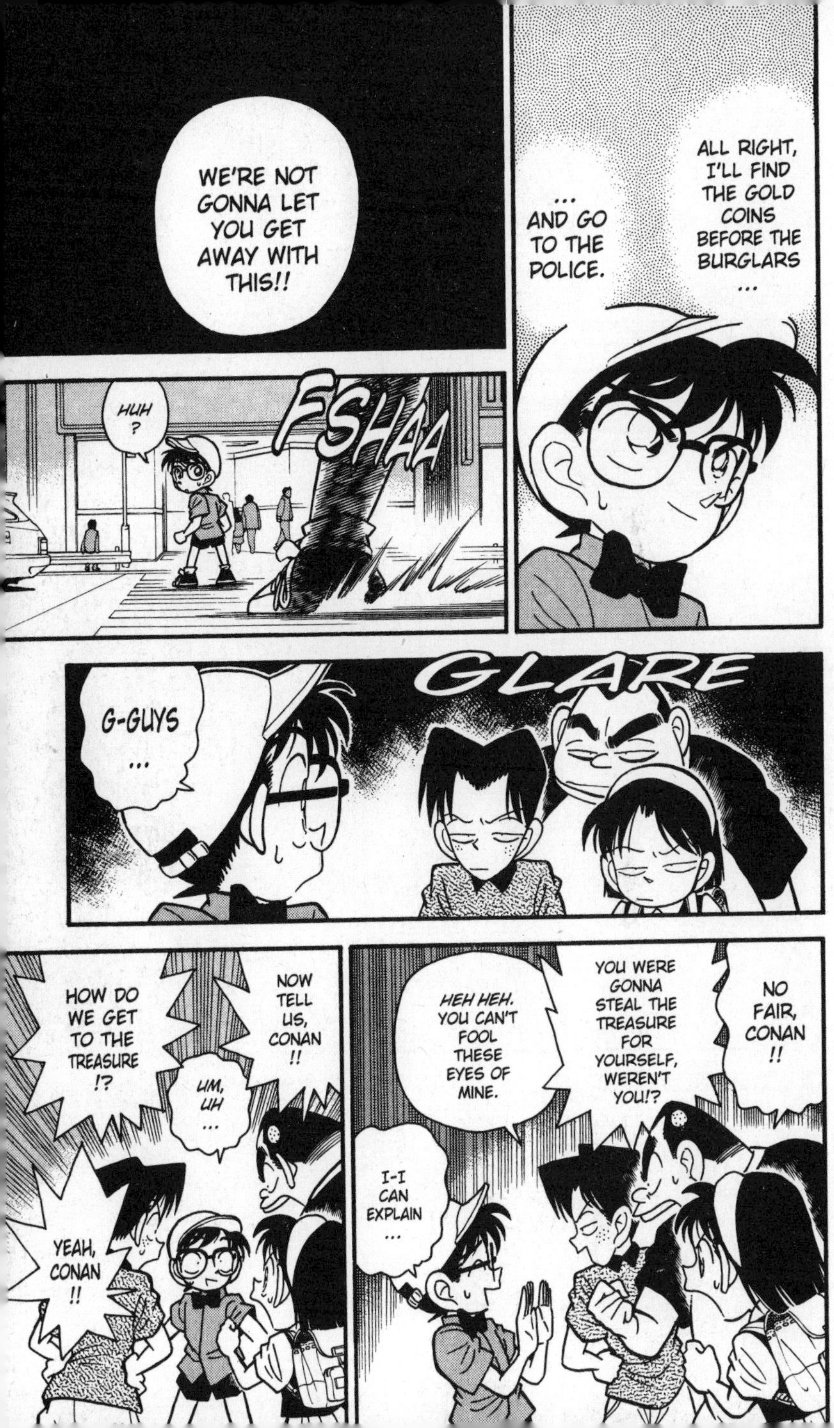
ALL RIGHT, I'LL FIND THE GOLD COINS BEFORE THE BURGLARS ...
... AND GO TO THE POLICE.
WE'RE NOT GONNA LET YOU GET AWAY WITH THIS!!
FSHAA
HUH ?
GLARE
G-GUYS ...
NO FAIR, CONAN !!
YOU WERE GONNA STEAL THE TREASURE FOR YOURSELF, WEREN'T YOU!?
HEH HEH. YOU CAN'T FOOL THESE EYES OF MINE.
I-I CAN EXPLAIN ...
NOW TELL US, CONAN !!
HOW DO WE GET TO THE TREASURE !?
UM, UH ...
YEAH, CONAN !!

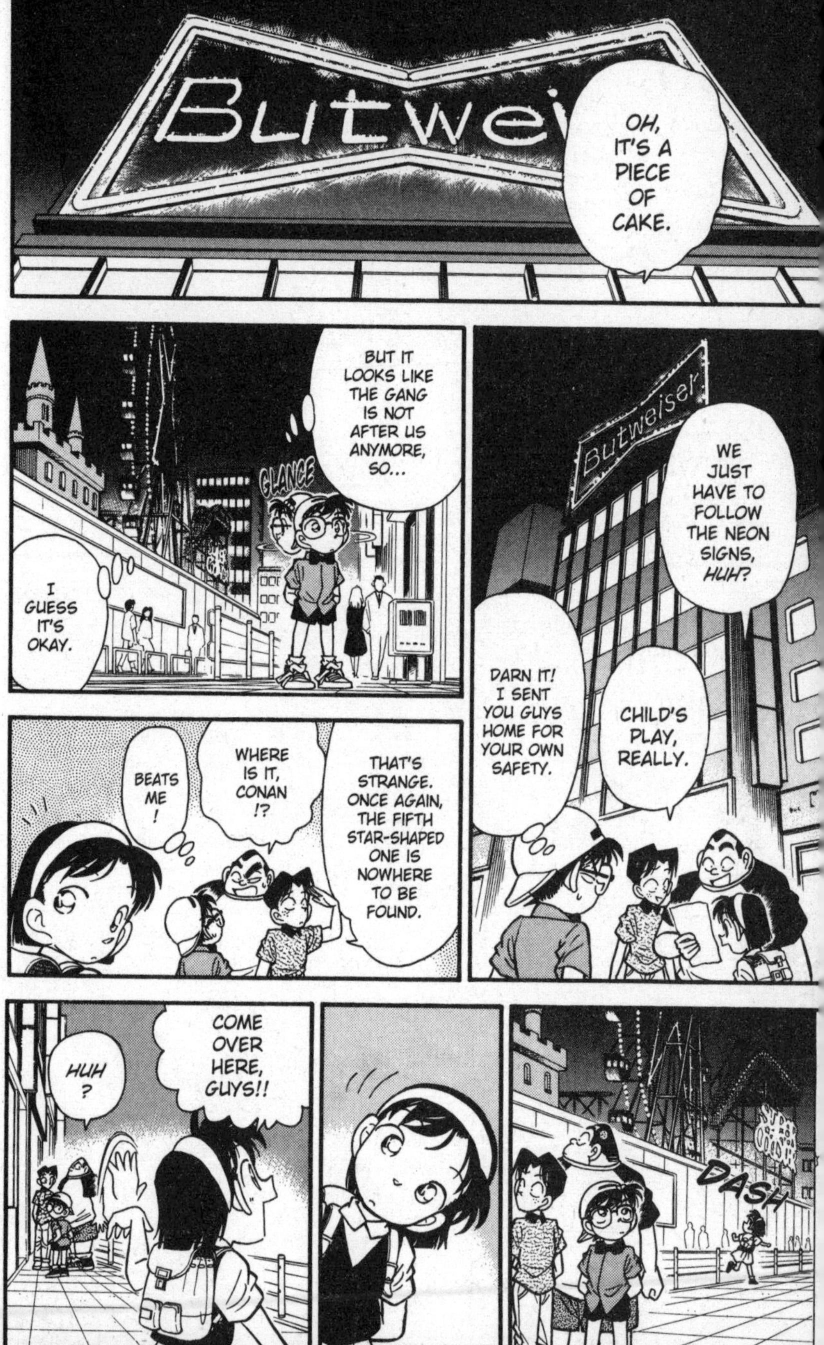
Butwei
OH, IT'S A PIECE OF CAKE.
Butweiser
WE JUST HAVE TO FOLLOW THE NEON SIGNS, *HUH?*
CHILD'S PLAY, REALLY.
DARN IT! I SENT YOU GUYS HOME FOR YOUR OWN SAFETY.
BUT IT LOOKS LIKE THE GANG IS NOT AFTER US ANYMORE, SO...
GLANCE
I GUESS IT'S OKAY.
THAT'S STRANGE. ONCE AGAIN, THE FIFTH STAR-SHAPED ONE IS NOWHERE TO BE FOUND.
WHERE IS IT, CONAN !?
BEATS ME !
DASH
COME OVER HERE, GUYS!!
HUH ?

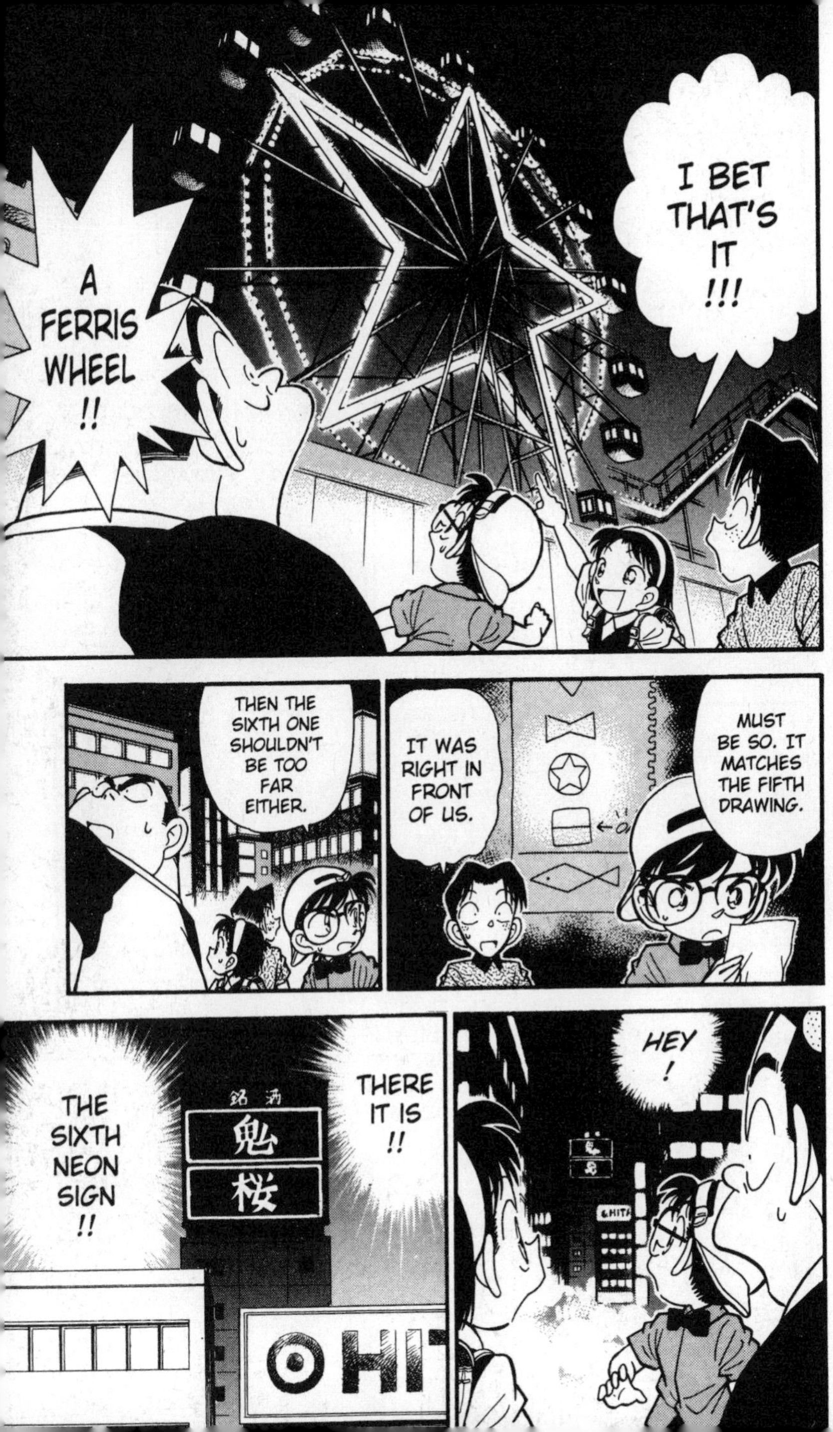
I BET THAT'S IT !!!
A FERRIS WHEEL !!
MUST BE SO. IT MATCHES THE FIFTH DRAWING.
IT WAS RIGHT IN FRONT OF US.
THEN THE SIXTH ONE SHOULDN'T BE TOO FAR EITHER.
HEY !
THERE IT IS !!
銘酒
鬼桜
THE SIXTH NEON SIGN !!

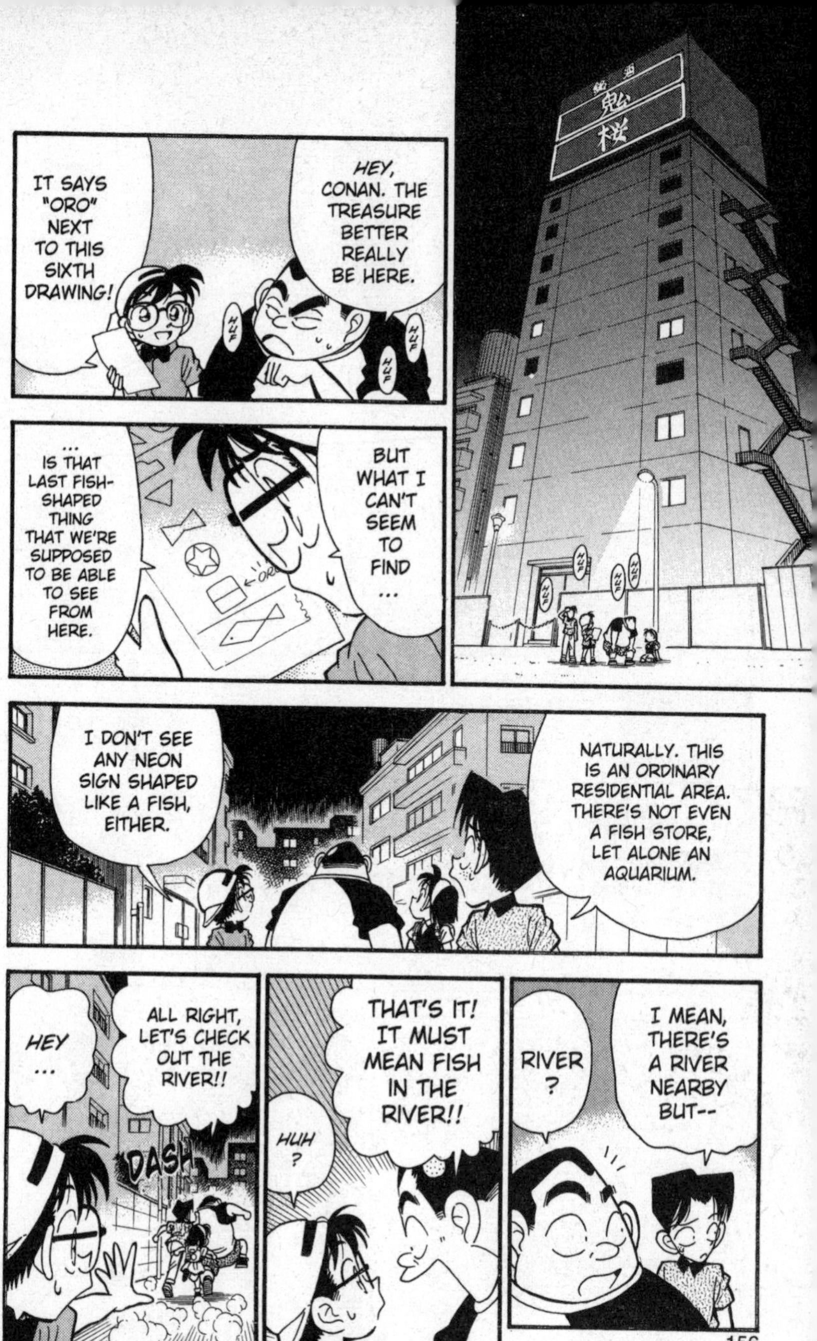
鬼桜
HUF
HUF
HUF
HUF
HEY, CONAN. THE TREASURE BETTER REALLY BE HERE.
IT SAYS "ORO" NEXT TO THIS SIXTH DRAWING!
HUF
HUF
HUF
BUT WHAT I CAN'T SEEM TO FIND ...
... IS THAT LAST FISH-SHAPED THING THAT WE'RE SUPPOSED TO BE ABLE TO SEE FROM HERE.
ORO
I DON'T SEE ANY NEON SIGN SHAPED LIKE A FISH, EITHER.
NATURALLY. THIS IS AN ORDINARY RESIDENTIAL AREA. THERE'S NOT EVEN A FISH STORE, LET ALONE AN AQUARIUM.
I MEAN, THERE'S A RIVER NEARBY BUT--
RIVER ?
THAT'S IT! IT MUST MEAN FISH IN THE RIVER!!
HUH ?
ALL RIGHT, LET'S CHECK OUT THE RIVER!!
HEY ...
DASH

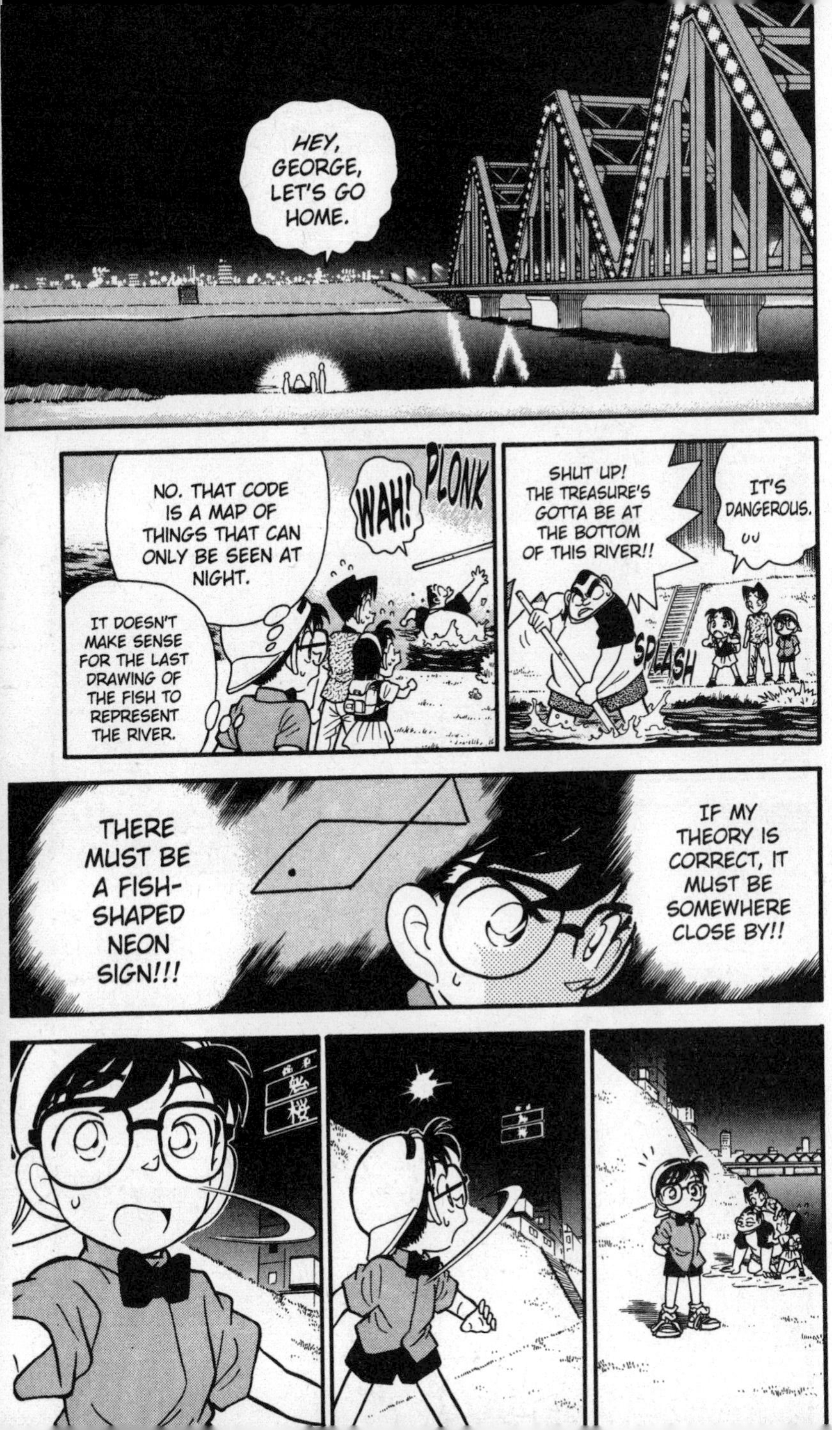
HEY, GEORGE, LET'S GO HOME.
IT'S DANGEROUS.
SHUT UP! THE TREASURE'S GOTTA BE AT THE BOTTOM OF THIS RIVER!!
SPLASH
PLONK
WAH!
NO. THAT CODE IS A MAP OF THINGS THAT CAN ONLY BE SEEN AT NIGHT.
IT DOESN'T MAKE SENSE FOR THE LAST DRAWING OF THE FISH TO REPRESENT THE RIVER.
IF MY THEORY IS CORRECT, IT MUST BE SOMEWHERE CLOSE BY!!
THERE MUST BE A FISH-SHAPED NEON SIGN!!!

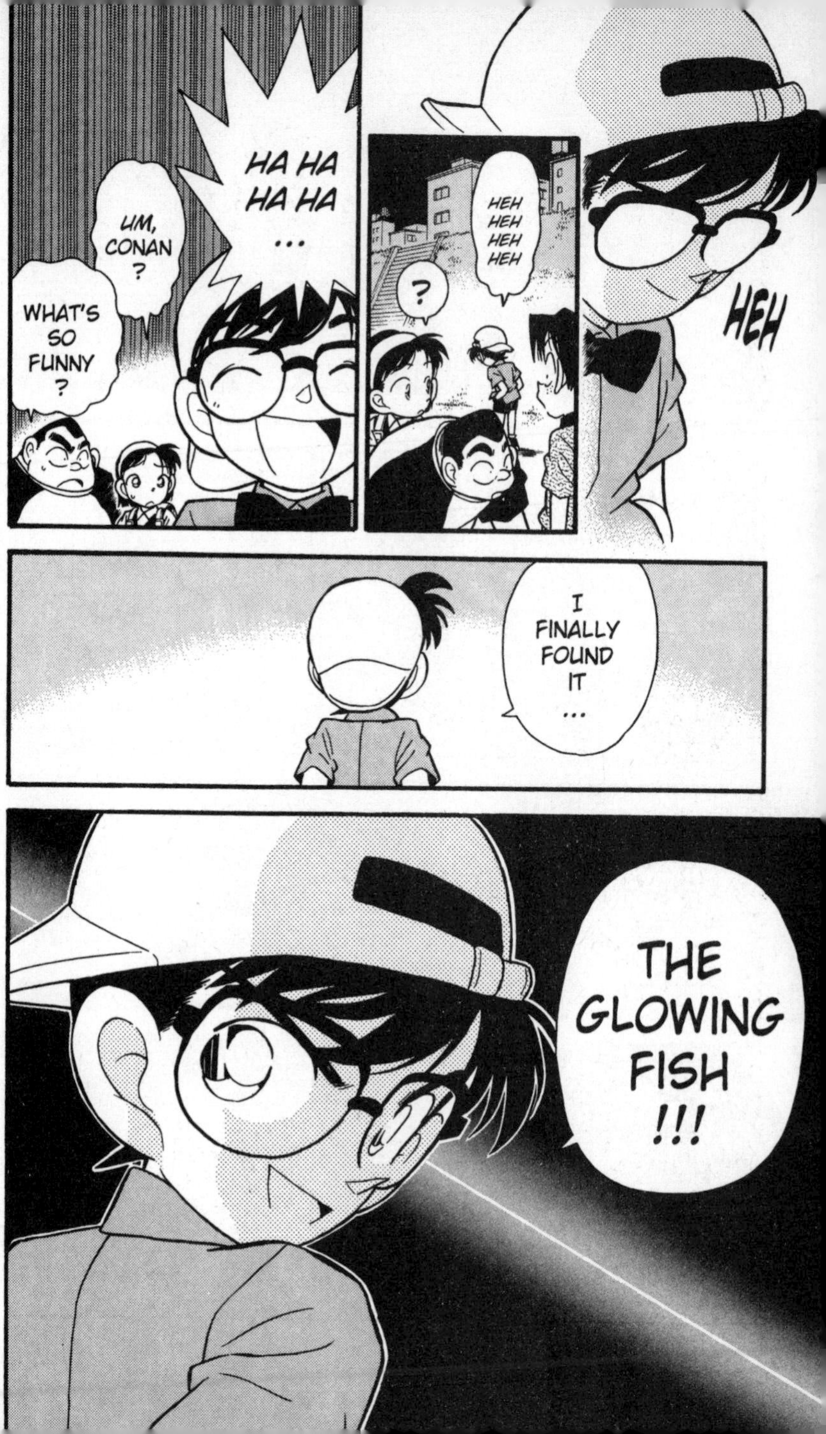
HEH
HEH HEH HEH HEH
?
HA HA HA HA ...
UM, CONAN ?
WHAT'S SO FUNNY ?
I FINALLY FOUND IT ...
THE GLOWING FISH !!!

FILE 10: THE GLOWING FISH

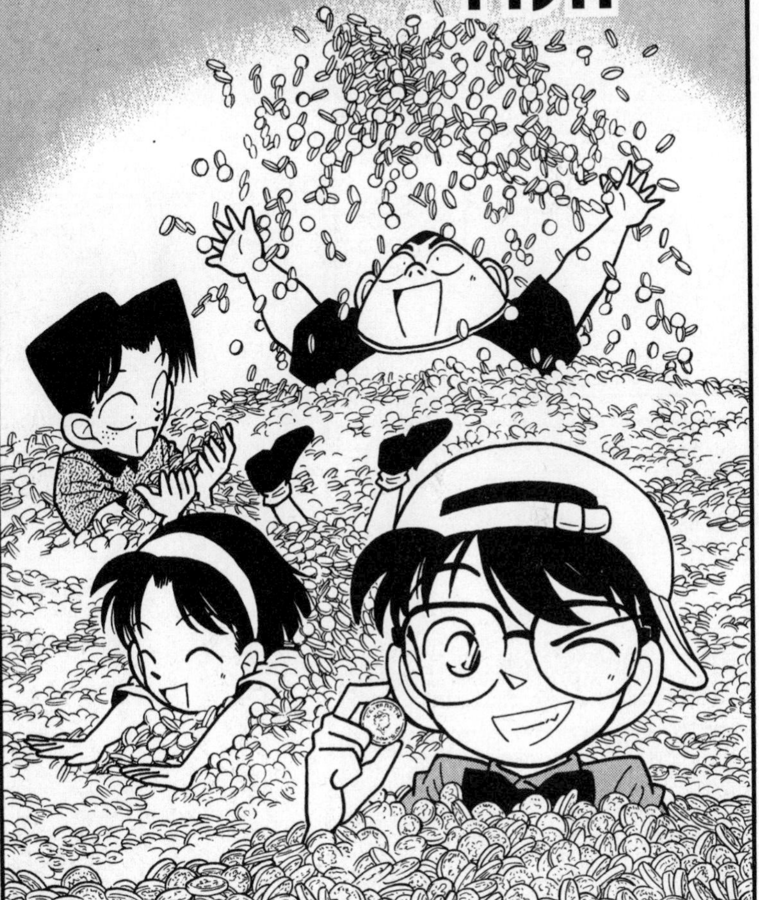

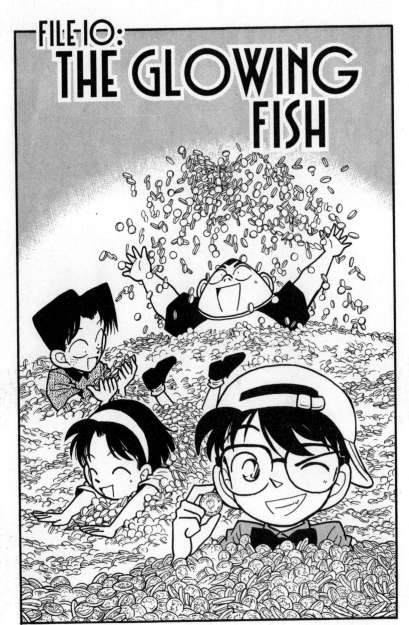

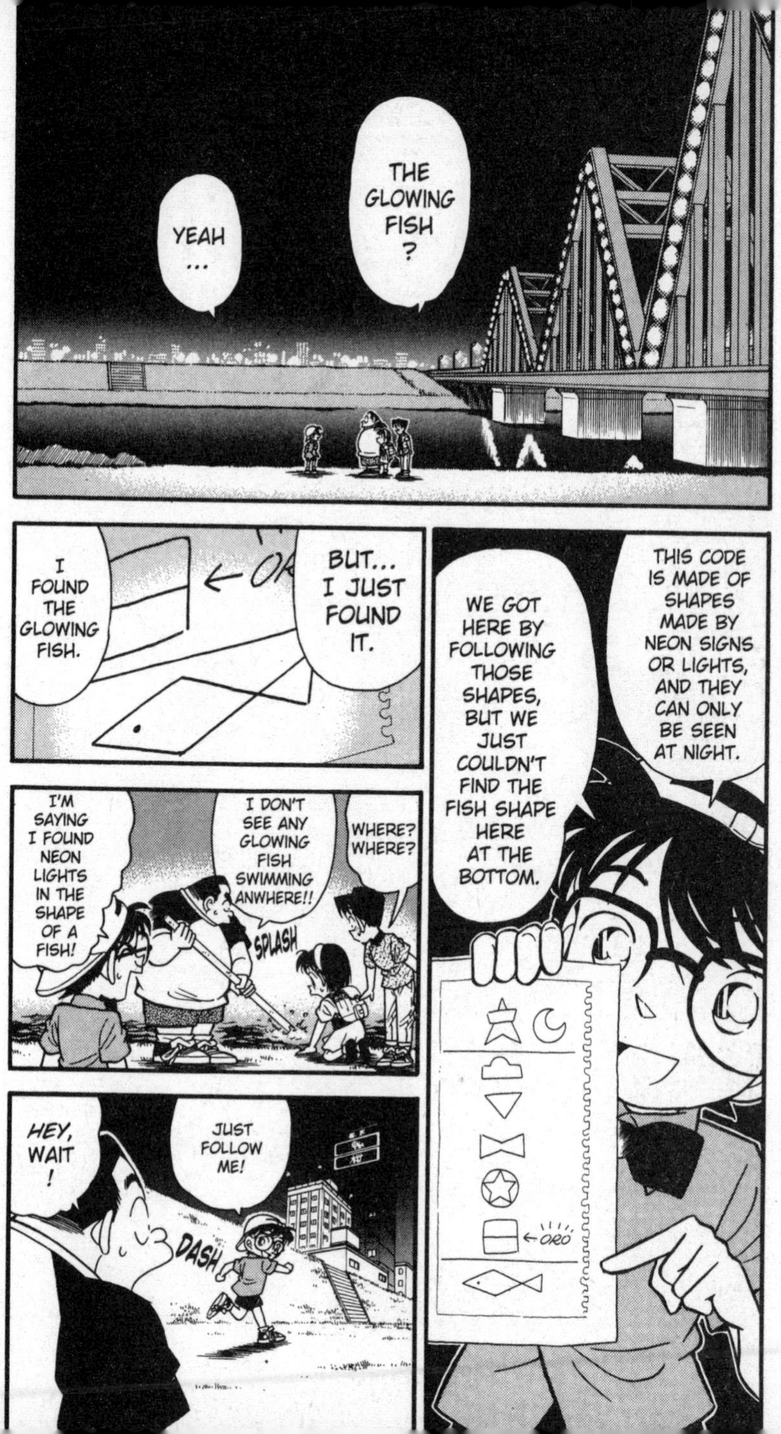
THE GLOWING FISH?
YEAH...
THIS CODE IS MADE OF SHAPES MADE BY NEON SIGNS OR LIGHTS, AND THEY CAN ONLY BE SEEN AT NIGHT.
WE GOT HERE BY FOLLOWING THOSE SHAPES, BUT WE JUST COULDN'T FIND THE FISH SHAPE HERE AT THE BOTTOM.
ORO
BUT... I JUST FOUND IT.
I FOUND THE GLOWING FISH.
WHERE? WHERE?
I DON'T SEE ANY GLOWING FISH SWIMMING ANWHERE!!
SPLASH
I'M SAYING I FOUND NEON LIGHTS IN THE SHAPE OF A FISH!
JUST FOLLOW ME!
DASH
HEY, WAIT!

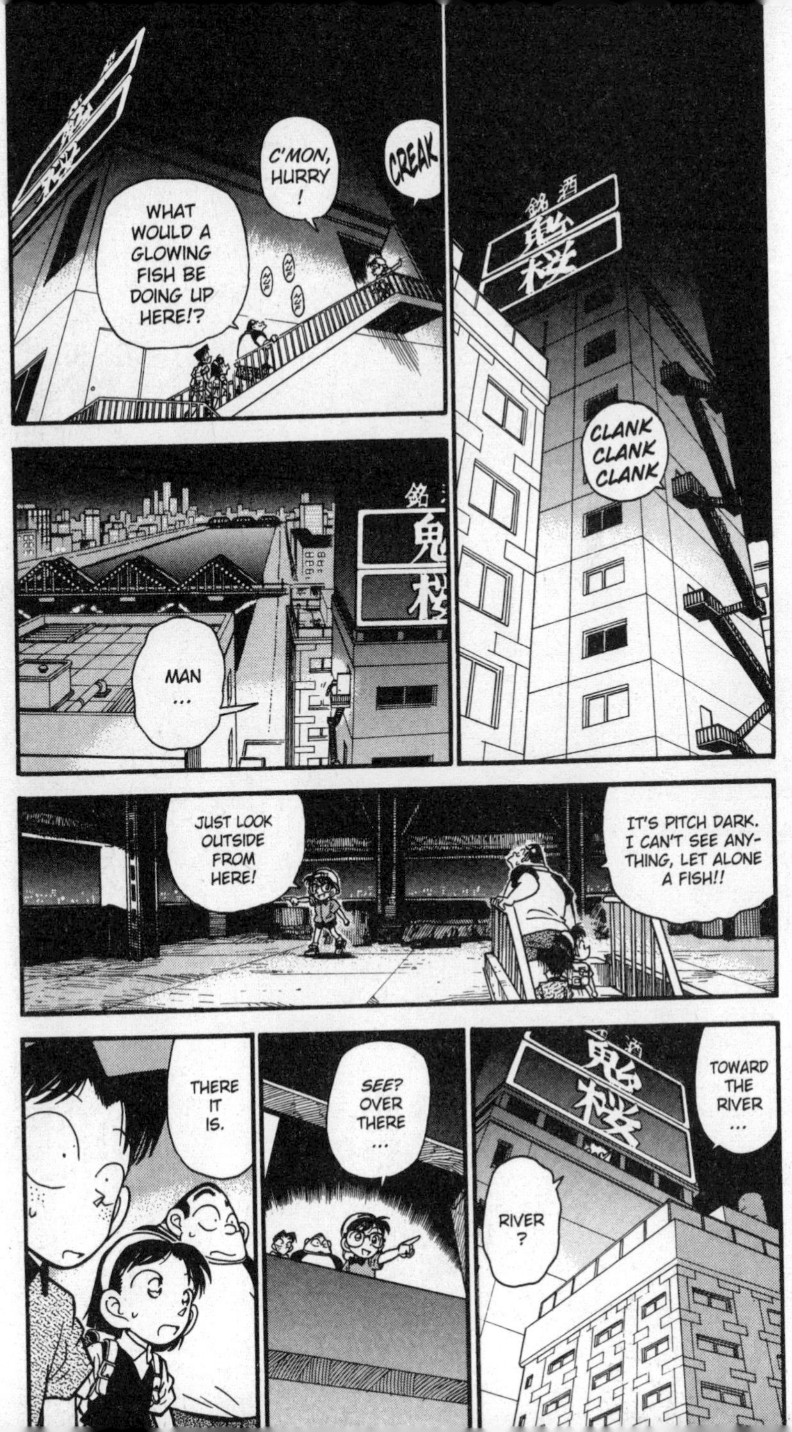
銘酒
鬼桜
CLANK CLANK CLANK
CREAK
C'MON, HURRY!
WHAT WOULD A GLOWING FISH BE DOING UP HERE!?
MAN...
IT'S PITCH DARK. I CAN'T SEE ANY-THING, LET ALONE A FISH!!
JUST LOOK OUTSIDE FROM HERE!
TOWARD THE RIVER...
RIVER?
SEE? OVER THERE...
THERE IT IS.

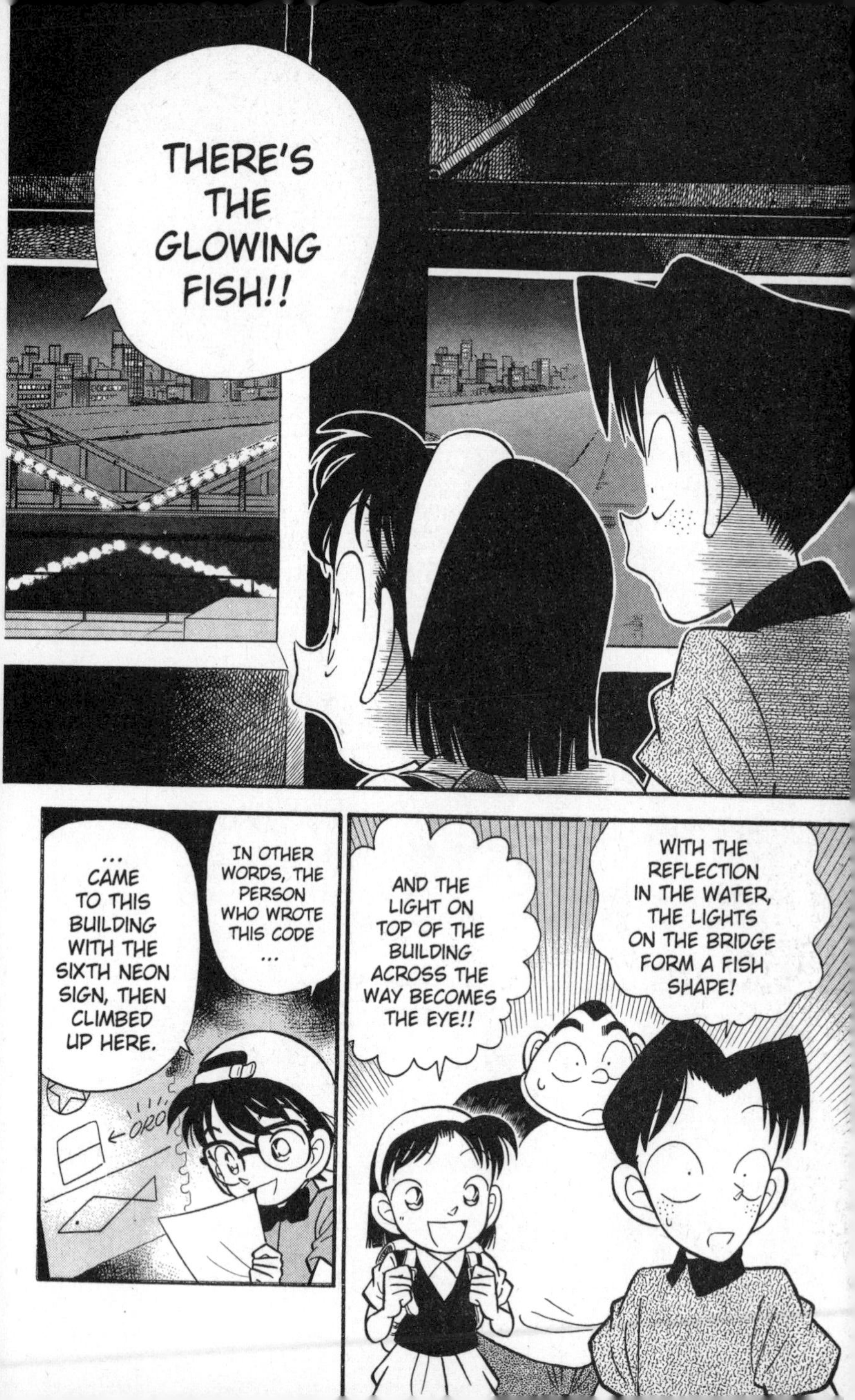
THERE'S THE GLOWING FISH!!
WITH THE REFLECTION IN THE WATER, THE LIGHTS ON THE BRIDGE FORM A FISH SHAPE!
AND THE LIGHT ON TOP OF THE BUILDING ACROSS THE WAY BECOMES THE EYE!!
IN OTHER WORDS, THE PERSON WHO WROTE THIS CODE ...
... CAME TO THIS BUILDING WITH THE SIXTH NEON SIGN, THEN CLIMBED UP HERE.
←ORO

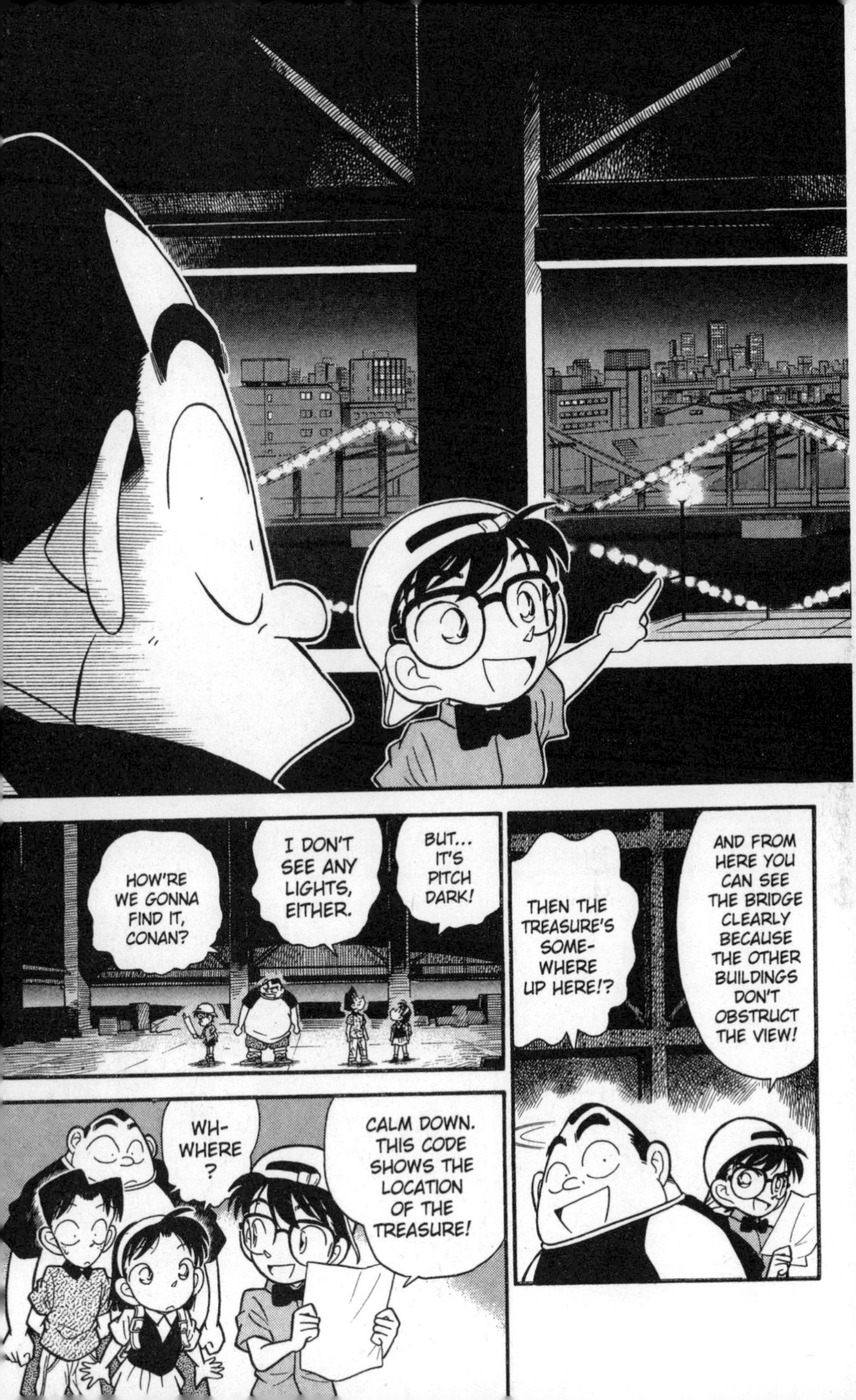
AND FROM HERE YOU CAN SEE THE BRIDGE CLEARLY BECAUSE THE OTHER BUILDINGS DON'T OBSTRUCT THE VIEW!
THEN THE TREASURE'S SOME-WHERE UP HERE!?
BUT... IT'S PITCH DARK!
I DON'T SEE ANY LIGHTS, EITHER.
HOW'RE WE GONNA FIND IT, CONAN?
CALM DOWN. THIS CODE SHOWS THE LOCATION OF THE TREASURE!
WH-WHERE ?

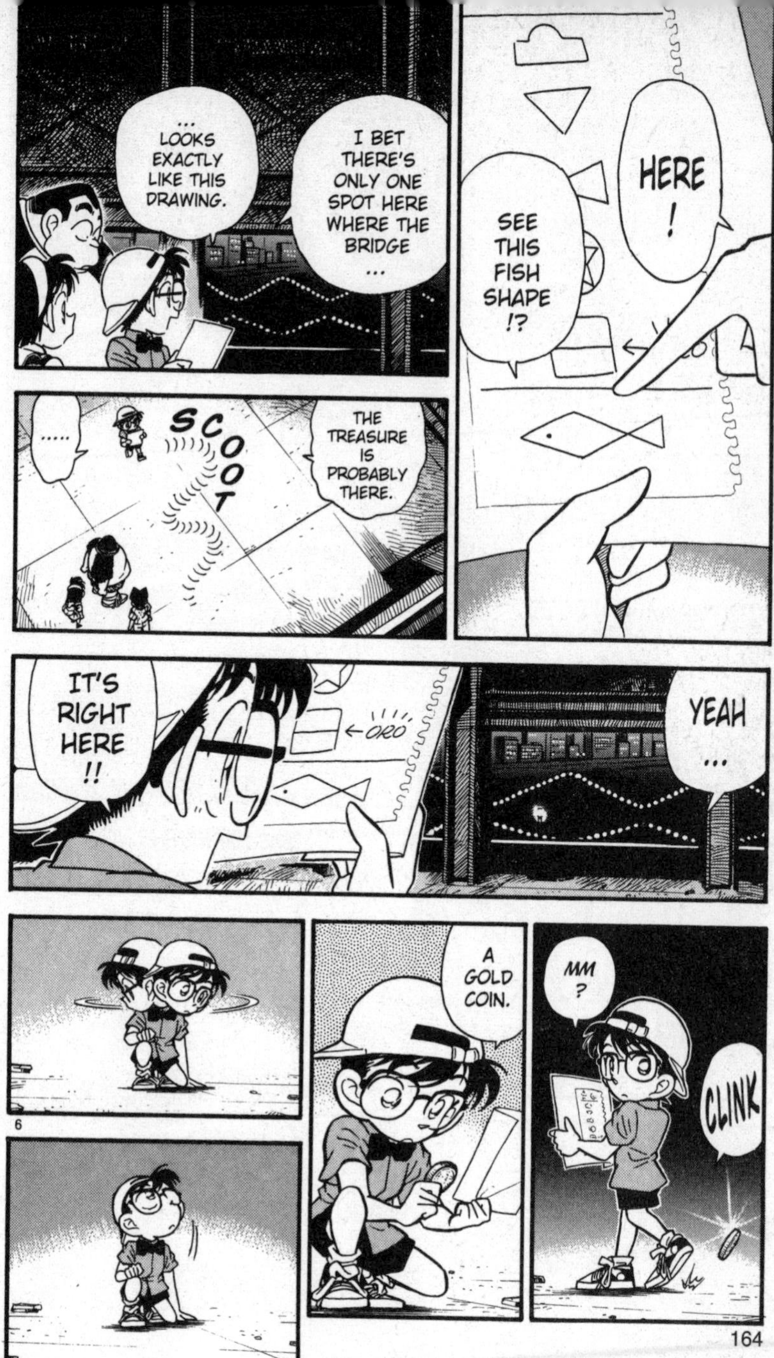
HERE !
SEE THIS FISH SHAPE !?
I BET THERE'S ONLY ONE SPOT HERE WHERE THE BRIDGE ...
... LOOKS EXACTLY LIKE THIS DRAWING.
THE TREASURE IS PROBABLY THERE.
SCOOOT
.....
YEAH ...
←ORO
IT'S RIGHT HERE !!
MM ?
CLINK
A GOLD COIN.

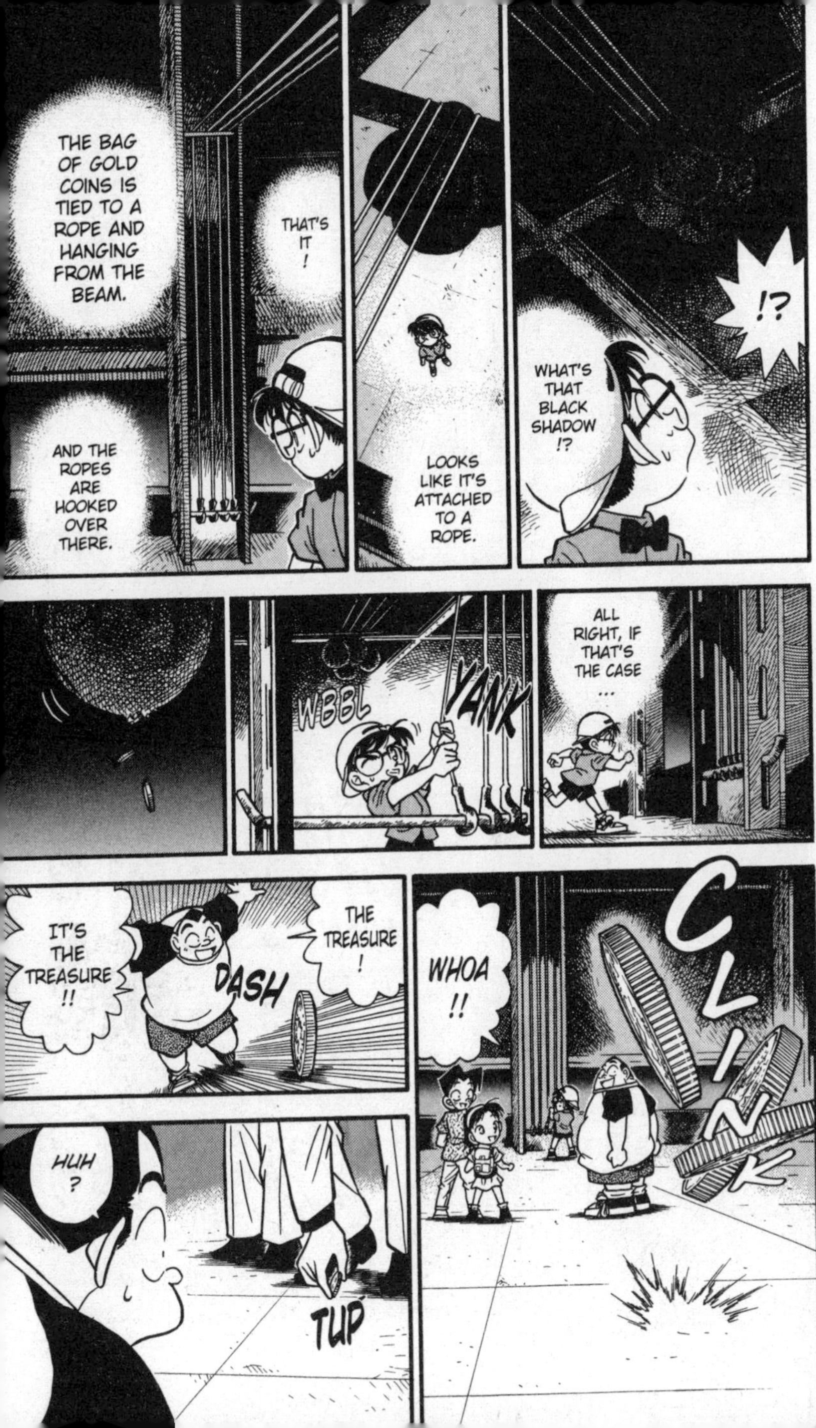
!?
WHAT'S THAT BLACK SHADOW !?
LOOKS LIKE IT'S ATTACHED TO A ROPE.
THAT'S IT !
THE BAG OF GOLD COINS IS TIED TO A ROPE AND HANGING FROM THE BEAM.
AND THE ROPES ARE HOOKED OVER THERE.
ALL RIGHT, IF THAT'S THE CASE ...
YANK
WBBL
CLINK
WHOA !!
THE TREASURE !
DASH
IT'S THE TREASURE !!
HUH ?
TUP

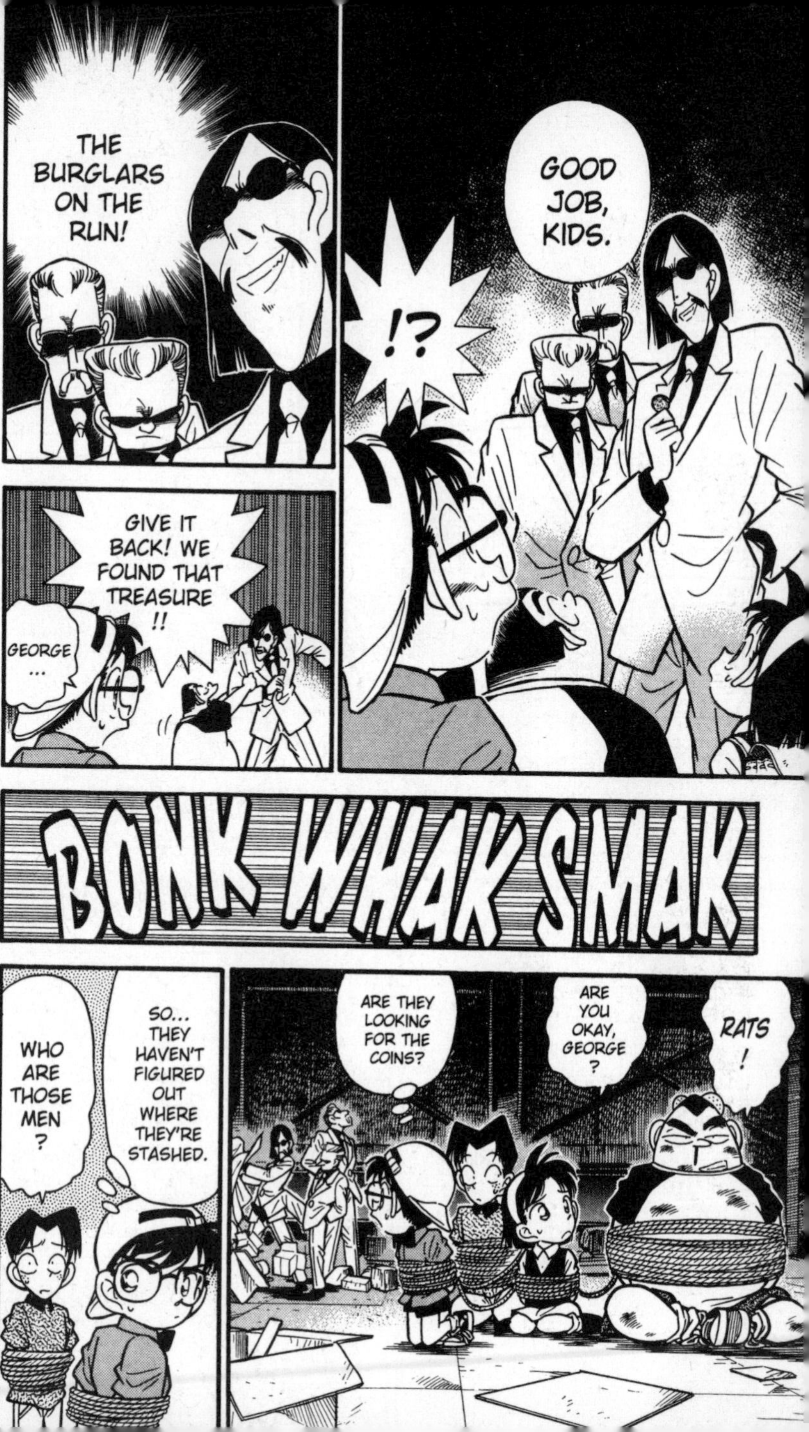
GOOD JOB, KIDS.
!?
THE BURGLARS ON THE RUN!
GIVE IT BACK! WE FOUND THAT TREASURE !!
GEORGE ...
BONK WHAK SMAK
RATS !
ARE YOU OKAY, GEORGE ?
ARE THEY LOOKING FOR THE COINS?
SO... THEY HAVEN'T FIGURED OUT WHERE THEY'RE STASHED.
WHO ARE THOSE MEN ?

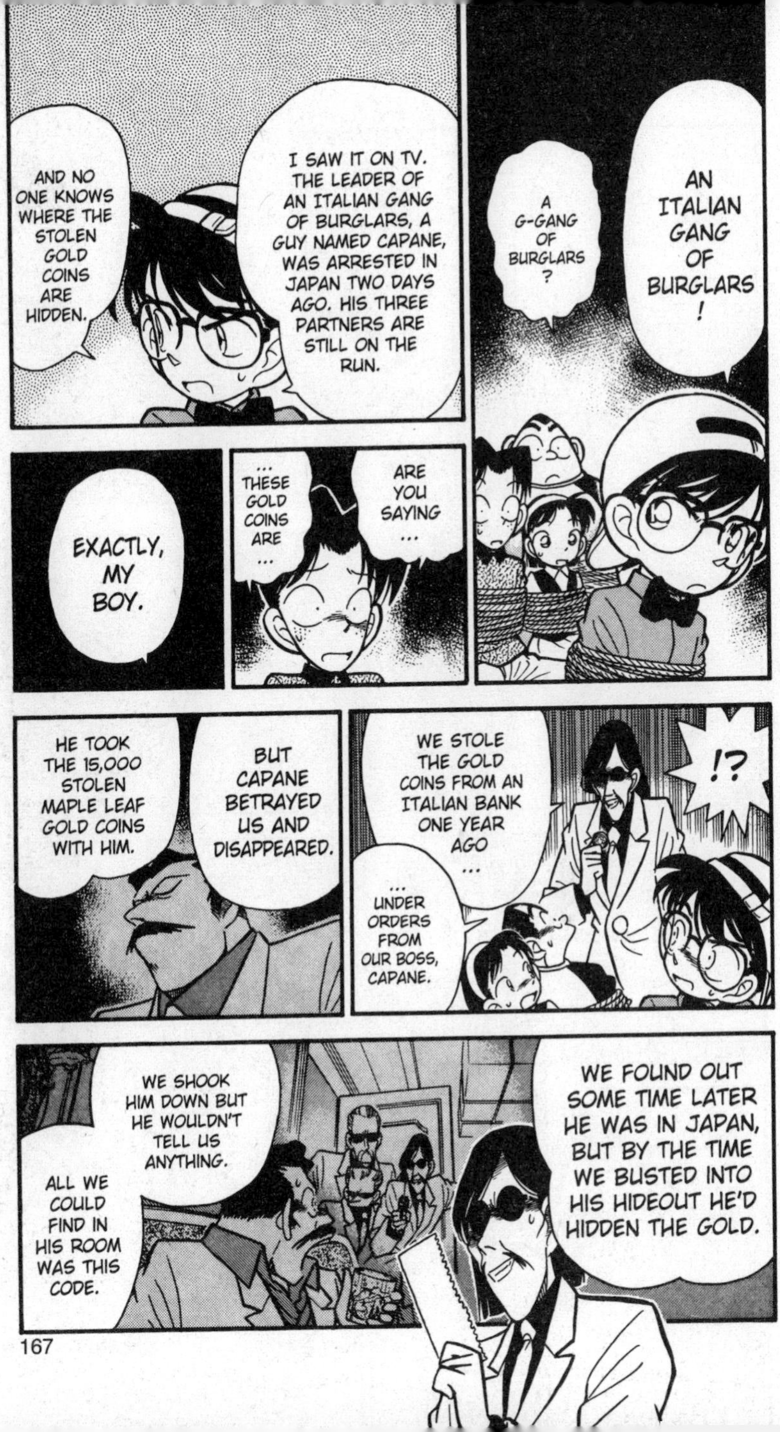
AN ITALIAN GANG OF BURGLARS !
A G-GANG OF BURGLARS ?
I SAW IT ON TV. THE LEADER OF AN ITALIAN GANG OF BURGLARS, A GUY NAMED CAPANE, WAS ARRESTED IN JAPAN TWO DAYS AGO. HIS THREE PARTNERS ARE STILL ON THE RUN.
AND NO ONE KNOWS WHERE THE STOLEN GOLD COINS ARE HIDDEN.
ARE YOU SAYING ...
... THESE GOLD COINS ARE ...
EXACTLY, MY BOY.
!?
WE STOLE THE GOLD COINS FROM AN ITALIAN BANK ONE YEAR AGO ...
... UNDER ORDERS FROM OUR BOSS, CAPANE.
BUT CAPANE BETRAYED US AND DISAPPEARED.
HE TOOK THE 15,000 STOLEN MAPLE LEAF GOLD COINS WITH HIM.
WE FOUND OUT SOME TIME LATER HE WAS IN JAPAN, BUT BY THE TIME WE BUSTED INTO HIS HIDEOUT HE'D HIDDEN THE GOLD.
WE SHOOK HIM DOWN BUT HE WOULDN'T TELL US ANYTHING.
ALL WE COULD FIND IN HIS ROOM WAS THIS CODE.

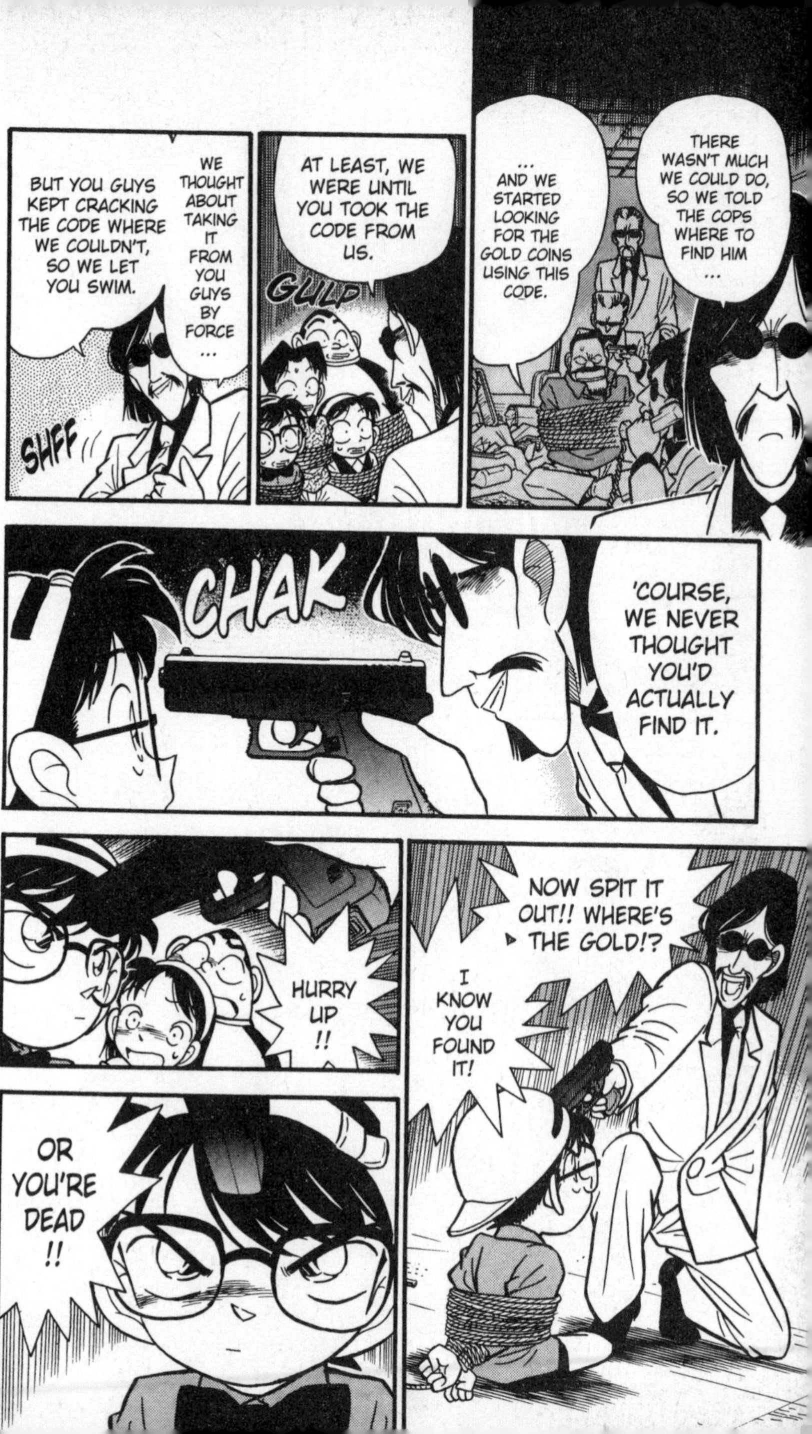
THERE WASN'T MUCH WE COULD DO, SO WE TOLD THE COPS WHERE TO FIND HIM ...
... AND WE STARTED LOOKING FOR THE GOLD COINS USING THIS CODE.
AT LEAST, WE WERE UNTIL YOU TOOK THE CODE FROM US.
GULP
WE THOUGHT ABOUT TAKING IT FROM YOU GUYS BY FORCE ...
BUT YOU GUYS KEPT CRACKING THE CODE WHERE WE COULDN'T, SO WE LET YOU SWIM.
SHFF
'COURSE, WE NEVER THOUGHT YOU'D ACTUALLY FIND IT.
CHAK
NOW SPIT IT OUT!! WHERE'S THE GOLD!?
I KNOW YOU FOUND IT!
HURRY UP !!
OR YOU'RE DEAD !!

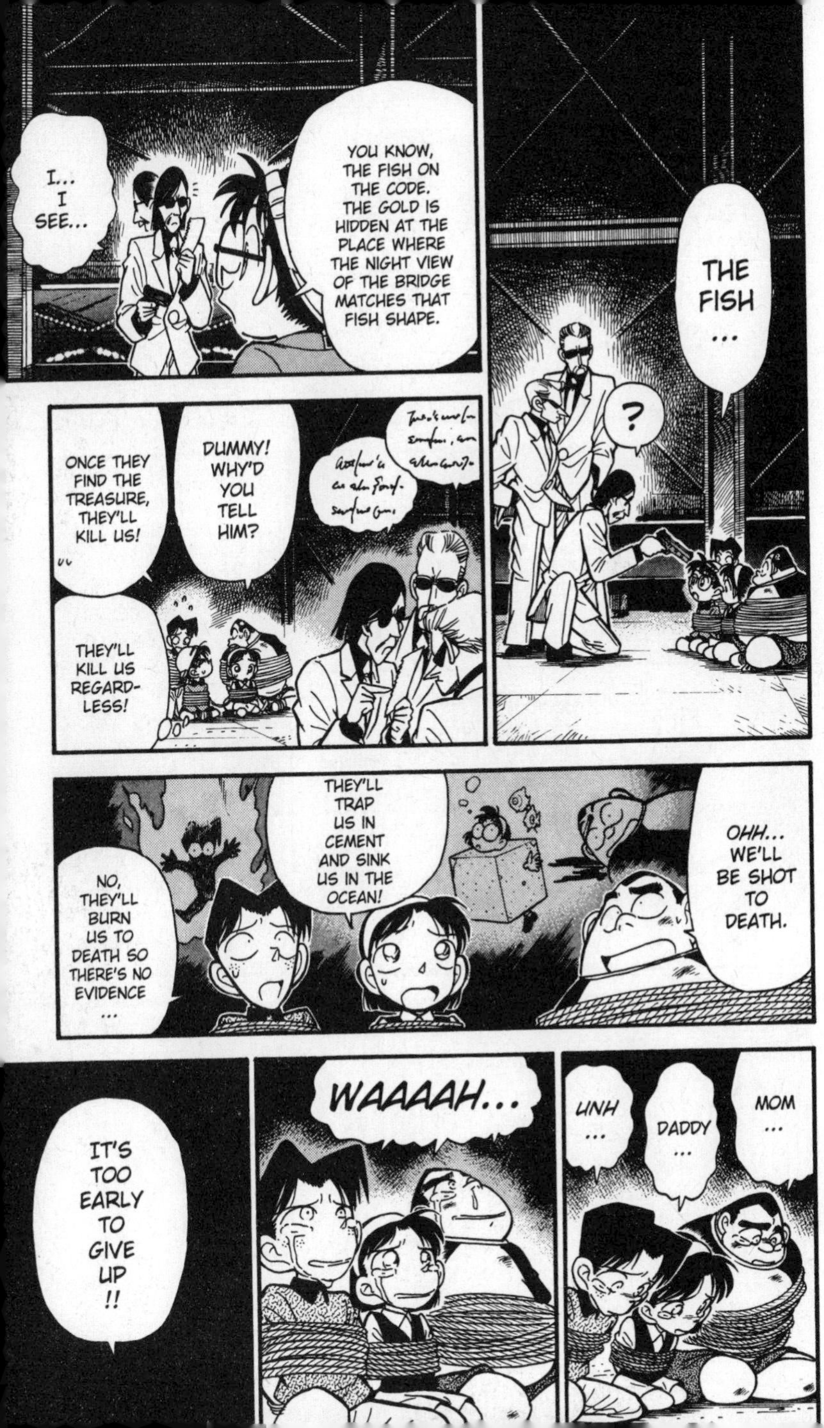
THE FISH ...
?
YOU KNOW, THE FISH ON THE CODE. THE GOLD IS HIDDEN AT THE PLACE WHERE THE NIGHT VIEW OF THE BRIDGE MATCHES THAT FISH SHAPE.
I... I SEE...
DUMMY! WHY'D YOU TELL HIM?
ONCE THEY FIND THE TREASURE, THEY'LL KILL US!
THEY'LL KILL US REGARDLESS!
OHH... WE'LL BE SHOT TO DEATH.
THEY'LL TRAP US IN CEMENT AND SINK US IN THE OCEAN!
NO, THEY'LL BURN US TO DEATH SO THERE'S NO EVIDENCE ...
MOM ...
DADDY ...
UNH ...
WAAAAH...
IT'S TOO EARLY TO GIVE UP !!

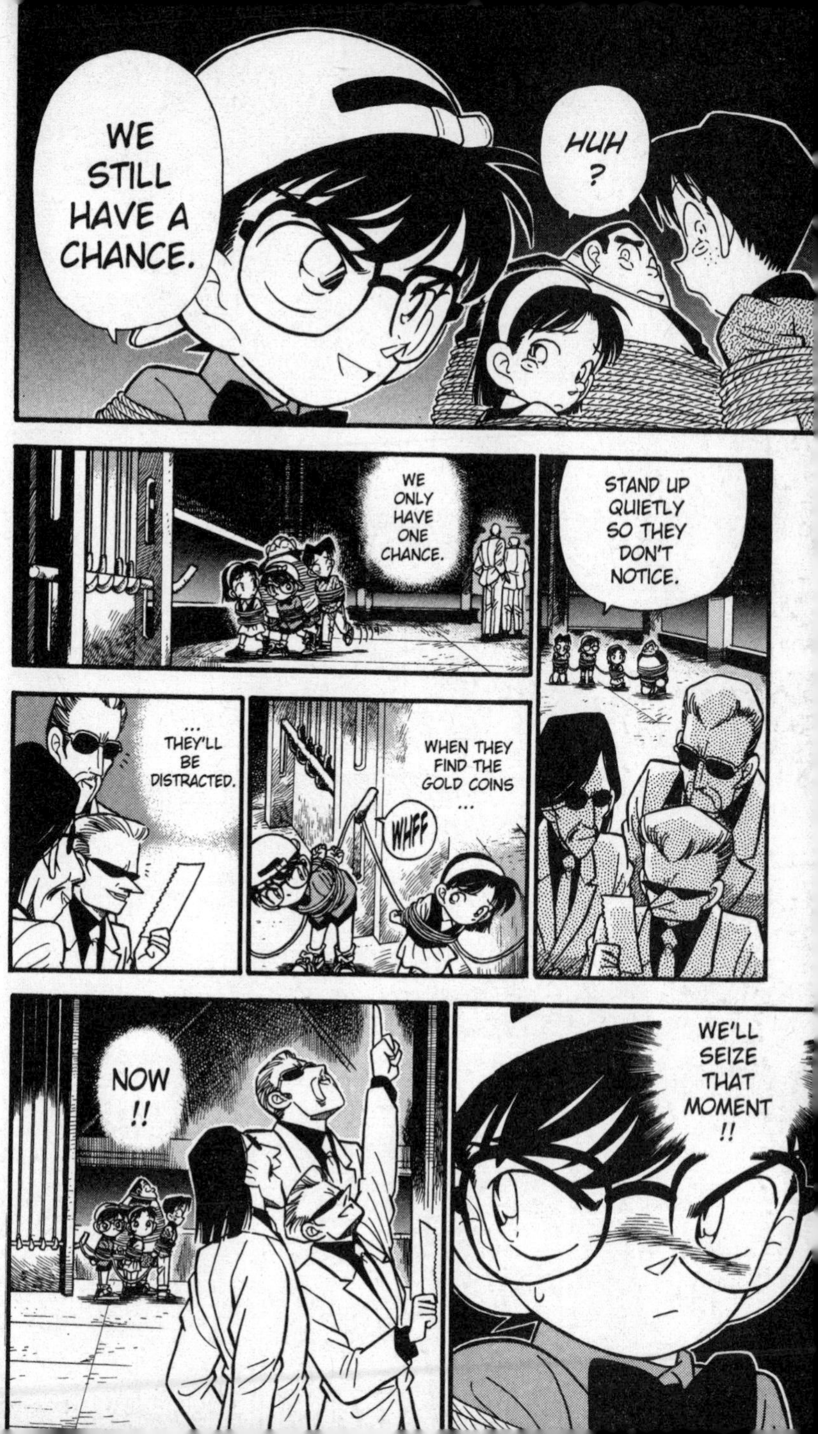
HUH ?
WE STILL HAVE A CHANCE.
STAND UP QUIETLY SO THEY DON'T NOTICE.
WE ONLY HAVE ONE CHANCE.
WHEN THEY FIND THE GOLD COINS ...
WHFF
... THEY'LL BE DISTRACTED.
WE'LL SEIZE THAT MOMENT !!
NOW !!

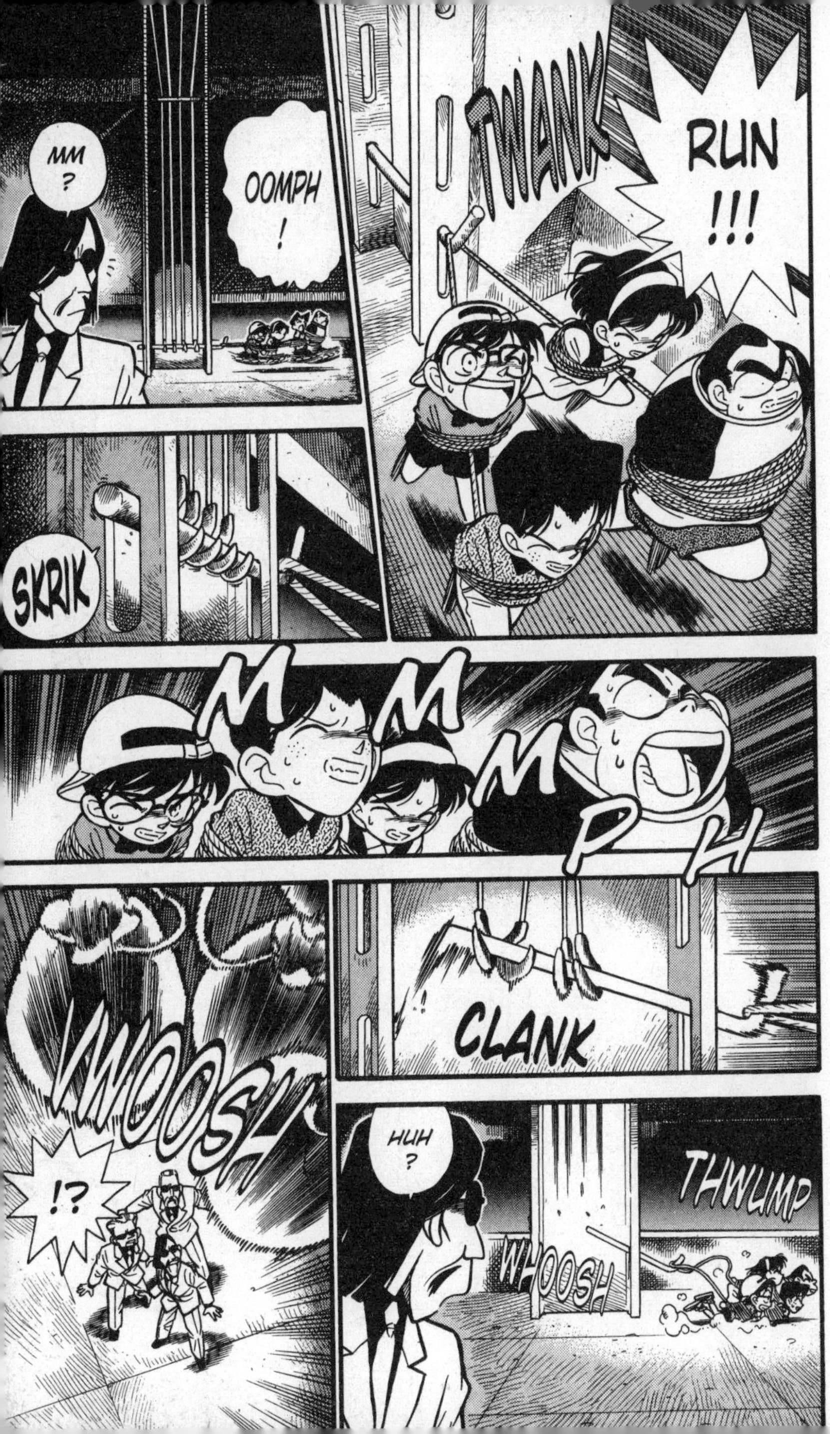
RUN !!!
TWANK
OOMPH !
MM ?
SKRIK
MMMPH
CLANK
THWUMP
HUH ?
WHOOSH
WOOSH
!?

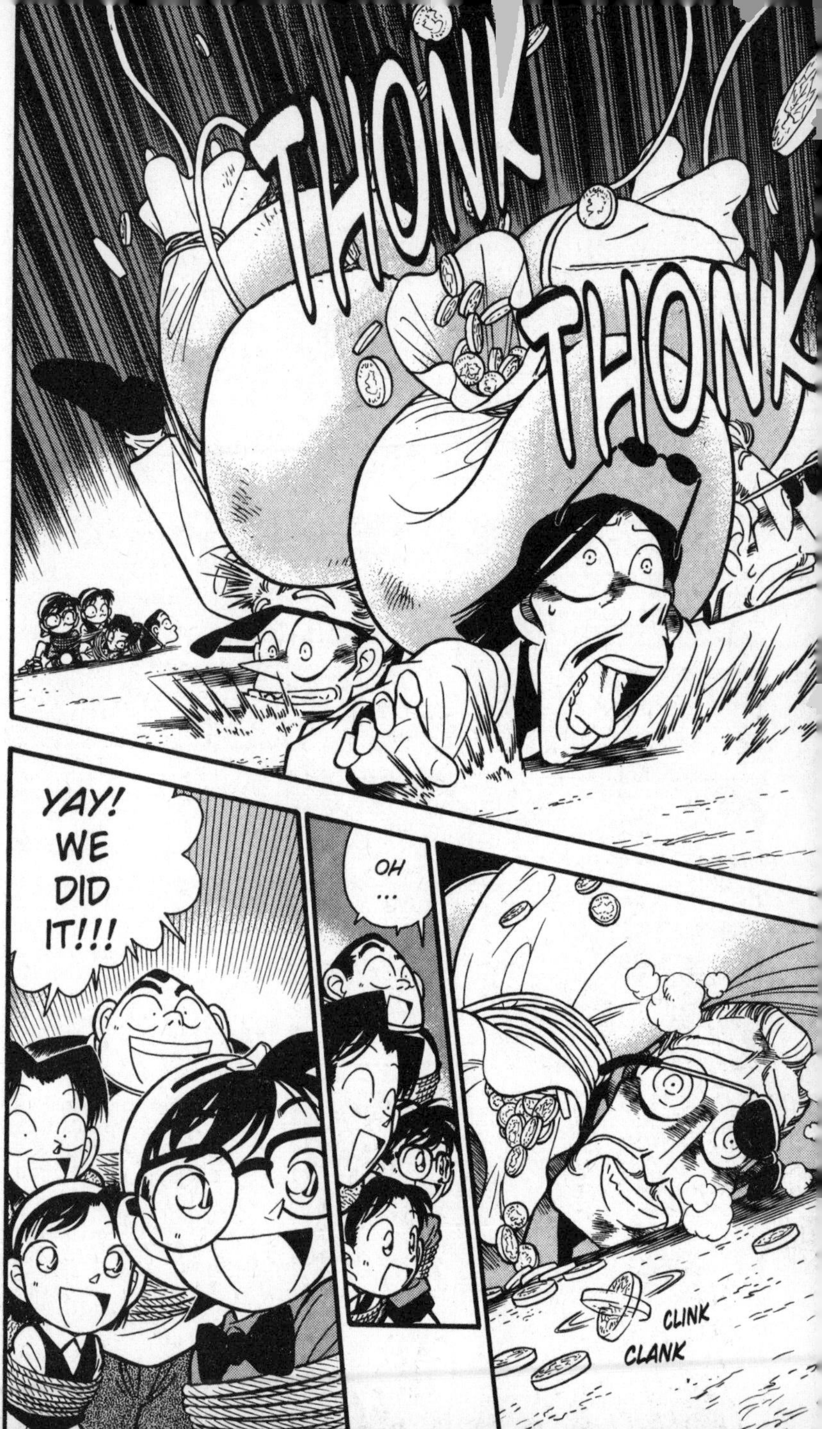
THONK
THONK
CLINK
CLANK
OH ...
YAY! WE DID IT!!!

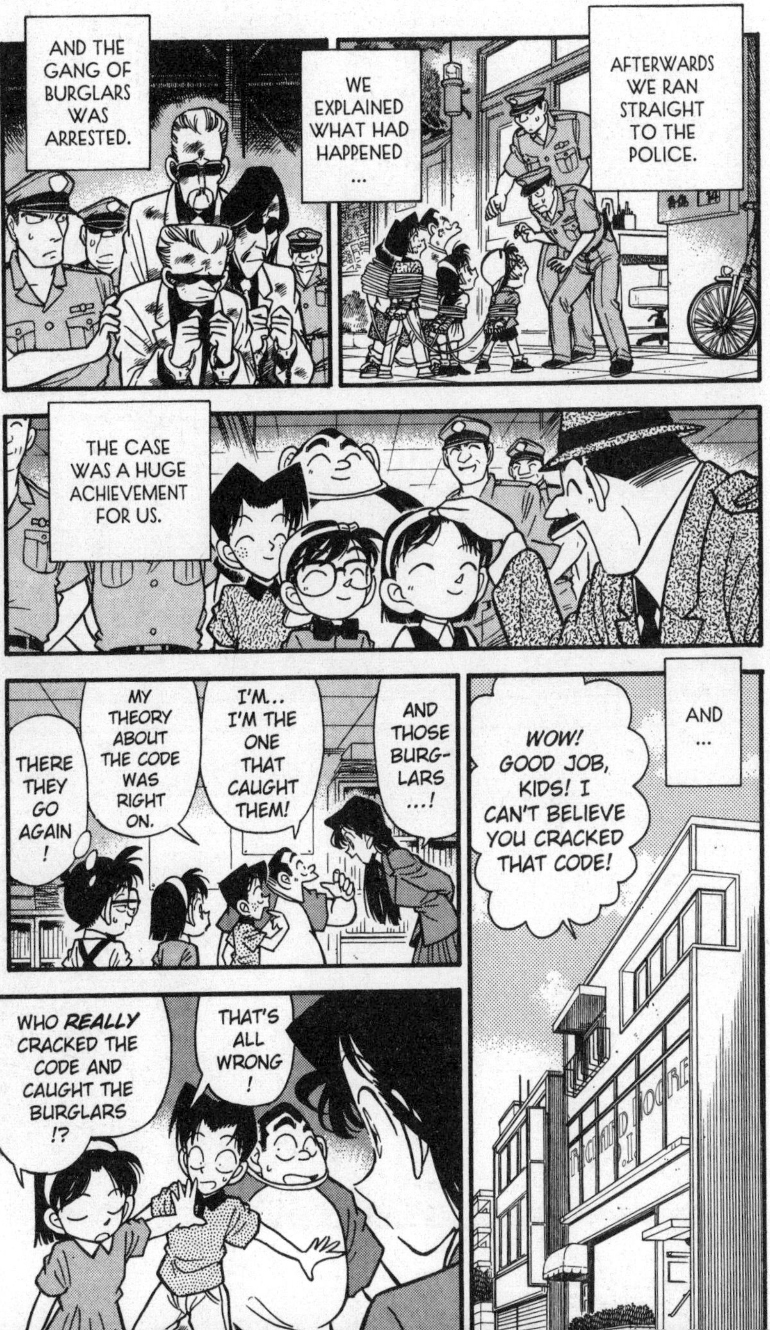
AFTERWARDS WE RAN STRAIGHT TO THE POLICE.
WE EXPLAINED WHAT HAD HAPPENED ...
AND THE GANG OF BURGLARS WAS ARRESTED.
THE CASE WAS A HUGE ACHIEVEMENT FOR US.
AND ...
WOW! GOOD JOB, KIDS! I CAN'T BELIEVE YOU CRACKED THAT CODE!
RICHARD MOORE D.I.
AND THOSE BURGLARS ...!
I'M... I'M THE ONE THAT CAUGHT THEM!
MY THEORY ABOUT THE CODE WAS RIGHT ON.
THERE THEY GO AGAIN!
THAT'S ALL WRONG!
WHO **REALLY** CRACKED THE CODE AND CAUGHT THE BURGLARS!?

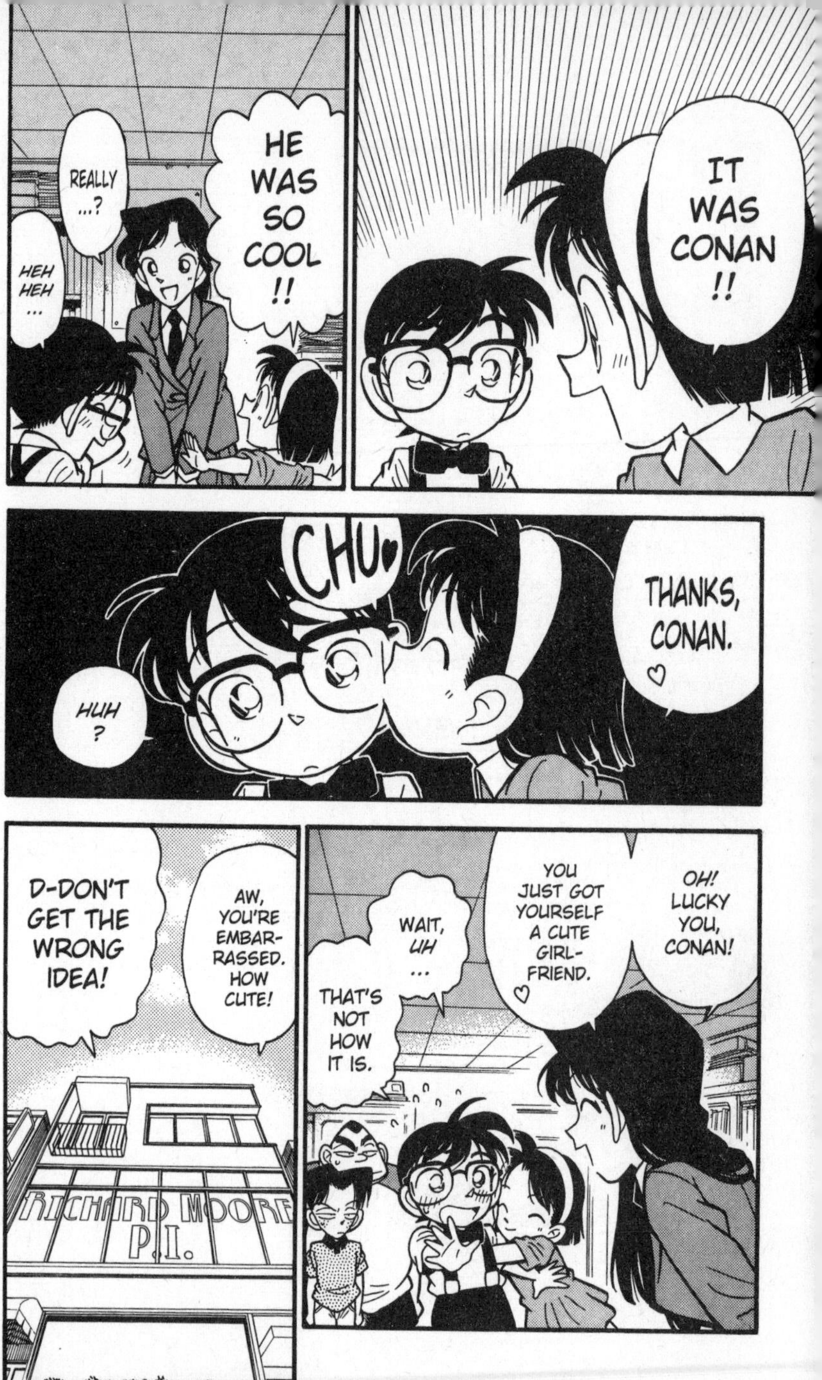
IT WAS CONAN !!
HE WAS SO COOL !!
REALLY ...?
HEH HEH ...
THANKS, CONAN. ♡
CHU♡
HUH ?
OH! LUCKY YOU, CONAN!
YOU JUST GOT YOURSELF A CUTE GIRL-FRIEND. ♡
WAIT, UH ...
THAT'S NOT HOW IT IS.
AW, YOU'RE EMBAR-RASSED. HOW CUTE!
D-DON'T GET THE WRONG IDEA!
RICHARD MOORE P.I.

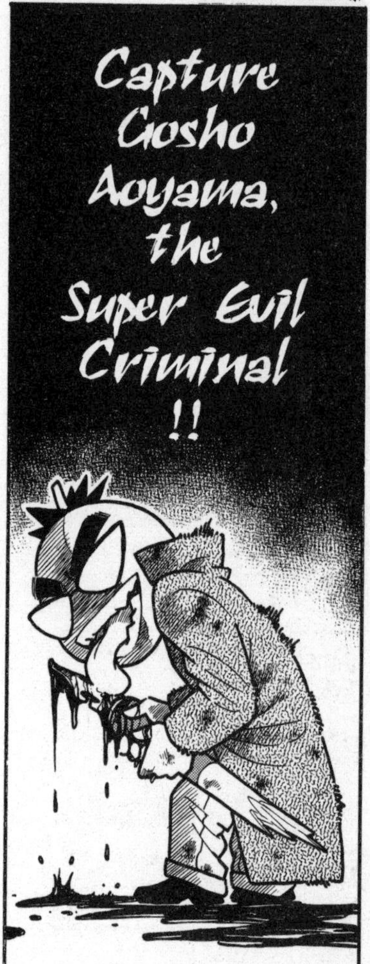
Capture Gosho Aoyama, the Super Evil Criminal !!
Gosho Aoyama Detectives:
Yutaka Tani
Masaki Negishi
Eiichi Yamagishi
Kōichi Kishida
Keiji Aso

THE ALCOHOLIC DETECTIVE YUTAKA TANI SERIES FILE 1995

A SUPPRESSED DESIRE TO KILL

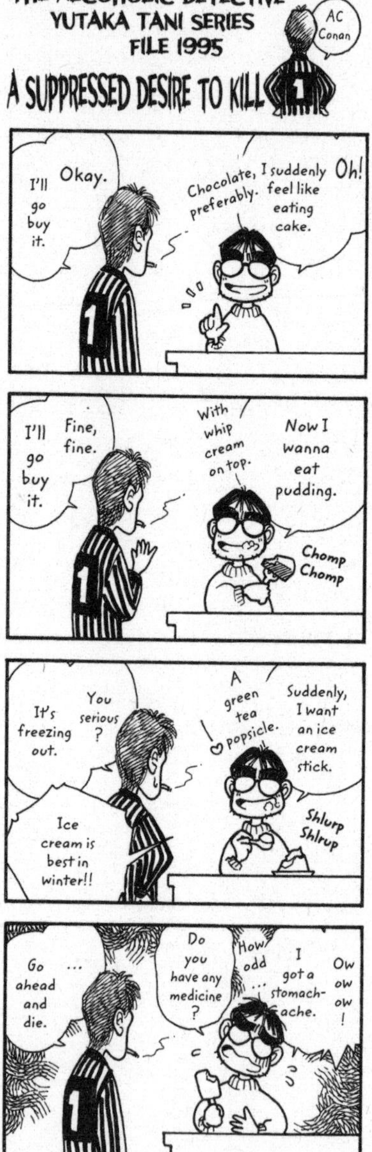
AC Conan
Oh!
I suddenly feel like eating cake.
Chocolate, preferably.
Okay.
I'll go buy it.
Now I wanna eat pudding.
With whip cream on top.
Chomp Chomp
Fine, fine.
I'll go buy it.
Suddenly, I want an ice cream stick.
A green tea popsicle.
Shlurp Shlrup
You serious?
It's freezing out.
Ice cream is best in winter!!
Ow ow ow!
I got a stomach-ache.
How odd...
Do you have any medicine?
Go ahead and die...

The Report from Gishimasa -- the ever-expanding Fat Detective

Is this what Aoyama Sensei is like?

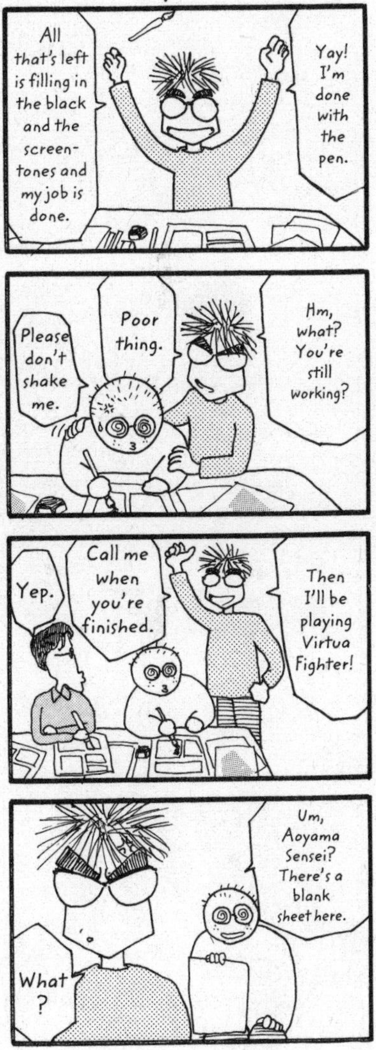
Yay! I'm done with the pen.
All that's left is filling in the black and the screentones and my job is done.
Hm, what? You're still working?
Poor thing.
Please don't shake me.
Then I'll be playing Virtua Fighter!
Call me when you're finished.
Yep.
Um, Aoyama Sensei? There's a blank sheet here.
What ?

Detective Yamachan's Puppet Show

We're All Friends

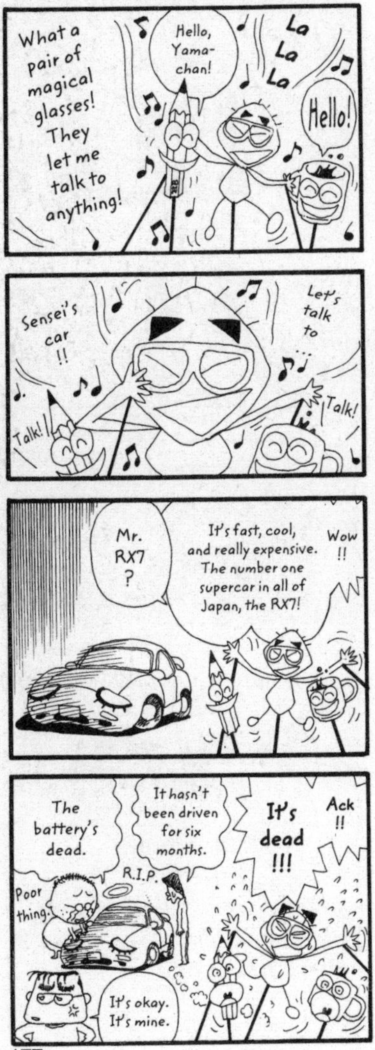
Hello!
La La La
Hello, Yama-chan!
What a pair of magical glasses! They let me talk to anything!
Let's talk to...
Talk!
Sensei's car !!
Talk!
Wow !!
It's fast, cool, and really expensive. The number one supercar in all of Japan, the RX7!
Mr. RX7 ?
Ack !!
It's dead !!!
It hasn't been driven for six months.
The battery's dead.
R.I.P.
Poor thing.
It's okay. It's mine.

~~BIG HEAD~~ YOUTHFUL STORYTELLER DETECTIVE

What is Youth?

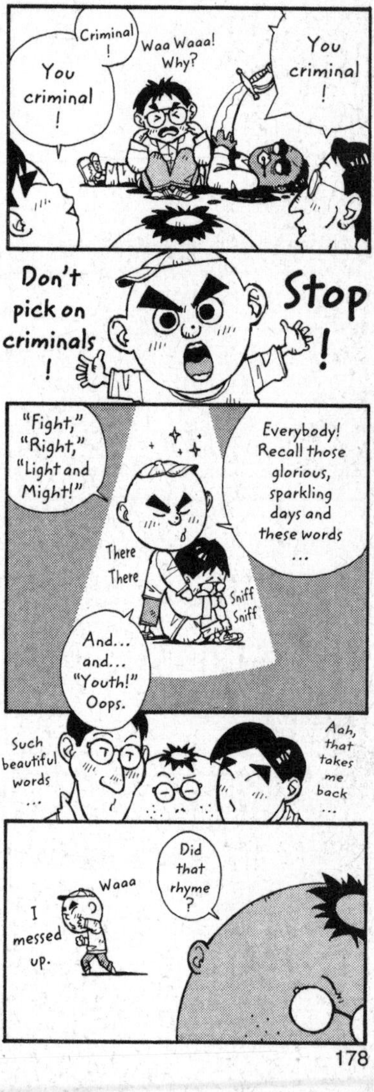
You criminal !
Waa Waaa! Why?
Criminal !
You criminal !
Stop !
Don't pick on criminals !
Everybody! Recall those glorious, sparkling days and these words ...
"Fight," "Right," "Light and Might!"
There There
Sniff Sniff
And... and... "Youth!" Oops.
Aah, that takes me back ...
Such beautiful words ...
Did that rhyme ?
Waaa
I messed up.

Keiji Aso: Head Detective

DON'T SAY BANZAI!

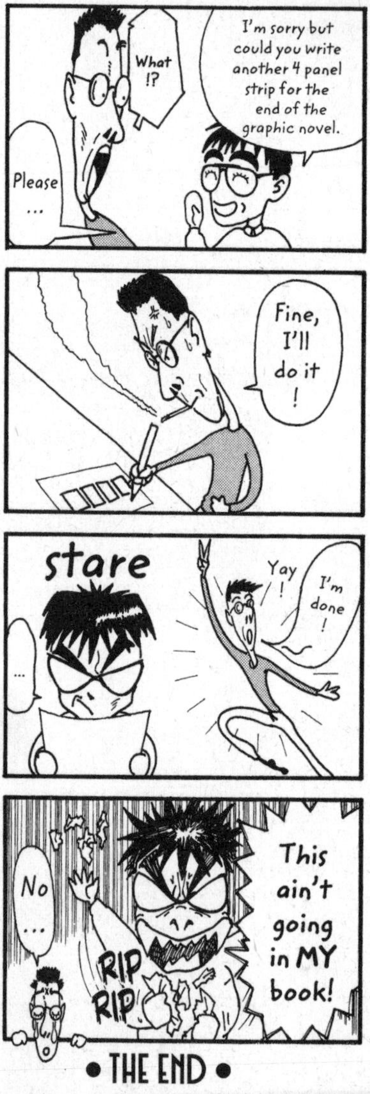
I'm sorry but could you write another 4 panel strip for the end of the graphic novel.
What !?
Please ...
Fine, I'll do it !
I'm done !
Yay !
stare
...
This ain't going in MY book!
RIP RIP
No ...

• THE END •

Hello, Aoyama here.

Some folks claim that Dr. Watson's name should be rendered in Japanese as "wa-to-su-n." I've decided to go with "wa-to-so-n," the way it was written in the books that I read as a child. I wish the way names are written wouldn't change so much just for the sake of pronunciation. Even the name Poirot is being rendered now as "po-wa-ro" instead of "po-a-ro" as it has always been. But if they ever change the rendering of "Holmes" from "ho--mu-zu" to "ho-u-mu-zu" I think I'll cry.

Gosho Aoyama's
Mystery Library

4

ARSENE LUPIN

The gentleman thief Arsene Lupin—a man who can crack a smile even when he's about to face certain death!! Heavy-duty safes and security systems mean nothing to the protean Lupin. He's so masterful at the art of disguise that he sometimes even forgets what his own face looks like! He's so proficient at changing his voice and his handwriting that he'll never be caught! Arsene Lupin has even transformed himself into an officer of the law to solve a crime or two. And despite the difficult circumstances of his upbringing he still hasn't lost his sense of justice. Offering aid to the weak and defeating the strong, he has a particular weakness for a damsel in distress. To come to the aid of a fair maiden, he'll throw himself into all matter of danger. Arsene Lupin is indeed a daring grand master thief! By the way, have you readers figured out where Rachel Moore's original name Ran Mori came from? It's inspired from the name of the creator of Arsene Lupin, Maurice Leblanc. Rendered in Japanese it is "Mo—ri-su Ru-bu-ran." I recommend reading **The Extraordinary Adventures of Arsene Lupin, Gentleman Burglar.**

CASE CLOSED IS A STEAL
THE PROOF IS IN THE PRICE

CATCH THE CAPERS ON DVD FOR UNDER $30 A SEASON!

You should be watching funimation.com/case-closed

Based on the original graphic novel "Meitantei Konan" by Gosho Aoyama published by Shogakukan Inc.
© Gosho Aoyama / Shogakukan • YTV • TMS. Produced by TMS Entertainment Co., Ltd Under license to FUNimation® Productions, Ltd. All Rights Reserved.

FUNIMATION

Ranma ½

Rumiko Takahashi's smash hit now back in a 2-in-1 edition

Story and art by
Rumiko Takahashi
From the creator of *Inuyasha* and *RIN-NE*.

Available now!

One day, teenage martial artist Ranma Saotome went on a training mission with his father and ended up taking a dive into some cursed springs at a legendary training ground in China. Now, every time he's splashed with cold water, he changes into a girl. His father, Genma, changes into a panda! What's a half-guy, half-girl to do?

viz.com/ranma

RANMA1/2 © 1988 Rumiko TAKAHASHI/SHOGAKUKAN

MAGI
The labyrinth of magic

Story & Art by
SHINOBU OHTAKA

A **fantasy adventure** inspired by
One Thousand and One Nights

Deep within the deserts lie the mysterious Dungeons, vast stores of riches there for the taking by anyone lucky enough to find them and brave enough to venture into the depths from where few have ever returned. Plucky young adventurer **Aladdin** means to find the Dungeons and their riches, but Aladdin may be just as mysterious as the treasures he seeks.

MANGA STARTS ON SUNDAY
SHONEN SUNDAY
www.shonensunday.com

Available NOW!

RATED
T
FOR TEEN
ratings.viz.com

VIZ MEDIA
www.viz.com

MAGI © 2009 Shinobu OHTAKA/SHOGAKUKAN

Hey! You're Reading in the Wrong Direction!

This is the **end** of this graphic novel!

To properly enjoy this VIZ graphic novel, please turn it around and begin reading from **right to left.** Unlike English, Japanese is read right to left, so Japanese comics are read in reverse order from the way English comics are typically read.

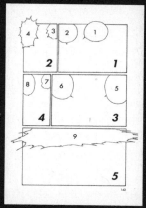

Follow the action this way

This book has been printed in the original Japanese format in order to preserve the orientation of the original artwork. Have fun with it!